ı St.
'A 98662

Tel 360 891 8313

MacArthur
and Defeat
in the Philippines

———————

MacArthur and Defeat in the Philippines

RICHARD CONNAUGHTON

THE OVERLOOK PRESS
WOODSTOCK & NEW YORK

First published in the United States in 2001 by
The Overlook Press, Peter Mayer Publishers, Inc.
Woodstock & New York

WOODSTOCK:
One Overlook Drive
Woodstock, NY 12498
www.overlookpress.com
[for individual orders, bulk and special sales, contact our Woodstock office]

NEW YORK:
141 Wooster Street
New York, NY 10012

Library of Congress Cataloging-in-Publication Data

Connaughton, R. M. (Richard Michael).
MacArthur and defeat in the Philippines / Richard Connaughton.
p. cm.
Includes bibliographical references and index.
1. World War, 1939–1945—Campaigns—Philippines.
2. MacArthur, Douglas, 1880–1964. I.Title.

Manufactured in the United States of America
FIRST EDITION
1 3 5 7 9 8 6 4 2
ISBN 1-58567-118-5

This book is dedicated to the memory of
Doctor John Lewis Pimlott
1948-1997

CONTENTS

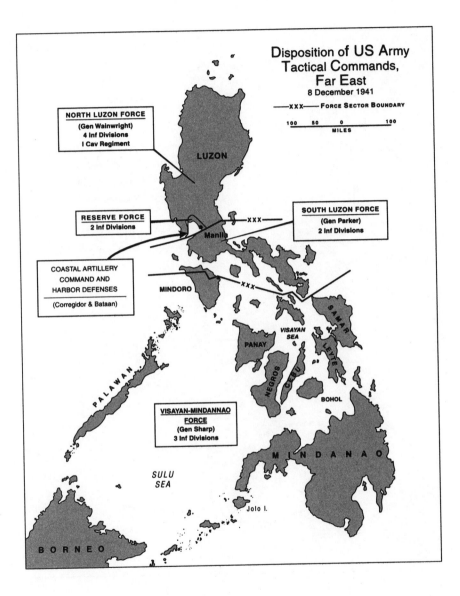

Disposition of US Army Tactical Commands, Far East

8 December 1941

—XXX— Force Sector Boundary

100   50   0   100
MILES

NORTH LUZON FORCE
(Gen Wainwright)
4 Inf Divisions
I Cav Regiment

LUZON

RESERVE FORCE
2 Inf Divisions

Manila

SOUTH LUZON FORCE
(Gen Parker)
2 Inf Divisions

COASTAL ARTILLERY COMMAND AND HARBOR DEFENSES
(Corregidor & Bataan)

MINDORO

VISAYAN SEA

SAMAR

PANAY

LEYTE

PALAWAN

NEGROS

CEBU

BOHOL

VISAYAN-MINDANNAO FORCE
(Gen Sharp)
3 Inf Divisions

MINDANAO

SULU SEA

Jolo I.

BORNEO

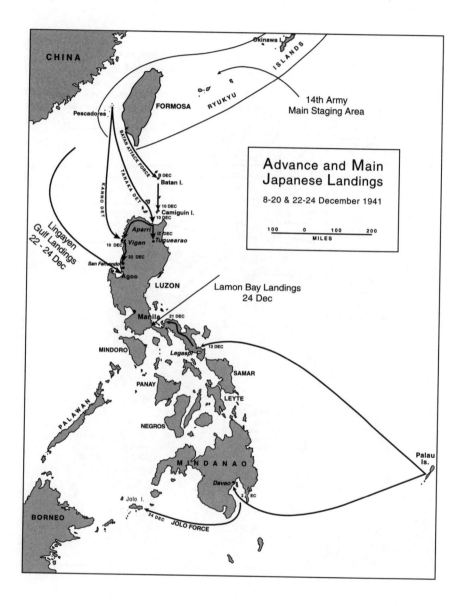

CHINA

Okinawa I.

RYUKYU ISLANDS

FORMOSA

14th Army
Main Staging Area

Pescadores

BATAN ATTACK FORCE

KANNO DET

TANAKA DET

8 DEC
Batan I.

10 DEC
Camiguin I.
10 DEC

12 DEC
Aparri
10 DEC
Vigan
Tuguearao

22 DEC

San Fernando

Agoo

Lingayen
Gulf Landings
22 - 24 Dec

LUZON

Lamon Bay Landings
24 Dec

Manila   21 DEC

MINDORO

Legaspi   12 DEC

SAMAR

PANAY

LEYTE

NEGROS

PALAWAN

MINDANAO

Palau
Is.

Davao

21 DEC

Jolo I.

24 DEC   JOLO FORCE

BORNEO

**Advance and Main
Japanese Landings**

8-20 & 22-24 December 1941

100   0   100   200
MILES

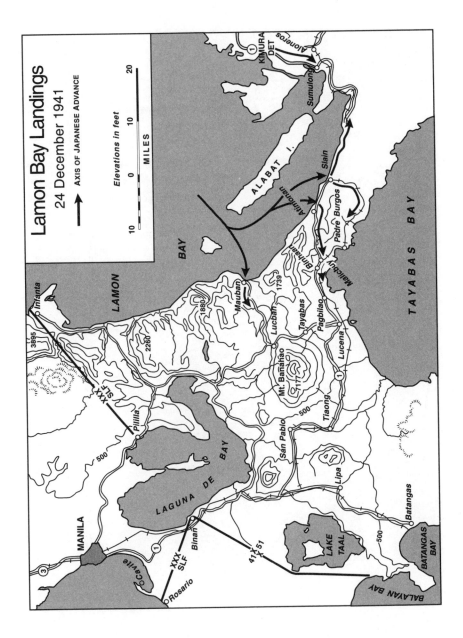

Lamon Bay Landings
24 December 1941
→ AXIS OF JAPANESE ADVANCE

Elevations in feet

MILES
10   0   10   20

LAMON   BAY

ALABAT I.

TAYABAS   BAY

Infanta
3895

500

Pililla
XXX SLF.

2260

1880

Mauban

Lucban

Mt. Banahao
4177

San Pablo

500

Tiaong

Tayabas

1739

Binñan

Atimonan

Slain

Padre Burgos

Malicbuy

Pagbilao

Lucena

LAGUNA   DE   BAY

MANILA

Cavite

Rosario

Binan
XXX SLF

41 X 51

500

Lipa

LAKE
TAAL

Batangas

BATANGAS
BAY

BALAYAN BAY

KIMURA
DET
Aloneros

Sumulong

1

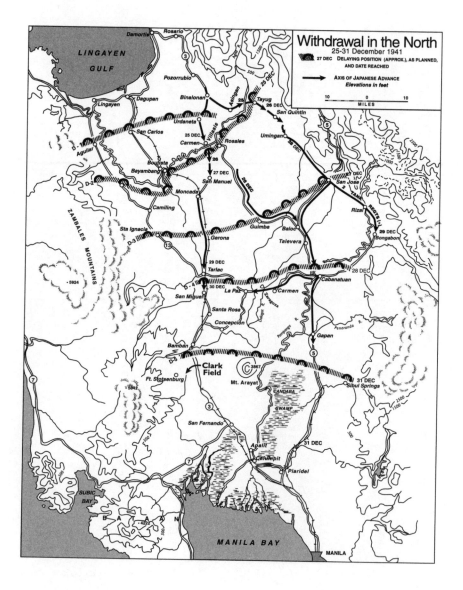

Withdrawal in the North
25-31 December 1941

27 DEC DELAYING POSITION (APPROX.), AS PLANNED, AND DATE REACHED

AXIS OF JAPANESE ADVANCE

Elevations in feet

10   0   10
MILES

LINGAYEN GULF

Damortis
Rosario
Pozorrubio
Binalonan
Asingan   25 DEC
Tayug   26 DEC
San Quintin
Lingayen
Dagupan
Urdaneta
San Carlos
Villasis   25 DEC
Carmen   Rosales
Umingan   28 DEC
Aguilar   D-1
Bautista   26
Bayambang
27 DEC   San Manuel
San Jose   27 DEC
Moncada   26 DEC
Rizal   29 DEC
Bongabon
D-2
Camiling
Guimba   Baloc
Sta Ignacia   D-3
Gerona   Talevera
29 DEC   Bongabon
ZAMBALES MOUNTAINS
13
• 5924
29 DEC   Tarlac   28 DEC
D-4   30 DEC   La Paz   Carmen   Cabanatuan
San Miguel   Santa Rosa
Concepcion   Gapan   28 DEC
5
Bamban   31 DEC
D-5   Sibul Springs
Clark Field   • 3867
Ft. Stotsenburg   Mt. Arayat
• 5842   CANDABA SWAMP
3
31 DEC
San Fernando   Apalit   31 DEC
7   Calumpit
SUBIC BAY   Plaridel
B A T A A N   • 4222
MANILA BAY   MANILA

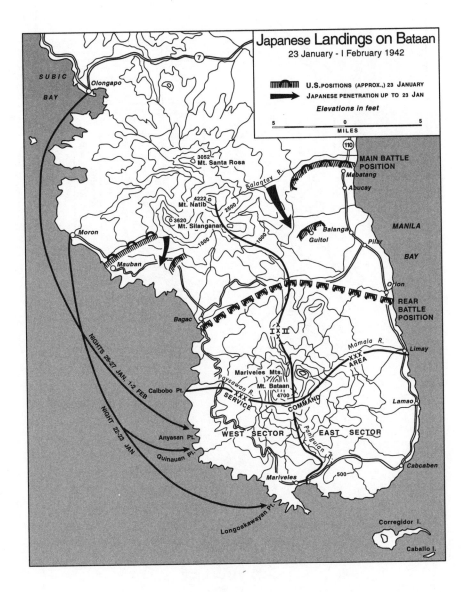

Japanese Landings on Bataan
23 January - I February 1942

U.S. POSITIONS (APPROX.,) 23 JANUARY
JAPANESE PENETRATION UP TO 23 JAN

Elevations in feet

5   0   5
         MILES

SUBIC
BAY

Olongapo

7

3052
Mt. Santa Rosa

Balantay R.

110

MAIN BATTLE
POSITION

Mabatang

Abucay

MANILA

4222
Mt. Natib

2500

3620
Mt. Silanganan

1500

1000

Moron

Mauban

Balanga
Guitol

Pilar

BAY

Orion

REAR
BATTLE
POSITION

Bagac

IX II
X

Mamala R.

Limay

XXX
AREA

NIGHTS 26-27 JAN, 1-2 FEB

Calbobo Pt.

Mariveles Mts.

Paysawan R.

Mt. Bataan

4700

XXX
SERVICE

COMMAND

Lamao

NIGHT 22-23 JAN

Anyasan Pt.

Quinauan Pt.

WEST SECTOR

Pantigan R.

EAST SECTOR

Cabcaben

Mariveles

500

Longoskawayan Pt.

Corregidor I.

Caballo I.

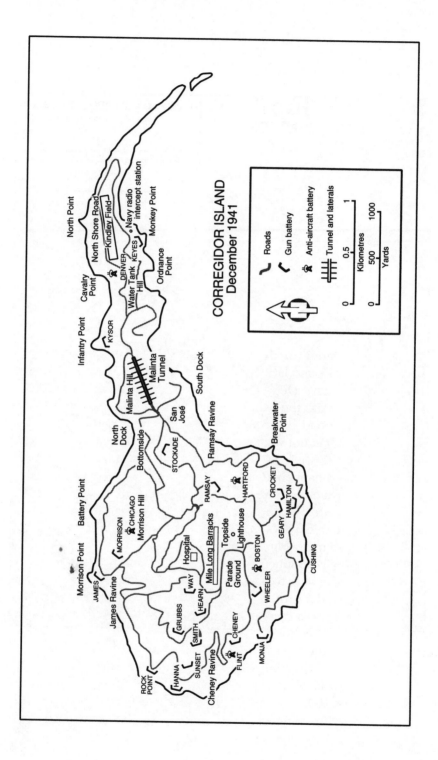

CORREGIDOR ISLAND
December 1941

Roads
Gun battery
Anti-aircraft battery
Tunnel and laterals

Kilometres
0   0.5   1

Yards
0   500   1000

North Point

North Shore Road
Kindley Field
Navy radio intercept station
DENVER
KEYES
Monkey Point
Water Tank
Ordnance Point

Cavalry Point

Infantry Point

KYSOR

Malinta Hill
Malinta Tunnel

South Dock

North Dock

Bottomside

San José

Ramsay Ravine

Battery Point

STOCKADE

Breakwater Point

Morrison Point

CHICAGO
Morrison Hill
MORRISON

RAMSAY

HARTFORD

CROCKET
HAMILTON
GEARY

James Ravine

JAMES

Hospital

Mile Long Barracks
Topside
Lighthouse
Parade Ground

WAY

HEARN

BOSTON

WHEELER

CUSHING

GRUBBS

SMITH

CHENEY

MONJA

ROCK POINT

HANNA

SUNSET

Cheney Ravine

FLINT

FOREWORD

Immediately prior to the 50th anniversary of the liberation of Manila in 1945, the late Dr. John Pimlott, Dr. Duncan Anderson (both of Sandhurst's Department of War Studies) and I received a commission to write the history of that liberation. Individuals in the Philippines who had been closely associated with that episode and who previously had not wished to recount their own personal stories, began to indicate their preparedness to give their very often grim accounts of what happened in February 1945. There was an element of immediacy which left the would-be authors with a matter of fourteen weeks to write *The Battle for Manila*. It was therefore not a deep and heavy academic work but a straightforward story of a tragic event in the lives of so many *Manileños*.

While in Manila conducting interviews, my mind turned to perhaps the obvious question as to the origins of the tragedy of Manila's liberation by General MacArthur. Although the process had been begun by the Japanese, it was a case of a city that was destroyed in order to be saved. This new book is the prequel to *The Battle for Manila* and begins in 1880, the year of MacArthur's birth, and runs through to 1942, to the fall of the Philippines in the first of the two campaigns of the Second World War. It is a weightier book than *The Battle for Manila* because there was sufficient time available to study the political and military machinations which led to America's stunning defeat by the Japanese. I began the prequel with a totally open mind. The conclusions that I have drawn are based on the analysis of the available material. So essential was the requirement for veracity that a number of experts in this field were co-opted to read and comment upon the drafts. To that end, I am extremely grateful for the generous assistance and advice provided by: Dr. Bernard D. Cole, Chairman, Department of National Security Policy and Professor of Maritime History and Strategy at the National Defense University, Washington; Colonel Adolf Carlson of the War College, Carlisle, Pennsylvania; James W. Zobel, Archivist at the MacArthur Memorial, Norfolk, Virginia; Professor Ricardo Trota Jose of the University of the Philippines; and Dr. Duncan Anderson of the Department of War Studies, Sandhurst. However, the responsibility for all errors and omissions are entirely mine.

In addition, I would like to thank: John J. Slonaker, Chief, Historical Reference Branch and David Keough of the Manuscript Branch, both at the U.S. Army Military History Institute; Kathy Lloyd of the U.S. Naval Historical Center; Ben Frank, formerly of the U.S. Marine Corps Historical Center; and Clive Richards, MoD Air Historical Branch. Thanks to Rosemary Best for reading the manuscript and to Gina, without whose work production skills and enthusiasm this book would never have come to fruition. Finally, I wish to record my gratitude to the Ayala Corporation, Roderick Hall, Consuelo McHugh, Memorare Manila and Ambassador John Rocha for their generous assistance in offsetting the research costs of *MacArthur and Defeat in the Philippines*.

RICHARD CONNAUGHTON
Nettlecombe, Dorset

MacArthur
and Defeat
in the Philippines

———————

1

GRAND STRATEGIES

On Monday 8 December 1941, Manila time,[1] the Pacific War, which had begun so emphatically with the infamous attack on Pearl Harbor, flowed outwards to the Philippine Islands. At 2 a.m. on that fateful Monday, American fighter and bomber pilots left a party at the Manila Hotel. Why was the U.S.A., this most decidedly anti-colonial state, in the Philippines? Rudyard Kipling, Britain's imperial bard, wrote his poem *The White Man's Burden* in response to the U.S.A.'s annexation of the Philippines in 1898,

> Take up the white man's burden
> —Ye dare not stoop to less
> Nor call too loud on Freedom
> To cloke your weariness;
> By all ye cry or whisper,
> By all ye leave or do,
> The silent, sullen peoples Shall weigh your
> Gods and you.

For a more pedestrian answer, it is necessary to go back to the years when the commanding general of the Manila-based United States Army Forces in the Far East (USAFFE), the sixty-one year old Lieutenant General Douglas MacArthur, was growing up in the 1880s and 1890s.

The completion of the Trans-Siberian Railway in 1895 changed the regional power balance in the Far East. In time, Russia would be able to move men and materiel from the west into Siberia and from there to capitalize upon the perceived collapse of the Chinese Empire. This development had the coincidental effect of putting Russia on a collision course with Japan's growing regional aspirations. In 1895, the German Kaiser pointedly commissioned a painting emphasizing the "Yellow Peril" and the threat posed to the interests of the European powers, which he then presented to the Tsar. The situation in the United States was seemingly less convoluted. The principle of isolationism had been established with the Founding Fathers. "We want with the outside world," said George Washington, "as little political connection as possible." But in reality the U.S.A. expanded steadily through the 19th century, starting with the purchase of Louisiana and Florida from France and Spain, then the 1867 purchase of Alaska from Russia, and a large parcel of land bounded by California and Texas taken from Mexico. The concept of "Manifest Destiny" had its origins in 1845 and was a stimulus to acquire the Oregon territories in 1846 and America's expansion out towards her natural domestic borders. However, with the exception of the New Mexico and California territories, U.S. expansion in the nineteenth century came about through purchase and not by conquest. Manifest Destiny was not a militarist concept. By the 1890s there was no further scope for reasonable expansion in Continental North America.

Until 1870, the use of steam power by the minuscule U.S. Navy had actually been forbidden. In 1880, there were only 48 ships in the USN capable of firing a shot in anger, but ten years later the situation had been transformed. This was in no small part attributable to the writings and influence of one man, Alfred Thayer Mahan, U.S. naval officer and theorist, who insisted that America's prosperity depended upon free access to world markets and that this could only be guaranteed through the development of a strong navy supported by an effective merchant marine. Mahan found influential backers for his assertive, expansive theories, including Theodore Roosevelt, Henry Cabot Lodge and John Hay. These white, Anglo-Saxon Protestants, mostly North-East Republicans,[2] believed the U.S.A. had the capability to become a global power and that this was its new manifest destiny. "The U.S. must not fall out of the line of march," said Lodge.

In 1895, there was a dispute with Britain regarding the Venezuela-British Guiana border, but America's principal source of aggravation

came from Spain. The 1895–1898 Cuban Revolution, brutally sup-
pressed by the Spaniards, came to a head on 15 February 1898 with
the (accidental) blowing up of the battleship *USS Maine* in Havana
harbor with the loss of 266 lives. On 25 April 1898, America declared
war on Spain and, on the 27th, the U.S. Asiatic Squadron of five cruisers and two gunboats, under Commodore George Dewey, left Hong
Kong for Manila, also part of the Spanish Empire. Dewey's purpose
was to prevent Spain's Pacific fleet from reinforcing the Caribbean. At
the Battle of Manila Bay, Dewey destroyed the Spanish fleet of four
cruisers and three gunboats and then blockaded the city of Manila
until the arrival of ground forces.

On 13 August 1898, after a token defense, the city surrendered.
Following Dewey's victory, Hawaii, which had applied to join the
Union in 1893, was annexed. In the summer of 1898, only forty per
cent of U.S. newspapers had been pro-annexation, but by year's end
that figure had increased to sixty per cent. The Treaty of Paris tidied
up America's conflict with Spain, which relinquished sovereignty over
Cuba, ceded Guam and Puerto Rico to the U.S.A. and sold the
Philippines for 20 million dollars. This sudden transformation of the
United States into not merely a Pacific but an Asiatic power was not
received with universal enthusiasm. President William McKinley
admitted he did not want the Philippines but, in effect being delivered on a plate, he thought it best to accept what had happened and
"by God's grace, do the best we could do for them."

In 1899 the Philippine Insurrection against the U.S.A. began, and
this caused a moral quandary and much heart-searching at home,
with considerable sympathy for the Filipinos' attempt to achieve their
freedom. American troops had been fired upon in the outskirts of
Manila and the subsequent American military response under Douglas MacArthur's father, Major General Arthur MacArthur, brought
the situation in the north under control by 1902. The conflict continued in the south of the country until 1905 when American forces
were confronted by fanatical Muslim tribesmen. It was no minor
insurgency. 100,000 American troops were engaged, of whom 4,243
were killed and 2,818 wounded[3] in action. The Filipinos lost 16,000
killed and a further 100,000 died from famine. The war effectively
ended American territorial expansion. Public opinion had reverted to
form, eschewing foreign adventurism, and regarding the Philippines
as a liability vulnerable to attack from Japan.

After William Howard Taft returned to Washington in 1904 after three years as civilian Governor of the Philippines, he commissioned Daniel Hudson Burnham, the architect of the city's post office and Union Station, to go to Manila. Burnham only stayed for forty days, but the results were profound. He laid down plans for a boulevard[4] running the length, north to south, of Manila's stunningly beautiful natural harbor. On the Luneta extension nearby, he catered for the social needs of the 15,000 Americans with an Army and Navy Club, an Elks Club for those of Masonic persuasion and, most important of all, he planned one of the world's famous hotels, the Manila,[5] "a hotel whose size, surroundings and appointments are intended to deliver Manila once and for all from the standing reproach of inhospitality toward a traveler."[6]

The *New York Medical Journal*, in an apparent damning with faint praise, judged Manila's climate to be healthier than that of Chicago and Philadelphia. But then again, Edwin W. Stephens, a Missouri editor, had written in 1908: "Manila is the most thoroughly typical American city I have ever visited outside the United States." The conclusion is that turn-of-the-century Americans did feel comfortable and at home in the Philippines,[7] perhaps because the cultural and racial differences within the city were reflected in a *de facto* caste system. There were the Spaniards who had been born in Spain *(peninsulares)*, Spaniards born in the Philippines *(insulares)*, those of mixed Spanish and Malay birth, of which Manuel Quezon was one, the *mestizos*, and the bulk of people of Malay stock who spoke dialects. There was also an appreciable number of Chinese. What these disparate groups had in common was the belief in, and practice of, the extended family. It was automatic that the local population, when on trips, would stay with family, so there had been no overwhelming need for hotels. The Manila Hotel formed part of the white enclave which excluded native citizens. Generally, Filipinos could not join the Manila Polo Club, the Manila Golf Club or the Army and Navy Club. There were exceptions to this rule, a rule which was bent in order to include within the American social circle Filipino citizens predominantly of Spanish ancestry—the *peninsulares* and *insulares*. Filipinos were not technically barred from visiting or staying at the Manila Hotel. There is the story of a prosperous Negros sugar planter inviting Visayan congressman José Romero to lunch in the hotel dining room. Becoming conscious of a child staring at them, they heard him say to his mother: "What are those Filipinos doing in here?"[8]

There was a convention that American men could have *queridas,* female mistresses, but they should not marry Filipinas. It was quite common for unaccompanied American men to have "a bit on the side." General Wood, who became Governor of the Philippines, makes mention of his adversary, General Pershing, having fathered two or three illegitimate children whilst posted to the islands.[9] There was the example of an American Sergeant who did marry a Filipina woman and had six children. The Asian Exclusion Act and his State's laws against mixed marriages prevented repatriation and re-enlistment. "He was doomed by his marriage to stay in the Philippines until he died."[10]

In 1912, the same year the Manila Hotel was opened, the U.S. Army in the Philippines was established as a permanent overseas colonial force. The total U.S. army manpower in the Philippines was 19,002 (compared with a total U.S. Army strength of 91,461) of which 13,007 were U.S. and 5,995 Philippine Scouts.[11] The Scouts had an authorized establishment ceiling of 12,000 but rarely exceeded 6,000. Unusually, the Regiments were permanently based in the Philippines and the men came and went on trickle postings, first for three years, then two. The two-year tour involved a rapid and destabilizing turnover of personnel.[12] Although the Philippines had a Governor-General, jurisdiction was exercised from Washington by the War Department's Bureau of Insular Affairs. This unusual reversal of the accepted civil-military relationship reflected the predominance of the military and their stake in the government of the Philippines.

If the mind can conjure a state on its toes, prepared to act decisively and quickly to optimize every opportunity, that was Japan at the end of the nineteenth century, a Japan convinced that the Dynastic collapse of China would not be permanent and hence the need to act when the right opportunity either presented itself or was engineered. After a short war, 1894–95, fought with exceptional military competence by Japan's armed forces in Manchuria and Korea, the feeble Chinese sought peace. Under the bilateral Treaty of Shimonoseki of 17 April 1895, China recognized Korean independence, thus paving the way for Japan to exercise what was in effect a protectorate over Korea. In addition, China paid Japan £25 million in reparations and ceded Formosa to Japan, as well as the Pescadores, and the Liaotung Peninsula in Manchuria upon which lies the warm-water port, Port Arthur.

Germany, France and Russia saw Japanese territorial ambitions as something to be nipped in the bud. Fleets were moved, the Russian army mobilized in the Amur region and, on 20 April 1895, a form of ultimatum was delivered to Tokyo. The Japanese Emperor recognized that Japan by herself did not have the power to resist the European coalition and consequently was obliged to withdraw from the Treaty of Shimonoseki. "I have," he said, "yielded to the dictates of magnanimity and accepted the advice of the three powers." As a result of the triple intervention, Russia took over the Liaotung Peninsula and Germany the Shantung Peninsula.

As a sweetener for the retrocession of the Liaotung Peninsula and for the return of Port Arthur into the limp hand of China, China paid Japan £5 million (60 million tael). The indemnities far exceeded Japan's war expenses and, as shall be seen, were wisely invested. What this episode taught Japan was the need for her to find an ally. That much became clear from the events of December 1897 when a Russian fleet appeared off Port Arthur as a preliminary to leasing the ice-free harbor and for building a railway northward to Harbin to connect with the Trans-Siberian. The 1902 marriage of convenience between Britain and Japan, whilst a shock to the world powers, was perfectly logical. The Japanese had a substantial army while Britain did not, and the British had a substantial navy while Japan did not. Moreover, Britain and Japan shared a common interest in containing Russia. Russia was seen as a threat not only to Britain's interests in China but also in India. Japan's perception of the Russian threat was altogether more immediate both in time and in space since she had a burgeoning population accompanied by a huge expansion of her industrial and trade base. Japan's market for the sale of her manufactured goods and source of food for her extra mouths were in East Asia. If the area were to be closed to Japan, the country would be brought to its knees. Of the East Asian markets, the most important to her were Manchuria and Korea. She attempted to negotiate with St. Petersburg but was rebuffed.

Japan had used her Chinese war indemnities well, investing in new battleships ordered from British yards. On 8 February 1904, she launched concurrent attacks against Russian forces over the beaches at Chemulpo (now known as Inchon) in Korea, and, led by Admiral Togo's flagship the *Mikasa*, against the Russian fleet at Port Arthur on the Liaotung Peninsula, though neglecting to declare war until 10 February 1904. Russia fought a disastrous, limited war with only a small percentage of her forces engaged, at the end of a 6,000-mile railway, while the Japanese fought a total war over short lines of communications but with limited national resources. Both were therefore

amenable to the entreaties of President Theodore Roosevelt to negotiate peace.

The Russo-Japanese War proved to be a watershed for Japan and
the U.S.A. due to the latter's role as negotiator at the Portsmouth
peace conference. In defeating a significant European state, Japan
had profoundly altered the international balance of power. The war
had been a foretaste of what was to come—the machine guns, trench
tactics, barbed wire and pounding artillery. The majority of military
observers who witnessed all this dismissed what they saw as irrelevant
to European warfare because the Russians had been so inept and the
Japanese so fanatical. One exception was the British observer Major-
General Ian Hamilton who, after the Battle of Liaoyang wrote: "I
have today seen the most stupendous spectacle it is possible for the
mortal brain to conceive—Asia advancing, Europe falling back, the
wall of mist and the writing thereon."[13]

General Arthur MacArthur, then Commander of the Division of
the Pacific at San Francisco, pleaded to be allowed to observe the war
but, by the time the visit was authorized and MacArthur arrived in
Manchuria, it was mid-March 1905 and all was over, bar the negotiat-
ing. On 6 August 1905 the Japanese and Russian delegations assembled aboard the *Mayflower* at Portsmouth, New Hampshire and
remained locked in negotiation until 6 September when the peace
treaty was signed. At the outset of the war, Theodore Roosevelt had
favored Japan but at war's end he had adopted a more balanced view,
having been persuaded of the threat posed by her as a political and
economic competitor. Europe judged him favorably as an arbitra-
tor: he won the Nobel Peace Prize. Others saw inequity in the peace
that he had brokered, best summed up in an article in the *New York
Times*: "The judgement of all observers here, whether pro-Japanese
or pro-Russian, is that the victory is as astonishing a thing as ever was
seen in diplomatic history. A nation hopelessly beaten in every battle of the war, one army captured and the other overwhelmingly
routed, with a navy swept from the seas, dictated her own terms to
victory." In Japan, the humiliating rewards for the victors—half of
frozen Sakhalin but obligatory withdrawal from Manchuria and no
indemnity—caused widespread anti-American rioting. This is the
point, September 1905, when the lines were drawn between Japan
and the U.S.A., the point at which fatal rivalry in the Pacific was iden-
tifiable. In March 1905, Roosevelt told Representative J.A.T. Hull,
Chairman of the House Committee on Military Affairs: "It may be

that the Japanese have designs on the Philippines. I hope not. I am inclined to believe not. But I believe we should put our naval and military preparations in such shape that we can hold the Philippines against any foe."[14] In 1906, the militarist, Giichi Tanaka began a study of possible Japanese operations targeting the Philippines.[15] In 1902, Washington had passed legislation against further immigration of Chinese and more pointedly, in 1906, the San Francisco School Board, reflecting the decades-old fear of the yellow horde in California, passed a rule segregating Japanese students in a separate elementary school.[16] In the 1907 War Plan Orange, Japan formally became recognized as a potential enemy of the United States of America.

In 1905, Secretary of War William Taft approved an overseas tour which would take Major General Arthur MacArthur, his wife "Pinky" (the former Mary Pinkney Hardy) and his aide-de-camp, his son Douglas—now a Lieutenant in the Corps of Engineers—on a grand tour of South East Asia. The General had encountered Taft in the Philippines in 1901 where the latter was civil governor. They had a difficult, tense relationship due, no doubt, to the General's outspokenness, particularly in making his animosity towards Germany public. It may therefore have been a matter of political convenience to have this potentially difficult general touring the military outposts of Southern China, Malaya, Burma, India and Ceylon from November 1905 to August 1906. On his return to his Headquarters in San Francisco, MacArthur senior resumed his duties but did not produce a substantive report of what he had seen and heard.[17] However, it is known that Arthur MacArthur told Taft that Japan's imperialistic ambitions were the core "problem of the Pacific" and that the Philippines required stronger defenses to prevent the territory's "strategic position from becoming a liability rather than an asset to the United States."[18] The "ordinary citizen"—the Japanese man in the street—had impressed his son Douglas. "But I had the uneasy feeling that the haughty, feudalistic samurai who were their leaders, were, through their victories, planting the seed of eventual Japanese conquest of the Orient."[19]

Japan's declaration of war upon Germany on 23 August 1914 came as a shock, not least to Germany who had been training Japan's army and to Britain, Japan's ally, who had been neither consulted nor informed in advance of Japan's intentions. The move marked a weakening of the Anglo-Japanese alliance. Tokyo's confidence and assurance had grown at such pace that she no longer needed the rickety prop provided by the colonial powers in London. Japan presented herself as the Asian hero and took the opportunity to take over Germany's few territorial interests in China and islands in the North Pacific (the Caroline, Mariana and Marshall Islands) thus potentially posing a strategic threat to the lines of communication between Hawaii and the Philippines. In January 1915, Japan presented China with her notorious 21 Demands, a plan for the annexation of China. Only the joint intervention of Britain and the U.S.A. forced Japan to back away, although her ultimate intentions remained alarmingly transparent. The assistant British military attaché in Peking, writing in 1918, recommended that London should take a realistic approach in her relationship with Tokyo: "If Japan is not given a free hand in some part of the Far East, there is a danger that she might actually go over to the enemy. With Russia a prostrate neutral between them, Japan and Germany would form an extremely strong combination, which would threaten the whole of the allies' possessions in Asia and even in Australasia." Isolationism had conspired to keep the United States out of the First World War until 1917 when the unrestricted German submarine campaign of February became one step too far. The infusion of fresh manpower helped to swing the tide against the Germans. Colonel Douglas MacArthur deployed to Europe as Chief of Staff of the 42nd (Rainbow) Division. By 1918 he had not only commanded 84th Infantry Brigade in the rank of Brigadier-General but also, on 6th November, was gazetted to command the 42nd Division. He had put down his marker.

At the Paris Peace Conference, Japan secured mandates over the former German territories but nothing to strengthen her hand in her relationship with China and the development of what she perceived to be her own, regional, Monroe Doctrine. Nationalists in Japan spoke openly of Japan having been denied her rights in 1895, 1905 and 1919. They castigated the international system which had been consistently unfair in its treatment of Japan and declared their view that if Japan was to advance she would have to do so unilaterally. Versailles stimulated the development of nationalist societies. By 1936 more than 750 active fascist groups were known to the police, the most dangerous and extreme of which were dominated by military officers.[20] Between 1905 and 1922, there had been a pronounced change in the nature of the Japanese soldier. No more was he a chivalrous and generous fighter and instead had become cold, vicious and callous.

Japan's growth in the early 1920s may not have been as dramatic as the U.S.A.'s but, in becoming a creditor nation, she was on the right economic path. Her manufacturing output increased 78 per cent, merchant shipping 70 per cent and the customers and markets which the war had prevented Britain from servicing fell serendipitously into the lap of Japan. The Anglo-Japanese Alliance fell due for renewal in 1922. The U.S.A. insisted that Britain should abrogate her treaty with Japan, which had outlived its purpose as a counter-balance to Russia and as a means for facilitating the concentration of the newest Royal Navy warships in European waters in the face of a new German naval threat. A combined Anglo-Japanese fleet posed too strong a challenge for the U.S.A. which, post-war, had chosen not to become involved in an arms race. That much was reflected in the 1921–22 Washington Conference and the resultant Washington Naval Treaty.

The Washington Conference was convened to reduce the number of capital ships in the world's navies, to halt the construction of battleships and to re-jig the relative strength of world navies in the proportion Britain and U.S.A. 5, Japan 3 and France and Italy 1.75. A ten-year suspension of building programs was proposed as well as a restriction on tonnages. The Conference was Pacific-centric, involving not only changes in naval policy but also implications for the future of Asia. By 1919, the majority of the USN was on the West Coast to meet any Japanese challenge. A nine-power treaty undertook to honor China's sovereignty and to support America's "open door" principles. Also superimposed upon this conference was a four-power treaty—Britain, U.S.A., Japan and France—involving a declaration of mutual respect for dependencies. It was a U.S. initiative aimed at safeguarding the Philippines. A subsidiary condition of the Washington disarmament conference had been the restriction placed upon further fortification of the Philippines. So sensitive was Congress to active participation in world affairs that the aforementioned "respect for dependencies" initiative barely achieved the requisite two-thirds Senate majority. A schism had also developed among Imperial Japanese Naval officers who saw in the USN the devil they needed to keep them up to the mark. The Washington Naval Treaty aimed to prevent the Japanese Navy from challenging the Americans but failed to do so. In the view of the Chief of the Naval General Staff, Admiral Kanji Kato, war with the United States began with the signing of the Washington Naval Treaty.[21]

A court martial of considerable significance took place in the

U.S.A. in 1925. The officer court martialled, Colonel Billy Mitchell, was a friend and former neighbor of the by now Major-General MacArthur who had been appointed a member of the Court—"One of the most distasteful orders I ever received."[22] Mitchell was the most outspoken proponent of the predominance of air power at the time, calling for the unified control of all air forces which, at that time, were divided among the Army and Navy. The greatest opposition to Mitchell's proposals came from the Navy, which may account for his vitriolic criticism of the War Department in general and Navy Department in particular when the Navy dirigible *Shenandoah* was lost in an electrical storm. What General MacArthur had to say at the time of the court martial was perceptive: "Neither ground nor sea forces can operate safely unless the air over them is controlled by our own air power."[23] Nevertheless, in December 1941, the air forces were still not under any semblance of unified control.

The collapse of the Manchu Dynasty in China in 1911 had led to high levels of disorder and instability. Japan sought to capitalize upon the fragility of China's condition by demanding control of the Shantung Peninsula. Ninety per cent of China's external investment came from Japan and China took 25 per cent of Japan's exports. In June 1928, following a long period of drift and lack of direction, Chiang Kai Shek, leader of the Chinese Nationalist Kuomintang Party, established a government in Nanking with a view to bringing order to the country. Chiang Kai Shek's wife and sister-in-law had graduated from American colleges and had converted to Christianity, which may possibly have contributed to his decision to cut the economic, Gordian knot with Japan in favor of economic ties with America. The timing of this intended realignment could not have been more inopportune for Japan. Japanese agriculture had adapted to the reality that the state was not gifted with endless acreage for agrarian development. What therefore passed as agriculture was built around the silk industry. In 1930, exports of silk fell by 40 per cent, representing a loss of 33 per cent of Japanese exports. Forty per cent of Japanese families depended upon the silk industry for their livelihoods. Tokyo realized that advancement could not be built upon something so vulnerable to the whim of market forces. Security could only be enhanced through expansion beyond Japan's borders.

In 1931, to the embarrassment of the Japanese government, junior army officers manipulated an incident in Manchuria as an excuse to occupy the region. This was the beginning of what for Japan would be "the Fifteen Years War."[24] In March 1932, the protectorate of Manchukuo was established, comprising a resource-rich land area larger than Japan, with a population of 30 million. The international community, afflicted by the Great Depression, had neither the will nor capabilities to intervene. The condemnation of Japan by the League of Nations in February 1933 merely led to Japan leaving the organization. In 1934, Japan denounced the Washington Conference, thereby unshackling herself from the restraints of that treaty. Provisions within that treaty meant that the United States could, two years following Japan's unilateral action, renew the fortification of the Philippines, but domestic politics supervened and the work did not begin.[25] Following the outbreak of war between Japan and China in 1937 reports of Japanese atrocities became an immediate source of tension with the U.S.A., notably the Rape of Nanking at year's end but also the Panay Incident.

In 1938, Russian and Japanese forces clashed at Changkufang where the Chinese, Korean and Siberian borders meet, to the west of Vladivostock. In the summer of 1939 there was a larger, more serious army-scale battle at Nomonhan on the borders of Manchuria and Outer Mongolia. The Soviets thrashed the unmechanized Japanese Army, armor being one of the few areas in the Japanese order of battle found wanting. The lesson of Nomonhan was that Japan should avoid the open plains of Siberia and seek out the closer terrain of the islands and peninsulas of the Pacific. Accordingly, in 1941 Japan came to a non-aggression agreement with the Soviets and an understanding among themselves that they would only implement the northern option if the Soviet Union was defeated by Germany in the west. Strategically, it made little sense for Japan to enter into armed conflict with the 40 Soviet divisions held back in Siberia for such a contingency. Since Japan no longer posed a serious threat to the Soviet Union, the Siberian divisions were released to the western sector, arriving in Moscow by 17 November 1941, just in time to halt the German forces outside the city.

Following the outbreak of war in Europe in 1939, Japan's association with Nazi Germany strengthened, culminating in the September 1940 Tripartite Pact, the Berlin-Rome-Tokyo Axis. The Pact considerably strengthened Japan's arm for it meant she could take America to the wire, and beyond, safe in the knowledge that, if America reacted with an armed attack, Japan would be supported by Germany and Italy. When Vichy France acceded to Tokyo's request to occupy Indo-

China as a means of gaining further leverage over China, Britain, the U.S.A. and the Netherlands froze Japanese assets and war materials. The strategic ramifications of this initiative were to turn off eighty-eight per cent of Japan's oil supply, since the U.S.A. had been a major supplier of Japan's oil. Japan had only two years of oil in reserve, yet the contemporary strategic estimate indicated three years being required to defeat China. Thus, her modern fleet which by 1941 had achieved parity with the U.S.A., though having the benefit of operating on interior lines, could not be guaranteed indefinite freedom of action. Secretary of State Cordell Hull agreed to restore Japan's oil supply in exchange for a guarantee of non-aggression from Japan—a guarantee which was not forthcoming. Japan found herself in a difficult position. If the embargo were not to be lifted, she faced the straight choice between taking the oil she needed and fighting the western powers or withdrawing from China with the strong prospect of stimulating a domestic coup by the military. There were no other measures. A partial withdrawal, say from Indo-China with an accompanying guarantee of no further southern expansion would weaken Japan strategically. Tokyo believed such a concession to be a sign of weakness, guaranteed to beget further demands from Washington. However, if Japan adopted an aggressive policy, she could secure in Java and Sumatra all the oil she would need to bring the China campaign to a satisfactory conclusion. Moreover, seizure of Malaya, where four-fifths of the world's rubber and two-thirds of its tin were produced, would be a mighty strategic blow.

What the U.S.A. did not want was a war on two fronts. Her policy was to contain a Japan whose strategic aims were thought to revolve around Russia and Indo-China. In 1940, America's army was so small that the officer corps was reasonably well acquainted one with another, certainly to the extent of recognizing their challengers for the limited amount of promotion available. Militarily, the U.S.A. was ranked twentieth in the world order, with America immediately behind the Netherlands. The more significant naval resources were fully stretched. The Atlantic, where the U-Boat war was in progress, made priority demands and, in the Pacific, that ocean's naval resources had to be deployed from California to Hawaii. Roosevelt toyed with the idea of offering Japan a *modus vivendi* conditional upon Japan's withdrawal from Indo-China. That option was not pursued for to have done so would have marked the abandonment of the Stimson Doctrine, which underwrote the sovereignty of China.

In the critical year of 1941, Roosevelt recognized the inevitability of war with Germany, yet he had also assured America's parents that their boys would not be sent into foreign wars. Moreover, eighty per cent of Americans opposed America entering the war. In August 1941, Roosevelt met Winston Churchill at the Atlantic Conference at Placentia Bay, Newfoundland. Churchill had crossed the Atlantic aboard the pride of the British navy, the 35,000-ton battleship *HMS Prince of Wales*. Churchill believed that he had "established warm and deep personal relations with our great friend" but was nonetheless depressed by the "President's many assurances and no closer to war."[26] In fact the U.S.A. did move closer to war with Germany. Selective service was extended and more USN vessels were assigned to convoy escort duties in the Atlantic. An attack on the *USS Greer* on 4 September 1941 led to the President authorizing the USN to attack Axis warships on sight and, in November 1941, the neutrality laws were revised to allow U.S.-registered ships to enter hostile war zones.

Japan's evolving concept of a Greater East Asia Co-Prosperity Sphere was no more to the advantage of the countries in the sphere than the western system it sought to replace. The invasion plans being finalized were aimed at colonial territory whose inhabitants existed in varying degrees of subservience. But Japan had no intention of releasing the people of South-East Asia from colonial bondage and merely looked to replace western leadership with her own. It was the Imperial Japanese Army which formulated Japan's aggressive philosophy, rather than the Imperial Japanese Navy. But the Army, extremely nationalist, prickly and highly volatile, had its expansionist plans limited more or less to Manchuria and Korea, while the Navy pursued a Pacific-wide strategy which demanded secure lines of communication and resources. By September 1940, Roosevelt's oil embargo threatened to undermine the Imperial Japanese Navy's Pacific strategy, yet in a letter to Admiral Shimada in December 1940, Admiral Yamamoto wrote: "To be stunned, enraged and discomforted by America's economic pressure at this belated hour is like a schoolboy who unthinkingly acts on the impulse of the moment."[27] Admiral Yamamoto knew from his own experiences that an America stung by an infamous attack would quickly gear itself up and be able to sustain total war far longer than Japan. Yamamoto gave the military planners six months only in which to defeat the U.S.A. It was for that reason that a pre-emptive strike was launched upon an unprepared U.S.

Pacific Fleet. When, on the morning of 7 December 1941 Honolulu time, the carrier *Akagi* signaled to her carrier group the launching of their maritime aircraft against Hawaii, she flew from her masthead the battle flag the *Mikasa* had flown when she initiated Japan's 1904 pre-emptive strike against the Russian fleet at Port Arthur.

The tragedy of the War in the Pacific is that it might well, through a process of sensible compromise, have been avoided. It was an unnecessary war which, from its outset, Japan was by no means certain she could win. Japan "entered the war in December 1941 not so much in the hope of victory, but because the spirit of the nation demanded nothing less."[28]

2

EARLY DAYS

Douglas MacArthur served his first tour in the Philippines in 1903. He enjoyed two months graduation furlough before this tour with his parents at Fort Mason, during which time he met a military legend recently arrived from Manila, Captain John J. Pershing. Here was the epitome of the well cut, military action man who had already carved out a reputation for fearlessness in Cuba and in Mindanao against fanatical Moro tribesmen. The meeting passed without mention in MacArthur's autobiography *Reminiscences*, but Pershing was sufficiently "favorably impressed by the manly, efficient appearance of the second lieutenant," to record the event in his unpublished autobiography.[1]

MacArthur had graduated top of his class at West Point[2] as a second lieutenant in the Corps of Engineers. He had no natural affinity with engineering, but had been persuaded that this was the most assured course for rapid promotion. Whilst at West Point, his mother had taken up residence just outside the entrance to the Academy, testimony to the closeness and interdependence of the family. Her eldest son, Arthur III, had joined the U.S. Navy, participating in the battle of Santiago. A mother's boy with an awareness that he was something special, Douglas was already tending to become a remote and reserved individual. Whilst at West Point he leaned very heavily upon a mother not averse to managing his career. But the reason she had gone to West Point was to preserve the links, companionship and integrity of the family.

Much has been written of Major General Arthur MacArthur's 1900–1901 disagreements with William Howard Taft who headed the Philippine Commission before becoming Civil Governor. It was, for Arthur, an unfortunate clash of personalities, for Taft was not only a close personal friend of President Theodore Roosevelt but would become his Secretary of War.[3] The friction between the two men broke Arthur MacArthur's career. "Broke" is a relative term for although it is true that some unspectacular appointments intervened between his departure from Manila and retirement, he nonetheless rose by an act of Congress to the rank of Lieutenant-General, the highest military rank then attainable.[4] That, and his retrospectively awarded Medal of Honor, provided the son with targets to achieve.

General MacArthur's achievements during the fourteen months he was military governor had been particularly distinguished. He had a difficult course to steer because a clash of interests between the cultural rather than religious differences of the new order as represented by American Protestantism and the old order as represented by Spanish Roman Catholicism appeared inevitable. When the 325 lb. Taft arrived in June 1900, he took over a number of important initiatives that MacArthur had begun, such as tackling the draconian Spanish civil code, the introduction of a basic form of education, and establishing a commission to set up a bilateral trade relationship between the U.S.A. and the islands. MacArthur's most lasting civil achievement, and the one most appreciated by the Filipinos,[5] was his preparedness to work with them and to take them into his confidence. It was a limited form of contact but an important first step, as Taft himself recognized. Both men set out to befriend Manila's political elite, the *illustrados*, and, with promises of power-sharing in the future, were able to separate them from the rebels.

Militarily, MacArthur had a reputation as an uncompromising warrior in battle yet humane towards the defeated. Two years of bitter, bloody insurrection eventually reached an impasse when General Emilio Aguinaldo's guerrillas could no longer go forward, but nor would they contemplate surrender. MacArthur agreed to a plan of Captain Frederick Funston to capture Aguinaldo through trickery. Surprisingly, the ruse worked, and when Aguinaldo was brought before MacArthur, the guerrilla leader was offered, and accepted, an amnesty. Moreover, he took an oath of allegiance to the United

States. Rumors of this began to percolate out into the countryside. In order to verify the unlikely story, one of Aguinaldo's lieutenants, under safe conduct, visited MacArthur at Malacañan Palace. The dapper *mestizo* guerrilla stood in front of MacArthur's desk and requested to see his leader. MacArthur said "he's over there," pointing to the door across the corridor from his office. When the two met, Aguinaldo instructed his visitor to tell the guerrillas to disperse peacefully.[6] The name of the emissary from the guerrillas was Manuel Quezon.

The young MacArthur spent his year engaged on defense projects throughout the island. He admitted to being charmed by the Philippines. "The delightful hospitality, the respect and affection expressed for my father, the amazingly attractive result of a mixture of Spanish culture and American industry, the languorous laze that seemed to glamorize even the most routine chores of life, the fun-loving men, the moonbeam delicacy of its lovely women, fastened me with a grip that has never relaxed."[7]

The Philippines were, for the young men of MacArthur's vintage, the new frontier. MacArthur had, of course, accompanied his parents on their remote postings on the old western frontier and, "like all frontiersmen, I was expert with a pistol." That was just as well for he recounts how, in a moment of carelessness on Guimaris Island at the mouth of Iloilo Harbor, he had been confronted by a pair of "desperadoes" but, being equal to the moment, "I dropped them both dead in their tracks." Alerted by the noise, his Irish foreman had come rushing up and, surveying the scene, drawled, "Begging this Loo'tenant's paddon, but all the rest of the Loo'tenant's life is pure velvut."[8]

Perhaps it did happen, but there are also, in the early part of his memoirs, events which he remembers which others could not recall. Another striking feature of the memoirs is the absence of evidence of real and lasting friendships. Traditionally at college, bonds are established which last a military career and beyond. But already we discern in this intensely ambitious young man someone with his vision fixed on the stars. Outside his own family, he seems to have had no great need for people other than the tight circle of military staff he gathered around himself. Those he dealt with fell into two categories, inferiors and competitors. Yet for one so full of confidence and self-awareness, he unashamedly wrote the most servile of letters to those he regarded as peers or superiors. John Gunther saw in MacArthur the traits of Julius Caesar: "strong will, imperiousness, narcissism" while William Manchester titled his biography of MacArthur, *American Caesar*. Like Patton, MacArthur knew his history and would doubtless have recalled that Caesar was stabbed in the back by his associates. He certainly became wary of those around him, convinced that there were parties deliberately frustrating his plans and ambitions.

In October 1904, suffering from malaria and ringworm, MacArthur left Manila for San Francisco and then the Engineer School at Washington Army Barracks,[10] where he also worked for President Roosevelt's military assistant. In August 1907 he was posted to Milwaukee, where he was able to live at home with his parents, his father being between appointments. It was whilst at Milwaukee, working on engineer bread-and-butter projects such as rivers and harbors, that the rather obvious dawned upon MacArthur: from a career point of view he was drifting. Whoever had recommended a career in army engineers as a fast-track to promotion must have done so tongue in cheek. His mind drifted from the job in hand and his superior recorded the fact in only a "fair" efficiency report: "his duties are not performed in a satisfactory manner." This blemish to his career was seen as irredeemable by his mortified mother who called upon the Chairman of the Union Pacific Railway to facilitate an emergency career change for her darling, without telling him. Although his ego had been severely bruised, he had no plans to leave the army, and soldiered-on at his new post, Fort Leavenworth, Kansas, where he would remain for the next four years.

His father retired in June 1909 at the age of 64, but had only three more years to live. Whilst attending the 24th Wisconsin Volunteer Regiment's 50th Anniversary Reunion on 5 September 1912 he collapsed and died. "My whole world changed that night. Never have I been able to heal the wound in my heart."[18] His mother had been in poor health for some time and a supernumerary appointment was arranged for Douglas in the office of the Chief of Staff, Medal of Honor winner and physician Major-General Leonard Wood. Wood was an original thinker, pro air power, a Republican, politically astute and one who recognized the importance of good relations with the media. MacArthur lived in awe of the man. In April 1914, following a change of government and a two-day clash of arms between Mexican forces and American marines, Wood sent Captain MacArthur on a reconnaissance to Vera Cruz, Mexico. Brigadier Frederick Funston, captor of Aguinaldo, had arrived there with his Brigade as a preliminary to a more significant commitment of forces led by Wood, who had completed his term of duty as Chief of Staff. MacArthur got into a scrape on his reconnaissance and had to fight his way out. He had a way with words and wrote a short but highly embellished account of what he had done, which some cynics suspected had the intention of winning him the Medal of Honor. He wrote to Wood, telling him of his achievement, and commented how:[11] "General Funston is handling things well and there is room for little criticism, but I miss the inspiration, my dear General, of your own clear-cut decisive methods. I hope sincerely that affairs will shape themselves so that you will shortly take the field for the campaign which, if death does not call you, can have but one ending—the White House."[12]

The Navy and Marines awarded themselves a profusion of fifty-five Medals of Honor for the two day set-to at Vera Cruz, including one for the naval commander, Admiral Fletcher, who had remained aboard his flagship during the operation.[13] MacArthur had three nominations for the Medal of Honor, including one from Wood himself. As MacArthur wrote in a matter of fact way: "The War Department disagreed."[14] What he did not reveal was a major tantrum in which he declared himself "incensed" over the Board's "rigid narrow mindedness and lack of imagination." He won few friends for what biographer James describes as "a pattern of behavior (which) was becoming increasingly evident in him which would brand him in the eyes of many officers as a pleader for special consideration and a sensitive, self-righteous protester against any infringements upon what he felt were his prerogatives."[15] The need for two eyewitnesses to corroborate his claim was waived as being "impractical" but he was still ruled ineligible for the award by a majority view that it had been inadvisable for him to have conducted the reconnaissance in question "without the knowledge of the commanding general on the ground." However, in December 1915, MacArthur was promoted to Major.

In June 1917, Major-General John J. Pershing sailed for France to command American forces on the Western Front. Major-General Frederick Funston, who, it was assumed, would lead American forces against Germany, had died of a heart attack at the age of 52 in February. General Wood's criticism of the Administration—he said, "We have no leadership in Washington"—effectively debarred him from a leadership role in France. Meanwhile MacArthur was in Washington attracting attention. His work with censorship brought him into regular contact with the press. When one pressman asked him, with the threat of a war looming, whether he would take an important staff post in Washington, he replied to the contrary: "The real promotions will go to the men who go to France."[16]

Whilst in France, initially as divisional Chief of Staff, MacArthur displayed his capacity for heroism and style. He dressed informally, outrageously—one of his nicknames was the Beau Brummel of the AEF[17]—as if a peacock, saying "look at me." He wore no helmet, carried no gas mask or weapon, except a riding crop.

On a rare occasion when he was not in the front line, MacArthur was at a railhead overseeing the evacuation of soldiers when General Pershing made a surprise visit. Pershing shouted out to MacArthur, "This Division is a disgrace! The men are poorly disciplined and they are not properly trained. The whole outfit is just about the worst I have seen. They're a filthy rabble." MacArthur sought to excuse his men by telling Pershing, whom of course he knew well, that the men had only just been taken out of the line. Pershing became apoplectic. "Young man, I do not like your attitude!" MacArthur apologized saying he was only telling the truth, to which Pershing responded, "MacArthur, I'm going to hold you personally responsible for getting discipline and order into this division—or God help the whole pack of you."[18] Pershing had a number of undesirable habits: he was a womanizer, he was notoriously unpunctual and he bawled out senior officers in the presence of their subordinates in the belief it kept them on their toes.

Though no malice was intended, no one had ever so publicly humiliated the rising star. Certainly MacArthur had enemies in Pershing's headquarters, but Pershing would brook no criticism of him among his staff officers. "Stop all this nonsense. MacArthur is the greatest leader of troops we have, and I intend to make him a division commander."[19]

When the Armistice came, the majority of Brigadier Generals commanding divisions—including MacArthur—reverted to their substantive rank. Thus MacArthur was denied his second star when he resumed command of his former brigade—the 84th. But he had had a good war, in which his reputation had been greatly enhanced. He won 12 American decorations, including two Purple Hearts[20] (gassed on both occasions), seven Silver Stars and the Distinguished Service Medal, and nineteen awards from Allied nations—he was the AEF's most decorated soldier. But it was insufficient. He wanted the Medal of Honor. A review board met in January 1919 and again decided he was ineligible for the award. Angered, MacArthur attributed this failure to "enmity . . . on the part of certain senior members of Pershing's GHQ Staff."[21]

MacArthur returned from war in April 1919. An old comrade of his, General Peyton C. Marsh, was Chief of Staff and he gave the thirty-nine year old MacArthur the unlooked-for appointment of Superintendent of West Point. Here, it seemed, was a round peg for a round hole, but MacArthur knew differently. It was a prestigious post which locked in his wartime rank as a substantive Brigadier-General[22] with seniority over the majority of his peers, but he saw himself as a doer rather than a teacher and he had real concerns as to how he would manage his former, elderly professors, many of whom formed an academic gerontocracy. Nevertheless, MacArthur had a strong attachment to his alma mater and could not resist a challenge, particularly the mission given to him by March to revitalize and revamp the academy. A monastic quiet pervaded the Superintendent's house at West Point with, unusually, a Mother Superior in residence. Pinky was now sixty-seven and passed regularly from bouts of good health to sickliness.

As a wartime exigency, the former four-year syllabus had been reduced to one year. MacArthur was now required to oversee the planning and development of a three-year course. The faculty steadfastly resisted his reforming zeal, and what should have proved to be a challenging and rewarding appointment became quite the contrary. A chill from Washington merely added to MacArthur's sense of isolation and loneliness when the pacifist yet pliant Secretary of War Newton D. Baker and Chief of Staff March were replaced in 1921 by a Bostonian, John Weeks, unknown to MacArthur, and by General "Black Jack" Pershing, who was perhaps too well known.

On 22 November 1921, Pershing warned MacArthur to be prepared for overseas service in June 1922.[23] Although there were no rules of tenure, a Superintendent could expect to serve out a four-year tour at West Point. The reason why MacArthur was being short-toured became the subject of intense speculation in political and military circles. MacArthur attributed the new orders to the Washington conspiracy against him and with this, together with his local difficulties, he felt highly vulnerable. It was at this point that he met Louise Cromwell Brooks. Louise had divorced her wealthy contractor husband in 1919. The super-rich mother of two children, she had lived out the war in Paris where she became romantically acquainted with General John J. Pershing. When Pershing returned to the U.S.A., Louise came too and acted as his official hostess. Many thought they would marry, but that seemed not to be the view of the widower Pershing. Besides, Louise had been attracted to Pershing's aide, Colonel John G. Quekemeyer—that is until she met Douglas MacArthur in January 1922 at a social event near West Point. Several weeks later, after a home football game, a sport which MacArthur adored, he proposed marriage, to which Louise immediately agreed. "If he hadn't proposed the first time we met," Louise told reporters, "I would have done it myself.[24] On 15 January, Louise announced their engagement and two weeks later Pershing announced MacArthur's posting to the Philippines.[25]

Rumors abounded that Pershing's posting of MacArthur was out of spite for stealing his mistress. That is improbable because, by then, Pershing had another established mistress, the Romanian artist Michelline Resco whom he had met in France.[26] What is possible is that it was a blow aimed at Louise. Pershing took grave offence at her dumping of Quekemeyer, whom he treated like a son, in preference to MacArthur. He attempted to get Louise to change her mind and it seems that banishment to the socially-retarded, disease-ridden environment of Manila and its enervating heat may have been intended to be a punishment. But it could have been that the Philippine posting had been Pershing's intention for MacArthur all along.

The couple were married at Palm Beach on St. Valentine's Day, 14 February 1922. Standing side by side, the slim, godlike figure of MacArthur in white uniform seemed at odds with the fuller figure of his wife, ten years his junior. A headline in the next day's *New York Times* screamed MARS MARRIES MILLIONS, but it was an unlikely and ill-conceived union. Among the 200 guests, the only representative that could be identified as being on the groom's "side" was the West Point Chaplain, Clayton Wheat. Pinky was not present, not, as was widely assumed, due to her objection to her son marrying a divorcee, but because she had not fully recovered from a heart attack[27] in November 1921.

Another myth arose, following a comment Louise made the morning after the wedding night. At breakfast, Louise confided in the best man, her brother, Marine Captain Jimmy Cromwell: "He may be a general in the army but he's a buck private in the boudoir."[28] Louise's words were ones of appreciation, not criticism, for while it is unlikely that she had had any sexual experience of a "buck private," the thought did conjure in her mind's eye the earthiness of a basic, grass roots, direct approach.[29] When the marriage did eventually fail in 1929, this, and others of Louise's public comments, were seized upon by enemies and political opponents alike to link MacArthur's political ambitions to his perceived failure as a lover.

MacArthur's tenure as Superintendent at West Point ended as intended on 30 June 1922. His relationship with Pershing plumbed new depths when Pershing wrote his efficiency report, placing his former protégé thirty-eighth in a pecking order of forty-six, mostly long-in-the-tooth Brigadier-Generals. Under normal circumstances, MacArthur might have anticipated a grading of excellent and a rec-ommendation for promotion. Instead he was graded with the kiss-of-death rating "above average."

Neither MacArthur nor his bride relished the tour in Manila. Louise was more used to Paris and Washington and, while Douglas had fond memories of the place, he had been assigned a non-job as Commander of the newly-established Military District of Manila, manned by a mere battalion of troops. The one bright spot was the presence in Manila, as Governor General, of an old friend, General Leonard Wood. He had failed to obtain the Republican nomination for President in 1920, and so reluctantly assumed office in Manila in 1921.[30] However, relations between Wood and the Philippine cabinet had deteriorated due to Wood's unsympathetic reaction to Philippine aspirations for independence. Wood proved to be a hard taskmaster who maintained a distinct division between Americans and Filipinos. He would not talk to the latter on official business unless an American was also present. In exasperation, the leading politicians, Manuel Quezon and Sergio Osmeña, engineered the tendering of the resigna-tions of the President of the Senate and the entire cabinet. Non-plussed, Wood accepted the resignations and ran the government, arguably more efficiently than before, on his own.

MacArthur's position was therefore difficult. He very much wanted to gain the confidence of the Filipino élite like his father, in order to be accepted as a *compadre*, part of the expanded Philippine family. It was a fine line to tread, since the last thing he wanted was to antago-nize his friend Leonard Wood. Although MacArthur's relations with the Filipinos were entirely social—he deliberately eschewed the dis-cussion of politics—he nonetheless encountered what he described as resentment and even antagonism from the upper ranks of expatriate society who still regarded men of Quezon's caliber as socially unacceptable.

The accommodation assigned to the MacArthurs was a large Spanish *adobe* building, 1 Calle Victoria, known as the Casa on the Wall due to it being built against the southern extremity of the great wall of Intramuros. Originally the Spanish cavalry barracks and prison, now, in addition to being their home, it was also the military headquarters of the District of Manila. Louise decorated the house lavishly with heavy furniture, made by the inmates of Bilibid Prison, and Chinese carpets. Two hundred and fifty yards to the west of their home lay the social center of Manila—the Manila Hotel. Louise also bought a two-room beach cottage at Pasay, which she then decorated in vibrant colors, for the more informal entertainment which she also enjoyed. The problem was that Douglas, other than mixing with Quezon and his circle of friends, had no interest in the social whirl upon which Louise had thrived. What social life there was tended to be men only.[31] Douglas went to inter-unit boxing matches and his presence was also occasionally required as president, at the Army and Navy Club. So, ironically, it was the reluctant Douglas who suffered a social life while his wife who craved one was left out in the cold.

Louise's ostracism was also due to her inability to act as an army wife. Most of the army wives had to live on their husband's pay which, even given a low-cost posting to Manila, never seemed to stretch far enough. Louise's extravagance was notorious even before she landed in Manila. So massive had been the quantity of her baggage crammed into the holds of the modest *Logan*, that there had only been room for one trunk each as accompanied baggage for the other family passengers. She appeared oblivious of the consideration due to others. There was an orphanage run by nuns which produced small quantities of hand-made lace, which the army wives had a habit of buying as mementos to take back home. Louise, greatly taken by the delicate craftsmanship, bought the entire output for two years.

The marriage began to show signs of strain. Seldom together with her husband, Louise pursued her own interests and good causes. The mistreatment of the ponies which pulled the local *caromata* appalled her and her solution was to get the civil police to exert authority over the drivers. She did in fact arrest one for cruelty.[32] Another cause to attract her attention was the welfare of half-breed children with American fathers. Socially, the MacArthurs' one common denominator was the Quezon family. Friendship with the Quezons was the one concession Louise made towards social discourse with Filipinos and she had given sympathetic support to them when their first daughter died. They both grew to like Louise, her disregard for authority, her laid-back attitude to life, but also her resolute determination.

Louise wrote to friends at home about how she found life in Manila extremely dull and had plans to persuade Douglas to leave the army. She turned to Wood to complain of Pershing's treatment of MacArthur, but all he could do was sympathize.[33] Louise's exasperation was further fuelled when her daughter caught malaria. Then, quite suddenly, what appeared to be a lifeline was thrown to her. Her mother-in-law, whom she had now grown to resent, suffered a further bout of illness with a prognosis that she might not recover. In February 1923, the MacArthur family left Manila to be with her. Arguably it was more concern for his mother's health than concern for his wife which prompted MacArthur's attempt to terminate his Manila posting. Later in her life Louise blamed Pinky for having been "an interfering mother-in-law who eventually succeeded in disrupting our married life." In what manner that was done was never made clear, but Pinky did have an unhealthy hold upon her favorite son, one which any wife would resent. Pinky duly recovered from her heart ailment and both Douglas and Louise, having failed to find an ear sufficiently sympathetic to change their posting, re-embarked for Manila. It had been the last occasion the MacArthur brothers would meet. Arthur's death from appendicitis in December merely served to strengthen the bond between the mother and her last surviving child.

MacArthur returned to a new military organization in Manila, formed in April 1922. The War Department had gathered its limited resources—the two regiments of Filipino Scouts, the 45th and 57th, and the sole U.S. infantry regiment, the 31st—into the Philippine Division of two brigades. MacArthur was given command of the twenty-third Brigade. This return to proper soldiering seemed to spur him to consider the fundamental matter of the defense of the Philippines. There was an unspoken taboo on what might appear to have been the obvious solution—to recruit Filipinos locally. Certainly the Scouts were first-class soldiers, outperforming their American compatriots in military skills. A 1923 report to the War Department read: "all companies of the 57th Infantry (PS) qualified 100% in rifle and machine gun marksmanship. I believe this is the first regiment in the Army of the United States to make such a remarkable record."[34]

Indeed, by comparison with the demoralized, complaining, poorly trained American 31st Infantry, the Philippine Scouts were in a class of their own. However, they had not been recruited to their permitted ceiling because of a fear among white Americans of putting weapons in Filipino hands. Then there was the post-war revival of American isolationism. When, in 1924, the comedian Will Rogers wrote "why don't we let people alone and quit trying to hold what they call a protectorate over them? Let people go their own way and have their own form of government. We haven't got any business in the Philippines. We are not such a howling success of running our own government"—he was not trying to be funny. The underlying message was that a state cannot pursue an isolationist policy and also maintain an empire with all its concomitant, entangling commitments. There was a critical, geographical reality that could not be ignored. The 1,150-mile long Philippine Archipelago, comprising over 7,000[35] islands, is over 5,000 miles from Pearl Harbor and 7,000 miles from San Francisco. Manila, on the most important island of Luzon, is by comparison less than 700 miles distant from Hong Kong and Formosa and 1,800 miles from Tokyo. By 1924 it was manifestly evident to the United States that her most probable enemy in the Pacific would be Japan. The War Plan Orange Strategy for the defense of the Philippines, revised in 1924, required the military to hold Manila Bay until reinforced and relieved by a vengeful fleet which would steam to their aid from Hawaii's Pearl Harbor.

As early as 1907, Theodore Roosevelt had written to Taft saying he believed that the Philippines could not be defended and they ought to be given their independence "with perhaps some form of international guarantee."[36] Now Japanese occupation of Germany's Pacific Islands after the First World War threatened the U.S.A.'s line of communication with her protectorate. Governor Leonard Wood forecast that the outcome would be "abandonment of American posts, American soldiers, an American fleet, American citizens in the Far East."[37] But there were genuine economic concerns tied to the retention of the Philippines, primarily that Asian markets were an essential component in the United States' economy. The military presence represented a statement, emphasizing the United States' interests: they were a deterrent force which could, if necessary, be written off. According to a contemporary report: "It seems probable that a Japanese major effort could succeed in taking both the Philippines and Guam before our Fleet could arrive in the Western Pacific, but it is believed that the collapse of our forces, both naval and military, would be justified by the damage done to the enemy."[38] This statement became a prevailing attitude. Little was done in the meantime, locally, to coordinate Joint Army-Navy plans so that when the attack did come, as seemed likely, maximum damage could not be inflicted upon the enemy.

MacArthur the engineer was given the additional task of mapping the Bataan Peninsula as part of the fleshing-out of the regional strategic plan, and it was an impressive achievement for a man in his forties to have surveyed forty miles of inhospitable, jungle-clad, mountainous terrain.[39] The job gave him enormous satisfaction, but the time spent away from his brigade meant that he lost touch and was unaware of a simmering dispute in its ranks. He *was* in his office on 7 July 1924, when news arrived that 222 Scouts had declared they would soldier no more. The mutiny has to be seen in the context of a general dissatisfaction among the Filipinos at their treatment by the Americans. A report concluded that the normally loyal and dependable Scouts' disaffection was due to "discrimination against the Philippine soldier in pay, allowance and benefit." There was little economic headroom to make more than cosmetic improvements. Predictably, yet inaccurately, General Wood maintained that Filipino politicians had encouraged the mutineers. Very few commanders' careers survive a mutiny in their ranks. Not only did MacArthur survive but he was appointed divisional commander. It was an imaginative gesture, for one of the few options available to improve the lot of the locally employed soldiers was to put someone over them who was sympathetic to their situation.

His efficiency reports were now glowing and he had made up the ground lost at West Point. What had not been made up was an improvement in his relationship with Louise. Unlike Pershing, MacArthur was a most punctilious officer. Louise, however, had a relaxed attitude to timekeeping. On one occasion, when she was still putting on her face at her dressing table when they should have been on their way to a dinner engagement, MacArthur stood impatiently behind her, arms folded, telling her to get a move on. Louise, the liberated flapper, was not to be harassed by anyone. Taking up her hand mirror she stood up, turned, and smashed it over his head.[40]

Meanwhile, in Washington, Pinky had written to Pershing about "my Boy's promotion to Major-General." Pershing's obligatory retirement at the age of 64 was due on 13 September 1924 but Pinky

shamelessly remarked how he was "looking still so young and won-
derfully handsome! I think you will never grow old." She reminded
Pershing that MacArthur was seventh on the list for promotion and
asked if he couldn't "find it convenient to give him his promotion
during your regime as Chief of Staff.[41] General Leonard Wood also
wrote directly to the Secretary of War in May 1924, drawing John
Weeks' attention to MacArthur's excellent qualities and qualifications
for promotion. Weeks replied to the effect that MacArthur's promotion should be anticipated soon.[42]

On 23 September 1924 the War Department announced the
44-year-old MacArthur's promotion to Major-General with effect
from 17 January 1925. He would be the youngest of the army's
twenty-one Major-Generals and, as one newspaper noted, "stands a
splendid chance of some day becoming head of the army."[43] In January the MacArthurs, accompanied by five Filipino servants, sailed
from Manila aboard the Transport *Thomas*, its holds crammed full
with Louise's trunks, furniture and carpets. "The other Army wives
aboard ship returned home seething, laceless, servantless again, limited to one trunk, and with their own Filipino furniture piled up back
on the dock."[44] In the Army, like all hierarchical organizations, rank
has its privileges. Was MacArthur as insensitive towards his subordinates as his wife, or did he not want to cross swords with her?

3

A WHIFF OF POLITICS

In May 1925, MacArthur assumed command of the IV Corps Area with its headquarters in Atlanta, Georgia. Within a few months he was re-assigned to the more important III Corps Area with its head-quarters in Washington DC. It is debatable whether it was a matter of great shrewdness or acute stupidity to move this increasingly political General into the center of the political universe. Domestically it suited the MacArthurs because it meant that they could live on Louise's Baltimore estate; in addition it gave Douglas convenient access to his mother in Washington. MacArthur attempted to adapt to Louise's interests and somewhat different friends but he could not pretend that he found his wife's way of life anything other than trivial. He had three beliefs: in himself, his country, and his Service. There was never any chance that he would acquiesce in Louise's persistent attempts to secure his resignation from the Service in order to enter business. Divorce became inevitable, and it took place in Reno, Nevada, in June 1929 on the extraordinary grounds of his "failure to provide" for this immensely rich woman.

After stepping in to take the American Olympic team to the Netherlands and being in Washington long enough to gain the "lasting hostility of two powerful groups in the United States, the Communists and the Pacifists,"[1] MacArthur was ordered back to the Philippines as Department Commander to relieve Major General

William Lassiter. Governor General Henry L. Stimson liked Lassiter. Between 1922 and 1928 there had been considerable confusion regarding Pacific War aims in general and the defense of the Western Pacific in particular. The tendency had been to strengthen the position in the Eastern Pacific and for the Western Pacific to adopt its own defensive posture in a process which can be best summarized as self-help. On 21 August 1928, Lassiter produced a report[2] on the Defense of the Philippines which represented a movement away from the static front thinking of the First World War. The military's mission, effective 26 June 1928, and confirmed in that order of priority in 1929, was in three parts: a.) To hold the entrance to Manila Bay in conjunction with the Asiatic Detachment (USN); b.) To hold Manila Bay in conjunction with the Asiatic Detachment as long as possible consistent with the accomplishment of a, above; c.) To support the Civil Government. Lassiter established the germ of an idea later developed by Major-General Grunert and then seized upon by MacArthur.

> The function of *Mobile Troops*[3] is, in conjunction with the naval and air forces, to close the back entrances to the Manila Bay area. They cannot accomplish anything by sitting down behind a trench system covering a restricted locality and waiting for the enemy to come to attack them. Their only hope of effective action, as against the enemy's presumably greatly superior numbers, is to strike him most at his vulnerable, that is, at the beach.

On the face of it, the numbers were not there to provide for a Mobile Force capable of making an impression on Japanese landings,[4] and Lassiter recognized this, as is shown by a letter he sent to Chief of Staff General Summerall:[5]

> The Oriental is no longer inert, and passive to the dominance of the white man. He now insists on being able to run his own affairs . . . it is of primary importance for us, not only to assure ourselves of the loyalty and dependability of the native troops and the Constabulary, but to be assured that these forces can be quickly expanded by trained reservists and that the general population of the country will throw its weight on our side.

Although Stimson opposed MacArthur's appointment, MacArthur later wrote that he found him "a preparedness man, and supported my military training program with understanding and vigor. We became fast friends."[6] It is in fact unlikely that Stimson would have cared to admit MacArthur as a friend, and Perret insists that "MacArthur did not like Stimson, but Stimson positively disliked MacArthur."[7] With MacArthur, anyway, "friendship" was a relative statement, and insofar as he found it at all it was among his subordinates. On this tour he began a lasting friendship with one of his junior staff officers, First Lieutenant Thomas J. Davis.

President Coolidge had appointed Stimson as Governor-General at the express request of Manuel Quezon, who had gone to Washington specifically for that purpose. Quezon had no wish to repeat the experience of working with a Governor General like the obdurate and "racist" Leonard Wood, and Stimson lived up to Quezon's expectations. He developed a good rapport with the Filipinos and, while not in favor of independence, he did envisage a looser form of association. However, the encouraging foundations being laid between the two were not to last. Coolidge did not seek re-election and in February 1929 the new President-elect, Herbert Hoover, nominated Stimson as his Secretary of State. Keen as ever to keep in with the obvious movers and shakers, MacArthur sent what James described as his trademark, the "White House benediction." "I hope and believe," wrote the General, "it is but a stepping stone to that last and highest call of America, the Presidency." MacArthur concluded, "My association with you has been so delightful personally and so inspiring professionally that no matter who may succeed you in Malacañan I shall have a sense of unreplaceable loss."[8] MacArthur had an undoubted view as to who should replace Stimson in the Malacañan Palace— himself. If MacArthur were to put his cap in the ring and be selected, it would be an end to his aspiration to become Chief of Staff of the Army, since the Governor General had to be a civilian. But he did not trust the schemers in Washington, whom he felt were likely to prevent his selection as Chief of Staff.

Quezon and his wife Aurora had grown to like and respect the General. During this tour his interests had broadened and he had expressed himself sympathetically on a number of non-military issues, particularly trade and revenue. But Quezon was not greatly taken with the prospect of another military Governor General. Not only was the Wood experience too fresh in his memory but also, in the longer perspective, there was the recollection of life under Spanish generals.

Thus Quezon was not wholehearted in his support of MacArthur.

MacArthur sensed this and did his best to guide him in the presentation of his case, writing out a radiogram for Quezon to send Stimson. MacArthur stressed that his "personal interests in this matter are a minimum":

> I have carefully canvassed all shades of Filipino thought with reference to the appointment of a new Governor General. In all circles, political, industrial and labor, I find an almost unanimous agreement on General MacArthur. I know of no man who so thoroughly commands the confidence both of the American people and the Filipinoes. His appointment would be a masterstroke of statesmanship and diplomacy. It would not only insure harmonious cooperation but would give promise of constructive accomplishments which would transcend anything which these Islands have ever known. I solicit your cooperation in pressing these views upon the President. I am confident that General MacArthur's great interest in Philippine affairs would cause him to consent to retiring from active military service to accept this great national duty. Please regard this radiogram as absolutely confidential except for the President.[9]

Quezon is unlikely to have sent a radiogram couched in such phraseology. If he did ever send it, Stimson is unlikely to have considered MacArthur a serious candidate. MacArthur could scheme and an appointment as Governor General was seen by some as the first of three steps towards the Presidency, not that he gave any overt indication of that being his aim. There were kingmakers in Washington, however, who did see MacArthur eventually becoming a Republican Presidential Candidate. "According to close friends, General MacArthur has his eyes on the White House for eight or twelve years hence," confided the *New York Times*, "via a successful administration as Governor General for four years, followed by a Cabinet post either as Secretary of State or Secretary of War."[10] This is the path blazed by Taft 30 years previously.

Eventually, Hoover appointed Secretary of War, Dwight F. Davis, as Governor General and underwhelmed MacArthur with the offer of Chief of Engineers. MacArthur believed that if he accepted the post he could say goodbye to his rekindled ambition of becoming Chief of Staff. There was an inherent risk in refusing the President's offer but MacArthur knew precisely where he stood in the pecking order, and turned down the engineer post. General Charles P. Summerall, the Chief of Staff, had to retire due to age by the end of 1930. MacArthur was the senior ranking Major General among those candidates able to serve the full term of four years. Sure enough, on 5 August 1930 MacArthur received a radiogram: "President has just announced your detail as Chief of Staff to succeed General Summerall." He explained in his memoirs how he backed into the limelight:

> I did not want to return to Washington, even though it meant the four stars of a general, and my first inclination was to try to beg off. I knew the dreadful ordeal that faced the new Chief of Staff, and shrank from it. I wished from the bottom of my heart to stay with troops in a field command. But my mother who made her home in Washington, sensed what was in my mind and cabled me to accept. She said my father would be ashamed if I showed timidity. That settled it.[11]

The Manila Hotel was the venue for a banquet in MacArthur's honor. The leading white and Filipino dignitaries said nice things about him and he responded with a speech full of his own homespun philosophy. Speaking of change, he reflected upon "the shift of the center of interest from the Atlantic to the Pacific."[12] In this and other matters, he was out of touch with reality. On 19 September he once again took his leave of Manila, and was then sworn in as Chief of Staff on 21 November. The new 50-year-old four-star general moved into his official Quarters Number One at Fort Meyer, across the Potomac from the capital. He arranged for a sun porch and elevator to be fitted for the benefit of Pinky.[13] Meanwhile, in great secrecy he ensconced the new love of his life for the past five months in a comfortable apartment in Georgetown, close to his office. Her name was Isabel "Dimples" Rosario Cooper.

MacArthur fully recognized the "dreadful ordeal" he was about to face but was less than honest in appearing to suggest that it was an ordeal he wished to avoid. October 1929 had witnessed the Wall Street stock market crash, the effects of which reverberated through to the spring of 1930, culminating in a catastrophic slump and recession. MacArthur saw as his principal aim the protection of the core force of the Army in a bitterly fought battle for survival. There was little scope for the research and development of new concepts; armor trials and development of army aviation were all sacrificed. MacArthur maintained that the value of military aviation "as an instrument of war was still undemonstrated."[14] though. In fact, throughout his term as Chief of Staff, his position on the subject of military aviation was not

as black and white as he portrayed. Also MacArtl
ment with his opposite number, Admiral Willian
the Army Air Corps was responsible for coastal
air forces will be based on the fleet and move wi
element in performing the essential missions of tl
Army air forces will be land based and employed ;
Army in carrying out its mission of defending the

It is impossible to conceive of a more divisiv̄ ᴍꜱ̄ᴛ ᴜᴍent than
the annual budgetary round, guaranteed to put the Services at each
other's throats. At times of particularly acute economic stringency,
the need to defend corners and to protect turf is of paramount importance. The unification of the War and Navy Departments into a
Department of National Defense was routinely examined during the
1920s–1930s but rejected in essence for no other reasons than that
soldiers did not want to be commanded by sailors and, that for sailors,
their nightmare scenario was soldiers commanding fleets. The principal, official reason for rejecting the consolidation of the War and
Navy Departments was "the interposing the head of this department
between the services concerned and the President."[17] Unification
would have helped the Joint Planning Process but would have made
no advance in the vexed and combative environment of apportion-
ment of budget share. There was still in being the Joint Army and
Navy Board created in 1903 which fulfilled the standing inter-Service
war planning function to the satisfaction of both Services. Chairman-
ship alternated between the Services: Admiral Dewey had been the
first Chairman until his death in 1917 and MacArthur acted as Chairman for three years.

The post-war 1930s army numbered 130,000 enlisted men and
12,000 officers, half the strength authorized; the sixteenth largest in
the world, smaller than Greece's and Portugal's armies.[18] The quality
of the army was indifferent, as was their equipment and pay: there had
been no pay rises in a decade. In 1930, the War Department's share of
government spending fell to 7.5 per cent, half of what it had been at
the end of the war. But there were Pacifists and Congressmen who still
felt this sum to be excessive and MacArthur needed all his guile and
gravitas to defend the army's corner. Among the particularly dogged
Congressional opponents during MacArthur's term as Chief of Staff
were the curmudgeonly Harold Ickes and the combative Ross Collins.[19] Secretary of the Interior Ickes from Chicago found MacArthur's
snobbishness abhorrent and admitted how, in later years, it had given

great kick . . . to break the news to MacArthur that the President had rejected a number of his budget requests.[20] Among the many clashes between MacArthur and Ickes, none was more emotive than Ickes' attempt to take the Arlington National Cemetery away from the War Department and into his bailiwick of the National Park Service. Roosevelt gave Ickes control of General Lee's mansion overlooking the cemetery but the military graves remained the responsibility of the War Department.[21] Ickes was an obsessive Empire builder. In 1939 he would win a very significant victory over the War Department and not for the better.

By 1932, the economy was in free fall. Hoover attempted to stabilize the situation by balancing the budget, outgoings matching income. The War Department, the recipient of tax dollars and the biggest employer among the federal departments, became a rather obvious sacrificial cow. The already low salaries were cut by a further ten per cent, a move considered justifiable when unemployment had risen to twenty per cent. Ross Collins of Mississippi proposed ending retirement pensions for those officers who had private means in excess of ten thousand dollars a year. Proposals were also aired to abolish Pershing's special pension of eighteen thousand dollars. MacArthur's sturdy defense of principle earned him the gratitude and change of heart by Pershing who had been foremost among those who had opposed MacArthur's appointment.

Eric Larrabee summarized MacArthur's politics at that time as "neither especially intense nor extensive; they followed the upper-middle-class norms of the time, those of a conservative Hoover Republican."[22] What MacArthur did intensively loathe was Communism. The Bonus Marchers, "an army of disillusioned and lost men who had served in the war . . . seeking desperately to influence Congress to grant an *immediate* cash bonus for veterans,"[23] had been in the capital since May. Approximately 3½ million veterans possessed redemption certificates worth about one thousand dollars, redeemable either on death or in 1945. They sought redemption of these certificates at this, the time of their greatest need. "The American Communist Party," wrote MacArthur, "planned a riot of such proportions that it was hoped the United States Army, in its efforts to maintain peace, would have to fire on the marchers. In this way, the Communists hoped to incite revolutionary action."[24] There had been Communist interference but MacArthur overstated the influence the Communists held over the marchers' predominantly apolitical leadership.[25]

MacArthur had brought onto his staff in the War Department Building (shared with the Navy Department and the Department of State) an officer who had been a Lieutenant Colonel during the war, reverted to the rank of Captain in 1919 and had again risen to the rank of Major, albeit one long in the tooth and apparently passed over. "Douglas MacArthur," he wrote of his boss,

> was a forceful—some thought an overpowering—individual, blessed with a fast and facile mind, interested in both the military and the political side of our government. From the beginning, I found that he was well acquainted with most of the people in government in almost every department. Working with him brought an additional dimension to my experience. My duties were beginning to verge on the political, even to the edge of partisan politics.

He elaborated. "Most of the senior officers I had known always drew a clean cut line between the military and the political . . . but if General MacArthur ever recognized the existence of that line, he usually chose to ignore it."[26] The observer's name was Major Dwight D. Eisenhower.

There seems to be a general academic consensus that MacArthur did not display presidential pretensions until the Second World War. The autobiography of an officer serving in the Budget Branch of the War Department, Major Bradford Grethen Chynoweth, appears to challenge that supposition:

> When I was an Engineer Lieutenant, like most others, I put Douglas MacArthur on a pedestal. His image had been blurred when I heard him in 1930 in a speech for the San Antonio Chamber of Commerce. He spoke of the troubled conditions in our country and described in detail the kind of man we needed to elect in the forthcoming elections. I couldn't believe my ears! The man in the country who fitted exactly his specification was Douglas MacArthur.[27]

Chynoweth, whose family originated in Cornwall, England, accepted that in 1932, with an anti-military Congress, MacArthur had an unenviable job, but he made an important observation about MacArthur's brand of leadership. "He should have known that the entire General Staff, of which he was Chief, were also frustrated and unhappy about it. He should have exerted himself as a leader, to buck us up. He never came near us."[28]

If MacArthur's grip of the common touch with the military was slipping, his growing political interests were cause for adverse comment in political quarters. Governor Franklin Delano Roosevelt of New York was a distant cousin of MacArthur's and arguably became a Democrat because the Republican path to high office was already congested with other aspiring Roosevelts. They had little in common and maintained an enduring dislike of one another: "The day FDR died I rode home with General MacArthur. We talked of those who had disappeared from the scene since the war started, especially of FDR. As MacArthur got out of the car, he turned towards me and said, 'Well, the old man has gone—a man who never told the truth if a lie would suffice.' "[29]

Roosevelt, recently nominated the Democratic Party presidential candidate, was sitting at lunch in Albany in August 1932 with family and friends, among whom was Rexford G. Tugwell. The telephone rang and Roosevelt took a vitriolic call from Governor Huey Long of Louisiana. The guests listened to Roosevelt's pacification of Long. "It's all very well for us to laugh over Huey," he chided, "but actually we have to remember all the time that he really is one of the two dangerous men in the country." Tugwell remembered Roosevelt amplifying this point: ". . . referring to Hitler and his haranguing method, his unscrupulous use of specious appeals, his arousing of hate, envy, fear and all the animal passions." But who, Tugwell asked Roosevelt, was the second dangerous man? Was it the turbulent Father Coughlin? "Oh no," he said to my surprise, "the other is Douglas MacArthur." Roosevelt then went on to justify what he had just said to those present and, as remembered by Tugwell:

> There was latent, he thought, not far below the uneasy surface of our disrupted society, an impulse among a good many "strong" men, men used to having their way, mostly industrialists who directed affairs without being questioned, a feeling that democracy had run its course and that totalitarians had grasped the necessities of the time. People wanted strong leadership; they were sick of uncertainty, anxious for security, and willing to trade liberty for it.[30]

Attempts such as this at proposing General Douglas MacArthur as The Man on Horseback fall short of reality. Like Roosevelt, he was the consummate actor but he posed for effect, as an investment, not because he had any intention of challenging the stricken Hoover administration. But the month before this scene an event took place which did more to harm MacArthur's reputation than any other. It was an event that appears remote and not germane to a study of the Philippines but it reveals a great deal about the man who would later be in a position of considerable importance and responsibility in that country. The incident was the Bonus March of unemployed First World War Veterans of the self-styled Bonus Expeditionary Force (BEF).

The Bonus Marchers did elicit sympathy but there were significant reservations. Eisenhower observed: "Despite the fact that this was a national calamity affecting almost all citizens, some veterans seemed to feel that they should be regarded as a special class entitled to special privileges."[31] There were about 18–20,000 men accompanied by women and children. Some camped out across the Anacostia River while others chose to come into the capital where they occupied buildings earmarked for demolition close to the Capitol. To some Washingtonians, the squalor in which they existed, their placards and protests, had no more than nuisance value, but others saw a cancer that threatened the government and democratic ideals. MacArthur says he ordered the issue of tents and camp equipment and sent mobile kitchens across to the Anacostia Flats but was obliged to withdraw the kitchens due to an outburst in Congress. "There are more than 8,500,000 out of work in the United States, most of them with families. If the Government can feed those that are here, then we can expect an influx that will startle the whole country."[32]

Matters came to a head when the city police, who up to that point had been entirely responsible for dealing with the BEF, sought to evict them from the buildings they occupied in order that they might be demolished. Used to dealing with petty crime and traffic offences, they were no match for veterans of the battlefields of France. On 28 July 1932, the President, through the office of the Secretary of War, called out the army in support of the police to clear the area. In those days, the military staff of the War Department wore civilian clothes in the city. General MacArthur, who had decided to take personal command of the army detachment, sent a Filipino servant to Fort Myer to collect his uniform and told Eisenhower to get changed and report back for duty. Eisenhower recalled how he believed that his relationship was close enough to MacArthur for him to object to a four star general taking command of 5–600 soldiers in a "street corner" matter. MacArthur would have none of it, insisting this to be a question of

Federal Authority in the District of Columbia and moreover, there was "incipient revolution in the air."[33] To many people, his involvement was regarded as "a strange and vindictive performance."[34]

MacArthur looked immaculate in his uniform, sporting the ostentatious General Staff badge of his own design. He wore eight rows of medal ribbons. He had not aggregated the medals he had won more than once so he wore the ribbons of both Distinguished Service Crosses, all seven Silver Star ribbons and two Purple Hearts. Inexplicably he also wore the Philippine Campaign Medal that had been awarded to his father.[35] MacArthur did not take over direct command from Brigadier General Perry L. Miles commanding the 16th Infantry Brigade supported by a number of obsolescent Renault tanks (which were not used) accompanied by Major George S. Patton Jr. Nevertheless, he was at the front of the operation, acting as an "interested observer"[36] and it was he who ordered Miles' troops to cross the river.

Much of what followed has been either understated or embellished. The argument in this context as to whether MacArthur did or did not ignore orders by crossing the Anacostia Bridge to pursue the BEF is academic but we will rely here on the account of Major Eisenhower who was with MacArthur. The slow process of clearing the veterans from the disputed area and shepherding them in the direction of the Anacostia River began. "The veterans made no more vigorous protest than a little catcalling and jeering at the soldiers," wrote Eisenhower. "Instructions were received from the Secretary of War, who said he was speaking for the President, which forbade any troops to cross the bridge into the largest encampment of veterans on open ground beyond the bridge." According to Eisenhower, "these instructions were brought to the troops by Colonel Wright, Secretary of the General Staff, and then by General Moseley of the Assistant Secretary's office. In *neither instance did General MacArthur hear these instructions*.[37] He said he was too busy and did not want either himself or his staff bothered by people coming down and pretending to bring orders."

The column advanced over the bridge, whereupon the veterans torched their encampment. "The whole scene was pitiful," wrote Eisenhower. "The veterans, whether or not they were mistaken in marching on Washington, were ragged, ill-fed, and felt themselves badly abused." As MacArthur turned to get into his staff car, Eisenhower advised him that, as a result of what had happened there, newspaper reporters would want to talk to him. "I suggested it would be the better part of wisdom, if not of valor, to avoid meeting them." It was in Eisenhower's mind a political decision to use troops and the politicians should respond to the press. "He disagreed and saw the newspapermen that night."[38] MacArthur concluded his press conference by saying, "I have been in many riots,[39] but I think this is the first riot I was ever in or ever saw in which there was no real bloodshed. So far as I know, there is no man on either side who has been seriously injured."[40] As a result of this press conference, MacArthur had left the press with the general impression that he "himself had undertaken and directed the move against the veterans and that he was acting as something more than the agent of civilian authorities."[41]

The press gave him a hard time, even picturing him as the "savior on the white horse." Eisenhower observed that MacArthur had developed "an obsession that a high commander must protect his public image at all costs and must never admit his wrongs."[42] The reporting of two pressmen in particular, Drew Pearson and Robert S. Allen, so rankled that MacArthur filed a libel suit asking for a quarter of a million dollars in damages from each. The case never came to court, thanks to Dimples.

MacArthur had kept his affair with her a secret for four years but it had become increasingly difficult to confine the vivacious young lady, who had been a celebrity in Manila, to the confines of her apartment. She demanded more freedom and more expenses. Growing tired of her and her demands, MacArthur offered to pay for her repatriation. When she refused, he sent her a *Washington Times* classified section offering menial employment, and a scribbled note: "Apply to your father or brother for any future help."[43] Dimples moved out, taking with her MacArthur's love letters. Congressman Ross Collins came to the rescue, informing Pearson, "You know MacArthur's been keeping a girl in the Chastleton Apartments on 16th Street?"[44] Pearson discovered Dimples and moved her to Baltimore for safekeeping. Then "we just got in touch with MacArthur's attorney. That was all there was to it." MacArthur dropped the case. He paid Dimples $15,000 for his letters and gave Pearson a similar sum to offset his legal fees.

During his tour of duty as Chief of Staff, MacArthur made two visits to Europe—his own personal road to Damascus. These visits had such a profound effect upon him that he reported to the Secretary

of War: "The next war is certain to be one of maneuver and movement . . . The nation that does not command the air will face deadly
odds. Armies and navies to operate successfully must have air cover."[45]
Roosevelt, who had now succeeded Hoover, maintained his partiality
for the Navy but could be swayed by argument to support the cause
of the Air Corps. The President prided himself on his knowledge of
the navy and army, so much so that he treated his Secretaries and Service Chiefs as though what they had to say was redundant. One evening, MacArthur asked Roosevelt why it was that the President paid
little attention to his views on the military but sought his opinion about social reform, of which he knew little. "Douglas," came the
reply, "I don't bring these questions up for your advice but for your
reactions. To me you are the symbol of the conscience of the American people."[46]

Roosevelt inherited Hoover's 1934 budget. The Army requested
$321 million, Hoover agreed $277 million and Roosevelt reduced the
budget further to $187 million. MacArthur threatened resignation
and persuaded Secretary for War George Dern to make a budgetary
status quo speech on the radio. Roosevelt refused to see MacArthur,
to which the Chief of Staff threatened that unless he spoke to the
President by one o'clock that afternoon, he would resign as Chief of
Staff by two o'clock and tell the press association why at three.[47] The
President relented and MacArthur accompanied Dern into the President's office. Roosevelt tore into Dern for having criticized administration policy in public. "Under his lashing tongue, the Secretary grew
white and silent," wrote MacArthur who then intervened because "the
country's safety was at stake and I said so bluntly."[48]

MacArthur recalled that the President "was a scorcher when
aroused" but the Chief of Staff, almost his equal when the "tension
began to boil over," laid into him. "In my emotional exhaustion I
spoke recklessly and said something to the general effect that when
we lost the next war, and an American boy, lying in the mud with
an enemy bayonet through his belly and an enemy foot upon his
dying throat, spat out his last curse, I wanted the name not to be
MacArthur, but Roosevelt." The President roared back "You must not
talk that way to the President."[49] Recognizing he was in the wrong,
even before the last words had come out, MacArthur apologized and,
giving Roosevelt his resignation, made for the door. As he reached the
door, "his voice came with that cool detachment which so reflected

his extraordinary self control." "Don't be foolish Douglas; you and the budget must get together on this." MacArthur took his leave with a gleeful Dern in tow, who must have been taken aback by the sight of the Chief of Staff vomiting over the White House steps.

Meanwhile, Manuel Quezon had been actively pursuing independence for the Philippines from the United States. Quezon, however, was sufficiently astute to realize that there had to be an intermediate phase between colonial status and full independence, especially with Japan already on the move in Manchuria and the worldwide economic slump. The Philippines did not feature high on the Roosevelt agenda, but in March 1934, he signed into law the Tydings-McDuffie Act which provided an interim Commonwealth period until 4 July 1946, when complete independence would be guaranteed. United States basing and defense agreements were to remain in place throughout the Commonwealth Period but the Philippines would enjoy greater autonomy over domestic affairs. In Manila, Quezon persuaded the Philippine Legislature to approve Tydings-McDuffie (they had rejected its predecessor) and, in so doing, virtually guaranteed his own election as first president of the new Commonwealth.[50]

Quezon was in Washington in 1933 and again in the autumn of 1934, and it seemed quite natural that he should approach his friend MacArthur. Quezon put to MacArthur the question in the minds of all strategists debating the defense of the Western Pacific. "Can the Philippines be defended?" The answer of most strategists would have been in the negative, yet MacArthur's response was: "I *know* that the islands can be protected, provided of course you have the money which will be required."[51] The Chief of Staff was convinced in his own mind of the viability of General Wood's concept of a citizens' army on the Swiss model—that is, a small cadre of regular trainers and commanders supported by a large pool of reservists and conscripts eligible to be called to the colors in a national emergency. MacArthur knew well the difficulties his father had faced during the Aguinaldo insurgency. He knew that the Philippine terrain favored defense and recalled that it was self-sufficient. He told Quezon:[52] "If you have a small, regular force as a nucleus to be expanded by employing the citizen army in time of peril, no nation will dare attack you, for the cost of conquest will be more than the expected profit." What he was not allowing for were changes in the last two decades. He still thought of warfare in terms of 1918, not of an aggressor with modern equipment and in strength, against a predominantly amateur force whose native country was coming under ever increasing strain to support a growing population of 14 million.

Quezon asked MacArthur if he would consider assuming responsibility for the defense of the Philippines, to which MacArthur replied: "I am prepared to devote the remainder of my life if necessary to securing a proper defense for the Philippine Nation. No question that confronts it in ultimate analysis is of such importance."[53] About this time he declined Chiang Kai Shek's request to train five million men to fight the Japanese,[54] since he thought he would need 20 years whereas it would take only 10 to train the Philippine army. In fact there were but seven before the outbreak of war in the Pacific. The work on the Philippine national defense plan began in November 1934. The initial staff work was undertaken by Major Eisenhower from the Chief of Staff's office in conjunction with his West Point classmate Major James B. Ord, who was then at the Army War College at Fort MacNair. The Commandant of the War College, George Simonds, was MacArthur's preferred choice to relieve him as Chief of Staff, which also helped to ease communications.

When precisely MacArthur's appointment as Chief of Staff would end became a matter of intense political and military speculation. Roosevelt provided the answer on 12 December 1934 when, swayed by the arguments of his own people in Congress, he announced that MacArthur would have, in effect, a further year, "in order to obtain the benefit of General MacArthur's experience in handling War Department legislation in the coming session."[55]

The provision of a military mission to the Philippines with MacArthur at its head required enabling congressional approval. Rather than introduce separate legislation, Secretary Dern persuaded Senator Millard Tydings and Representative John McDuffie, Chairmen of Insular Affairs in the Senate and the House, to amend a 1926 Act of Congress permitting military assistance to certain Latin American countries, so as to embrace the Philippines.[56] MacArthur negotiated a salary of 36,000 pesos ($18,000) a year and annual allowances of 30,000 pesos ($15,000), more than Quezon would earn but the same as the Governor General.[57] ". . . He wanted to make certain that he would be the 'ranking American' in Manila. He wanted Quezon to guarantee that he would have the equal of every facility, perquisites—and honorarium—which the American Governor General had received"[58] if his military salary, which he retained, was discounted. But the Governor General did not have a performance-related bonus. MacArthur negotiated with Quezon, for his own benefit, a commission of just under half of one per cent of Philippine defense spending, subject to his Defense Plans being approved by the Commonwealth Government. MacArthur was no less demanding in his requirement for accommodation:

"The Governor General has, for his private residence, Malacañang Palace." Quezon paused to consider.

"We cannot build another Malacañang Palace. But perhaps we can give you comparable accommodation. What is it that they have at Malacañang that you would also like to have?"

"Malacañang has seven bedrooms," said MacArthur.

"All right," agreed Quezon, "we will give you seven bedrooms. What else?"

"Malacañang has a special study for the President."

"We can give you that too. What else?"

"Malacañang has a state dining room," MacArthur said. (Quezon, according to an aide present, was amazed at the detail of the General's knowledge of Malacañang.)

"That's not difficult," Quezon said. "We can prepare that. What else?"

"Malacañang is fully staffed with servants. There are also motor cars with drivers available."

Quezon nodded. "We can do that."[59]

But that was not all. MacArthur was a man immensely conscious and protective vis-à-vis rank, rewards, awards, status and protocol. As soon as he ceased to be Chief of Staff he would revert to his permanent rank, that is, he would lose two stars, falling in rank from four star General to two star Major General. However, he now secured from Quezon his agreement that he would eventually become a five-star General—a Field Marshal. He would become the Philippine Army's one-and-only Field Marshal. Never previously had any American held five-star rank. MacArthur gave instructions for the making of an extravagant uniform of black trousers with a contrasting white, sharkskin tunic with intricate filigree designs. The limiting factor here was the requirement for Quezon to have been elected leader of the Philippines before this appointment.

For a number of years Eisenhower believed that the idea of making MacArthur a Field Marshal had been Quezon's, but during the course of casual conversation with Quezon in Washington, after his escape from Corregidor, he discovered that not to have been the case. "I was surprised to learn from him that he had not initiated the idea at all; rather, Quezon said that MacArthur himself came up with the high sounding title."[60] Eisenhower was emphatically opposed to MacArthur's assumption of five-star rank, and tried "to persuade MacArthur to refuse the title since it was pompous and rather ridiculous to be the Field Marshal of a virtually non-existent Army."[61]

Meanwhile, Frank Murphy, the Governor General in Manila, indicated his wish not to become the new High Commissioner of the Philippine Commonwealth but to return to the States. In a private meeting with MacArthur in Hyde Park, September 1934, Roosevelt wondered whether the Chief of Staff might be interested in becoming High Commissioner. MacArthur claimed later that "It was a flattering proposal but involved my retirement from the Army, so I declined, stating that I had started as a soldier and felt that I should end as one."[62] But others have suggested differently. In the event, Murphy did not resign, and MacArthur had to be content with the post of Military Adviser to the Philippines. However, a clause in his contract allowed him to retire temporarily as military adviser if the civilian post of High Commissioner were to become available. MacArthur maintained an interest in the position almost until the outbreak of war. In fact he applied to hold both posts simultaneously. As Eisenhower said "the position might well prove to be the springboard for attaining an even more desirable position in official or industrial life."[63]

Secretary Dern and MacArthur made their plans to see Manuel Quezon inaugurated as the first President of the Philippine Commonwealth. Although elections had been postponed, when they were held Quezon and his Nacionalista Party won a handsome and expected victory. It is not certain that the letter now sent by Secretary Dern to the President was drafted by MacArthur but it transparently revealed his intention to avoid a humiliating drop in rank by smoothly proceeding upward, from four to five stars:

It is essential that General MacArthur leave for Manila in October in order that the new Commonwealth President can have the benefit of his fundamental advice in presenting to his legislature a National Defense Act for enactment. Mr. Quezon has specifically requested that he be permitted to leave at that time as otherwise he would be gravely embarrassed in handling the situation which will confront him. There is no necessity, however, to relieve him as Chief of Staff at that precise time. It is suggested therefore, that General MacArthur be relieved as Chief of Staff on December the 15th by which time I will recommend to you his successor, probably General Craig.[64]

Roosevelt replied to Dern the next day: "I entirely approve the general arrangement you suggest."[65] On 1 October 1935 MacArthur, accompanied by his ailing eighty-two-year-old mother, his sister-in-law Mary McCalla MacArthur, who was to care for Pinky, and a small staff[66] which included Major Dwight D. Eisenhower and his friend Major Jimmy Ord, left Washington by train for San Francisco. The next day, at a halt at Wyoming, MacArthur was handed a telegram sent by Dern's deputy at the War Department. Craig had been appointed Chief of Staff "effective this date."[67] According to Eisenhower, the news caused MacArthur to "express himself freely. It was an explosive denunciation of politics, bad manners, bad judgement, broken promises, arrogance, unconstitutionality, insensitivity, and the way the world had gone to hell."[68] Then he sent an eloquent telegram of congratulations to his successor.

Why Roosevelt should have treated MacArthur so badly, reneging on promises made to MacArthur and to the War Department, is difficult to fathom. Perhaps, in this rarified circle of super egos, Roosevelt was making the point that it was he who was supreme, the Commander-in-Chief.

Whatever the truth, it was a salutary indicator that the relationship between the President and the military emissary in the Philippines might not only be brittle but also duplicitous. That October 1935, one of Roosevelt's two dangerous men had effectively been removed from the continental United States and consigned to the Philippines on his final, momentous tour. That same year, an assassin effectively removed the other dangerous man, Senator Huey Long.

4

PLANS

The origins of America's Color Plans lay in a directive sent by Secretary of War Taft in April 1904 to the newly formed Joint Army Navy Planning Board. He required them to prioritize plans for "the execution of which in time of emergency the two staffs will be responsible."[1] Under the system of color coding, America was Blue and potential enemies were each color specific. Germany, the focus of attention at the time, was Black. By 1906, particularly at the Naval War College, Japan, orange, became the main adversary for all war planning and war games.[2] Until that time it was assumed there would be a European orientated threat to the security of the Philippines.[3] Plan Purple reflected America's concern that either Germany or Italy might exploit Mexico's instability. Plan Red was for war against Britain, France and Canada. By 1940 the realities of World War saw the emergence of the new, so-called Rainbow plans.

The plans and the approval of the plans were much more informal than might be imagined. Miller wrote of Orange: "The plan was a matter of common understanding more than a set of documents."[4] Plans would have been signed off by the two Service Secretaries but "no Orange Plan was ever enacted by Congress or signed by a President."[5] The Army and Navy, particularly at the War Colleges, where the bulk of the planning was being conducted,[6] had by 1934 begun to realize that the next war would be a two-ocean war. Thus a conflict in prioritization among the military and politicians was already discernible, which the absence of higher level political oversight allowed to bumble on unchallenged. The students and faculty members who worked on the nation's military plans were the cream of their peer group; future generals and admirals to whom the responsibility of translating their plans into action could well fall. At about the same time, the concerned staff at the Naval War College, Newport, Rhode Island, came to the conclusion that the Imperial Japanese Navy would not be defeated in one enormous Trafalgar or Tsushima battle. The implications of this for the Philippines were enormous. Without a forward base "the Philippines were not expected to hold out very long in a war with Japan."[7]

The early naval planners believed that as long as bases in Samoa, Hawaii and Alaska were held, Japan would be unable to threaten America's West Coast directly. The Philippines, however, lay well beyond this ring of confidence. It would take 68 days (or over 100 if the Panama Canal was inoperative) for the U.S. fleet to reach the Philippines, compared to the eight days the Imperial Japanese Navy would need from Japan or one to two days if launched from Formosa (Taiwan). Troop carrying convoys would take longer. Lingayen Gulf in Luzon was four days' sailing time from Formosa. This meant that the army would have to fight unsupported for over two months.[8] This assessment reflected the optimism and can-do philosophy of the time, which was only now being seriously challenged.

The President of the Naval War College was so concerned by what was being expected of the navy that on 27 February 1934 he sent an unsolicited letter to the Chief of Naval Operations stating that it was "highly questionable" that the navy could achieve its strategic mission against determined Orange opposition.[9] Concern at Newport percolated through to the Army War College in Washington. William Halsey had been a student at both Staff Colleges in 1933–34 when a mini rebellion occurred among his fellows. They argued that little was known of the Japanese and, instead of two months, maintained that it would take two to three years for the navy to begin to overthrow the Japanese occupation of the Philippines. The problem was that these working level concerns were not shared significantly higher up the command chain, nor was there an inter-Service consensus as to the way forward.

At the outbreak of war, the official position had the army believing that it would need to fall back to the home base to prepare for engaging in offensive operations in strength. The navy held the contrary view that the "long legged," heavily gunned U.S. navy-in-being was simply not inclined to give up the Philippines.[10] "Between the wars, the army was entirely pessimistic," wrote Admiral Thomas C. Hart, "while, at times, the navy took the position that it was possible to hold (the Philippines). However, the realistic concept that Japan would initially take Luzon prevailed."[11] One of the inter-Service problems was that the Services were not always working at the same level. The Army in the Philippines was concerned with a situation virtually of confined defense in the same way as were the British in Malaya and Hong Kong and the Dutch in Java. The allied navies, however, had the capability to concentrate and therefore were not concerned simply with national joint plans but also had to consider international combined plans.

Divergences in Army and Navy views were problematic enough, but now a pessimistic army was in the process of sending an optimistic Douglas MacArthur to the Philippines in 1935 with new defense plans. It is important to make the point that MacArthur was an advisor to the civil government. He was authorized to deal directly with the Secretary of War and the Chief of Staff, but his prime function was to advise President Quezon how best to defend the Philippines. He commanded nothing. American ground forces of the Philippine Department continued to be under command of an American Major General who was routinely pessimistic. In 1933, Brigadier General Embick, commanding the harbor defenses, complained of the progressive weakening of the military position in the Philippines:

As a result the Philippine Islands have become a military liability of a constantly increasing gravity. To carry out the present Orange Plan— with its provisions for the early dispatch of our fleet to Philippine waters—would be literally an act of madness . . . In the event of an Orange War, the best that could be hoped for would be that wise counsels would prevail, that our people would acquiesce in the temporary loss of the Philippines, and that the dispatch of our battle fleet would be delayed for two or three years needed for its augmentation.[12]

The defense of the Philippines in the mid 1930s reflected that age-old truism that it is the budget that drives strategy not the threat. However, it would be wrong to suggest that there had been no defensive preparations. Major General E.E. Booth, commanding general in the Philippines, wrote on 27 April 1934 of projects nearing completion on Corregidor, the rocky bastion guarding the approach to Manila harbor. "When the above are completed, it is believed that Corregidor and the other defenses in the mouth of Manila Bay will be as near complete for an emergency as it will ever be practicable to complete them until the emergency actually occurs."[13] It was not a ringing endorsement of their efficacy.

It was the very weakness of these defenses which prompted Embick to propose the withdrawal of U.S. forces to a strategic line Alaska-Oahu-Panama, a proposal that mirrored that made by the Army's War Plans Division seven years previously, that is, a withdrawal to the 180° meridian. But in 1934 a declaration was made, supported by the then Chief of Staff MacArthur and repeated in 1936, 1939 and 1940 to the effect that: "Depending on the availability of funds, the War Department desires to keep up existing strength, both in personnel and materiel, in the Philippines, and in particular to provide adequate protection for the harbor defenses of Manila Bay, but to go to no further expense for permanent improvements unless thereby ultimate saving will result."[14] Booth's successor, Major General Frank Parker, was more jingoistic and arguably realistic in an oblique sense when he said: "As long as our flag remains in these waters, it goes without saying that it must not be hauled down at the will of any foreign power without a fight to the finish."[15]

During his tenure as Chief of Staff, MacArthur had been entirely opposed to War Plan Orange but had not found it either expedient or necessary to attempt to convert the unconvertible. He claimed instead that he saw the President personally and told him "that if mobilization became necessary during my tenure of office that my first step would be to send two divisions from the Atlantic coast to reinforce the Philippines."[16] This was probably MacArthur talking up his position to a subordinate, Captain Bonner Fellers, liaison officer to Quezon. As Perret points out, two divisions were not available on the West Coast or anywhere else in the U.S.A. and it was the President as Commander in Chief who sent divisions to foreign fields, not the Army's Chief of Staff. But War Plan Orange was a broad plan, essentially a navy-blue tapestry upon which local military commanders embroidered their own colors, their concept of operations, commensurate with the overall mission and what resources would allow.

To that extent, MacArthur was broadly correct when he went on to say to Fellers that "the man who is in command at the time will be the man who will determine the main features of the campaign." When MacArthur spoke of the "man in command" he meant the Chief of Staff but the comment was more applicable to the position of the Commanding Generals in the Philippine and Hawaii Departments.

In Manila in July 1934, the first committee meeting on National Defense, a constituent part of the constitutional convention, gathered to consider the defense of the Philippines during the Commonwealth phase and future independence. The Philippine Legislature produced its own National Defense Bill in November, but Governor General Frank Murphy vetoed it as too immature. The most substantive investigation into effective and economical means of defending the Philippines had been initiated in Washington that month by MacArthur, who had given the task to Eisenhower and Ord. Philippine input was not marginalized because, as identified by L. Siguion Reyna, the technical adviser to the Philippines Secretary of the Interior, the main problem was one of attaining maximum effectiveness at minimum cost. He emphasized that the army had to be useful in times of war and peace "otherwise, it would be considered by the already overburdened taxpayer as a real parasite in time of peace."[17] A conscript army with only a small regular training cadre was the only realistic and self-selecting option. It was also apparent that, other than operating coastal patrol craft, a Philippines Navy was beyond the bounds of a tight budget.

There were three ways the Philippine Defense Forces might be organized. The first, as championed by Major Vicente Lim of the Philippine Scouts, the first Filipino graduate of West Point, proposed the army being started from scratch. It was ideal in principle but too expensive in practice.[18] The second option was to base the new army upon the well trained, professional Philippine Scouts, but on the eve of the founding of the Commonwealth, the Philippine element only comprised two dozen officers with limited staff training and no experience in major field commands. "Moreover, their allegiance was to the U.S.; they were still members of the United States Army."[19] The only realistic option was to make the Philippine Constabulary the foundation for the Philippine Army. New equipment had been made available and an increase in strength was authorized from 400 officers and 5047 men to 549 officers and 8512 men. Although, as a uniformed and disciplined body, the Constabulary was the best available option, it was by no means a perfect one. It had seen recent internal security action but it was essentially a body charged with the maintenance of domestic law and order. The Constabulary was trained to operate in small groups to hunt down small numbers of dissidents rather than for the larger operations associated with national defense. According to Eisenhower, the Constabulary comprised "some commissioned individuals who were natural leaders and who possessed a rather good background of military training," but they were essentially "trained as a police force." Lim's and the Scouts' objections were to do with the close association between the Constabulary and the provincial and local governments with whom they had intimate dealings: the Constabulary's "image was not entirely clean."[20]

When Eisenhower and Ord presented their first proposal for the Defense of the Philippines to MacArthur they had pared the force to the bone and come up with an annual cost of 22 million pesos ($11 million). MacArthur sent the plan back to them. He had agreed with Quezon that the new army would only cost the Philippine government 16 million pesos ($8 million) a year. The discrepancy meant reduced training periods and delay in the procurement of equipment such as organic transport, which served to extend the period of preparation over 20 years rather than over the ten-year life of the Commonwealth.

The plan proposed 20-year-old Filipino males being required to register for conscription in an exercise in nation building. (Preliminary military training was to be done in primary and secondary schools including training in sanitation, hygiene, citizenship and military discipline.) The intention was to call up 40,000 a year in two groups of 20,000. Over the ten year period, therefore, it was intended to have built up a citizen army of 400,000 men. The first intake would consist of only 3,000 men who would test the system. Besides, there was insufficient accommodation for the full intake. The army would be by nature territorial, that is, the conscripts would serve close to their homes in a plan that sought, if necessary, to deny any part of the Philippines to an invader. Initially, five Military Districts were planned, based not on the size of territory but upon population. The Military Districts would have their own training centers as well as their own mobilization and equipment depots. Divisions were light and small, through force of circumstance rather than design, though it was argued, unconvincingly, that this enhanced flexibility and ability to fight on the beaches. In addition, there was provision for an air corps of 150 fast bombers whose very existence, according to Mac-Arthur, would be "sufficient to keep major portions of a hostile navy completely outside these territorial waters."[21] Finally, there was to be an offshore patrol of 50 small and fast torpedo boats designed to deny Philippine waters to an enemy. In early October, Major General MacArthur, his staff and family, boarded SS *President Hoover* in San Francisco for Manila, taking with them MacArthur's proposed ten-year development plan for the Philippine defense forces.

The luxury of the liner *President Hoover* was a far cry from the Army Transport Ships which had been the usual means for Mac-Arthur and the military to travel the San Francisco-Manila route. But this time, the Philippine government was paying. MacArthur looked forward to his return to the Philippines with a genuine feeling of optimism, anticipation and the conviction that he had much to offer—not least his upbeat defense plan. Roosevelt's cruel deception had only served to convince him that new opportunities would be found among the appreciative population of the Philippines. He had the promise of luxurious accommodation, a very generous pay and remuneration package, and the genuine support and welcome generated by the majority of Filipinos compensated to some degree the severe bruising of his ego.

Gradually, aboard the *President Hoover*, Pinky's health deteriorated. The increasingly anxious MacArthur spent the best part of every day of the three week passage in her cabin. He was in no mood to appreciate the non-stop party-going enjoyed by the senior political figures who were on board, en route to Manila to participate in the new Commonwealth's inaugural celebration. However, early one evening he attended a sedate cocktail party hosted by the ship's captain in honor of the Mayor of Boston, James B. Curley. It was at this time of intense emotional vulnerability that he met a respectably wealthy 37-year-old spinster, Jean Marie Faircloth. The petite and attractive Miss Faircloth came from a Tennessee family, proud of its role in the Civil War. She was an active member of two Confederate associations and one of her grandfathers had fought against Arthur MacArthur at Missionary Ridge. But she, like Pinky, kept the Civil War in perspective, not allowing it to get in the way of friendship. "Captivating in personality . . . Poised in movement and cultured in conversation,"[22] she seemed to have all the attributes of a devoted army wife, content to support rather than to lead. They had fallen for one another before Jean disembarked at Shanghai to visit some English friends. MacArthur

implored her to travel on to Manila once her visit to China was concluded. She arrived as bidden, immediately prior to Quezon's inauguration on 15 November.

A banquet was held in Malacañang in honor of the military mission
on the evening of their arrival, at which Quezon announced that
MacArthur would serve as military adviser to the Commonwealth.
In his introduction, Quezon described MacArthur as "not only a
soldier—one of the greatest in the world today—but he is also a
statesman, a combination not easily found in one man." He was, continued Quezon, "a true friend of the Filipino people, and no American, whether in the Army or outside, knows the Philippines and the
Filipinos better than he does." Quezon was not enjoying the best of
relationships with Major General Frank Parker, commanding general
of the Philippine Department. MacArthur's presence there that night
and the fact that Roosevelt had allowed MacArthur to be the Commonwealth's military adviser was a clear indication of the President's and
the American government's support of the defense plans, reasoned
Quezon.[23] Even before the Commonwealth had been inaugurated,
Quezon formed an ad hoc national defense committee to study the
papers brought by MacArthur. The National Defense Act would be
the first measure to be approved by the Philippine National Assembly
once the Commonwealth was in being,[24] but it was not until nearly a
month after the advisory team's arrival that the papers were made
available to Frank Murphy.

The first real test of the Quezon-MacArthur friendship came during the run up to the inauguration. To the casual observer, it might
seem trivial but, in the field of precedence and protocol it was of inestimable importance: how many gun salutes should be accorded the
new Commonwealth President and his subordinates. The Head of
the Bureau of Insular Affairs suggested to MacArthur when he was
still Chief of Staff, that Quezon was not a sovereign head of government and therefore might reasonably be entitled to a 19-gun salute,
the same as Murphy and American State Governors. The 4-star
MacArthur told the 1-star Bureau Chief that Quezon should receive a
full 21-gun salute, explaining to Dern, the Secretary of War, that the
refusal of "a sovereign salute to the elective head of this people will
create a sense of resentment and insult in the breasts of all Filipinos."[25] The Bureau of Insular Affairs thereby deferred to Mac-
Arthur's wishes and, with the concurrence of Roosevelt, directed that
Quezon would be afforded a 21-gun salute and the playing of the

Philippine national anthem, effectively taking precedence over the High Commissioner. Secretary of War Dern arrived in Manila on 2 November and the strength of opposition encountered among American leaders to according Quezon a 21-gun salute caused him to have second thoughts so that, on 9 November, he cabled Roosevelt. Dern informed the President that, with the exception of MacArthur, all ranking American civil and military dignitaries believed the recognition of Quezon with such high honors "would subordinate the status of the High Commissioner who is the representative of the United States Government in the Philippines, thereby making his position difficult and untenable."[26]

Roosevelt changed his mind. The 21-gun salute would be reserved for the President of the United States, in recognition of his "direct supervision and control over foreign affairs." Three days later, and after further reflection, the President told Dern that, although Murphy and Quezon would enjoy equal rank and honors, it would be Murphy who was to be *primus inter pares* because "it is proper that the High Commissioner be regarded as the senior official and therefore that as between the two he take precedence over the President of the Commonwealth."[27] Quezon reacted by refusing to take part in his own inauguration, now but a few days distant. Only some speedy, conciliatory diplomacy was to save the day, though one of Murphy's allies insisted that "nothing . . . could have kept the President from that occasion except his own demise."[28]

American antipathy towards Quezon in the Philippines arose from a suspicion of Murphy's that MacArthur and Quezon were out to undermine the provisions of the Tydings-McDuffie Act by treating the 10-year Commonwealth period as a euphemism for full-blown independence.[29] There was built-in ambiguity, gray areas, between American responsibilities in the Philippines for foreign relations, economics and defense; the role of the High Commissioner to advise on these and other matters; and Quezon's undeclared perception of himself as Head of State. As Friend remarked, "sovereignty, like pregnancy, could not be partial; . . . one either was or was not sovereign."[30] In 1937, Roosevelt blocked Quezon's attendance as Philippine Head of State at King George VI's coronation in London, thus making the point that Quezon was not a sovereign being.

Perhaps the pacifist Democrat Murphy and the Republican Major General MacArthur were bound to dislike one another. The situation was not helped by MacArthur's pursuit of the former's job or by

MacArthur's criticism of Murphy's performance in that appointment. One of MacArthur's partisan subordinates wrote of the manner in which MacArthur's hostility towards Murphy was replicated. Apparently, Murphy "betrayed his jealousy of MacArthur's stature in the Islands by initiating a personal campaign of pressure on President Roosevelt to cause the General's removal."[31] When Murphy was eventually favored with the sight of MacArthur's defense plan, he was not greatly excited by what he saw. Moreover, when the *Report on National Defense in the Philippines* was eventually published in 1936, Murphy was among a number who wondered whether MacArthur was indeed in the real world.

Meanwhile, on the morning of 15 November 1935 three hundred thousand spectators had gathered in the sunken garden opposite the Legislative Building to witness Quezon's inauguration ceremony, attended by Vice President John Nance Gardner, Secretary for War George H. Dern, the Speaker of the House, Joseph W. Byrnes, seventeen Senators and twenty-six Congressmen. It was, at that time, the largest American Congressional group ever to be sent out in one single delegation. They were away from their offices for well over two months. The Pan Am China Clipper service, which took five days from Manila to San Francisco, was not inaugurated until the end of November 1935.[32] After President Quezon took the oath of office there followed an enormous civic-military parade and generous hospitality. At a formal dinner held that night at the Manila Polo Club, two vaudeville actors, unkempt and in rags, holding toy guns, approached MacArthur at his table. After they had saluted, the United Press's Revel S. Moore announced: "General MacArthur, I want you to meet the Philippine Army." "Thanks," replied MacArthur, hiding his acute lack of amusement, "I didn't know I had even two soldiers to start with."[33]

Two weeks after the celebration Pinky died in the Manila Hotel of cerebral thrombosis. MacArthur, the solitary, vulnerable and emotional general, took the death of his mother very hard and suffered severe depression. Eisenhower observed how her passing "affected the General's spirit for many months."[34] He ordered her suite to be locked, and it remained unoccupied for a year. The saving grace was the presence of Jean Faircloth and it was a natural process for him to transfer the love and deep affection he had held for his mother to Jean.

It became common for Miss Faircloth to be seen with the General, not that they went out often other than for their regular cinema visits. MacArthur's mundane lifestyle suited Jean, she did not challenge him in the way that Louise had done. The age disparity of 20 years seems to have had little effect on their relationship. They both had a passion for western movies and would watch up to six a week, otherwise, listening to records was popular, Bing Crosby in particular. He treated her like royalty and called her Ma'am. She reciprocated with the pet name "Sir Boss," after the benevolent autocrat in *A Connecticut Yankee at King Arthur's Court*, or, more formally, "Gin'ral" in her soft Tennessee accent.[35] The General smoked like a chimney, nowadays it was usually a pipe. He was virtually abstemious, drinking a glass of gin and lime juice—a ginster—prior to dinner. Of their divergent individual tastes, MacArthur would go to a boxing match at the Olympic Stadium if there was a good fight in prospect, while Jean adored dancing—something which MacArthur had done under protest in Louise's time but now steadfastly refused to consider. MacArthur vetted Jean's dance partners: his aides were deemed suitable, as was the harmless Sergio Osmeña. It seems certain that MacArthur would have drawn the line at Manuel Quezon, had the President not had a penchant for dancing with younger women.

The President would appear several nights a week at the Manila Hotel's Fiesta Pavilion accompanied by male friends and almost invariably by his social aide, Colonel Nieto. Nieto's job was to ask the prettier ladies to dance with the President. Quezon had a passion for the tango. When he took to the floor, other dancers made way for him and his selected partner. A woman friend recalled that: "He was a small man but very lithe, very graceful and he danced the tango beautifully." At the annual, two-week carnival held opposite the hotel in the Luneta Park, the President would attend every night in disguise and dance incognito with the prettiest of girls. When someone once remonstrated with him that his behavior was unbecoming, he replied that the burden of the problems of state was lightened by feminine company.[36] But he was, as John Gunther observed:

a good deal more than a playboy . . . He is full of nerve and nerves. He is one of the world's best ballroom dancers, and also one of its supplest practical politicians. He loves cards and alcohol; also he loves his country and his career. He likes to laugh—even at himself—but he is, or was, a quite genuine revolutionary, as much the father of his country as Kemal Ataturk.[37]

Nothing was permitted to impede the progress towards the adoption of Quezon's defense plan. On 25 November 1935, he told the National Assembly of the Commonwealth at its first session, "self defense is the supreme right of mankind, no more sacred to the individual than the nation."[38] The speech contained all the hallmarks of MacArthur rhetoric, which is understandable since the Military Mission prepared the speech which received only cosmetic amendment by Quezon. The new Commonwealth President was prepared to put his reputation on the line in pursuit of a national defense policy. He relied explicitly upon MacArthur to provide professional reassurance that the Philippines was indeed defensible, placing enormous trust and confidence upon his military adviser. When Murphy once asked Aurora Quezon to explain to him the intricate relationship that existed between MacArthur and the Quezons, she said to him: "Frank, you don't seem to understand. Douglas is our brother."[39]

Very little time was allowed to digest the forty-six page document on its express journey towards acceptance. In the media, the former guerilla leader, Emilio Aguinaldo challenged the cost. In 1936, sixteen million Pesos was 37 per cent of the Philippine budget, more than was spent that year on the previously highest spending department, education. Aguinaldo insisted that the formation of a national army was a useless pretense. The Government should rely upon the Americans to defend the Philippines until 1946 when the country should put itself under the auspices of the spirit of international justice. This continuing confidence in the international order and the Kellogg-Briand Pact to foster international peace and security was a common, international, left-of-center philosophy and one supported by Murphy.

In practice, the Philippines could not afford its proposed defense program unless it raised taxes. The situation in the countryside was volatile, the people inclined to violence by despair born of hunger and poverty as average incomes plummeted below subsistence levels. Malnutrition, dysentery and tuberculosis grew to epidemic proportions.[40] The principal dissenter to the bill was Camilio Osias, a pacifist who claimed that one third of the amount of money allocated to defense was sufficient to provide for all schoolchildren of elementary age for ten years. He insisted that defense monies would be better used dealing with disease and hunger rather than on American defense obligations. He poured scorn on the proposed pay scale of conscripts, five centavos a day, insufficient to buy a pack of cigarettes.

Moreover, to take twenty year old males away from the farms for five and a half months robbed agricultural families of essential labor at harvest time. If, argued Osias, drawing on U.S. Senator Nye's supportive opinion, the Philippines had no army and only a small internal security police force, the Philippines could rely upon international opinion for its defense. To prepare for peace, he argued, the nation had to implement peace.[41] His was virtually a lone voice. At almost midnight on 20 December 1935, the National Assembly passed the National Defense Act, which was signed by Quezon the next day in the presence of Sergio Osmeña and Douglas MacArthur. The intention was to establish a standing force of 10,000 troops and reserves of 400,000 by 1946. The standing or regular force would include the 6,000-man Philippine Constabulary.

Now came the hard part, implementing the defense plan. The first step was to create the framework of the new army by redesignating the Headquarters of the Philippine Constabulary, as Headquarters Philippine Army, and designating the Constabulary's division as Philippine Constabulary Division of the Army. The second step was to restructure a new Philippine Military Academy from the old Philippine Constabulary Academy. The third step was the appointment of a General Staff for the Philippine Army. Three Philippine-born assistant Chiefs of Staff were appointed.[42] The 1918 census which indicated 109,000 Filipino males would become 20 years old in 1936 was found to have been flawed. Making due allowances for those who would dodge conscription, a lesser figure was anticipated. However, by the final count made on 10 April 1936, 153,489 young men had come forward. So ecstatic was Quezon that he decided the full quota of 40,000 men would be trained in 1937. Quezon and MacArthur concerned themselves only with generalities. The detail fell to Eisenhower and Ord. When they approached MacArthur and pointed out all their estimates had been instantly nullified by Quezon's action—more trainers, more barracks, more money would be required—MacArthur sent them away, telling them to get on with it.[43] "The full quota would be trained in 1937, which meant that 128 cadres—each of two officers, eight enlisted men, and two Philippine Scouts non-commissioned officers—had to be organized, each to train from 100 to 198 trainees."[44] "Disregarding entirely the cost of arms and ammunition for these men after they have been trained, the additional training and maintenance cost involved will be about ten million pesos . . . Another acute embarrassment arises from the fact that we have no money whatsoever immediately available for construction," complained an increasingly exasperated Eisenhower.[45]

The Commanding General of the Philippine Department had been ordered by Washington to assist the Military Mission. The new commanding general, Major General Lucius R. Holbrook, had not made the most tactful of approaches when he asked the Adjutant General whether MacArthur took precedence over him and the Commander of the Asiatic Fleet. After due discussion in Washington in April 1936, the Adjutant General responded in Holbrook's favor. Manila's priority in Washington's pecking order had been put in perspective. "Only on rare occasions would the Philippine President and his military adviser obtain priority for any of their defense requests, no matter how urgent they seemed in Manila."[46] Room could only be found for 500–600 Filipinos for training in American camps at Commonwealth expense in the Philippines and in 1936 only four American officers were made available to assist in the training of the new Philippine Army. Difficulties with Philippine Scouts' terms and conditions of service whilst on training detachment with the Philippine Army were more easily overcome to allow eleven of the twenty-five Filipino officers to assist the Philippine Army.[47]

There was nothing in MacArthur's first formal report to Quezon in April 1936 to suggest that the plan was not going better than intended, having "exceeded original anticipation." As to the vexed and sensitive issue of cost, MacArthur reassured Quezon that the defense plan "makes every possible concession to economy consistent with efficiency. The result is that in the world today there is no other defensive system that provides an equal security at remotely comparable cost to the people maintaining it."[48] Once fully developed, the new defense plan would be so powerful as to deter any potential invader. MacArthur's planning duo of Eisenhower and Ord knew otherwise, regarding MacArthur's upbeat report, distributed widely in the U.S.A. and in the Philippines, as having been economical with the truth. ". . . we had barely gotten started, and there was no Philippine Army to speak of. Few of the camps had been built, and the system of registering the Filipinos for training had barely been functioning."[49] On 18 June, MacArthur's appointment as Field Marshal was made official, but not until 24 August 1936 did Aurora Quezon present the Field Marshal, resplendent and bemedalled in his new uniform, with the Field Marshal's gold baton. In his acceptance speech, MacArthur emphasized the importance of military preparedness. Once MacArthur had sat down, the Japanese Consul General, who was present at the ceremony, turned to an acquaintance at his side and said, "it is the same speech the Japanese generals make before the Diet when they want more money for the army."[50]

Criticism of the defense plan and of its architect continued to develop both in the Philippines and in the United States. MacArthur's willing assumption of the rank of Field Marshal—"he is tickled pink and feels he's made a lot of face locally"[51]—did nothing to help his credibility among some notably hostile senior military figures in Washington. Among the reasons Eisenhower and Ord advanced against their own local promotion (Eisenhower was promoted Lieutenant Colonel of right in 1936) were the beliefs "that in a locality where we were serving with so many American officers, most of whom believe that the attempt to create a Philippine army is somewhat ridiculous, the acceptance by us of high rank in an army which is not yet formed would serve to belittle our effort. Moreover, it would seriously handicap every effort on our part to secure necessary cooperation from commanders and staffs in the American army."[52] MacArthur's successor as Chief of Staff, General Malin Craig, owed him nothing, and the present Head of the War Plans Division, Brigadier General Stanley D. Embick, was clear eyed about the Philippine situation. Craig, Embick and most of the General Staff believed that a military establishment capable of being maintained by the Philippines Government "would be wholly ineffective in itself to protect the Philippine Islands against Japan." Two reasons were given. First, the Philippines was an archipelago, not a compact land unit as Switzerland, and an enemy could dominate the intervening seas to prevent Philippine armed forces from concentrating, which meant outlying islands could be captured one by one. Second there was no Philippine industrial base, which meant munitions and equipment would have to be procured abroad to support armed forces which did not include a navy capable of keeping open lines of communication. The War Plans Division conceded that the only value of MacArthur's Philippine armed forces would be that "of supplementing military (including naval) measures the United States might be induced to take for the defense of the Philippines ... If the United States does not intend to assume responsibility for the defense of the new Philippine state, it should announce that fact at an early date."[53] The United States was committed to the defense of the Philippines until independence in 1946, at which point the Philippine Defense Forces would be fully autonomous. There was already the idea abroad in some quarters in Manila of advancing the date of independence. The War Planners, aware of the ongoing threat to Philippine security from ethnic insurgency, believed that the maintenance of internal order was what was required and that the Philippine Government should look to improving the Philippine Constabulary through gradual expansion rather than create a new national defense force. Embick recommended that the 90,000 rifles and 4500 Browning automatics MacArthur needed each year from 1936 to 1939 should not be sold. The Mission had provisionally agreed to purchase from the Army Department heavy, obsolete First World War Enfield rifles of British design at 8 pesos each. They could not afford the standard U.S. Army M1903 Springfield rifle which cost ten times as much, let alone the new Garand M-1 which MacArthur had been instrumental in acquiring for the U.S. Army. The War Planners were concerned about the dispersal plans of these arms, fearing they might fall into rebellious hands, affecting the stability of the Manila government, impinge upon American sovereignty over the Philippines and create an unfavorable international impression. In the end, they decided that the Japanese were more of a threat than insurrection.

Eventually it was therefore agreed that the Philippines could have its arms but the price charged for the Enfields became 18 and not 8 pesos.[54] Because of these and other continuing cost escalations, such as building cost overruns, Eisenhower and Ord attempted to get MacArthur to go and see the War Department in Washington to fight his corner. The two unhappy officers were having similar difficulties on the Filipino side, where initial enthusiasm for defense had faded with the memory of the recent inauguration. Eisenhower remarked how they both had "learned to expect from the Filipinos with whom we deal a minimum of performance from a maximum of promise. From the President on down, each official seems to act individually and on the spur of the moment with respect to any detail in which he is interested and without regard for possible effects upon other activities or upon the army as a whole."[55] Ord had chaired the Philippine Defense Planning Committee at the Army War College and had done the groundwork upon which MacArthur superimposed his plan. Ord, the extrovert, had been brought up in Mexico and spoke fluent Spanish, the language of politics and business in the Philippines. The introverted Eisenhower needed Ord's "quickness of mind" and it soon became apparent that, though junior in rank, cerebrally and effectually Ord was the senior of the two. It was he who acted as intermediary between the military and the Assemblymen. "Ord was the best man in the entire outfit . . . Ike did well but he didn't have the knowledge of things."[56]

Coordination between MacArthur and Quezon had begun to break down. Quezon would make defense decisions unbeknown to the Mission. A contributory factor to this problem was MacArthur's refusal to visit the President on a regular basis because, according to Eisenhower, MacArthur thought "it would not be in keeping with his rank and position for him to do so."[57] The reason MacArthur was not prepared to take issue with Washington was due to his conviction that the Republican, Alf Landon, would trounce Roosevelt in the November 1936 elections. MacArthur was inclined to make judgements and stay with them irrespective of more recent, more authoritative indications to the contrary. He read the famously inaccurate poll in the *Literary Digest* and told his subordinates, Eisenhower and Ord, that Landon would win by a landslide. When they, in unison, repeated an opinion that Landon "cannot even carry Kansas," he "got perfectly furious" and told them they were stupid. MacArthur could not contemplate a Roosevelt victory because he was set to go with Quezon to Washington after Landon's inauguration to secure their own New Deal for the Philippines. Eventually it became clear that Landon was not going to win. "Boy, did the general backpedal rapidly," wrote Eisenhower. He "accused the *Literary Digest* of 'crookedness' when he heard Wall Street odds had gone up to 4-1 on Roosevelt against Landon." MacArthur had bet heavily on a Landon victory. What saddened Eisenhower was his failure to express "any regret for his bawling out of a couple of months ago." They had been told not to go out on a limb unnecessarily. They were "fearful and small-minded people who are afraid to express judgements that are obvious from the evidence at hand."[58] The more the pressure, the more the likelihood of a bawling out, which was increasingly directed towards Eisenhower.

MacArthur was undoubtedly a visionary, and among the first to appreciate the potential of the Pacific Rim. He, as a red blooded American, wanted his country to be there at the forefront of a region in transition. It was a matter of prestige. In his Report on National Defense in the Philippines, 27 April 1936, he commented:

So the industrial and economic revolution in East Asia, with its growing demand for credits and manufactured goods has begun just in time, if intelligently handled, to cushion the shock of compulsory readjustment in Europe and America, if not to postpone indefinitely the necessity for such readjustment. For many years the new markets will sustain a capacity to absorb vast quantities of manufactured products, paying for these in equivalent quantities of raw materials that occidental countries grow increasingly to need.[59]

There were also elements of paternalism and the American Way in the National Defense Act of the Philippine Commonwealth. MacArthur said, "its purpose is to preserve the integrity of the only Christian state in the Far East—to perpetuate the ideals of religious freedom, personal liberty and republican government that have under American tutelage, flowered here in fruition."[60]

MacArthur did not believe the Philippines to be an attractive economic resource[61] but he held an exaggerated belief that she could become an international focus for trade, investment and economic development in the way that Hong Kong would become. "They comprise an important, in some respects the most important, section of the great and vaguely defined region known as the Far East."[62] The General was fast becoming a modest private investor himself and a high proportion of his new Filipino acquaintances were property owners and investors. "Of all Western nations, none is more fortunate in the location and character of its contact with the Far East than is the United States in its position in the Philippine Islands." The obvious problem was that the Philippines could not defend its position with the Philippine Division alone. It is for this reason that MacArthur's Defense Plan was an essential ingredient in beginning to provide his philosophy with any form of rationale. On 25 July 1936, MacArthur wrote to General Hugh Drum, the man assumed to be Malin Craig's replacement, and who was still in Hawaii. MacArthur enunciated his opinion that the line of defense in the Pacific should run from the Philippines to Alaska. Such a posture would nullify "the threat of the mandated islands held by Japan, and will give the United States a position of such mastery in the Pacific as to give pause to any force of aggression." Clearly MacArthur thought such a step would deter Japanese aggression and that "the United States can look with perfect security upon the developments in the Pacific situation in the decades to come."[63] The problem with deterrence is that it is by nature threat-related and therefore risks giving rise to conflict which may not have arisen if the deterrent had not been created. "The present American garrisons," he continued to Drum,

> are manifestly unable to insure even reasonably adequate protection in the face of strong attack and Department Commanders in the past have almost in desperation developed plans for attempting, after the beginning of an emergency, to raise, train, and equip additional forces from local manpower. All schemes of this kind heretofore proposed have offered little real promise of success but the successful development of the Commonwealth Army changes completely the situation here.

MacArthur believed that with the development of his plan, "the American Army, for the first time in 35 years, will be in a position not only to adequately protect from predatory attack, but what is equally important to thoroughly protect a Navy Base."[64] MacArthur had the idea of developing the Manila Bay area as an equivalent base to that at Singapore, with the means of sustaining the fleet there. This concept took little account of the fleet's utter disdain of Manila Bay as a suitable location for a substantial naval base.

On 3 August 1936, MacArthur chose an address to the faculty and student body of the Command and General Staff School at Baguio to defend his defense plan. Beneath the confident delivery and rhetoric there lay a critical mismatch between the dream and the reality, ". . . it would be an impossibility for any potential enemy to bring to the Philippine area anything like a preponderant portion of his army. He would indeed have difficulty in concentrating into the vital area as large a force as the Philippine Army which would oppose him. Any conceivable expeditionary force might actually find itself outnumbered."[65] The General drew an analogy with Great Britain and how the sea had been the crucial factor in determining that Britain had never "been compelled to drive off a land attack from its shores."[66] In his speech, MacArthur understated the role and function of a strong navy not so much from a defender's as from an attacker's point of view. He continued, pointing out the failure of the Allied landings against poor opposition at Gallipoli in the First World War: ". . . it emphasized again for all students of warfare the tremendous difficulties attendant upon overseas operations and to indicate the degree of reluctance with which any General Staff would commit a major portion of its army to a venture of this character."[67] The General and Naval Staff in Washington were at this time reasonably confident that the Imperial Japanese Staff would, if they attacked the Philippines, come over the beaches of Northern Luzon.[68]

MacArthur's strategic vision was, as Jose maintains, based on what he saw as probabilities, not possibilities.[69] His view of what would happen, where and when became a constant. Alternative contingency planning in the event that his predictions proved wrong went unexplored. There was little provision for the fog of war or examination of other courses open to a potential enemy. Bonner Fellers, disciple to MacArthur and aide to Quezon, minimized the role of air power and the threat of amphibious landing. The thinking was decidedly shallow, based as it was on the assertion that amphibious operations involved withdrawal of ships from trade routes, thus harming international trade, and that an offensive operation such as this would leave the enemy flanks exposed. Bonner Fellers recited MacArthur's argument that the geography of the Philippines, properly employed and defended, could impose unacceptable damage upon an aggressor.[70] Integrated coastal and field artillery acting in cooperation with infantry would stop an attack on the beaches. The thinking was sound; failure to resource the idea meant that it just did not work in practice. The strongest part of MacArthur's argument lay in the comparison he made with the Philippine insurrection, albeit forty years previously.

> In that campaign, a poorly equipped and loosely organized force of irregulars, which probably never exceeded 20,000 in its total strength, compelled the American Government, with its bases thoroughly established here and with complete command of the ocean, to support large forces here engaged in bitter field campaign for a period of several years—force which at one time numbered almost 100,000 men. Had the Filipino Army been properly organized and adequately equipped, the resources in men and money expended by the American Government would have been multiplied many fold.[71]

In his lecture, MacArthur did discuss the cost of his proposed defense program but in a very clinical and precise manner which left no latitude for cost overruns or for enhancements to the original plan.

Only MacArthur could have taken his flawed defense concept as far forward as he did. "He was regarded as probably America's most brilliant military mind. And he knew his Philippines. If anybody's word of a defense program for the Philippines should carry weight, his was certainly that word."[72] As a concept, it had gained sufficient momentum to remain in being when other evolutionary advances, such as the development of air power, superimposed themselves upon MacArthur's thoughts. The belated arrival of the U.S. Army Air Corps in strength in the Philippines with all its attendant, exaggerated hopes, meant that Japan's invasion of the Philippines was no longer a probability. It became a certainty. The establishment of a long-range, American air force based in the Philippines was a threat to Japanese aspirations in south east Asia which the Japanese felt obliged to remove. When Major Kotoshi Doba, Fifth Air Force, was interrogated after the war and asked why the Japanese Army attacked the Philippines, he replied: "Our bases in Formosa could have been easily attacked by the American air force. It was necessary to eliminate this danger."[73]

It could be that one contributory factor towards Hugh Drum being overlooked as Chief of Staff was because he was too close in his thinking to MacArthur. On 4 September 1936, he wrote to "Field Marshal Douglas MacArthur." "Dear Mac," he began, ". . . In the last few years I have been indicating the same prophecy claiming that there are no more fish in the Atlantic Ocean—the Pacific is the happy hunting (trading) ground . . . I for one am willing to take this burden (the Philippines) to retain our hold in the Orient as some assurance of securing our share of its trade."[74] In his letter, Drum told MacArthur of the death of Dern, the Secretary for War. One of Dern's last letters to MacArthur was written on 11 June 1936. "I cannot close without expressing my keen delight that you are a Master Mason . . . when you have an opportunity, I recommend that you also take the Scottish Rites Degrees."[75] It was a bad time for MacArthur to lose the support of a kindred spirit. Masonry was one of two facets that MacArthur had in common with Roosevelt; the other was acting ability.

One of MacArthur's weaknesses was founded upon a belief that he himself fostered, that he knew the Far East and its people. It is debatable that he even fully grasped the situation in the Philippines and the true capabilities of its peasant stock. The Swiss may have had to overcome the problems of three national languages but the Filipino tribes and their thousand islands had eight languages and eighty dialects.

Although convergence between the Americans and the ruling Filipino classes was progressing in Manila, there remained many gaps. Again, one of the reasons for the failure of the military training regime in such distant places as Mindanao was that the assessments were made based on educational standards in Manila. No one in the higher civil and military planning organization considered the possibility that schools in the remoter corners of the Philippines were not producing youths capable of being trained.[76]

One of the first to recommend the recall of MacArthur was Harold E. Fey in a June 1936 article in *The Nation*.[77] In a later article he argued that the development of a Philippine Army might endanger relations of the United States with other nations—including Japan.[78] The voices of dissent soon became more regular and more widespread. Why, the General Staff wanted to know, was MacArthur not discussing policy issues with them before submitting his shopping lists for the new Philippine Army. Craig, and representatives of the Army and State Departments recommended to the President that MacArthur be brought home to account for his actions. Roosevelt declined to take their advice. The last thing he wanted on the eve of the election was the dramatic resignation of MacArthur in the full glare of Washington's media. In November 1936, Assistant Secretary of State Francis B. Sayre, son-in-law of Woodrow Wilson, put to Roosevelt the idea of a bilateral agreement with Japan not to further militarize their Pacific islands. Although the plan was idealistic, Roosevelt conceded that it was the best option for protecting the Philippines. Perhaps the President did realize that the very sovereignty that he was unwilling to concede contributed to the overall vulnerability of the islands and that the challenge posed by a strong America within Japan's own sphere of influence would seem something that could not be ignored. In those days it would not have entered the minds of many that Japan would contemplate taking America on, but Roosevelt was the exception. Realistically, he believed that, even defended by American forces, the archipelago would be taken quickly by the Japanese. His best hope was to evacuate what assets he could with a view after perhaps two years to "gradually move westward in an island-hopping operation," and recapture Manila.[79]

With Roosevelt successfully returned to office, MacArthur now hoped that none of his freely expressed, partisan comments on behalf of Landon had percolated through to the White House. MacArthur and Quezon were both going to the U.S. on what could be a difficult

visit. The excuse was an invitation by Paul V. McNutt, who was to succeed Murphy as High Commissioner, to attend his inauguration ceremony in Washington. Quezon, who sailed from Manila on 25 January,
took with him a large national delegation and, in the course of his
journey, created grave offense in Washington by accepting the honors
due to the head of a sovereign state. His biggest bombshell was
reserved for his arrival in Los Angeles when he told reporters that he
wanted the Philippines independent by the end of 1938. Many
Americans would have been agreeable to Quezon's proposition but,
politically and militarily, the division ran deep. The Executive branch
of the American Government opposed any advance of independence
day, while it was actively encouraged by the Legislative branch.[80]
However large the number who saw the Philippines as being an
entangling commitment which they would be happy to forego, the
challenging manner of Quezon's announcement made it virtually
impossible for the President to accede to his demand. That reality
suited people with business interests in the Philippines as well as the
influential, conservative, Spanish-Catholic group in Manila. Quezon
went to New York prior to Washington, which was probably just as
well because no invitation to him had been forthcoming from Roosevelt. Roosevelt said he did not know why Quezon was in America
and, further, he had no intention of seeing him.[81] A continued rebuff
would have been particularly hurtful because Quezon had a deep
trust of Roosevelt,[82] but MacArthur intervened. He asked to pay his
personal respects to the President and was grudgingly given 5-10
minutes. The meeting lasted two hours and involved the verbal combat to which MacArthur had grown accustomed whilst Chief of Staff.
MacArthur told the President that he could not afford to humili-
ate the President of the new Commonwealth, since he might in the
future need him as an ally. Roosevelt relented and invited Quezon to
an informal lunch, but the same day withdrew the invitation. Only
after MacArthur once again intervened did Quezon get to see the
President. He received no encouragement for his notion of early
independence either from the President or on Capitol Hill, which
MacArthur and others persuaded him to abandon. Perhaps it was
never intended to be a serious proposition but merely a device with
which to extract economic concessions. There were indeed some but
otherwise the Washington visit was disappointing. (Quezon sought an
extension of privileged trade concessions for 15-20 years after inde-

pendence). MacArthur was no more successful with his shopping list in the War Department.

Not all observers were prepared to allow the arrival of America's first Field Marshal to pass by without comment. MacArthur chose not to respond, until there were ribald comments and descriptions in the press of the uniform which he had had a hand in designing.

> I have never worn and never expect to wear any other than the uniform of the United States Army specifically prescribed for my rank and orga-nization. My sensitiveness may be due partly to the veneration in which I hold the American uniform in which I have seen so many of my com-rades in arms die and in which I myself, was twice wounded on the battlefields of France.[83]

He had not held the uniform in veneration in France where he wore non-regulation items, and in the Philippines he had indeed worn his Field Marshal's uniform. The point can be stretched to agree that gas inhalation equates to being wounded in so far as soldiers gassed in combat were entitled to the award of the Purple Heart. What this exchange revealed was that when riled, MacArthur was prepared to stretch the truth to defend his position.

The bandwagon rolled on to Mexico, where the Mexicans wanted to see MacArthur, not Quezon. The problem of the General upstag-ing the President was solved by the former's return to New York. Quezon continued with an extended tour of Europe, before arriving back in Manila in August 1937 after an absence of seven months. For his part, MacArthur had two appointments of a personal nature. He laid Pinky finally to rest next to his father in Arlington Military Ceme-tery, Virginia and, on the morning of 30 April 1937, accompanied by his aides Major Howard J. Hutter and Captain T.J. Davis, he arrived at the Municipal Building in Manhattan. Where he married Jean Marie Faircloth[84] in a civil ceremony. They had a wedding breakfast at the Astor Hotel and honeymooned on the journey back to Manila. Demands for MacArthur's removal had not abated. Craig and Embick were of the opinion he should go, as was his old adversary Ickes who criticized him as a virtual mercenary greedy for power, in search of a private army to command.[85]

5

———

TO BUILD AN ARMY

After returning to the Philippines on 30 May 1937, it is said[1] that the fifty-seven year old MacArthur caught Jean up in his arms and gallantly carried her over the threshold of their home, past the Field Marshal's baton sitting prominently in a glass case at the entrance. The apartment on the sixth floor of the Manila Hotel came with a complimentary servant and included three bedrooms, drawing room, dining room, breakfast room and a library which contained MacArthur's books and awards as well as his father's own substantial collection. A wide terrace led out from the drawing room, providing a magnificent view over Manila Bay. The drawing room and terrace combined provided room for several hundred people,[2] though only once, soon after their marriage, did the MacArthurs entertain on such a scale. Small dinner parties tended to be the norm and guests were usually upper-class Filipinos rather than Americans. When not entertaining, the couple could invariably be found out on the terrace between 5 and 7 p.m. The General would pace up and down as though on sentry duty, talking to Jean or simply lost in thought. MacArthur was no workaholic; he rarely reached his desk before eleven. After a late lunch hour, he went home again.[3]

The penthouse was undoubtedly the premier accommodation in the Philippines: "more beautiful and more elegant than Malacañang itself."[4] New features included wall-to-wall carpeting and air conditioning. Air conditioning had not been fully developed at that time and could not be regulated. If it was on, it was like living in a refrigerator. The auditor-general insisted that the hotel should bill MacArthur, not the government, for his use of the penthouse. The sum involved was considerable; $1000–1500 per month at 1937 values. After one month in occupation, the Hotel Corporation advised Quezon that there was a problem with MacArthur and his penthouse, since Quezon had promised MacArthur free accommodation. The solution was to have MacArthur elected Chairman of the Manila Hotel Board of Directors, with free quarters, but no salary.[5] He attended the monthly meetings, which tended to be lengthy affairs although business matters were dealt with expeditiously. The rest of the time would be given over to MacArthur briefing the many dignitaries who were Board members on current affairs both globally and as they affected the Pacific.

In July 1937, Japan invaded northern China. Shanghai fell in an ever-widening general war, and, by the end of the year, Japanese forces had occupied Nanking and set about the slaughter of non-combatants. A reporter aboard *President Coolidge* bringing MacArthur back to the Philippines had asked whether he believed a general world war to be in the offing. MacArthur dismissed the idea. "I do not agree with those who predict an imminent war. The complete state of preparedness of practically all nations is the surest preventive of war."[7] Under MacArthur's plans for the defense of the Philippines, the Commonwealth would not be in such a state until 1946. Would a potential enemy be prepared to wait? Confidence in the defense plan was shaken by what the Japanese were doing in China. "The progress of that campaign eventually changed the attitude of many of the Filipinos in responsible positions."[8]

The preparation of MacArthur's army did not stand close examination. The budget would never be equal to the aspiration and yet there were elements within the Philippine Assembly who argued not only that the *plan* was too expensive but so too was MacArthur. They insisted that the Philippines would be in a better position to call upon international assistance if the archipelago were defenseless rather than having self-contained defense forces. In truth, there was insufficient in terms of materiel and manpower to move the program on as planned, despite MacArthur's broad and generous charter to obtain assistance from the Philippine Department. General Holbrook remained uncooperative rather than openly obstructive, but it is

unlikely that the training resources of the Philippine Division would
have greatly enhanced the overall situation. The shortage of trainers
was a significant problem that was never overcome. The idea of feeding the new army with the output from self-sustaining government
farms and supporting it regionally through local industries and diver-
sified local agriculture was impractical. High illiteracy, language in-
compatibility, and the absence of any concept of rudimentary health
and hygiene meant that the training program of the first intake of
conscripts had to be drastically altered. The heavy, constant rains,
which should not have come as a surprise, also hindered the intake
program. The conscripts were issued with shoes, white socks, khaki
shorts and khaki sport shirt, an abaca waist belt, *guinit* (coconut fiber)
helmet and cotton undershirt and drawers. Each man was to have a
blue denim fatigue uniform with low cut rubber shoes, a blanket and
a mosquito net. All except the khaki clothing was of Philippine manufacture.[9] The hats, like the plan, were sound in theory but were not
waterproof[10] and shone in the sunlight.

During the three months of MacArthur's absence, Eisenhower and
Ord had juggled with the budget. The $8 million for 1937 had been
fully used by July of that year and the two staff officers set about making a realistic appraisal for 1938. MacArthur had promised Quezon
that the military budget year-on-year for ten years would not exceed
$8 million so the news the General heard on his return was not what
he wanted, nor did he relish presenting the truth to Quezon. He sent
Ord to Washington to plead with the War Department for greater
consideration and more assistance—something he himself had been
unable to achieve. Meanwhile, Eisenhower completed the sums for
the 1938 defense budget and it came to $14½ million—over 50 per
cent above forecast. What was more alarming was the realization that
this amount would be needed each year for the next five years. Construction costs would tail off, but the slack would more than be taken
up by the provision of mobilization centers, warehousing and the
need to make unforeseen improvements. Provision for the Off-Shore
Patrol and the Air Corps had barely moved forward. In a letter to Ord
in Washington, Eisenhower wrote: "Possibly you and I, two years ago,
did not hold out as insistently as we should have for the 22,000,000
pesos figure. In our own defense, however, we can remember that
our studies and conclusions were academic ones and we had no
means of demonstrating their accuracy."[11] In view of the guarantees

he had received from MacArthur, the news came as a profound shock to Quezon.

It speaks legions for MacArthur's powers of persuasion that he was able to convince Quezon that the enormous hike in costs was due to the deteriorating security situation elsewhere in the world, forcing up equipment costs, and also to Quezon's own aspiration to complete the ten-year program in five years. Quezon, who allegedly told his aide Bonner Fellers that he would rather lose an arm and a leg than go before the Assembly and ask it to increase the military budget, was no less persuasive when he used an Eisenhower draft to explain to it that the cost of the full defense cycle had been reassessed as $130,000,000 and not $80,000,000[12] and that the program was to be completed in five not ten years. Quezon told the Assembly that there was no need for concern and, in the sublime political speak Eisenhower had crafted for him, he explained how, "regardless of the aggregate authorized for the full development of our national defense, the annual appropriations will be adjusted each year to the annual revenue, so that all other authorized government services and activities may develop in harmony with the growth of the populations and the expansion of our culture."[13]

There is a another story, about how angry MacArthur became at Eisenhower's and Ord's unauthorized and unacceptable budget increase: "By their misrepresentation it appeared to President Quezon that General MacArthur had broken faith." The account then tells what happened next, when Eisenhower and Ord appeared in front of the General: " 'What goes on here? I am neither a knave nor a fool.' " He said to them he ought to send them home but since he had chosen them as members of his staff and brought them to the Philippines he would keep them but he would never again trust them."[14] There is no evidence to support this version, and it is disturbing that the original source could only have been MacArthur. Hunt, a pro-MacArthur writer suggests, rather unconvincingly, that Eisenhower and Ord "coveted" MacArthur's job. How would Hunt have known that unless he had either been told by MacArthur or had other evidence? Hunt had access to material that is no longer available. This is true of much of the research into MacArthur at this time. Key linkages are simply missing. This military budget debate took place at a time of increasing criticism of the MacArthur Plan both in the U.S.A. and the Philippines. MacArthur dismissed the pacifist view as admittedly vocal but not influential. He held true to his constant theme that only the Filipino would defend the Philippines: no one else would fight for him.[15] It is unlikely that MacArthur believed everything he said for he was often targeting his comments at specific audiences. It is difficult to separate the deeply held conviction from the rhetoric. Such arbitrary dismissal of the opposition's point of view which, if it had come from any other than pacifist sources might have been taken more seriously was unfortunate. ". . . It did not seem possible to them (MacArthur and his staff) that within two years Quezon might be faced with the dilemma of 'full development' of the defense system, or maintenance of 'all other authorized government services,' but not both.[16]" In Washington, his old adversaries, the columnists Drew Pearson and Robert S. Allen, alleged that MacArthur was the real power behind Quezon, who did what MacArthur wanted. Rumors abounded of MacArthur's imminent recall to the United States. On 20 August 1937, Quezon radioed the President:

> I am deeply disturbed by persistent rumors which have come to me both in the States and since my return to Manila that the War Department contemplates the early relief of General MacArthur . . . in view of the important issues involved, and my certain knowledge that his relief in the near future would constitute a serious psychological and material blow to the continued preparation of these islands for their place among the family of nations.[17]

In fact MacArthur had already been informed by Malin Craig that he was to be recalled: "Upon completion by you of two years of absence on foreign service you are to be brought home for duty in the United States. The return of your assistants is not contemplated right now."[18] Craig promised to make available to MacArthur any command for which he might express a preference.

There was a growing opinion that America should not be drawn into a war through irresponsible provocation or to protect American business interests in the Far East. There were many who took Frank Murphy's view that it was positively dangerous to arm 400,000 Filipinos. Major J. Lawton Collins, who had served in the Philippines and was at the Army War College in 1937, provided a neat summary of the strategic situation: "Manila Bay is too big to defend from the land point of view; there are too many beaches and too many ways it can be attacked. Yet we have poured hundreds of millions of dollars into the organization of the defense of Corregidor [the island at the mouth of the Bay], and we all agree we cannot hold it. To me, that is a tremendous indictment against the Army and Navy."[19] Among the defenses of Corregidor was a sophisticated series of lateral tunnels based on a central tunnel known as the Malinta Tunnel. The tunnels had been built in contravention of the Washington Naval Treaty's non-fortification clause, being listed in the records as a "public works project."

MacArthur made a polite response to Craig's letter confirming his sadness at having to leave. After pondering the options, MacArthur first applied to be assigned to the IX Corps area (Pacific Coast) but, after quiet reflection, on 16 September, he formally requested retirement for a multitude of reasons—poor health, his work as military adviser was almost complete, he didn't want to create a blockage to others' promotion prospects, he wanted to pursue cultural interests. But the bottom line was probably his inability to contemplate a lesser position than his current one.[20] In an earlier signal to the Chief of Staff, MacArthur pointed out that if war came, he would be just as available on the retired as on the active list. If he were to be recalled to arms, he would have achieved something which eluded his mentor Leonard Wood. "I am convinced however that the United States will not become involved in war during my day," he wrote, adding a typically ingratiating comment: "The magnificent leadership of President Roosevelt practically assures against such a calamity."[21] On 11 October, his application was approved and the War Department set his retirement date as 31 December 1937. He would retire in the rank of General. The President wrote to thank him for his outstanding services to the nation.

It was never really fully determined who had actually pushed MacArthur. Bonner Fellers, confidante and conspiracy theorist, now a Captain at West Point, wrote to MacArthur on 31 December 1937.[22] "Few realize the understanding, the tact, the mental control and the infinite patience you have been forced to exercise," he oozed:

> 1. Consensus of WD opinion is that you were ordered back as the WD felt your assignment Manila was not considered commensurate with the grade of Major General. 2. One Colonel blames the Catholic Church. 3. My best source says General Craig who did display far more than routine interest in the case, is not without blame; to which I am forced to subscribe.

I feel there was close cooperation among Murphy and the Church, White House officials and the C of S (Chief of Staff) and I regret to say the AHC [McNutt, the American High Commissioner].

The balance of probability is that Bonner Fellers was wrong on all or almost all, counts. Craig advised Roosevelt against sacking Mac-Arthur for he feared the loose cannon effect. MacArthur's resignation or retirement "would leave MacArthur free to press ahead with his plans, and the War Department would have less opportunity than ever to control him."[23] Murphy had returned to Michigan in the Spring of 1936. While his concept of an undefended, neutral Philippines dependent upon international law and order for its protection was diametrically opposed to MacArthur's basic idea—if they want it, they'll have to fight for it—he was not in the center of events so, while he may well have been a collaborator, it is unlikely that he led the movement to bring MacArthur home. The moving force would have had to have been in Washington with access to the President.

Which actor actually played the role of Brutus will never be known but there is some residual, circumstantial evidence. Brigadier General Charles Burnett, the new head of the Bureau of Insular Affairs, told MacArthur in a letter that he knew the individual's identity and left as a clue, "I have never known a dirtier piece of politics."[24] Who, therefore, was capable of dirty politics of such a high order? James believes "the most obvious nominee would be Ickes."[25] Ickes' loathing of MacArthur remained undiminished and he now regarded his adversary as having become positively dictatorial[26] in Manila. MacArthur was therefore in a position to obstruct Ickes' plan to bring the Philippines under the jurisdiction of the Department of the Interior and away from the War Department. MacArthur's removal from the scene would help bring this plan about, which did indeed occur in 1939. It was not to be a change for the better.

As to his future as a retired officer, MacArthur decided that he wanted to continue as military adviser to the Philippines. There had been a proposal that he consider becoming a Republican presidential candidate, and others relating to business openings and on the lecture circuit, but he decided to stay put. His task would become manifestly more difficult because he would no longer be able to put his requests for personnel, materiel and general support directly to the War Department. Such requests had now to come from the Philippine Government, channeled through General Holbrook. In addition, his

military staff (thirty-two officers and eight enlisted men) were transferred to the Philippine Department, though they were allowed to
continue working for him. Clouds do have silver linings for in the
matter of social protocol, MacArthur's retirement in the rank of General meant that he took precedence below active officers of that rank
but higher than active Lieutenant Generals—one in the eye for
Major General Holbrook.[27] In a letter of 29 January 1938 to Paul
McNutt, MacArthur assured the High Commissioner that he "personally set very little store upon such matters" but established for the
record his entitlement to "a seventeen gun salute and four ruffles . . .
until death."[28]

While the Philippine National Assembly was content on 21st
November to thank MacArthur for his contribution to the organization of the Philippines' national defense, they declined to support his
continuing engagement after 31 December 1937 as Military Adviser
and Field Marshal. In his response, MacArthur thanked the Assembly for their "patriotic and spontaneous support,"[29] knowing that their
rejection of him was of little significance, since on that date Quezon
was to unilaterally issue an executive order appointing him military
adviser to the Philippines.

When the year ended, the tensions that had developed, principally
between Eisenhower and MacArthur, had not abated. MacArthur's
style was to create his own team around him and to hang on to them
as the paternal head of his own military family. Most people would
have been content to be sought after by a general of MacArthur's
reputation, particularly if his flattering annual efficiency reports compensated for a protracted tour. Eisenhower was, however, an exception. He had been working alongside MacArthur since 1933, and
after years of staff work, he wanted to serve again with troops since
turbulence in Europe and Asia meant the prospect of future conflict.
With only six months service with troops under his belt, his further
advancement would otherwise be circumscribed. Eisenhower was
more than flattered by MacArthur's reluctance to bring in somebody
new. "In addition to the implied compliment, this insistence revealed
a human quality in the General who even then was thought to be a
mysterious, romantic figure far above the frailty of dependence upon
others."[30]

The orderly mind of Eisenhower became increasingly taxed and
exasperated by MacArthur's idiosyncrasies. Although MacArthur had
been to West Point, he had not progressed to school at Leavenworth

or to the Army War College. By contrast, Eisenhower had been to almost every military school conceivable, alternating with staff work. Eisenhower understood the military system and procedures while MacArthur improvised: MacArthur also insisted upon being the center of attention. An entry in Eisenhower's diary of 1 July 1937 recalls the diarist having written a statement of accomplishments of the Philippine Army over the past six months. When MacArthur read it, he told Eisenhower to expand the report and prepare it for his signature so that he might give an interview to the *Herald*. "I fear that one of these days some editor will flatly refuse to take such statements for publication, because of little or no news value."[31] Eisenhower's pen was one of MacArthur's most valuable tools, yet MacArthur did not use his staff wisely or sympathetically. For instance he nominated Eisenhower as a representative of the Philippine Army in its dealings with the Boy Scouts.

Ord had met Brigadier General Embick in Washington. The Head of the War Plans Division left his visitor in no doubt that their plan was a non-starter and hence a good justification not to deliver equipment certain to fall into enemy hands.[32] It was Ord's return from the U.S.A. which proved to be the catalyst for the first of a number of eruptions among the increasingly truculent inner family. The General had heard of the possibility of Ord staying permanently in the United States, and expressed his readiness at a moment's notice to terminate the tours of any or all of the mission's members. He found the "conceit and self-centered" attitudes of various members of the mission, their sense of indispensability, and their individual selfishness in "looking out only for himself" intolerable. Eisenhower remarked how:

> It begins to look as though we were resented simply because we labor under the conviction, and act on it, that someone ought to know what is going on in this army and help them over the rough spots. However, from the beginning of this venture I've personally announced myself as ready and willing to go back to an assignment in the United States Army at any moment.[33]

By the end of 1937, having worked at MacArthur's pet project for two years, both his principal staff officers were in a state of despair and disillusionment. "The Philippine Government simply could not afford to build real security from attack," concluded Eisenhower. "We had to content ourselves with an attempt to produce a military adequate to deal with domestic revolt and to provide at least a passive type of defense around the perimeter of the Islands to slow up the advance of any aggressor until some friendly nation, presumably the United States,[34] came to their aid."

In the new year MacArthur decided to put on a reassuring, morale-raising display, presenting the new, fledgling army to its tax-paying public in Manila City. Trainees would be brought in from all corners, camp in the capital for 3 or 4 days and, after inspection, would take part in a grand, culminating parade. After the proposal had been turned over to Eisenhower and Ord for a feasibility study, they told him it was impossible to achieve within budget. "Carrying out this demonstration would take money that was desperately needed for more important purposes."[35] Nevertheless they were told to get on with it, and so began the initial staff work.

It was a massive enterprise involving the coordination of road transport and island shipping firms to bring the troops to the capital. One day Quezon called in Eisenhower from the small coordination office he manned in the Malacañang Palace. He had heard of the planned troop movement and asked Eisenhower what it was about. Eisenhower, assuming MacArthur had discussed the plan with the President, was astonished to find him in complete ignorance. An extremely angry President rang MacArthur immediately. Eisenhower returned to his other office at No 1 Calle Victoria, there to find MacArthur "exceedingly unhappy with his entire staff, saying he had never intended them to proceed with preparations for the parade but only to investigate the possibility quietly. The staff were to become the scapegoats, and Eisenhower was extremely agitated at this. MacArthur's response was conciliatory; putting his arm around Eisenhower's shoulder he said: "It's fun to see that Dutch temper take over. It's just a misunderstanding, and let's let it go at that."[36] Eisenhower wrote, "Because General MacArthur denied he had given us an order—which was certainly news to us—there was nothing to do except stop the proceedings. This misunderstanding caused considerable resentment," "and never again were we on the same warm and cordial terms."[37]

In the midst of these difficult times, on 21 February 1938, Jean presented her beleaguered husband with his only son and heir. Someone jokingly said to MacArthur, "I didn't know you had it in you." "Neither did I," said Douglas, laughing.[38] The Episcopalian Bishop of Manila christened their son Arthur MacArthur IV in their penthouse on 2 June 1938.[39] Churches, like medicine and funerals, were something MacArthur avoided. He was deeply religious, read the Bible every day, invoked the support of God in many of his rousing speeches, but rarely went inside a church. Jean had even adopted his nominal Episcopalianism at the expense of her Presbyterianism in the hope that he would change his ways. Manuel and Aurora Quezon were the godparents, confirming MacArthur and Quezon as *compadres*. This was ironic because Quezon's doubts and disillusionment with his military adviser were growing. Contemplating neutrality as a possible way forward, in July Quezon sailed for Tokyo to discuss that very prospect.

One of the consequences of establishing the 90 odd training stations, each handling approximately 200 conscripts at a time, was a communications problem. The road system in the Philippines, other than in parts of Luzon, was execrable. Many will say it still is. The solution was to buy a quantity of short take off and landing (STOL) aircraft to connect the training stations. Two instructors were borrowed from the Army Air Corps and a training field, Zablan Field, was established just outside the capital to train Filipino pilots. Eisenhower was attracted to the idea of flying and, unbeknown to his wife Mamie, started lessons in 1936. At the age of 46, he found his reflexes less responsive than those of younger men and was not to gain his private pilot's license until 19 July 1939. Eisenhower's first instructor was Lieutenant Jerry Lee, the founding father of the Philippine Army Air Corps. Lee was delighted to have Eisenhower's ear, for it was common knowledge that MacArthur, at that time, was not air-minded. Indeed, he hated flying because he never felt he was in control. "He was still for damn patrol boats to patrol the coastline of the Philippines," said Lee. "I was trying to promote the (Philippine) Air Force and point out to him that we could go out and meet incoming invaders . . . while the boats would have to stay around close, and it took a hell of a lot more to patrol the coastline of the Philippines with boats than it would with air. And Ike, of course, went along with me."[40] More than once Eisenhower would take the enthusiastic Lee up to talk to MacArthur who paced the terrace, invariably on *send* rather than *receive*. "Of course," recalled Lee, "you didn't get to talk much when you went to see MacArthur. He did the talking. And he called me 'Commodore' for some damned reason or other." Lee was unable to divert MacArthur from his vision of 50 torpedo boats speeding out to sink incoming Japanese transports in Lingayen Bay. The idea was not unreasonable: there just wasn't any money. Nevertheless, Lee rated MacArthur as "the greatest strategist we've ever had in this country."[41]

A practice had developed whereby, if a landing was not essential, an Air Corps aircraft would buzz a location and, once attention had been attracted, a package, a message attached to a rock—whatever—was thrown from the aircraft. Jimmy Ord intended to drop a note at the family home of the Fairchilds up in the mountains in Baguio. He mentioned this to Eisenhower and that he intended to take a Filipino student pilot.

"No you won't," said Eisenhower. "Get one of the American flight instructors. They'll be glad to do it."

Ord laughed. "Our Filipino boys are doing really well. I'll use one of them. I won't be gone more than a few hours. See you late this afternoon."

Whilst in the process of circling, the trainee pilot, Lt Pelagio Cruz, lost speed and crashed. Pilot and plane were not seriously damaged but Ord, leaning out of the back seat, suffered fatal whiplash injuries.[42]

It was a grand, military funeral. The President and High Commissioner were there to support the widow and her two children. MacArthur was not. Quezon authorized the posthumous award of the Philippines' highest military medal, the Distinguished Service Star, and the family received compensation for Ord's loss. Later, the camp in San Miguel, Tarlac, was named in Ord's honor.[43] Ord's death hit Eisenhower hard both in terms of losing a good friend and also because the planning now devolved entirely upon his shoulders. "Without my friend," wrote Eisenhower, "all the zest was gone."[44] A substitute staff officer for Ord, Captain Richard Sutherland, was found serving in Tientsin in China with the 15th Infantry. While Eisenhower appreciated his help, things would never be the same again. MacArthur was shrewd enough to recognize this. Sutherland formed the vanguard of a new team but he was less approachable than Ord had been. He soon felt competent and was itching to take over the reins. On 26 June 1938, Eisenhower took his family back for home leave and to cajole the American Army to provide more from the limited resources at its disposal.[45]

Eisenhower returned to Manila on 5 November 1938 having had some success with his military hardware shopping list. In September, Hitler had annexed the Sudetenland, in Czechoslovakia, with its three million German inhabitants. The persecution of German and Austrian Jews intensified. In Manila's Army-Navy Club, arguments

broke out between those pro-Hitler and the majority opposed to what
he was doing. After 400 years of Spanish domination it was unsurpris-
ing that a good proportion of Manila's Spanish community supported
Hitler through his association with Franco. "Almost without exception . . . the Spanish community was on Hitler's side . . . Hirohito got
little attention."[46]

During Eisenhower's absence an empathy or bond had developed
between MacArthur and the Yale-educated Sutherland. They found
they had much in common, working out "an operational division of
staff responsibility. The blue ribbon responsibility of operations and
planning went to Sutherland while Eisenhower attracted responsibility for the far less glamorous activities of supply and logistics."
This was a calculated snub to Eisenhower and a demotion by function. When Eisenhower remonstrated with MacArthur, insisting that
others would see the new arrangement as a reduction in his prestige, MacArthur responded that "Eisenhower was free to seek other
assignments if he chose." In difficulties with Quezon, MacArthur
became resentful of the personal working relationship developing
between him and Eisenhower, whom he called "traitor."[47] Quezon
persuaded Eisenhower that his early departure might prejudice all
that had been achieved to date, and there was also a mercenary reason to soldier-on and serve out the standard four-year tour in Manila:
the generous allowances paid by the Philippine Government. In
1945, Sutherland would brag that he had outwitted Eisenhower, but
by the time Sutherland had appeared on the scene, the "zest" had
gone and Ike was more than prepared to take on a new appointment
with troops at the appropriate moment.

On 3 September 1939 Eisenhower and a friend sat crouched over
an antiquated radio in the Manila Hotel when they heard in their
headphones Chamberlain's broadcast to Britain and the Empire that
Germany had not responded to their ultimatum to leave Poland and
"consequently this country is at war with Germany." Ike went to Mac-
Arthur. "General, in my opinion the United States cannot remain out
of this war for long. I want to go home as soon as possible. I want to
participate in the preparatory work that I am sure is going to be
intense." Eisenhower reminded MacArthur how, in the First World
War, he had been so highly valued as an instructor that he had not
seen combat; he did not want to miss out on a combat opportunity
again. MacArthur said he was making a mistake but was markedly less
resistant than Quezon who handed Eisenhower a blank contract as

though it were a blank check. "We'll tear up the old contract," said Quezon. "I've already signed this one and it is filled in—except what you want as your emoluments for remaining. You will write that in." "Mr. President," replied Eisenhower, "your offer is flattering. But no amount of money can make me change my mind. My entire life has been given to this one thing, my country and my profession. I want to be there if what I fear is going to come about actually happens."[48]

Eisenhower was royally dined at the Malacañang Palace and, for only the second time in memory, the MacArthurs came aboard ship to bid associates, the Eisenhowers and son John, farewell. If MacArthur did describe Eisenhower as "the best file clerk I ever had"[49] it would have been out of character, but they were so dissimilar that they were never likely to have established the rapport which developed between MacArthur and Sutherland. MacArthur did nothing apparently untoward, out of spite or disenchantment, to damage Eisenhower's career. Indeed, his efficiency report from MacArthur, 1 July 1936 to 30 June 1937, was positively glowing in praise. "A brilliant officer. Equally suited for command or staff duties . . . Is performing duties which in scope and responsibility are comparable to those applying to a general officer of the War Department General Staff. Well suited for civilian contacts." Under the heading "value to service," MacArthur had written, "In time of war, this officer should be promoted to general rank immediately."[50]

Major Richard J. Marshall arrived to take over Eisenhower's quartermaster responsibilities. In Sutherland and Richard Marshall, MacArthur had the beginnings of his own "Chaumont" team which, once fully constituted and after its flight from Corregidor, became known as the Bataan Gang—a term more often than not used as a pejorative. That September there was also news of an unwelcome nature for MacArthur. Major General Hugh Drum, the senior candidate, had been passed over for promotion to Chief of Staff. Roosevelt announced the new Army Chief of Staff was to be the Colonel whom MacArthur had sent into the military backwater of Chicago, General George C. Marshall. In October, High Commissioner McNutt, who originally opposed MacArthur's defense plan but, conditional upon the allocation of adequate resources, had since become an ardent supporter, returned to the U.S.A. to become Head of the Federal Security Administration. He and MacArthur had got on well together. Both were thirty-second-degree masons. In July, MacArthur had sent a broad hint to Stephen Early, Roosevelt's assistant, that he was ready, able and willing to replace McNutt.[51] The offer fell upon stony ground.

A practice mobilization exercise had been held in May 1939. The 40,000 "class of '37" was put on standby for call out for 10 days from 4 May. 23,270 men were called and 24,174 responded. This was a cadre exercise, companies being called out to represent battalion-sized units. MacArthur announced the mobilization to have been satisfactory, but it was patently obvious that the uneducated reservists had forgotten much of what they had learnt two years previously. However, he was called to Quezon's office for a discussion that lasted for six hours, a long session for a pair who met infrequently. Quezon had already been alerted to the problem by Vicente Lim (who would be appointed Deputy Chief of Staff on 3 May). Lim criticized MacArthur's plan because it concentrated too much on producing in the short term large quantities of enlisted men without the corresponding officers.[52] "We are building up an Army full of enlisted reserves without adequate trained officers,"[53] he complained. Conceptually, MacArthur's theory of building up a citizen army over a ten-year period had fallen apart. The results of the mobilization confirmed in Quezon's mind that he had been "hoodwinked" by MacArthur.[54]

The creation of a Department of National Defense in May 1939 was one of a number of shake-ups or significant directional changes which occurred at this time. The new department represented a *de facto* dilution of MacArthur's former position as Philippine Defense Adviser. The Chief of Staff, Major General Santos, someone with whom MacArthur felt he could work, had been replaced by Major General Basilio J. Valdes, no devotee of him or his plan. In the summer, the Constabulary was separated from the Army. It was a logical move if the Constabulary were to avoid losing its talented personnel to the Army, but it deprived the Army of access to good men at a time of great need. The reality was that the Constabulary had an apparently unending cycle of internal security disorders to handle while the Army was preparing itself for a mission which an increasing number believed it could not achieve. Quezon began to listen increasingly to his pessimistic deputy, Sergio Osmeña, who consistently and convincingly questioned the feasibility of MacArthur's plans. Then, suddenly and very perceptibly, the Quezon dam cracked. Based upon his observation about what was happening in Europe, Quezon told the National Assembly during the Autumn of 1939 that he had become

convinced "of the futility of spending money to carry on our program
of defending the Philippines from foreign aggression, and this objective cannot be attained with the limited resources of the country for
many years to come." His Secretary of Defense, Teofilo Sison,
insisted that the defense of the Philippines was an American responsibility until the Philippines achieved independence. The 1940
Defense Budget was 14 per cent down on 1939, and the 1941 budget
progressively lower than that of 1940.[55] In fact the reduction of the
defense budget was not only due to a revaluation of defense prospects
but was also part of a concerted effort on Quezon's part to send the
right message to Japan. Defense spending in 1936 accounted for 37
per cent of the national budget, 28.6 per cent in 1937, 23.8 per cent
in 1938 and 15 per cent in 1939. The number of trainees had been
reduced from 40,000 a year to a more manageable 29,500.[56]

On 28 June 1939, MacArthur gave a statement to the press in
Manila defending his position, repeating the popular, definitive speech
he made in 1936. The problem was, it took no account of the virtual
subjection of China by Japan in the interim. It confirmed in the
minds of a substantial proportion of undecided, educated Filipinos
that politically and militarily MacArthur was out of touch. He
claimed, "It will cost the enemy, in my opinion, at least half a million
men as casualties and upwards of five billions of dollars in money to
pursue such an adventure[invading the Philippines] with any hope of
success." Yet Japan had been content to bear the financial and human
costs of invading a country with a population of 450 million people
and an army of 2,500,000 men. What was likely to deter a country
which saw as its own manifest destiny the political and economic
domination of the Far East? The cost of invading the Philippines,
with a population of 16 million and a conscript army planned to be
less than 400,000, would seem paltry. "It has been assumed, in my
opinion erroneously, that Japan covets these islands. Just why has
never been satisfactorily explained. Proponents of such a theory fail
fully to credit the logic of the Japanese mind."

In his strategic assessment, MacArthur argued that the possession
of the Philippine archipelago would seriously weaken the Japanese
Empire. "It would split that empire militarily into two parts, separated by a broad stretch of ocean and between it would lie its present
military enemy, China." Yet the neutralization of China, a prerequisite
before a Japanese advance southward, appeared to have been
achieved already. MacArthur is on record as having emphasized the

economic benefits accruing from maintaining the United States' interest in the region. It is difficult to comprehend why that same argument and logic did not equally apply to Japan, desperately seeking markets in which to expand. If Japan truly did not covet the Archipelago, why was so much effort being made to defend it? The New York *Herald Tribune* assessed MacArthur's comments as being "not only cursory" but also as falling below expected levels of objectivity.[57] The whole MacArthur thesis rested upon the categorical claim that Japan did not covet the Philippines. "If the Japanese do not covet the Philippines," wrote Robert Aura Smith, "their entire policy, both military and political, has not only been a series of meaningless contortions, but has been systematically misrepresented, not by outside alarmists, but by the Japanese themselves."[58]

The Philippine Army had attracted the lion's share of attention over the past three years but there had been modest developments in the creation of the Philippine Army Off-shore Patrol and the Philippine Army Air Corps. What was notable about MacArthur's proposed 50-boat navy was that it would be the army's navy—that is the extent of what MacArthur definitely knew on the subject. MacArthur chose as his project manager, a friend of Eisenhower's and someone who would become a firm family friend, Sid Huff, who had retired from the USN as a Lieutenant following a heart attack during the course of a game of golf with Eisenhower. Called into MacArthur's office, Huff was told to sit down while MacArthur lit a cigarette and put it down on his desk before commencing his famous perambulations while he talked:

"I want a Filipino navy of motor torpedo boats, Sid. If I get you the money, how many can you get built in ten years?"

"General, never in my life have I ever seen a torpedo boat."

"That's all right. You will. Sid, I don't know anything about torpedo boats. But I want you to start work on plans for a navy. You're a navy man and you know what to do . . ."

Huff went outside into the heat of Manila's December sun, trying to compose himself. "If it had been any other man I would have asked myself: 'Is he kidding?' But I didn't because I had been talking to MacArthur . . . I began to think I could do it because MacArthur told me to do it."[59]

The first thing Huff discovered was that the U.S. Navy did not have any boats but was in the process of developing them. The U.S. Navy wanted $112,000 a boat. Huff wanted two initially, to be used as test boats, but not only was the cost prohibitive, he suspected the

U.S. Navy would use the money to experiment on prototypes rather than in the production of tested boats. Instead, orders were placed with the British company Thorneycroft for two torpedo boats, one small, one large. These, described by Quezon in a December 1938 press conference as "very dangerous boats," arrived in 1939.[60] The boats were also so expensive that contracts were placed with local Philippine yards to copy them, but only one prototype had been completed by the time of the Japanese invasion in December 1941.

The first aircraft procured for the Philippine Army Air Corps were four observation-trainers, followed by a further seven in 1938. In March 1939, the businessman Joseph R. McMicking Jr donated a bronze plaque to Zablan field, on which were to be engraved the names of the Air Force's top pilots. McMicking was also an accomplished pilot and a social acquaintance of the MacArthurs. He would become the most unlikely and enigmatic member of the Bataan Gang. With one exception, all the Philippine Army Air Corps' aircraft were Stearman biplanes, twin-seat training aircraft with a dual attack capability. The aircraft came equipped with machine guns and bomb racks but they were not state-of-the-art attack aircraft.[61] They reflected the priority of the time—the training of pilots who had "a very poor appreciation of speed, distance or anything mechanical."[62]

Set against the German military performance in Spain and Poland, and Japan's in China, these tentative developments could not have been at all reassuring to those who knew about military potential and capabilities. A 1939 Study Group at the Army War College, Washington, confirmed the view that the islands would probably be lost early in the war.[63] In the ensuing discussion, the Commandant, Major General John L. DeWitt, gave the class of '39 the benefit of his blunt thoughts on the government and the leadership in the islands:

I don't think that after 1946 the Philippines will be either a Commonwealth, colony or republic with reference to the United States, but of Japan. I believe the government there today is as near a dictatorship as it can be . . . The recent victory of Franco in Spain will lead to a development of fascism in the Philippines through Spanish influence [and] activity of the German colony in Manila . . . If he [Manuel Quezon] is alive at the end of that time [1946] we are liable to see a prompt joining of the so-called Rome-Berlin-Japanese axis by the Philippine Government of Japan . . . I don't think we, as a nation, can depend on them after 1946.[64]

DeWitt's forecast was as wrong as it possibly could have been. Naturally, fate and the course of the war bore consequences impossible to predict in advance but the reason why, in the end and when up against it, the Filipinos were the only Asians to take on and to fight the Japanese seriously, was largely preordained. By virtue of the Tydings-McDuffie Act, America guaranteed the Philippines their own sovereignty in 1946. The arrival of the Japanese postponed this cherished aspiration indefinitely. The Filipinos had great respect for the American concern to improve the lot of the Filipinos, their health and their education. They had been associated with the west for 400 years, and had a strong desire to relate as closely as possible to western culture. In a loose understanding of the term, they saw themselves as the Americans' *compadres*, sharing joy, despair, risks and triumph. But what DeWitt had completely discounted in his assessment of Filipino loyalty to the United States was the MacArthur factor.

> MacArthur, the personification of the best of Americanism to the majority of Filipinos, became the repository of Filipino allegiance because, like the saints and apostles, he was the tangible sign of a complex abstraction. His dramatic flair captivated the imagination of the Filipinos, and his brilliant manipulation of symbols and language permitted him to become a symbol himself.[65]

It was MacArthur's undoubted eloquence, the ability on occasions to talk nonsense with confidence, which served not only to delude others but also himself.

Another major contributory factor towards the crisis in the Philippines was the fact that there were divergent ideas in both capital cities. Quezon's attempt to test his options, early or delayed independence, sent confused messages back to the United States where, according to a *Fortune* magazine poll, 46.3 per cent believed that the U.S. should defend the Philippines, 37.2 believed it should not and 16.5 per cent were undecided.[66] Quezon was adept at identifying the conundrum but was unable to find a solution. On 13 October 1937 he had told the National Assembly that the U.S.A. was unable to grant the Philippines additional governmental powers without endangering her own interests and security, while the Philippines' decision-making facilities had been limited by the provisions of the Commonwealth. A variation on that theme appeared contemporaneously in the *Rock-*

ford (Illinois) Star. "The hard and practical fact is that Filipinos are dependent upon American prestige for their continued independence; that we are unable to release complete control of our prestige in the Pacific, and all that implies in trade routes, is to stand."

Quezon's attempt to secure immediate independence was blocked by Roosevelt and the State Department and the notion of a prolonged dependence was declined by Congress. Quezon found himself squeezed by the two principal institutions in the United States which share power. The executive argued that with the international situation deteriorating, it was not possible to grant the Philippines independence. Congress's objection was financial. As long as the Philippines remained under U.S. jurisdiction Philippine goods were imported into the United States duty free. Moreover, the United States in effect gave to the Philippines each year approximately $15 million arising from the collection of taxes on coconut oil. The money had strings as its use was restricted to "meeting new or additional expenditures which will be necessary in adjusting Philippine economy to a position independent of trade preferences in the United States."[67] There were similar neutralizing influences in the Philippines:

> Politicians against delay for fear of losing votes, and businessmen against advance for fear of dislocating the economy. Worse still: in the haphazard tessellation of American Far Eastern policy there was no clear design for the Philippines. The executive branch was mildly internationalist and would denounce Japan; the legislative branch, stoutly isolationist, would appease her. The Navy was asking for a stronger offensive capability; the Army for a contracted defense perimeter.[68]

It is understandable that America's Far Eastern policy was difficult to identify. The country was barely out of recession before being ruffled again by a mini-recession in 1938, while the political bias towards the east coast, and by association the Atlantic, drew attention towards Europe. There was, after all, a war there with Germany, against whom America had fought as recently as 21 years ago. At that time, Japan had been America's ally, albeit a passive and undemonstrative one. While Washington faced the reality of a possible resumption of the unfinished war in Europe there was no conflict directly involving American interests in the Far East and it was certainly policy to avoid at all cost the prospect of ultimately becoming involved in a war on two fronts. Words were heard deploring Japanese expansion in the

Far East yet, out of a fear of provoking Japan, Congress voted down a bill which would have established an improved naval base on Guam. Besides, MacArthur had been consistent in his insistence that Japan did not covet the Philippines.

Francis Bowes Sayre, Woodrow Wilson's chip-off-the-old-block son-in-law, now became the next High Commissioner in the Philippines. He and his family arrived in Manila 21 October 1939. As Assistant Secretary of State Sayre had been involved in and informed about Philippine Affairs since 1934. This was rather more than could be said of the Department of the Interior officials who, since 1 July 1939, had assumed jurisdiction for Philippine affairs. Sayre recognized that in the Interior, "there was a striking scarcity of men who had lived in the Philippines and knew Philippine problems."[69] MacArthur said they ran the Philippines as though it were a National Park. The fact is that, faced with war in Europe and China, America's overt foreign policy was to appear to sit resolutely upon her hands.[70]

The Philippines was not a high priority either in political thinking or in the allocation of scarce resources. Guam and Panama were ranked higher in importance. America was militarily weak in 1939, unable to buttress her foreign policy with threats of the use of force. The Air Corps and Navy were equipped mostly with outdated aircraft, the Army was skeletal and the Navy, though relatively stronger, had fewer ships than permitted by the restrictive Washington Naval Conference. Reinforcement and the building up of Philippine defenses were not realistic options when there were potential threats closer to the continental United States. The only workable policy which might have spared the Philippines would have been American withdrawal from there, acceding to Quezon's request for the granting of early independence. America would have appeared enlightened and magnanimous, and there would have been no American flag to taunt or to tempt the Japanese to remove it. However, this was not a view shared by the influential outgoing High Commissioner, Paul McNutt: "If our flag comes down, trouble will follow for at least a generation."[71] There was also no guarantee that Japan would have respected Philippine neutrality. Any southern advance strategy could not have avoided the absorption of the Philippine archipelago.

6

RELATIVE VALUES

Francis Sayre sailed in September 1939 aboard *President Cleveland* for Manila. In theory the Washington end of the chain of command to which he was linked had been spelled out in September by Roosevelt and confirmed by him in May 1940. Normal correspondence was to go through the Philippine section of the Division of Territories and Island Possessions, Department of the Interior. "This will not, however, diminish your authority or materially affect your direct responsibility to me as defined in my previous communication of September 7th, and will not preclude direct communication with me whenever you deem it advisable." Sayre's concern was the Head of the Department of the Interior. There had arisen "a coolness if not a hostility toward myself on the part of Harold Ickes . . . the ill feeling toward me boded no good, and I greatly regretted it." Sayre believed Ickes' hostility stemmed from Sayre's friendly relationship with the President whose 17 May letter "was one Secretary Ickes never forgave."[1] Sayre also became less than popular with Cordell Hull and the State Department. Sayre had left Manila on 18 April 1940 for talks in Tokyo because of his concerns over Japan's aggressive actions in East Asia and so he could explain to Japan the Philippines' immigration restrictions. The visit met with the approval of the President but it was intended to be nothing more than a fact-finding mission by one of the United States' regional representatives. It was perhaps naive to imagine that the arrival during this tense period in Tokyo of the son-in-law of Woodrow Wilson would not be seen as having a great deal more significance. Sayre had a meeting with the anglophile Foreign Minister Arita Hachiro, who found it difficult to believe Sayre's claim to be speaking "unofficially and privately."[2] Sayre's obvious professional interest in assessing the possibility of brokering a peace between Japan and China did little to dissuade the Japanese from making this assumption. When news of Sayre's meetings appeared in the press—he was received by the Emperor—the State Department's rage was evident in Cordell Hull's response. "There was no thought, repeat no thought here that Sayre should or would embark upon discussions with Japanese officials of any subject of high policy. We are at a loss to understand why he did so . . ."[3]

The *President Cleveland* called at Shanghai, where Admiral Thomas C. Hart, Commander in Chief of the Asiatic Fleet, came aboard. Hart felt that Sayre did not like him because he was not "tied to the tail of his kite."[4] Their relations, however, did develop better than most of Sayre's with the military. Hart was not convinced, however, that Sayre was going to be able to master Filipino social life—certainly not with Manuel Quezon. Overall, Hart found Sayre too stiff, too formal, not "one of the boys,"[5] all factors he believed would undermine the new High Commissioner's effectiveness. At the next port of call, Hong Kong, Sayre was in his element as guest of Governor Northcote. The British had made some acknowledgement of the fact they were at war by the ladies not wearing white gloves at the formal dinner that evening.[6] On 21 October, the *President Cleveland* docked at Manila where a large reception party headed by President and Mrs. Quezon was there to meet the new High Commissioner.

The first meeting was warm and friendly although, by this time, the ravages of tuberculosis, said to have originated from the shouting matches with Leonard Wood, had perceptibly weakened the President. "In stature he was short—of average height for Filipinos; but in every other way he was far from average," wrote Sayre. "Filled with dynamic energy and restlessness, he was always the center of movement and activity." With their backgrounds, they were as unlikely to bond as oil and water. Sayre was a practical rather than a nominal Christian, a free trader and committed democrat. He arrived suspecting that Quezon and the oligarchy which he dominated might replicate the national socialism sweeping Europe, but this discounted the Philippine social ethos. However, this suspicion led slowly but surely to a breakdown in relations between them. "He was a dictator," wrote Sayre, "but happily a benevolent one. A man of impulses and moods, he was often insensitive to reason and logic. He was temperamental to the last degree—a prima donna of the first order. Always he was adroit and dramatic, and knew exactly how to play his cards to win his public."[7]

On 8 January 1940, Quezon told Sayre of what had taken place during a lunchtime meeting and discussion he had had the previous week with MacArthur, the General Staff, Sison and Sutherland.

"What would be the position of a Philippine army of 300,000 in 1946 if Japan decided to attack?" asked Quezon of MacArthur.

"It would require an expenditure of anywhere from 30–50 million pesos to carry on six months' resistance against an army such as Japan's, and all manner of military and other supplies would have to be imported," MacArthur was said to have replied.

"And how could I import such supplies without a navy if Japan were attacking us?"

"It would be hoped that Great Britain or some other naval power would come to the rescue and would not permit Japan to make such an invasion." MacArthur was therefore acknowledging what others had been saying for some time. No longer was he adamant in his assertion that the Philippines could defend itself.

"But if that were the fact, why the necessity of maintaining and paying for an expensive army?" President Quezon asked. "Does your plan of defense include Mindanao?"

General MacArthur gave President Quezon no satisfactory reply.[8] The very existence of the MacArthur plan was intended to deter an enemy from attempting an invasion of the Philippines. (After the war, MacArthur insisted that it was the boldness of his defense plans which had prompted the Japanese attack.)[9] Colonel Segundo, the Philippine Army Head of Intelligence, noted ruefully that MacArthur "pretends his plan is self-sufficient."

Quezon, who had been stunned by the *blitzkrieg* effect of armored maneuver warfare supported by air power in overrunning Poland the previous summer, explained to Sayre that he wanted to maintain an adequate military defense but there were limits as to what could be afforded. He could not see the merit in maintaining an expensive, highly trained army "if a great power decides to conquer a small one." Quezon explained how he had told MacArthur that the defense budget would not only not be increased but the cost of the constabulary might also have to be included in it. Sayre told Quezon that these matters were entirely within the President's jurisdiction but, as a dedicated pacifist, Sayre admitted that he could "take no exception to his conclusions."[10]

Such frigidity developed between Quezon and his Field Marshal that the President refused to see MacArthur and only communicated through his factotum, Jorge Vargas. "Jorge," said MacArthur, "some day your boss is going to want to see me more than I want to see him."[11] But at this time, when positions were being reassessed and occasionally changed, MacArthur reacted to the weight of criticism of his defense plan by acknowledging for the first time that the United States was ultimately responsible for the defense of the Philippines, and the function of the Philippine Army was as "a practical reserve for the small contingent of American forces stationed in this outpost."[12] But MacArthur was not a total convert. On his birthday he re-rehearsed in an interview his idea of a Philippine Switzerland protected by an army of 30 divisions of 300,000 trained men by 1946. MacArthur had also taken the Finnish defense against Russia as something the Philippine armed forces could emulate. He was unaware that Quezon had decided to reduce the defense budget, but he must have known that the intake of conscripts was now consistently and progressively falling behind target.[13] Quezon told Sayre that MacArthur's birthday interview had been crazy, while the outspoken Colonel Segundo said that it had been "all propaganda and had no value." An anonymous American businessman who had been on a vacation trip on Quezon's yacht *Casiana* sent a memo to Sayre. The American spoke of the discussion centering on Finland and how MacArthur by his comments had made "a fool of himself"—how it had been an "idiotic" statement.[14] Quezon now spoke openly of his disillusionment with MacArthur. He apologized to the Philippine General Staff: "I am sorry I did not consult you at the beginning. MacArthur has been bluffing all along."[15] Quezon confided in Admiral Hart that it was foolish for the Filipinos to say that they would be ready to defend their country in 1946; that they might arrive at that point in twenty-five or thirty years, but that anyone who said that it could be done from 1946 onward, irrespective of how much expenditure for the purpose the Commonwealth made in the meantime, was entirely wrong.[16] Admiral Hart's relationship with Quezon, although more irregular than had been the case with MacArthur, was one of mutual respect. "I like *El Presidente* immensely," admitted Hart, "and admire him quite a lot. He can be laughed about but not laughed off." Hart did observe and comment upon Quezon's dictatorial tendencies in some areas but he was "shrewd, with a quick and at times brilliant mentality, coupled with extraordinary political ability and understanding of the psychology of his people."[17] "No authoritative opinion, least of all that of our Army out here, agrees at all with [MacArthur's] statements," wrote Hart.[18] Despite military skepticism, the decision to defend the Philippines would be based upon a political rather than a military judgement. Politically, America had little option but to defend the Philippines, but Washington was not prepared to provide the resources required to satisfy that aim. Congress decided not to fortify Guam and the Philippines for fear of provoking Japan. The President's speech of 17 March 1940, outlining America's vital interest, did not include the Philippines.[19]

Isolated and ostracized, MacArthur withdrew to what Sayre described as his ivory tower. In a meeting between Sayre and Quezon on 28 February 1940, the President told the High Commissioner that the Philippines could no longer afford an annual outlay of 18 million pesos on defense and would therefore be reducing the budget by 1½ million pesos and by 3 million pesos in the next fiscal year. It was Quezon's intention to maintain the constabulary with its responsibility for internal security, to continue officer training and, to a limited extent, continue compulsory military service. Then the subject turned to MacArthur, who "was now serving (at a salary which exceeded that of the President) but under no written contract of any kind." In view of the altered plan, mused Quezon, MacArthur might tender his resignation, in which case Quezon "could not but accept it." In the event that MacArthur might appeal to Roosevelt, Quezon wondered if Sayre might write to Roosevelt and explain the situation. Sayre agreed, but because the matter was "so highly confidential and inflammable," he questioned the wisdom of putting the matter in writing. Sayre recommended that he should speak to Roosevelt on this subject the next time they met, to which Quezon agreed.[20]

The budget machinations and Quezon's disillusionment with both MacArthur and his Plan had been kept relatively secret until Quezon chose to give vent to his frustrations at the graduation ceremony of the Philippine Normal School held at the Rizal Stadium on Commonwealth Day. The Philippines was indefensible, he said, "even if every last Filipino were armed with modern weapons."[21] The President said that the Philippines could not be defended against the aggression of a first class power, the implication being that even after 1946, particularly after 1946, the Philippines would not be able to defend herself. He then said, rather curiously, that the Philippines could withstand another three hundred years of subjugation if necessary. Had Quezon turned full circle? Instead of looking for early independence, was he considering the option of extending the period before independence? Colonel Segundo thought so but Quezon, who had recently also discussed the possibility of neutrality with Sayre,[22] was obviously airing his options and thinking aloud in public. As Segundo observed, it was not an excessively risky ploy. "The people may question the necessity or prudence of further expenditure for national defense if such is not sufficient to defend the country. As he makes or unmakes public opinion, however, the effect may not be so bad."[23]

Sixty-year-old cavalryman Major-General George Grunert could be described as the classic regimental officer, wiry, highly professional and, despite his age, still ambitious. He was the same age as Douglas MacArthur whom he knew and respected. He joined the army as an enlisted man, thus he had not been a contemporary of MacArthur's at West Point though they were both serving in the Philippines in 1904. His record of service was impressive and reflected a man who had seen and been involved in the horrors of battle as well as one who had thought deeply to ensure that the next time, the enemy would be engaged in the most effective manner. After three years in Cuba he was with the 40th British Division at the Battle of Cambrai, 20 November–3 December 1917, where he saw the first mass use of armor. His military education continued as a student at the Army War College and the Command and General Staff School. He returned to the Army War College 1932–36 as a member of the faculty.

Grunert was promoted Major General in December 1939. By now he had a second tour in the Philippines under his belt, having held the prestigious appointment of Commanding Officer, 26th Cavalry Regiment, Philippine Scouts. He then progressed to command of the Philippine 23rd Infantry Brigade at Fort McKinley. At the end of that tour of duty, Chief of Staff Malin Craig, careful not to pre-empt Marshall's wishes, held out the possibility of Grunert's return to the Philippines.[24] On 14 February 1940, Grunert arrived in Manila where he assumed command of the Philippine Division. The Philippine Department Commanding General was Major General Walter Grant. His tour of duty was due to expire in May 1940. Much had been expected of Grant when he arrived in May 1938 but a combination of living in MacArthur's shadow and an all pervading atmosphere of financial stringency limited his achievements. In February Grant had a meeting with Admiral Hart. They were friends, having been at the Army War College together for two years. They both agreed "that the positions of our commands were not happy," although Hart pointed out that the new naval plans meant the navy would not "go as far from him as had been planned." Grant spoke of his disappointment at not being able to get reinforcements and "seemed to agree" when Hart said he believed, from his standpoint, the Army's most important defensive weapon would be fighter airplanes.[25] Grant provided the navy with essential support in obtaining $78,000 to build tunnels for the navy on Corregidor Island. Hart wrote to Admiral Stark insisting he "send the money now and pay the Treasury later."[26] The tunnels would not only provide a location for a Navy Command Post and storage area for weapons but also for radio communications and decoding equipment. The Navy provided decoding facilities for both Services.

Grant retired and, on 31 May 1940, George Grunert was appointed in his place as Philippine Department Commanding General. The timing was fortunate for, with MacArthur isolated, the Philippine Government still had need of military dialogue with the U.S.A. Grunert was now in a position to examine his own Department's War Plans and, with MacArthur marginalized, he felt emboldened to incorporate the Philippine assets coming on-stream into a comprehensive defense plan. This was a legitimate move since the Philippine Army was at the disposal of the United States until independence in 1946. What was unusual was that the proud MacArthur should be subjected to asset stripping.

The Department's first War Plan, War Plan Orange-1, was drawn up in 1934 when there was no Philippine Army in existence. War Plan Orange-2, which originated in 1936 and was finessed in 1938 and 1939, did allow for limited Philippine Army reinforcements to bring the Philippine Department up to its war strength of 31,000 men, but it made no substantive provision for using the conscripts being generated as part of MacArthur's defense plan. Grunert set about rectifying that situation, convening a conference on 19 June 1940 to draw up a new Military Strategic[27] Orange Plan—War Plan Orange-3. MacArthur was invited to be represented. Major William Dunckel from the Military Adviser's office attended the conference as probably also did the Deputy Chief of Staff, Lieutenant Colonel Richard Marshall. In Washington, where the Joint Board juggled with its options at the Grand Strategic level, the Orange Plan had been diffused into a wider range of five Plans, known as Rainbow, since June 1939. All five Plans assumed the United States would face a coalition rather than a single power but the pivotal consideration vis-à-vis which plan would be adopted rested upon what happened to Great Britain and the Empire. A principal war aim of the United States was to keep Great Britain in the War. On one matter the Joint Board was agreed: the greatest threat to America lay in the Western Hemisphere and, irrespective of whatever might subsequently happen in the Pacific, the priority would go to Europe and the Atlantic. "Though it was the Army planners who seemed most aware of the danger from Europe, it was the Navy that made the first move to strengthen America's Atlantic defenses."[28] The Joint Planners saw the requirement for the main effort being directed towards the Atlantic and to hold fast in the Pacific until Germany's defeat, when the limited resources could be switched to counter whatever developments arose in the Pacific. The defeat of Holland and France in the summer of 1940 showed the Joint Planners had good reason for their assessment of priorities.

Contrary to MacArthur's continuing denials that Japan coveted the Philippines, his own and the Philippine Army Staff had actually issued memoranda in 1937 suggesting that the Philippines *did* fall within the ambit of Japanese military ambitions—"a quiet, silent and apparently peaceful penetration at first, but a well planned, slowly creeping but absolutely certain territorial invasion."[29] It was not until Poland fell, however, that the Japanese military's aspiration was formalized into policy. The 1938 Joint Estimate for War Plan Orange took a reserved, cautious view of Japanese and American citizens of Japanese extraction living in the Philippine Islands, Hawaii, Panama and on the Pacific Coast. "There is little doubt as to their loyalty to Orange, as a large number of them are even suspected of being in the military service of Orange."[30]

The number of Japanese living in the Philippines was a little above 30,000, most of whom were of families which had settled before the First World War. The Japanese capacity for subversion and espionage was greater in the Philippines than anywhere else in the Far East. There were fewer than 6,000 Japanese in Malaya and only 6,300 in the Netherlands' East Indies.[31] The majority of Japanese lived in their own colony in Davao where they controlled half the Philippine hemp industry. There were no more than 2,000 Japanese living in Manila, mostly businessmen and entrepreneurs[32] whose economic power belied their numbers. The Japanese in Manila began to develop their economic strength from 1932 in what can only have been an intentional policy to establish a bazaar on every main street. By 1934, the Japanese share of Philippine retail trade increased from 5 to 27 per cent at the expense of Chinese traders. The Japanese were not obliged to make a profit. Tokyo gave them a 6 per cent return on their total sales. Rubber-soled shoes were dumped on the Philippines at fifteen cents a pair, the popular undershirt was sold to the Filipino at less than ten cents each and electric light bulbs could be purchased for less than a third of the cost of similar items of American or European manufacture. By 1934, the Japanese textile industry had taken over half of the Philippines market.[33]

In August 1937, the Davao Provincial Commander advised the Philippine Army Headquarters that, at a secret meeting of the Davao Japanese Association, the members had agreed to a means-tested scale of contributions for the benefit of "the Imperial Japanese Army in its war against China."[34] The Japanese Consul, Kiyoshi Uchiyama Kiyoshi and the Vice Consul, Jitaro Kihara, had done well to stem anti-Japanese sentiment through the twin processes of propaganda and protest. It was also in August 1937 that this inventive pair began to lose the propaganda battle, for it was then that several thousand Americans, Europeans and Filipinos who had fled Shanghai—many destitute—arrived in Manila with vivid accounts of Japanese brutality in China.

Kiyoshi's plan, presented to Tokyo, to improve relations with the Filipinos included such measures as to "publish a pro-Japanese newspaper, manipulate the representatives, join hands with the opposite factions, stir up anti-American sentiment, arouse public opinion in Japan, and . . . adopt other behind the scenes measures."[35] Money was lavishly invested in a bid to counter anti-Japanese feelings. At the forefront of this initiative was the man whom circumstantial evidence points to as the "official" head of Japanese espionage operations in the Philippines, the veteran Vice Consul and Consul General in Davao, Jitaro Kihara.[36] Kihara entertained generously, was recognized as a giver of gifts and was readily and freely accepted within the ranks of the Philippine hierarchy. One day in 1940, when Quezon was still undecided whether or not to run for a second term, he was visiting the site of a new house being built for him on Dewey Boulevard. Kihara was with him. Pointing out across Manila Bay, Quezon said to Kihara with a smile, "I hope the Japanese Army is not coming here straight across the bay." "You have no reason to worry, we will respect your house," replied Kihara evenly. Quezon examined his friend's face for the hint of a smile. There was none. On another occasion, Doña Aurora Quezon mentioned to Kihara the difficulties she was experiencing on her hacienda. Kihara readily offered to send her two Japanese agriculturists.[37] The Quezon hacienda was at Arayat, Pampanga, close to Clark Air Base.

While Kihara worked on good public relations out of the Consulate, there was an "unofficial" figure who, from the early 1930s, had inveigled his way into social and military circles in much the same way as had Kihara. Sony Shiko, a Major in the Imperial Japanese Army, established the Triangulo Photographic Studio and became one of Japan's most important agents in the Philippines. The Germans also sent military personnel into the Philippines via their Embassy in Tokyo to teach espionage techniques to insurgents. In 1940, the Falangist Movement's José del Castano arrived in Manila and began his work aimed at destabilizing the civil administration.[38] In addition, a great deal of intelligence was systematically gathered which, if properly processed and accessed, had the potential to provide the Japanese with a significant force multiplier. Corregidor had two one-million-gallon-capacity water tanks. Concealment was obviously a problem but a solution for the one outside the YMCA was to put tennis courts on top of it. These tennis courts became one of the most comprehensively bombed targets in the South West Pacific.

There were spies galore. Quezon's gardener and masseur were both Imperial Japanese Army officers.[39] Japanese ran most of the photographic businesses in the Philippines: the photographer at the Military Academy was Japanese. Many barbers to the government and the military were Japanese and they controlled a good proportion of filling stations. Manila became gripped by war fever. The founder of the Socialist Party, Pedro Abad Santos, claimed that the Japanese Fifth Column in the Philippines was actively engaged in the collection of information. Santos also claimed that Japanese agents were active in Bataan and Zambales and had reconnoitered Corregidor and Subic Bay.[40] Not wishing to excite the Japanese, Quezon played down rumors of Japanese Fifth Column activities, but the enemy was already within. Detailed intelligence reports of Philippine defenses were sent back to Imperial Japanese Army Headquarters on Ichigaya Heights, Tokyo.[41] Intelligence is only effective if it gets to those who need it. Although Japanese spying in the Philippines was comprehensive, the performance of the combat troops did not reveal their having derived much benefit from the intelligence gathered. The real value of Japanese intelligence may, indeed, have been overrated to explain in some part the USAFFE defeat.

A proposal to amend the terms of office of the President and Vice President from six to four years, with the right to stand for re-election provided no one should hold office for more than eight consecutive years, set alarm bells about a dictatorial conspiracy ringing in Sayre's mind, and on 25 July 1940 he wrote to Roosevelt of Quezon's intentions:

> The worst feature of this provision is that it is made applicable to the term of the President now in office. To change the constitutional provision regarding the tenure of office of the President in such a way that the term of the existing President can thereby be prolonged is to create a precedent of exceeding danger to democracy, for such a precedent opens the way for any strong President who desires to become a dictator to prolong his tenure of office indefinitely.[42]

It was not the best of timing to protest since Roosevelt himself was already deep into a campaign to be re-elected for a third time. Unsurprisingly, Roosevelt thought it best not to veto the Philippine constitutional amendment. In November 1941, Quezon would be duly re-elected. The problem for Sayre was that a copy of his letter of 25 July came into the hands of Secretary Ickes and, as Sayre understood it, a copy from Ickes' office found its way onto Quezon's desk where it had its effect. "Incidents such as this almost inevitably cooled President Quezon's relationship with me. There was never an open break—we always remained on friendly terms; but the old intimacy had gone."[43] Soon, there would be increasing attempts in Washington and Manila to have Sayre replaced by a more amenable spirit.

On 15 July, worried by the international situation and emboldened by the vote of confidence implicit in the June approval of the constitutional amendments, Quezon asked the Assembly to grant him emergency powers. On 16 July, in a speech delivered to students of the University of the Philippines, he criticized democracy. Two "fetishes" of democracy should be discarded; the first was the sanctity of individual liberty and the second was opposition parties. Quezon proposed a one party system.[44] He could not have selected more provocative material with which to generate a reaction from Sayre. The High Commissioner's error lay in going public. Quezon was scathing in his response, insisting that the Filipinos had to do their own thinking. Rather than maintain a dignified silence, Sayre returned to attack on other matters: fraud and the June amendments to the constitution. Quezon penned an inflammatory reply but, not wishing to offend Roosevelt did not send it, choosing instead to smolder quietly—for a short while.

Whereas the Department of Interior remained ambivalent towards Sayre, that was not the case in the State Department, which on this issue, supported him. Roosevelt took the heat out of the situation by supporting Sayre's stand for American sovereignty but cautioned Sayre against further clashes with Quezon. Sayre's problem of divided authority was an unenviable one for he received little guidance from Washington.

> The administration's inertia toward the Philippines continued through 1940. Considering that the colony contained over sixteen million people, that it was the eighth largest customer of the United States, and that it was supposedly the laboratory for the United States' political ideas in Asia, the Democratic administration gave it scant attention . . .

By the mid 1940s, MacArthur's relations with Quezon and Sayre had become so frigid as to be non existent. His relations with Admiral Hart should have been better. Hart was one of the few officers to call MacArthur by his Christian name, having known him for 40 years and also Douglas's sailor brother, Arthur. "Douglas," he said, "knows a lot of things which are not so; he is a very able and convincing talker—a combination which spells danger."[45] Despite his reservations, Hart got on reasonably well with MacArthur, due principally to his respect for his combative spirit. The Navy-Army link-up, however, was not via the Philippine Army Adviser's Office at 1 Calle Victoria but through George Grunert's Philippine Department in Fort Santiago.

Grunert enjoyed good relations with Quezon, Sayre and Hart. In that respect he was a somewhat unique individual. "Our habitual contacts ripened into warm friendship,"[46] wrote Sayre who recommended to Marshall Grunert's promotion to Lieutenant General.

"Not only do I think that the work of your Army here would be fur-
thered by such a step, but I also believe that General Grunert has
been proving himself such a competent and splendid leader that he
richly deserves promotion."[47] Hart found Grunert to be "frank and
outspoken, with the cards on the table.[48] ". . .(he) was entirely coop-
erative and willing to come halfway."[49] They enjoyed an amicable
relationship despite the obvious disconnection between their respective plans. Hart had received new naval plans, WPL 44, which meant
that until Manila Bay was better protected, the bulk of his cruiser-
destroyer detachment which had "limited ship characteristics" would
have to be held back to the south of Manila, unable in effect to provide support to Grunert's forces. That excluded the submarines which
in theory constituted most of the power and which were available to
support the Army. Grunert, aware of the need to build up his ground
forces under the rubric of WPO-3 went forth like an emboldened
poacher to assess the capabilities of the Philippine Army. Grunert's
relationship with MacArthur was delicate due to the latter's suspicion
of the former's intentions. Grunert's covert information gathering was
detected by the Philippine Army Chief of Staff, the outspoken Brigadier General Vicente Lim, who insisted that the Philippine Army be
brought into Grunert's contingency planning process.[50] Appropriately
chastised, the Department made arrangements for Grunert to meet
MacArthur on 1 July 1940.

Grunert was no doubt aware that if his hope of becoming wartime
Military Governor was to come to fruition, it would have to be at
MacArthur's expense. Quezon's undoubted hostility to the whole
idea of a Military Governor would be tackled once that first hurdle
had been negotiated. There must have been an element of personal
ambition wound up in his dynamic kick-start or, to use his word,
"hammering" of the Army Department in Washington. The Philippine Department, unlike the Philippine Army, was part of the United
States Army and therefore attracted more attention and better
resources. His perseverance in making demands upon Washington
helped to turn the Army's stand-off policy to one of engagement at a
time when the Navy's policy of engagement had been superseded by
one of disengagement. Early in 1940, a War Planning Department
report determined that "the principle reliance would be placed on air
power not only to deter an attack on Luzon but to defeat one if
made."[51] The planners recognized that in order to defeat a first
attack, an augmentation of strength was essential and it became the

raison d'être for Grunert's acquisitive raid upon the Philippine Army's manpower. More U.S. manpower, ammunition, anti-aircraft defense, Air Corps funding and the doubling of the strength of the Philippine Scouts to 12,000 were also sought. The majority of these communications with Washington fell upon stony ground to begin with, principally due to there being higher priority demands elsewhere.

Quezon now keen to remain under Uncle Sam's defensive umbrella for the longest practicable period, had no definite indication that the United States intended to keep it up over the Philippines. He tried again to invest in their defense the consolidated sugar revenues which had accumulated in the United States to provide an economic prop at the time of independence. Congress demurred, insisting that this $21 million be reserved for the intended purpose. On 1 September 1940,[52] Grunert wrote to Marshall complaining of the mostly negative response to his many requests, and requesting a positive indication be given to the Philippine Government of America's intention to defend the archipelago. He reiterated the need for air power, a strong submarine force, American military reinforcements, and an American training team to train Philippine Army units.

Grunert's letter was timely because it coincided not only with one from President Quezon to President Roosevelt asking for two hundred pesos per soldier for training purposes, similar to the support given to the National Guard, but also with the dawning realization in the War Department of the urgent need for a coherent American policy towards the Philippines. In the absence of such a policy, the planners, in a letter of 10 October 1940, re-rehearsed an idea aired in 1933 and 1939 of proposing to the President the withdrawal of American forces to the 180° meridian. Watson suggests that the 10 October memorandum had been "prepared with a view to providing a decision quite different from that recommended." It worked. Within a few weeks the authority was forthcoming to raise the strength of the Scouts to 12,000 (achieved by calling to the colors Scout reservists), to increase the Luzon infantry regiment by 600 men, for coast artillery units, for the augmentation of local defenses,[53] and the allocation of $1,250,000 for construction, principally at air bases.[54]

On 19 August, Grunert had revisited MacArthur's Headquarters bearing his new plan WPO-3.[55] Beach defense operations were to be conducted by the regular army in Luzon while the Philippine Army hurriedly mobilized. Once on a war footing, the Philippine Army would relieve the regulars and also contribute to an operational reserve aimed either at pushing the enemy into the sea or defeating them in an open land battle. It was envisaged that only limited forces would be required to withdraw into Bataan. Grunert's concept of forward defense was merely an outline. Its success was entirely dependent upon a sufficiency of trained soldiers, naval and air support, adequate materiel and combat supplies to sustain both Services, mobility and good communications. There remained nagging problems over the quality of the Commonwealth Army. It comprised one cadre Regular division of less than 500 officers and 3,700 men and ten Reserve divisions in which 15 per cent of officers had had no active duty training and half had had no training at all. There were some things within their control—e.g. discipline[56]—but there were other aspects over which they had no control—shortages of competent officers and NCOs, equipment, clothing and ammunition. On 2 November 1940, Grunert wrote to Marshall, whom he knew well enough to call George, about a wildly inaccurate press report claiming the Philippine Army comprised 12 front line divisions of "approximately 125,000 well-trained men ready for combat."

For adequate and efficient defense purposes, organized and equipped units of the Philippine Army should be mobilized now, deficiencies in personnel of such units made up by assignment of men now assigned to units for which no equipment is on hand and training instituted. After a year of training, under competent supervision, these units should be able to mobilize rapidly in an emergency qualified to undertake as units any necessary military operations. In order to provide adequate supervision of and assistance in this training, I need approximately five hundred American officers.[57]

The draft mobilization proclamation recommended by Grunert was prepared for Roosevelt's signature but, like so much else, was sat upon, despite the fact that on 27 September 1940, Japan entered into a spheres-of-interest tripartite agreement with Germany and Italy[58] and the Vichy French agreed to Japan's occupation of Northern Indochina. Roosevelt's response was to stop the export of iron and steel scrap to all but a few designated states. As for the 500 officers to train the Filipinos, Grunert was promised 75. Four anti-aircraft guns were all that arrived of the 20 promised. Marshall wrote that shortages in the Western Hemisphere "were so serious that adequate reinforcements for the Philippines at this time would have left the United States in a position of great peril."[59]

Sayre had little need to either work or communicate with MacArthur. Their contact was, as Sayre admitted, "social rather than official." Sayre had no great liking for MacArthur, "his personality lacked the open, democratic, American approach."[60] There is a letter of 5 April 1940 in which MacArthur congratulates and gives "heartiest felicitations to" Sayre for a talk given at the University of the Philippines,

> not only on its basic conceptions but also for the brilliant forensic eloquence with which they were expressed. It was splendid in every way and causes me an especial pride as having marked the leadership of the ranking American official in this part of the world.[61]

Six months later, MacArthur wrote to Sayre on hotel notepaper complaining that Grunert had been seated in a position senior to him at one of Betty Sayre's Red Cross luncheons also attended by Jean MacArthur. He emphasized that he was senior to both Admiral Smeallie and General Grunert, and although he insisted he cared little about such things, he went on: "These officers hold currently the rank of Rear Admiral and Major General, a two star rating entitling them to a salute of thirteen guns. My rank is that of General, two grades higher, entitling me to four stars and a salute of seventeen guns." MacArthur thought it would be unfortunate if misunderstandings over protocol should be "brought before the native public" and offered the ultimate sanction that, if the situation were not to be resolved, "it would be preferable for me and mine to abstain from such social activities as would bring this question to the fore."[62] Sayre responded on the same date claiming ignorance of the alleged slight,[63] to which MacArthur responded by return, apologizing for his "misinterpretation of the situation" and thanking Sayre for his note which "serves to strengthen and cement the feelings of esteem, confidence and admiration which I have always felt towards you in increasing measure."[64] Whatever the quantity of obsequious flattery poured out, MacArthur's eyes were still firmly set upon taking the lead role of the "ranking American official" in the Philippines; the post presently occupied by Francis B. Sayre.

Sayre wrote that, according to "the current talk in Manila, General MacArthur's star was rapidly descending and he was expected to drop out of the Philippine picture."[65] But that would be to underestimate MacArthur who sat, somewhat impatiently, at the extremity of his web, awaiting developments. He admitted to having been "brash and untrained" in the First World War. "Since then I have read everything I can get my hands on about war. This time, I am prepared."[66] His undoubted status at home and abroad, his enthusiasm, overweening confidence and command of language continued to allow him to present that which "ain't so" as being so. In a letter to Early in March 1941, he reviewed his past five years as military adviser, suggesting it was time to move on to new pastures. He rehearsed the idea that his job as adviser would end that year, when he would probably return to the United States. In all probability nothing was further from his mind, as was evident from a check list of his attributes which followed and which, if taken as correct, presented a strong case for his continuing presence in a region increasingly beset by risks and uncertainty.

> From Vladivostock to Singapore I am thoroughly familiar with the most intimate details, political, military and commercial. I have a personal acquaintance with everyone of importance in the Orient and I believe no American holds the friendship and respect of this part of the world more than myself. In the present situation these are assets which the President might utilize in his coordination of the Pacific problems. I can respond to any call here or elsewhere. I am in robust health and feel that I was never quite so able to return to the Government in full measure the years of training it has devoted to me.

He concluded his transparently obvious job application with fawning praise of Roosevelt, fully realizing that Early would show his letter to the President. "He has proved himself not only our greatest statesman but what to me is even more thrilling, our greatest military strategist."[67] When Early replied on 14 April,[68] he said that Roosevelt had remarked, "Isn't that fine. It's just what I would expect Douglas MacArthur to do." In a follow-on letter the next day, General P.G. Watson emphasized that the President wanted MacArthur in the Far East in a "military capacity rather than any other." "Your name's always outstanding and most seriously considered."[69]

Tension within the Commonwealth increased; Navy dependants

had been ordered home at the end of 1940, as had been the dependants of Federal officials in China; Army dependants followed in May 1941. Sayre reconsidered the situation vis-à-vis the remaining civilians. The unofficial American Coordinating Committee in America proposed that Americans who could leave should do so, but Grunert disagreed: Americans should "defend [their homes] against all odds." It was a view supported by the Department of State which did not wish to create an impression that the Philippines was alien territory or that they were more concerned with the lot of Americans rather than Filipinos. There was also a lame excuse about the shortage of shipping space, but the effect of this unwise decision was that those civilians who put their trust in the wisdom of the State Department suffered three and a half years of internment. Accordingly, Sayre's family remained, as did the MacArthur family, since MacArthur was not at that time serving in the American armed forces.[70]

Quezon used the 1940 Emergency Powers Act to create the Civilian Emergency Administration (CEA). Sayre objected but Quezon's action was supported by Ickes, and Roosevelt ultimately approved the move. At the same time, he responded to Quezon's request of nine months earlier, to use sugar excise tax and the gold devaluation fund for defense purposes. Roosevelt told him for the first time of a policy change, in that the War and Navy Departments would be working on plans to strengthen the archipelago's defenses and might pay for these defenses from the funds held in trust. The Joint Board's enthusiasm to access the more than $50 million involved was exceeded only by Congress's determination that they should not. Not until much later, 13 October 1941, too late, was "authority to use the sugar excise money . . . removed from the Bill by the Senate and a general authorization for approbation for defense inserted."[71]

On 23 April 1941, Sayre reported to the President "considerable uneasiness here over a possible Japanese invasion. Public opinion, at times jittery, was gratified as a result of the increased strength of the United States Army and Navy forces here." Sayre was also jittery, due to the rumors "emanating from Washington which have appeared in the newspapers here as to the appointment of someone to succeed me as High Commissioner."[72] Quezon faced with the choice of retaining Sayre or seeing the return of Justice Frank Murphy, Ickes' protegée, chose the former option. He wrote to Roosevelt, "While High Commissioner Sayre and I have had differences of opinion on certain public questions—a thing which is but natural to happen between persons of independent minds—our relations have always been on very friendly terms." Sayre's experience, continued Quezon, "makes his continued presence in this country as America's representative in this critical time, of great value both to the Government of the United States and the Government of the Commonwealth." Sayre thanked Quezon for the letter but it did little to change their adversarial positions, particularly on the economy, civil defense and Quezon's authority to act independently in areas where Sayre believed he had no authority for independent action. Quezon's letter, however, had a dramatic effect in Washington, dealing a fatal blow to the Ickes conspiracy.

The War Department responded where it could to the urgent entreaties for support coming both from Grunert and from Mac-Arthur. The Philippine Army urgently needed artillery and in a memo-randum to the President on 29 March 1941, the new Secretary of War, Henry Stimson recommended the release of obsolescent 8 inch coastal artillery to MacArthur. It is evident from his note that the Europe-first policy remained a primary consideration. "The amount of equipment is relatively small. It does not affect our present com-mitment to the British Government and cannot materially affect future arrangements . . . your approval of this transfer is recom-mended."[73] Quezon had cancelled the 1940 mobilization, but in March 1941, 25,000 Filipino reservists were recalled to the colors for ten days of intensive training. Grunert supplemented the Philippine Army's inadequate training cadre from regular army resources and arranged for coastal artillery reservists to hold their two-week camp on Corregidor with the regular United States coastal artillery units.

MacArthur remained estranged from Quezon. Communication between the two continued to be conducted through Jorge Vargas. Then MacArthur conveyed to Quezon a tantalizing proposition he had allegedly heard from a secretary to Roosevelt: that MacArthur was being considered either as Military Governor or Commander in Chief of the military in the Philippines. MacArthur's real purpose in wanting a face-to-face meeting with Quezon was probably his con-cern that Sayre and Grunert would attempt to persuade Quezon, that in the event of war, he should place the military and civilian establish-ment under Grunert. At their meeting Quezon was horrified by MacArthur's attempt to ingratiate himself by getting the military to vote for Quezon in the November election. "I could consider it a dis-grace to my administration if anybody used trainees to support my candidacy."[74] Quezon refused to give any undertaking with regard to MacArthur's future. If he wanted to return to the United States in the six months prior to the expiry of his contract, the Commonwealth Government would continue to pay his salary.[75]

The stocks and maintenance reserves of ammunition, anti-aircraft equipment and aircraft in the Philippines were parlous, but all that could be elicited from Washington was sympathy.[76] On 29 May 1941, Brigadier General Leonard T. Gerow, acting head of the War Plans Department, proposed closer contact between MacArthur and Grunert. Grunert had made a similar proposal on 21 May which coincided with an informal approach made in a letter to Stimson from John Stevenot, a Manila telephone official. Marshall wrote a personal letter to Grunert advising him to improve the level of liaison between him and MacArthur.[77] "Additionally, the 1940 revision of the Philippine Department Plan Orange (WPO-3), recently received, indicates extensive use of organized units of the Philippine Army. A knowledge of the provision of this plan is restricted to officers of the United States Army."[78]

In a Memorandum of 6 June 1941, Gerow told Marshall of letters he had received from MacArthur recommending the creation of a new American military command embracing all Army activities in the Far East and that he, MacArthur, be assigned as the Commanding General. Gerow suggested that if MacArthur were to be recalled to duty he be offered Grunert's job which "does not expire until February, 1942."[79] A letter from MacArthur dated 29 May 1941 was already en route to Marshall. Although MacArthur may well have "disliked, mistrusted and resented George Marshall,"[80] it is evident from Marshall's treatment of MacArthur that this antipathy was not reciprocated. Not having had an immediate response to his letter to Roosevelt asking to be recalled to active duty,[81] MacArthur told Marshall that the plans to absorb the Philippine Army into the United States Army inferred his redundancy and therefore he proposed closing the Military Mission. Marshall replied that he and the Secretary of War were concerned about the developments in the Far East and admitted having come to the conclusion three months earlier that his experience made him "the logical selection for the Army Commander in the Far East should the situation approach a crisis." It was evident all the important parties were agreeable, for Marshall concluded: "This letter is also an acknowledgement of your letters to the President and to the Secretary of War. Please keep its contents confidential for the present."[82] Two days after this letter, 22 June, Germany invaded Russia, thereby easing Japan's concern of having to fight enemies on the northern and southern fronts.[83] In Tokyo on 2 July, an imperial conference had been convened, at which it was decided that Japanese forces would prepare to advance south against Malaya, Singapore, Java and the Philippines. The operational planning began in earnest but Admiral Kichisaburo Nomura, Japanese Ambassador to the United States, was instructed to maintain dialogue with Secretary of State Cordell Hull in case diplomacy might render armed conflict unnecessary.[84]

In a 4 July speech, Sayre made his most positive recognition to date of the inevitability of war and the need for the United States to be prepared. According to Hart, "he showed a decided change in mental attitude towards the possibilities in the international situation."[85] It is true that he had Europe in mind and was convinced of the necessity of not engaging Japan in war in the Far East. Shortly afterwards, the U.S. Navy announced that the entrances to Manila and Subic Bays had been mined. Shipping could only negotiate the minefields in daylight under the supervision of naval vessels. On 23 July, Grunert sent Marshall details of his 61st birthday celebrations held two days earlier and attended by Sayre, Quezon and many of the senior civil and military dignitaries, but not MacArthur. Grunert sought to explain to the Chief of Staff that, should a copy of the *Philippines Herald* 16-page birthday supplement "come your way or be brought to your notice," he did not wish it to appear that he was a party to "a self-aggrandizement program."[86] But bearing in mind the rumors floating around of MacArthur being resurrected phoenix-like from the ashes, that is precisely how it appeared. The newspaper declared: "In recent months the armed forces have been strengthened and developed here. Hardened by rigorous training, the troops, both American and Filipino have been forged into an efficient combat team, ready now to guard these islands against an aggressor." Grunert, was described by Quezon as "a real soldier and therefore a leader of men," who, according to Sayre, "has our unlimited confidence in his faithful and able execution of the tremendous tasks of national defense."[87]

On 26 July, Roosevelt issued executive orders freezing all Japanese assets in the United States and the Philippines[88] and closed the Panama Canal to Japanese shipping. The export of oil, iron and rubber by Americans to Japan was forbidden. Roosevelt asked Britain and Holland to follow suit by imposing similar embargoes.[89] The

President had not intended to completely shut off Japan's oil supplies, since the Navy and Churchill had warned him that if he did so, Japan would "run amok." So he assured Ambassador Nomura that low-grade gasoline supplies to Japan would continue at 1936 levels. On this occasion, however, Roosevelt was not equal to the scheming hawks in his cabinet, notably Dean Acheson and Ickes who, through bureaucratic chicanery, ensured that the embargo became complete, and thus war a little more certain.

At this moment, the United States did not possess the essential military capabilities to deter Japan from taking a calculated gamble into war. Yet there was an insensitivity, a determined reluctance to recognize Japan's advanced capabilities, or to treat Japan as a serious threat. There were undoubtedly racial overtones. However, the United States Ambassador in Tokyo, Joseph Grew, was convinced that both states could step back from the brink of disaster without prejudice to their core interests.

On 28 August 1941, Prime Minister Prince Konoye proposed a meeting with Roosevelt in Hawaii to thrash out their differences. While these tentative political approaches were being made, the Imperial Japanese Army had not only reconciled itself to war with the United States but also favored such action. The moderate Konoye knew that time was running out but, crucially, he had the backing of Emperor Hirohito which might well have been sufficient to hold the army in check. Roosevelt agreed to a meeting with Konoye aboard a battleship off Alaska, but the initiative was torpedoed by the State Department. They discounted Grew's warnings not to put too much pressure on Japan, doubted the value of any meeting between Roosevelt and Konoye and ignored warnings that Japan would go to war out of desperation. The Department stipulated that if there were to be an Alaska meeting, agreements had to be made prior to, and not during, the meeting. Konoye demurred, insisting that the purpose of the meeting was to thrash out differences. Konoye resigned and, on 17 October, General Hideki Tojo became Prime and War Minister.[90]

The Japanese Foreign Ministry's "Purple" coding machine had been in service since 1939. It took the American Army Signal Intelligence Service (SIS) eighteen months to break the diplomatic code, and it then had eight machines built to decode Purple traffic. The Army and Navy each retained two in Washington, three went to London for use at Britain's discretion and one was set up in the Navy tunnel, under naval control, on Corregidor.[91] On 26 July 1941, Magic (as the decryptions were called) intercepted a message from the Japanese Foreign Minister in Tokyo to the Japanese Ambassador in Berlin. The Foreign Minister described the situation in the Western Pacific as being strained and warned that Tokyo would not be able to bear the strain much longer. Japan, he said, "must take immediate steps to break asunder this ever-strengthening chain of encirclement which is being woven under the guidance of and with the participation of England and the United States, acting like a cunning dragon seemingly asleep."[92]

The Philippine "Magic" intercepted many naval reports sent by Japanese Consul Katsumi Nihro to Tokyo. The Japanese had sufficient agents in the Philippines to keep under surveillance selected naval personnel in addition to a number of people who had entered the country as tourists. The Japanese were keen to know why precisely the United States Navy wanted to requisition half the American Consulate space in Manila for espionage work. They also believed that in mid July 1941 investigations regarding Japanese shipping or Japanese people were being conducted by British and American sources principally through the British Honorary Consul, Francisco Brown.

Aware of the possibility of Japanese assets being frozen, it was decided on 25 July 1941 to keep a large proportion of them in cash in order to finance intelligence work. When the freezing occurred the next day—predicted in Manila as only the first of a number of retaliatory steps—Consul Nihro warned Tokyo that he could not maintain business as usual. The next week, on 2 August, he requested permission to control the allocation of secret funds at his discretion. The Japanese put great store on their cultural propaganda program. A Mr. Negishi was recruited in July 1941 to engage in intelligence as well as cultural work. Three candidates seeking office in the Philippine Assembly requested Japanese financial assistance. Tokyo was asked on 13 July 1941 for 40,000 yen and for the authority to assist the candidates—subject to further investigation assessing their prospects of being successful in the elections.

Of paramount importance was the movement of military personnel and equipment. On 10 July, Tokyo was informed of the unloading of coastal guns, ten gun platforms and more than 20 light tanks, as well as the arrival of the *President Taft* bringing 800–1000 soldiers to the Philippines. On 25 July, the Japanese assessed there were 460 aircraft and 1,300 pilots stationed in the Philippines, with a regular Army force of approximately 10,000 men. The Philippine Army with reserves was assessed to be about 130,000 men, with the potential in an emergency of raising 100,000 men. On 2 August, an agent observed that American Army and Naval planes had not been camouflaged. On 4 August 1941, the crew of the *President Coolidge* told of having brought approximately 600 more American soldiers to Manila. Naval and military preparations in the Cavite Naval Yard were under close surveillance by the Japanese. A report was made to Tokyo on 15 July 1941 that construction there would be delayed due to lightning having struck the master electric dynamo.[93]

At the Washington Staff Conference between 29 January–29 March 1941, the British and Americans had been working on a combined strategy known as ABC-1.[94] The British proposed three objectives. First, the European Theater was to be the vital one, where a solution must first be sought. Second, the general policy should therefore be to defeat Germany and Italy and only then deal with Japan. Third, the security of the Far Eastern position, including Australia and New Zealand, was essential to the cohesion of the British Empire and the maintenance of its war effort. Singapore was seen to be the key to the defense of these interests and its retention must be assured.[95] There had been no disagreement on the first two points but the position of Singapore raised issues of national interest and underlined different approaches to conflict—the British being comfortable with long wars while resource-rich America looked for short wars. If Washington was prepared to accept the temporary loss of the Philippines she was not prepared to fight to retain a jewel in Britain's imperial crown.

At a follow-on meeting held in Singapore in April with Air Marshal Sir Robert Brooke-Popham in the Chair, and where Hart was represented by Captain William R. Purnell, an attempt was made by the local commanders to determine a Far East strategy undetrimental to the policy of Europe first—a policy incidentally which Roosevelt had not then endorsed. The British wanted Admiral Hart's Asiatic Fleet substantially reinforced so that, in conjunction with the Dutch, it would act against, or deter, any Japanese designs on Singapore. The American Army and Navy were resolutely disinclined to reinforce the Far East but, as a compromise if war came, were agreeable to augmenting their fleets in the Atlantic and Mediterranean in order to release Royal Navy ships for the protection of Singapore and the Malay Barrier.[96] America was not convinced of Singapore's strategic importance and therefore a mutual decision emerged for each country to attend to its own national interest: Britain to concentrate on Singapore and America on the Philippines. No planning was made for the early recapture of the Philippines in the likely event of its loss. At the end of the Singapore meeting, the delegates endorsed ABC-1, which went on to form the basis of Rainbow 5: "A strategic defensive in the Far East, with the U.S. Fleet employed offensively in the manner best calculated to weaken Japanese economic power, and to support the defense of the Malay Barrier by directing Japanese strength away from Malaya." The implication of this decision was that when the U.S. Asiatic Fleet deployed southward, it[97] would come under the operational control of the Royal Navy.

On 26 July, Sayre received a radiogram from Washington. "The President on July 26th issued order calling Philippine Army into service of United States at time to be fixed by General MacArthur who has been called to active duty and designated as Commanding General Forces in the Far East, including the Philippine Department and Philippine Army. Please advise President Quezon."[98] When Sayre told Quezon of MacArthur's new role he refused to believe it but, once the inevitability of what he had been told sank home, he put all past animosity behind him. The War Department established the new Far East Command, United States Army Forces in the Far East (USAFFE), that same day, and appointed MacArthur the commander in the rank of Major General. MacArthur was back. On 28 July he heard he had been given the temporary rank of Lieutenant General, "although my retired rank was that of full general. Bureaucracy has a strange way of working sometimes, but I had reached a stage of life when I cared little for the reasons of administrators."[99]

7

INTERNAL CONFLICTS

A t seven thirty in the morning on 27 July, MacArthur sat down to his customary breakfast and picked up the *Manila Tribune*. He read the lead story which confirmed the Japanese occupation of Saigon and that the Japanese had called up one million reservists. It was his own name in a box at the bottom left hand corner which caught his attention. A bulletin from Washington (where, at that moment, it was still that busy 26 July) reported that Roosevelt was mobilizing the armed forces in the Philippines and that MacArthur was to be the Commanding General. The penthouse doorbell rang and a house boy brought him two War Department telegrams which confirmed what he had read and authorized him to spend $10 million on Philippine defenses.[1] Next, the hated telephone rang—it was Sutherland. "Dick, I told you so. Destiny is with me. Stay with me and rise to glory."[2] There are variations of this statement but they all include the word "destiny"; a noun that can be both kind and cruel. Soon Sutherland and Marshall arrived to find an effervescent MacArthur already poring over a map spread on the table. Sutherland said: "You know, General, it adds up to an insurmountable task." MacArthur turned to him and said: "These islands must and will be defended. I can but do my best."[3]

MacArthur's appointment had a dramatic effect upon the Philippines. A large minority of Americans were appalled by the news but reassured by the fact that Hart outranked MacArthur. But for most, past defeatism was replaced by the infectious optimism exuded by MacArthur. Quezon came round to MacArthur's penthouse and embraced him, "All that we have, all that we are, is yours."[4] The only plan then available was Grunert's extended citadel defense plan. He had been "hammering" to organize an anti-aircraft defense but the formation of USAFFE meant "this puts it up to that headquarters to plan and organize for the future."[5] Not until 6 October did he reveal his feelings about being superceded by MacArthur. In a letter to his friend General James G. Harbord, Grunert wrote: "He will get 100% loyalty and efficiency from me. I know of no one more entitled to command the United States Army Forces of the Far East than he. Naturally I would have liked the command myself." Proud of his achievements and the plans being turned over to MacArthur, Grunert observed that as "Department Commander, I still retain the responsibility for the training of the regular troops, and the training of the inducted Philippine Army troops has been added thereto."[6] But it would have been out of character for MacArthur to wish to share the spotlight, and later that month he asked Marshall to relieve Grunert and to designate the Philippine Department "an administrative echelon analogous to a Corps area . . . It would be advantageous to relieve him, as I am loath, as long as he is here, to contract the functions of the Department Commander."[7] The War Department concurred; Grunert was short-toured and recalled and on 31 October MacArthur assumed his responsibilities in addition to retaining command of USAFFE.[8] Destiny had been kinder to Grunert than he could have imagined when he was effectively bundled out of the Philippines.

MacArthur, now sixty-one, a soldier for forty-two years, twenty-three of which had been in the rank of General, selected his own team and kept track of rising stars in the Army Register. He appointed Lieutenant Colonel Richard Sutherland Chief of Staff and Colonel Carl Seals, Adjutant General. In September, he rejected a signals officer he was offered because he required "the highest talent in your senior command"[9] and rejected the credentials of the man proposed as chief surgeon.[10] Yet, in his apparent pursuit of excellence, he allowed his choice to be tempered by qualities other than professional expertise. The appointment of Lieutenant Colonel Lewis C. Beebe, an infantryman, as his logistician (G-4) was arguably not an inspired choice. Richard Marshall continued as Deputy Chief of Staff with oversight of the broad field of logistics and administration. The

Personnel post (G-1) was filled by Colonel Charles P. Stivers. The choice to lead the Intelligence branch (G-2) was an unconventional officer with the distinctive English name of Charles A. Willoughby. The name belied the fact that he claimed, probably fraudulently, that he came from a German family, Tscheppe-Weidenbach. He had joined the ranks in 1913 as a means of attaining American citizenship but he retained his German formality, part of the pretense of coming from high, aristocratic stock, and wore *pince-nez*—earning him the nickname "Sir Charles." Willoughby was one of a number who had been cross-posted from Grunert's headquarters. He was, according to Gunther, "tall and stout as an ox," emotional, melancholic and prone to fly into tantrums. Once, when he was dining with the Gunthers, he suddenly proposed a toast to "the second greatest military commander in the world, Francisco Franco."[11] Security considerations, specifically the "need to know" principle, excluded MacArthur's head of intelligence from Magic distribution. Only MacArthur and Hart received decrypted Japanese intercepts. Sutherland was added to the access list in late July 1941, immediately prior to his promotion from Lieutenant Colonel to Brigadier General.[12]

Other appointments were: Colonel Constant L. Irvin (Operations and Training, G-3), Beebe (Logistics, G-4), Seals (Adjutant General), Brigadier General Edward P. King (field artillery) and Colonel William Marquat (anti-aircraft defense), Colonel Spencer B. Akin, (chief signals officer), Colonel Hugh J. Casey (chief engineer), Colonel Charles C. Drake (Quartermaster) and Colonel George Hirsh (Ordnance). The commander of the Philippine Department's air units was Brigadier General Henry B. Clagett, but he had a drinking problem and so had to go. MacArthur was offered three names from which to choose a "qualified commander to take over your increased airforce unit's extended field of operations."[13] Major General Lewis H. Brereton, Major General Jacob Enfickel, and Brigadier General Walter H. Frank. MacArthur selected Major General Lewis H. Brereton to replace him, but the commander of the Third Air Force would not arrive until 4 November. It was a delay MacArthur was prepared to accept for he knew Brereton from the Rainbow Division days of 1918 when he commanded the supporting air observation squadron. Huff, the former naval officer and aide, became a Lieutenant Colonel, and a second aide, Captain Le Grande Diller, was also taken on board.

Later in the war, in 1943, MacArthur used the term "my staff" to

Marshall, to which Marshall replied that MacArthur had a court rather than a staff. News correspondent Clark Lee would have agreed because he identified a number of shared characteristics among those whom MacArthur gathered around him: "each carries a chip on both shoulders, is highly and sometimes childishly sensitive and is convinced that the General is the greatest man who ever lived." MacArthur endeavored to choose his people carefully although initially he had to make do with what he saw as the best available in the Theater, since the best overall went to Europe. Men who might seek publicity for themselves were not tolerated. "MacArthur did not select the brightest, most capable, and most promising officers in the Army to serve under him," continued Lee. "Most of the men on his staff were never heard of in the Army before they joined him, and never will be again."[14]

When the historian Louis Morton interviewed Sutherland after the war, he asked about the records of the first Philippine Campaign. The Chief of Staff said that the G-1, G-2 and G-4 records were probably available in the War Department, but Morton would never get his hands on the G-3 records (Operations and Training). "They are the most important body of records on the operation and are in MacArthur's possession." Sutherland told Morton that MacArthur did not want a history of the First Philippine Campaign, but did not know the reason why. MacArthur would never allow anything to be released which was in any way critical of him or of his command; the emphasis would always be upon the General's decisions and plans. Apparently, within his Headquarters, MacArthur handled only two things personally—publicity and politics—and all accounts and histories relating to these areas would reflect MacArthur's point of view. Everything outside publicity and politics was left to Sutherland. His staff had complete discretion in the fields of strategy, planning, operations and logistics. MacArthur was content to be briefed on an operation prior to its commencement but he rarely changed the plans or offered objections. According to Sutherland, only once did he disagree with a plan, and then he told Sutherland to go ahead anyhow.[15]

The most important publisher of news and current affairs in the U.S.A. was undoubtedly Henry Luce, owner and founder of *Time*, *Life* and *Fortune*. Henry Luce's parents had been missionaries in China, which accounts for his special interest in the Far East. In February 1941,[16] *Time* had produced an article on the Philippine Army

and its prospects. It was not an optimistic report but it was undoubtedly one that MacArthur, a devoted reader of *Time* and *Life*, would
have read. It was a story which caught the imagination of Henry Luce
who, together with his vivacious and talented wife, Clare Boothe
Luce, visited the Philippines in July 1941 to ascertain the facts for
himself. The MacArthurs entertained the Luces in their penthouse in
the Manila Hotel. Apparently, the General held forth for the duration
of the entire meal, which annoyed Luce who himself, given half a
chance, was inclined to dominate table talk. After bidding farewell,
the Luces descended in the MacArthur private elevator when, suddenly, Henry Luce pressed the Stop button between floors. He stood
there, his brows furrowed in quiet meditation.

"What are you doing?" inquired his wife.

"I'm trying to decide whether MacArthur is a great fraud or a
genius." Thirty seconds later Luce pushed the elevator's Down button.

"Well?" demanded his wife.

"He's both," concluded Luce as he stepped out into the hotel
lobby.[17]

Luce was among a number of newsmen who visited Manila at this
time who were amazed at the lack of preparation. "God help you,"
said Luce, "because no one else is going to—and you're in a terrible
spot."[18] Vincent Sheean of the *New York Herald Tribune* saw no anti-
aircraft guns and no air-raid shelters. He observed the contrast
between MacArthur and Sayre, the former "emphasized his every
statement with gesture and ornate imaging: he harkened and heard,
coming nearer every hour, the trumpets of immortality," while the latter played down the prospect of war.[19] "It was with genuine relief that
I took the clipper from Manila to go home. I was filled with appre-
hensions and had seen nothing (outside of China) to allay them. By
now I was quite certain that Japan intended to make war soon . . . I
thought the attack would be formidable and would have great
successes."[20]

In September 1941, Clare Boothe Luce returned to Manila to
write a profile of MacArthur for *Life*. MacArthur agreed to give the
interview, subject to his seeing the article prior to publication.
MacArthur was utterly attentive and detailed Diller to show her the
sights of Manila. One of his staff officers, Willoughby, actually bedded
the beautiful Mrs. Luce.[21] She said he was the only man she might
have run away with. While her papers show that Willoughby became

besotted, it was a fling which Mrs. Luce took in her stride without further thought or interest.[22] The Luce MacArthur relationship was respectful, mutually admiring and understandably platonic. She was a shrewd observer of the man whose "temperament was flawed by an egotism that demanded obedience not only to his orders, but to his ideas and his person as well. He plainly relished idolatry."[23] She noted the pallor of his skin, indicating how little time he spent outside, his trembling hands and the vanity which required him to comb his thinning black hair from left ear to right, thereby covering a large bald spot. What surprised her most was the face. It was not martial but rather "intellectual (and) aesthetic."[24] She asked him what his formula was for offensive warfare. "Did you ever hear the baseball expression 'Hit 'em where they ain't?'[25] That's my formula." There is no record whether her understanding was further advanced by this statement but she then asked him how he would describe a defensive strategy.

"Defeat."[26]

Fate had put him into the Philippines, which he likened to "the key that turns the lock that opens the door to the mastery of the Pacific." He took the analogy further by adding that "the man who holds a key, no matter what its special nature, from a strategic military opening to a boudoir door, is in a dangerous position,"[27] She took some photographs of the man who said he never posed for photographs, standing on the walls of Intramuros, close to his office, his eyes fixed beyond the horizon as though challenging unseen Japanese to chance their arm. True to her word, Mrs. Luce sent MacArthur the draft article. He was greatly upset by the more personal comments, particularly on his hair, and after the deletions he demanded what was left was a fawning, reverential profile.[28] Mrs. Luce was not happy with the finished product and apologized in a note to the editor, Noel Busch. She justified her less-than-honest article because she believed that United States power in the Pacific depended upon praising the emperor MacArthur's new clothes. She had found many unpleasant things that could be written about him but desisted because she had seen how, in the Far East, America's military prestige was "now indissolubly linked with the military (and personal) prestige of the General."[29] For MacArthur it had been a God-sent opportunity to appeal to the American public through the respected medium of *Life* to support his idea of turning the Philippines into a great redoubt, ready to "foil the enemy" by the spring of 1942.[30] Unfortunately, the article was published on 6 December 1941, too late to make an impact.

Suddenly, many of the past reservations in Washington about America's ability to hold the Philippines simply evaporated. The idea gained momentum that if the Philippine defenses were strengthened, this "pistol pointing at Japan's heart" would deter a Japanese advance southward through the China Sea. There was also the Russian factor. The sending of American troops and planes to the Southwest Pacific to tie down the Japanese would take pressure off Stalin. Stimson attributes the Administration's reappraisal of the Philippine situation to two main causes. One was MacArthur's "contagious optimism" and the other was "the sudden and startling success of American Flying Fortresses (B-17s) in operations from the British Isles."[31] Stimson had reflected long and hard on the question "whether we should make every effort possible in the Far East or whether, like the Navy, we should treat that as doomed and let it go."[32] Marshall, who had believed the reinforcement of the Philippines would be "a strategic error of the first magnitude," like Stimson, had changed his mind, promising MacArthur "every possible assistance within our power." Marshall's change of heart, of pivotal importance, had been brought about by Vichy France's granting of air and sea bases in Indochina to Japan, from where the Japanese could attack the lines of communication into China, the Dutch East Indies, Malaya and the Philippines. From that action followed the imposition of economic sanctions against Japan which in turn were a provocation for Japanese attacks into Malaya, the Dutch East Indies and the Philippines. Marshall recognized the lack of preparedness in the Philippines and, despite the preoccupation with Europe, determined that the time had come to reorganize the Army's defenses in the Philippines. The view in the War Department was that if the Philippines and Singapore were to fall, the Allies would fall back upon the Dutch East Indies, recover and then counter attack. Why they assumed the lightly defended Dutch East Indies would not also succumb to the Japanese is unclear. The Philippines took on a whole new purpose, and equipment previously denied was authorized for release. On 6 October Stimson told Hull that we "needed three months to secure our position," suggesting the Philippines would be ready to face a Japanese attack in early January 1942. MacArthur planned on being prepared, with all elements of defense in place, in April 1942. Within this thesis lay a number of important misconceptions.

American intelligence assessments in the event of war, forecast the Japanese landing 100,000 men with a view to seizing the harbor defenses of Manila Bay "prior to or coincident with a declaration of war." Surprise would be a key feature in the attainment of Japanese objectives of suppressing naval and air forces, the strategic occupation of the Philippines and the denial to the United States of a naval base on the archipelago. "Climatic conditions alone considered, December and January are the months most favored for land operations."[33] Yet, despite this and other strong intelligence indicators, the War Department assessed that the Japanese would not move before April 1942. There were no contingency plans in the event that the enemy came early and, if they did, there were no follow-on plans to relieve the United States military forces in the Philippines. It is a reasonable assumption that the forces being assembled in the Philippines were a forlorn hope; they were expendable after they had taken the highest possible toll of the Japanese invaders. MacArthur admitted that he had a struggle to get ready now that his ten year plan to prepare for the defense of the Philippines had been halved. "Too late, Washington had come to realize the danger. Men and munitions were finally being shipped to the Pacific, but the crucial question was, would they arrive in time and in sufficient strength?"[34]

Small wonder that "the U.S. Navy hated MacArthur, really hated him."[35] Early in the war, the Navy came round to the idea of having an overall joint commander in the Pacific with MacArthur and his army under command. There was a thought in the Navy that Marshall shared their loathing of MacArthur and they were initially delighted when he appeared to support their idea of a Joint Command. He had one condition. "If we are going to have an overall commander in the Pacific, there isn't any question about it, you will have to pick MacArthur—on the basis of pure competence alone."[36] For Brigadier General Leonard Gerow of War Plans Division, the matter was rather academic. In his 3 October 1941 strategic concept of the Philippine Islands for the Secretary of War, he maintained that the presence of "adequate heavy bombardment" would deter a Japanese advance southward until the Philippines had been neutralized, but added that "the U.S. Army and Philippine forces now authorized, including adequate support aviation, anti-aircraft, tanks and anti-tank units, will make the neutralization so expensive that the Japanese will hesitate to make the attempt."[37]

The so-called "sudden and startling success of the B-17 bomber,

the Flying Fortress, was revealed as a fiction during Roosevelt's
Atlantic Charter meeting with Churchill in August 1941. Twenty
B-17Cs had entered service with 90 Squadron, Royal Air Force in
May 1941, and their first operational raid was against Wilhelmshaven
on 8 July 1941. By September 1941, 90 Squadron had completed
twenty-six raids, including a number against the docked German
battleships *Scharnhorst* and *Gneisenau* at Brest. This series of raids
was:

> far from successful. In fifty-one sorties by individual aircraft, twenty-six
> were aborted with no bombs dropped. There were difficulties with
> the Norden bomb-sight, numerous mechanical failures, and the guns
> tended to freeze up at altitude. The most serious defect of all was the
> inadequate defensive armament. All guns were manually operated and
> there was a blind spot at the tail. It was decided to abandon operations
> over Europe.[38]

There were undoubtedly operational and conceptual differences
between the Americans and British as to how the B-17 should be used,
but the early B-17s were not impressive. The most critical problem
was the absence of a tail gunner, and one long ton of bombs dropped
cost eight B-17s: no wonder Goebbels derisively described the
Fortresses as "flying coffins."[39] A veil of silence was drawn over the
failure of the B-17 in the European theater. One third of Boeing's production line of B-17s had been earmarked for the Royal Air Force, but
now they were surplus to requirement and Britain was more than content to see them assigned to the Philippines where, in conjunction
with Royal Navy reinforcements in the region, they might more effectively enhance the defense and security of Singapore.

At the 6 September 1941 Imperial Japanese Conference, the decision was taken that Japan should prepare for war with a view to being
ready by the end of October. In less than two months the war plans
for Southern Operations had been largely completed. Imperial General Headquarters (IGHQ) had re-examined their existing operational plans, adapted and matched forces to operations, redeployed
troops, organized or supplemented air and sea transportation, prepared and made logistical plans including the commandeering of
ships and modification of holds to increase ships' capacity to carry
men and horses. On 6 November 1941, IGHQ issued the Order of
Battle of the Southern Army.

ORDER OF BATTLE, SOUTHERN ARMY, NOVEMBER 1941

UNIT	ZONES OF ACTION	COMMANDING GENERAL	CORE
Southern Army		Gen Hisaichi Terauchi	
Fourteenth Army	Philippines Operational Area	Lt Gen Masaharu Homma	16th, 48th Infantry Divisions; 65th Independent Mixed Brigade
Fifteenth Army	Thailand and Burma	Lt Gen Shojiro Iida	33rd, 55th (−) Divisions
Sixteenth Army	Netherlands East Indies	Lt Gen Hitoshi Imamura	2nd Division; 56th Independent Mixed Brigade
Twenty-Fifth Army	Malaya	Lt Gen Tomoyuki Yamashita	Imperial Guard Division; 5th, 18th Divisions
21st Division		Lt Gen Hisaichi Tanaka	[Directly attached to Army; from North China]
3rd Air Group		Lt Gen Michio Sugawara	Four fighter regiments; three light bomber regiments; three heavy bomber regiments; one reconnaissance regiment
5th Air Group		Lt Gen Hideyoshi Obata	Two fighter regiments; three light bomber regiments; two heavy bomber regiments; [and one reconnaissance regiment]
Miscellaneous			[Directly attached to Army: 21st Independent Mixed Brigade; 21st Independent Air Unit; 4th Independent Mixed Brigade]

Source: Saburo Hayashi

The Japanese objectives were to neutralize the Far Eastern bases of America and Great Britain followed by those of the Dutch, and to occupy the Philippines, Guam, Hong Kong, Malaya, Burma, Java, Sumatra, the Celebes, Borneo, the Bismarck Islands, Dutch Timor, "etc." Joint army and naval forces would launch simultaneous attacks against the Philippines and Malaya although Malaya was to have priority in Army air operations. Troops had almost entirely been committed to operational tasks: there was very little by way of reserve. Vice Admiral Takahashi's Third Fleet had the mission of taking the Philippines, Borneo and Celebes, while the Malay Peninsula had been assigned to Vice Admiral Kondo. Once the two Vice Admirals' missions had been satisfactorily completed, they and the Pearl Harbor Striking Force were to combine and seize the ultimate objective of Java. Guam and Wake were the separate missions of Vice Admiral Inouye's Fourth Fleet.[40]

Due cognizance had been given to the possibility of a diplomatic solution to Japan's increasing problems, in which case operations planned to be launched on X-Day would be cancelled. It was intended that offensive air operations were to be launched on X-Day against Allied air bases "to crush their power in one fell swoop." As operations progressed satisfactorily, air bases would redeploy, those in Southern Formosa to the Philippines, those in French Indo-China to Malaya. The main logistical base for Southern Operations was French Indo-China, supported from and by Formosa and Canton. Separate plans dwelt upon wider operations in China and contingency plans in the event of the Soviet Union entering the war. To all intents and purposes, the Imperial Japanese Forces were ready to commence Southern Operations in November 1941. They awaited the word of when X-Day would be.[41]

Meanwhile, in the Philippines, progress towards war was far less smooth and orderly. Quezon was undoubtedly unwell and his tendency to blow hot or cold was often a reflection of his acute illness and depression. On 15 September 1941, Sayre told President Roosevelt, "President Quezon has had another setback in his long and slow recovery. He has to limit himself strictly in his activities and has lost the vigor and fire that goes with robust health. I fear he may never recover them."[42] Increasingly, Quezon shunned Manila, staying in his residence at Baguio where the climate was more favorable towards his chest condition. His relationship with Sayre remained brittle, especially over the long-running dispute about responsibilities for civil defense. It was the one security item most likely to excite the emotions of Quezon. In a letter of 26 September, Roosevelt wrote to reassure Quezon: "I wish I could tell you at length of the increased belief that the Philippines can be adequately defended."[43]

Power and authority both within the Commonwealth and its links to America were hopelessly diffused:[44]

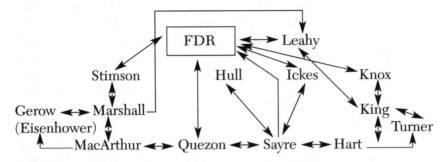

The situation was exacerbated by the continuous, often trivial machinations between the Army and the Navy. It is an oversimplification to point the finger of blame entirely at MacArthur. Hart was much concerned to protect Navy turf but he was not as intensely defensive and protective as MacArthur. Even with Grunert, whom he had found:

> Entirely cooperative and willing to come half way . . . little progress was made toward cooperative action between the arms where it was most needed—the respective air detachments. The main reason was that Army Air was building up rapidly, in fighters particularly, absorbing many partially trained pilots and was, in general, in such a preliminary state that cooperation seemed not yet timely.[45]

The nub of the problem lay in the diametrically opposed plans: the Army saw itself sitting tight and fighting it out with the Japanese while the Asiatic Fleet planned to withdraw to the safer waters in the south. The exception was of course the relatively large submarine force whose coordination with Army defensive plans was a *sine qua non*.

The short, wiry, 63-year-old, four-star Admiral Hart outranked the three-star Lieutenant General MacArthur yet it was the latter who luxuriated in the Manila Hotel's penthouse suite while the former had far less grand quarters three floors below. In terms of responsibilities, MacArthur's were increasing while Hart's, already limited, were not.

United States naval forces based on Manila comprised one heavy cruiser, one light cruiser, 13 destroyers, 17 submarines, 24 patrol planes with a range of 2,000 miles and one seaplane tender.[46] On 1 October, MacArthur had written to the Adjutant General about Rainbow 5. He mentioned how the Islands were being organized into a Theater of Operations of eleven to thirteen divisions, equivalent to an army of approximately 200,000 men. The General distanced himself from Grunert's War Plan Orange-3 for a "citadel-type defense" on the grounds that Manila Bay and Luzon could not be defended if an enemy was able to seize parts of the archipelago in the south. The citadel defense would be expanded to include all the Philippines less Mindanao, Palawan and some lesser islands. According to MacArthur, the wide scope of possible enemy operations, particularly aviation, meant revising the plans for the defense of the Philippines; "and the strength and composition of the defense forces projected here are believed to be sufficient to accomplish such a mission." To what extent MacArthur had come under pressure from Quezon is not clear but, to the Philippine Government, the concept of expendability, of trading space for time was understandably unattractive. MacArthur concluded his letter: "the extent of the Philippine Coastal Frontier should be defined as the land and sea areas necessary for the defense of the Philippine Archipelago, and the Joint mission and the Army mission should be changed accordingly."[47]

Both commanders recognized that they were on the threshold of a world war. Hart confessed himself to being in a quandary because the naval equivalent of Rainbow 5, WPL 46, gave the Asiatic Fleet a mission to support the defense of the Philippines and gave to its commander the decision as to "what components to deploy initially to that end." Hart recognized that if he employed his cruisers and destroyers in all-out defense of the Philippines their early loss could be guaranteed, whereas they might more usefully be employed as a combined fleet with the British and Dutch. On 17 September 1941, he proposed deploying his cruisers, two thirds of the destroyers and all large auxiliaries, less submarine tenders, to the South West. By this time, the British Admiralty had planned heavy reinforcements and, in that context, Hart's plan was approved. But on 27 October 1941, Hart changed his mind, proposing that the entire fleet fight the coming war from Manila Bay, which would have meant employing all American naval assets in direct defense of the Philippines. Hart had taken account of the build-up of the Army Air Force, assuming that Manila

Bay would therefore become protected from attack. It was also a reflection of the slow progress among the allies in planning combined operations, as well as a warrior sailor's belief that territory should not be abandoned without a fight. Conceptually, Hart's change of idea would have coincided with the Army plans and expectations of their Navy but, "our Navy vetoed the idea."[48]

On 22 September 1941, Hart had an interview with MacArthur to discuss war plans and progress with allied conferences to date. It was a meeting Hart could not have enjoyed. MacArthur's mannerisms were not the most endearing, as observed by his Chief Clerk, who was with him from October 1941. "Out of his blazing ego poured a steady torrent of self centered oratory: elegant, polished and sculpted. His voice crackled and shuddered with taut emotion, lightning flashed from his eyes as he paced nervously, leaving his visitors to listen with apprehensive dismay and discomfort."[49]

MacArthur received Admiral Hart dressed in his bathrobe with a big letter "A," seemingly for Army, on its front but in fact reflecting MacArthur's "A" for sporting achievement at West Point. He had a dinner engagement that night with Sayre. Since MacArthur's appointment, an official relationship developed between the two by force of circumstance. MacArthur still disliked Sayre but, as Hart observed, it "looks as if he may intend to get Sayre out of the picture, as much as he can, if MacA becomes Military Governor, and that he may already be laying a foundation. Sayre complains that MacA won't cooperate in any way."[50] In a Situation Paper written by Woodbury Willoughby of the High Commissioner's Office on the vexed subject of Civil Defense, it was observed that "General MacArthur's actions, despite his repeated protestations of willingness to cooperate, clearly indicate that he does not desire to do so and further that he seriously lacks appreciation of the need for joint planning."[51]

Hart explained to MacArthur how his submarines would make an initial deployment at the appropriate time around Luzon and off enemy ports but that the surface elements would have to withdraw to the south west. The return northward of the cruiser-destroyer detachment would depend upon the then prevailing circumstances. When he had finished, MacArthur replied to the effect that the Navy had its plans and the Army had its plans and both had their own airfields.[52] "He had no questions whatever, made no suggestions and offered no objections." The Army plan was to "meet them at the beaches where they would be weakest and fight to destruction [of the

Japanese] . . . The Commanding General thought that close collaboration was not vital. The Fleet was unable to accept that, as regards aircraft at least."[53]

A great deal happened between September and November in the relationship between MacArthur and Hart, as was evident from a missive sent by Hart to Admiral Stark on 20 November 1941. Hart had anticipated "a fine start" to it. As he explained to Stark, MacArthur's brother had been a shipmate and friend, and he had known "Douglas" a long time. Hart observed how MacArthur had got his own way, "when I gave in to him about Army and Navy football relations. (He says I cooperated!!)." Put into perspective, Hart believed that he was on as friendly terms with MacArthur as anyone in the Commonwealth. The Admiral observed how the General had long been unpopular with the American colony and had rarely been seen at social gatherings. The two certainly lived close enough to have friendly chats but it seemed that MacArthur's idea was "cooperate, yes of course, all you want, but the Army has its job, the Navy has its job, not much in common."[54]

In October 1941, a minor glitch between Army and Navy occurred, to which MacArthur overreacted. The situation in Shanghai had become tense and delicately poised as Japanese forces encircling the city threatened to move in. As the predominant Service in Shanghai, including the 4th Marines, the Navy carried particular responsibilities for military law and order in the city. Instructions were disseminated regarding control of U.S. Army liberty parties landed from westbound ships but, due to a clerical error, instead of MacArthur's headquarters being designated an information addressee, the message was sent to USAFFE as an action addressee. MacArthur wrote to Hart.

> Your order, although directly affecting personnel of my command, was issued without prior discussion with me, my first information having been received through the copy which was sent to my headquarters. Although I have since discussed this matter with you informally I wish to make a record of my insistent protest against your assumption of command over officers and enlisted men of the Army . . . your order in its present form . . . is illegal and cannot therefore be recognized by Army personnel.[55]

Hart apologized for the mistake but MacArthur still found it necessary to repeat chapter and verse to Hart's superior, Admiral Stark, the Chief Naval Officer.

Once this particular cloud disappeared, another soon arose to take its place. In a letter to MacArthur of 23 October 1941, Hart recapitulated Philippine Department and Sixteenth Naval District agreements of 24 May 1941 regarding air cooperation over water. These had included cooperation with reconnaissance, the attack by Army bombers on enemy naval forces off Luzon and the support of Army and Navy bombers by Army pursuit planes. As Hart explained, since both Army and Navy air assets either had increased or were scheduled to do so, the agreements "should go further" in order to counter the sea threat. "There must be exceedingly close cooperation between the Army's aircraft which operate over the water, those of the Navy, the submarines and even the Navy's surface ships." Hart proposed putting Navy aircraft assigned to attack land objectives under the Army's full tactical command while Army aircraft assigned to maritime operations should come under Navy control and in addition, the air effort should be coordinated.[56] Two weeks later, MacArthur replied that he found "the proposal entirely objectionable."[57]

MacArthur's veto was in line with a War Plans memorandum that had been drawn up for the Chief of Staff on 13 October 1941. In fact, so closely in line was it with MacArthur's thinking that it is not impossible that MacArthur had drafted the document. The paper rehearsed the fact that the Army now had in the Philippines a Lieutenant General "of outstanding military ability" and who "has spent the past six years in the Philippines and is thoroughly familiar with the defense problems of the area." Under MacArthur's command would be the main striking force. Therefore, "it is recommended that you request Admiral Stark to accept Army command over all U.S. naval forces in the Philippines, including the Asiatic Fleet."[58] Marshall, the realist, made no such move. On 7 November, MacArthur sent Marshall copies of his correspondence with Hart. "It is," he wrote, "quite possible that Hart is operating under instructions from higher authority. His letter would indicate that the Navy may be seeking strategic control in this area." MacArthur was becoming paranoid about the Navy in general and Hart in particular. When MacArthur had been invited to one of Quezon's parties, Sutherland sent a Colonel from USAFFE to talk to Quezon's aide. "Tell him General MacArthur will accept, but he's got to sit on Quezon's right, not Admiral Hart. Make that clear. If MacArthur should go over and find that he was seated on the left, he isn't staying."[59] While the Services bickered, anticipated conspiracies and dabbled in matters of monumental insignificance, the coordinated Japanese attack upon them was but one month away.

If MacArthur believed he would elicit Marshall's support in his dogmatic, sometimes petulant, struggle for ascendancy, he would be disappointed. In a signal of 29 November, Marshall told him in no uncertain terms how Stimson and he had been disturbed to receive his communication of 7 November. "It is the desire of the War Department that in matters of sea patrolling and action not, repeat not, directly concerned with immediate threats against the Philippine Islands, that you will within your means provide the desired air support for naval operations." In his return signal of 1 December, MacArthur sought to explain how it was his "considered opinion that in view of the mission and the forces involved, the most effective results can normally be obtained here by a coordination of mission rather than by unity of command under the navy." Then, by way of an apology, he added: "If therefore my position has in any way prejudiced or embarrassed you, do not hesitate to so inform me in order that I may effect readjustment." Given MacArthur's insatiable ego, he remained surprisingly deferential to his superior, Marshall, who, it will be recalled, the then 4-star Chief of Staff had once sent as a Colonel to Illinois. The reason they had a working relationship may be that despite MacArthur harboring suspicions of Marshall, they were totally different people with different temperaments. Marshall was a most undemonstrative man, not given to self dramatization. Once, after having his portrait painted by a friend, he protested at what he saw: "You have endowed me with more of a MacArthur personality than my own less colorful characteristics, and I fear you strove too hard to make good my deficiencies." Marshall did not resent MacArthur's showmanship for he believed it could be a beneficial attribute for a field commander.[60] Washington was not in a strong position to preach joint operations, since it was not until February 1942 that a Joint Chiefs of Staff Committee was established comprising Marshall, Admiral Ernest J. King and General H.H. Arnold, and even then there was no chairman.

Hart maintained that MacArthur resented his rank, "big Admiral, and small Fleet," but he was aware of the thinking in Washington of establishing a Joint Headquarters in Manila for which MacArthur must have been a leading candidate to command. Without specifically addressing his concerns he outlined MacArthur's defects to Stark, in November

We have in high place here a man who is basically of the lone-wolf characteristics, with prima donna complexes. It's hard for him to be anything
but king. Has a brilliant and quick mind and a vast amount of general
knowledge, so that it's natural for him to have developed a mental superiority complex. Talks well and at great length on many subjects and
enjoys it largely. Probably is very ambitious and inclined to look well
ahead. But while a brilliant one, it is also an erratic mind—and while
knowledge has come, wisdom tends to linger. All in all, it is to be feared
that an imbalance will appear which may be dangerous and that is the
main thought that I should pass to you. If you use it, remember it is
about a man I've looked upon as a friend—and hope I may again.[61]

The calling of the Philippine Army into the service of the United
States proved to be not only MacArthur's salvation but also led to the
restoration of an orderly relationship between him and Quezon.
There was little that was orderly, however, among the components of
the military, and there could rarely have been a more disparate and
unbalanced land force. The majority of the 22,000 U.S. Army troops
in the Philippines belonged to Coast Artillery Regiments, the Army
Air Corps or the Philippine Division comprising the Philippine
Scouts and the 31st Infantry. The Philippine Army required time for
training, instructors and resources, yet received insufficient amounts
of all three. It was also illusory to believe that the Philippine Army
became an integrated part of the U.S. Army.

The Philippine Scouts were one of the two best military units in
the region. They comprised the 45th and 57th Infantry, the 23rd and
24th Artillery regiments as well as the 86th and 88th (both under
strength), the 26th Cavalry and support arms and services. They were
consistently regarded as being combat-ready, well disciplined and
having good morale. But they had little in the way of modern weapons and equipment, though unarguably "well trained to use what they
had."[62] The 26th Cavalry was still horse-mounted but reconnaissance
troops were equipped with scout cars. The assimilation of the Philippine Army into the service of the United States from mid-1941, however, undid the unit-building and coherence of the Philippine Scouts.
Officers and non-commissioned officers had to be detached to train
the twelve provisional divisions of the Philippine Army and precious
equipment went with them. By the end of August 1941, two thirds of
the officers and almost half of the non-commissioned officers from
the Philippine Division were training the new divisions of the Philippine Army.

The other quality military unit was the 4th Marines, part of the Navy Department and therefore under Hart's rather than MacArthur's command. It had been in Shanghai for almost 15 years and comprised two small battalions of approximately 800 men. The regiment's vulnerability and the fear that the Japanese would create an "incident" led to its withdrawal to Subic Bay on 30 November to protect the Olongapo Naval Station and the naval base at Marivelos.[63]

On 30 August 1941, MacArthur told Marshall how disappointed he was with the training standards in the Philippine Division, after he had gone to see 31st Infantry maneuvers, which makes the point that he was not all politics and publicity but keen to see what was going on. The 31st Infantry

> never operated as a unified whole for combat training; infantry and artillery are in separate garrisons and have not trained together; training for cooperative missions between air and ground troops has been very limited; a division Command Post Exercise last week, said to be the first one in several years, showed the most glaring deficiencies . . . I consider it at present incapable of acceptable offensive operation as a division.[64]

These comments were of course an adverse reflection upon General Grunert. MacArthur told the Chief of Staff with some economy with the truth, that the Philippine Army units, which had of course been within MacArthur's command, "are now mobilizing in a most satisfactory manner and the whole program is progressing by leaps and bounds."[65] Two months later, MacArthur's situation report to Marshall told how "morale had been exceptionally high and all ranks show a real eagerness to learn. In consequence, training has progressed even beyond expectations." MacArthur could be excused if this optimism had been intended for public consumption but these were private letters to the Chief of Staff. Was he being deliberately dishonest to support his reputation or did he, as many observers suggest, live within his own self-generated wall of mist? He knew what was going on but the effective mobilization and training of the Philippine Army was crucial to the satisfactory execution of MacArthur's revised plan. What he saw was unlikely to protect his reputation as a warrior who got results. In a letter to Grunert, he complained bitterly at having found large groups of trainees and their officers standing and sitting around doing nothing. In at least one large group of hundreds of officers and men there was a complete lack of decisiveness in instructional procedure. Some American officers were practically ignorant of what was going on, and a pall of inactivity was evident.[66]

The problem of American enlisted men in the Philippines was that the good life in which they became inextricably bound during the two-year tour of duty was entirely contrary to what was required in the interest of military efficiency and preparedness. Private Paul P. Rogers, who was to become MacArthur's Chief Clerk, was among the great influx of reinforcements. He arrived on 21 October 1941 and was assigned to MacArthur's headquarters. At breakfast he found "a table set with linen, good china and flatware. Filipino mess boys served breakfast: platters of papayas, bananas and oranges; biscuits, rolls and toast; eggs, fried and scrambled; ham, sausage and bacon; and milk, coffee and juice. As they ate, the soldiers complained of the poor quality and poor service."[67] All three of 31st Infantry battalions were located in Manila; the regimental headquarters and the 1st battalion in Intramuros and the other two battalions at Fort McKinley to the southeast of the city. Soldiers were paid $21 a month, which was sufficient to afford a Filipino as a personal orderly to launder and to keep barrack spaces clean. The working day began with an 0700 reveille, lunch was at 1130, after which the men were free to siesta or to do whatever they wanted for the remainder of the day. Some of the men on second tours lived with Filipino girls in their *barrios* (villages). That was certainly well nigh universally true of the Air Corps. Enlisted men bought or built for $50 their own *nipa* huts. The military authorities condoned their men living with one woman in the *barrios*. Alcoholism and venereal disease were endemic in the 31st Infantry. Living off the base with a temporary partner served to reduce the incidence of both and so a food allowance was paid to encourage this form of cohabitation.[68]

While no American field artillery units arrived in time to fight in the Philippines,[69] two national guard tank battalions did. The 192nd and 194th Tank Battalions were equipped with the new M-3 Stuart light tanks, 54 tanks per battalion. The new tank was a ton heavier than the version upon which the men had been trained, with dual-mounted machine guns fixed in sponsons and fired by remote control

by the driver, an anti-aircraft gun and a 37mm gun as its main arma-
ment. Each battalion was supplemented by 23 half-tracks. For the
first two months after the arrival of the 194th on September 26, there
was only sufficient gas for 200 miles of motoring.

Among the Colonels designated for divisional command in the
expanded Philippine Army the assignments no one wanted were the
three divisions of the Visayan-Mindanao Force, the 61st, 81st and
101st. Colonel Bradford Chynoweth, formerly on MacArthur's staff in
Washington, had joked with his friend Colonel Pete Vachon that
these were backwaters too far from the potential hot spot of Luzon to
ever see action. The Visayan-Mindanao Force was a token force with
a mission to "defend against marauding raids and to prevent seizure
of landing forces against Luzon."[70] After disembarking, in September,
Colonel Bradford Chynoweth made his way to the Army and Navy
Club where he encountered his old friend and Head of Personnel at
USAFFE, Colonel C.P. Stivers, who told him his destination was
Mindanao and the 61st Division. Chynoweth pressed Stivers for more
details of his command.

"Do my troops have the new M-1 rifle?" he wanted to know. Stivers
roared with laughter. "No, and it's easy to see from that question that
you haven't been in the Islands long this time. These troops don't
even have Springfields!"

"Well," demanded Chynoweth, "for God's sake, what do they have?"
Stivers told him the whole ghastly truth. Those troops who had rifles
had the long, unmanageable 1917 Enfields. There were still insufficient Enfields to provide one for each man by the time mobilization
had been completed. The division's artillery, ancient mountain guns on
wooden wheels, had been obsolete for a quarter of a century. There
was no transportation, few American officers and few trained officers
of any kind. When he made acquaintance once again with MacArthur
the next day, the message on equipment was just as bleak. But
MacArthur did highlight one positive advantage Chynoweth's troops
had, and that was that they would be fighting over the terrain on which
they had trained. Chynoweth left MacArthur's presence inspired, like
so many before him, by his enthusiasm and rhetoric. After telling his
staff at Fort San Pedro, "of the unbelievable mobility they would
achieve, and the decentralized, all-out instruction which would fit
them for blitzkrieg in spite of the handicaps of equipment shortages,"
he became visibly annoyed by his staff's polite skepticism. It fell upon

Lieutenant Colonel Allen Thayer, commanding 62nd Infantry, to tell
the newly arrived divisional commander the facts of life:

> Sir, I am afraid that you have been misinformed as to your division's
> potential. Certainly as to its immediate abilities. The troops have no
> basic training upon which to build—the regiments, at this point, are lit-
> tle more than mobs. Furthermore, the few Filipino officers and non-
> commissioned officers (except for the half dozen regulars from the
> Philippine Scouts) have had so little training themselves that they are
> useless as instructors. We have about a dozen American Reserve Offi-
> cers in the entire Division, who are fairly well trained but without com-
> bat experience. They speak only English. The Filipino officials speak
> mostly Tagalog, and many do not understand English too readily. The
> men speak a variety of dialects, understand English little or none and
> Tagalog only slightly better.

Chynoweth was to recall many times General MacArthur's reassuring words to him in Manila, that the troops of the 61st would be
fighting over the very terrain on which they had been trained, and
wondered "if the General had been merely trying to be encouraging,
or if he had been misled or misinformed by his own staff, for none of
these men had had *any* combat training on *any* beaches or terrain."
Not only were the Enfields in short supply but 15 per cent had broken extractors for which there were no replacements. The reservists,
who had had the benefit of five months' training, were of the standard
of an American recruit after three weeks' training. They could not
shoot, since they had been rationed to five rounds a man, but now all
ammunition stocks had to be reserved for the grim day when these
unassuming peasants, plucked from their paddy fields, were to confront arguably the best, most seasoned and highly motivated of the
world's combat troops.[71]
It would be reassuring to think that the neglect and unpreparedness encountered by Chynoweth was due to his division being posted
away from Luzon, the perceived seat of initial contact. Sadly, it was a
common story: "shortages and improvizations (were) much the same
throughout the archipelago."[72] Brigadier General Clyde A. Selleck
commanded the 71st Division from its activation on 14 November
1941. "The 71st Division of which one regiment was left in Negros,
included some 6,000 under-trained and under-equipped peasants
with some high school and college students from Negros. In the words

of Gen. Selleck, it was short of everything. It only had a sufficiency of spirit."[73]

There was no electricity or furniture of any description in the Division. His Engineer Battalion was obliged to work on the approach road to the division's camp rather than on combat training, and its Anti Tank Battalion was never organized. Indeed, not one Anti Tank Battalion in the whole of the Philippine Army was ever organized, and what was worse, most divisions went into combat without field artillery regiments. There was never any training at divisional level and not one division would be fully mobilized before the Japanese attack came. Companies and regiments were half to three-quarters their authorized strength.[74]

On 4 December, 71st Division was placed under Major General J.M. Wainwright's command in the North Luzon Force. "Official visits, written instructions, briefings on war plans were practically nil," wrote Selleck. "As Divisional Commander I made calls at higher headquarters to acquaint them with our state of unpreparedness and lack of equipment."[75] Wainwright's North Luzon Force attracted the bulk of the military assets with the remainder distributed down to Major General George M. Parker Junior's South Luzon Force and Brigadier General, later Major General, William F. Sharp's Visayan Mindanao Force. Nine Philippine divisions were therefore assigned to Luzon and only three for the defense of the Visayan-Mindanao area. MacArthur turned down the offer of an American National Guard division because, by his estimate, he had in the American and Philippine infantry sufficient bayonets to deal with any possible contingency. He also preferred the available shipping to be dedicated to the carriage of equipment and supplies. Curiously, although Congress extended the draft, it had required the discharge and repatriation of all selective servicemen over the age of twenty-four. As Eisenhower observed: "Days before the war began, these men left Manila for San Francisco."[76]

The official concept of B-17 operations was as a supplement to the coastal artillery, not as strategic bombers. Although they were armed, they needed fighter cover for strategic offense, but range was a problem since the aircraft in U.S. Pursuit Squadrons, unlike the Japanese, had not been fitted with drop tanks to extend their range. The Philippines was of course U.S. territory and it was technically possible to assign significant air elements without transgressing the understanding of "Europe First." In response to an inquiry from the Adjutant

General's Department as to how many additional squadrons the existing airfields could accommodate, MacArthur's Headquarters replied on 19 August 1941:

Immediately	10 Pursuit Squadrons
	7 Bombardment Squadrons
	3 Heavy Bombardment Squadrons
3 months' time	3 Heavy Bombardment Squadrons
6 months' time	3 Pursuit Squadrons
	2 Medium Bombardment Squadrons
	4 Heavy Bombardment Squadrons

Thus, the total enhancements which could be accommodated within 6 months (up to February 1942) were: 13 Pursuit Squadrons, 9 Medium Bombardment Squadrons and 10 Heavy Bombardment.

The first squadron of nine B-17Ds arrived in the Philippines in early September at approximately the same time that General Clagett completed a strategic study for MacArthur.[77] Clagett identified 61 potential target areas within non-stop range of air bases in the Philippines but, more ominously, also identified at least 47 hostile airfields (37 of which could take heavy bombers) capable of bombing the Philippines. Clagett believed that by M-Day each of the 37 fields could support the minimum of one group of 27 bombers and be targeted against the Philippines in a few hours. A study report in MacArthur's papers, "To bomb Tokyo effectively using B-17 type airplanes," demonstrated the elasticity of the notion of coastal defense and also MacArthur's offensive spirit.[78] There was rather more than an outside anticipation that Stalin would allow Vladivostok to be used as an air base from which B-17 raids would be launched upon Japan's paper cities.

In early 1941, there were only two major army airfields in the Philippines: Clark, approximately 50 miles northwest of Manila, and Nichols to the south of the capital. Nichols, unlike Clark which had a turf airstrip, had a paved runway, but neither was sufficiently large to accommodate B-17s safely. General Grunert had recognized that airfields were the key to the satisfactory defense of the archipelago. He planned six major fields, four on Luzon and two on Mindanao, and many smaller ones situated strategically throughout the islands. The $2,773,000 obtained in July 1941 for airfield construction had swelled to $4,654,350 by 30 November. The problem was that there was too much to do and too little time in which to do it. There was a shortage of engineer expertise, labor and equipment. Moreover, the rainy season in western Luzon, where most of the work had to be done, lasted from June to November.[79]

The build-up of air power was channeled into the upgraded Nichols and Clark fields in Luzon, fighters to the former and fighters and bombers to the latter. The problem was that the aircraft were arriving before the infrastructure was in place to support them. Marshall, Arnold and Brereton were all aware that they were taking a calculated risk.[80] There was little by way of air defense, no radar, little space for dispersal and no suitable alternative fields for large numbers of bombers. Provision had been made in fiscal year 1942 "for completion of three detector stations and one information center."[81] A signal to the Adjutant General on 6 October 1941 advised: "Initial shipment detectors received. Request dispatch of civilian technical team for use in connection with the installation and maintenance of aircraft warning service detector equipment be expedited." There was an increasing sense of urgency but this congestion and apparent confusion has to be viewed in the context of MacArthur's dictum that the Japanese would not attack before April 1942. On 30 October 1941, he instructed his Liaison Officer at the British Commander in Chief's Headquarters at Singapore to tell the Commander in Chief "that I am in entire accord with his suggestion believe that the present Japanese Cabinet is preparatory in nature and intended to place Japan in readiness for possible action, probably not to be anticipated before next spring."

When General Clyde Selleck assumed command of the 71st Division, food was procured locally. There was no comprehensive supply plan in existence. The problem facing the office of the Chief Quartermaster in Manila lay in requisitioning combat supplies and materiel for the massively expanded Philippine Army over long lines of communication. It was not simply the time factor which was the principal concern but essentially one of finance. Technically, the United States was responsible for the defense of the Philippines but limited defense funding was prioritized—mostly elsewhere. From August 1940, Quezon had attempted to secure the release of $50,000,000 sugar duty to start military preparations under the guidance of the U.S. Government. In September 1941, the War Department recommended that Congress authorize the release of these paltry funds, but Congress demurred until after the attack on Pearl Harbor. The Chief Quartermaster therefore had no funds with which to requisition supplies from the San Francisco depot for the Philippine Army. Only after the Philippine Army had begun mobilizing after 1 September 1941 did funds come on stream. Marshall authorized the purchase of essential items with special U.S. Army allocations from the President's Emergency Fund. However, due to low shipping priorities, no Quartermaster supplies requisitioned for the Philippine Army and the defense reserves ever reached the Philippines.[82]

MacArthur's eleventh hour change of plan from the limited War Plan Orange-3 defense of the Manila area to a wider one embracing the protection of all the islands was sound in theory but, given the prevailing supply situation, was not logistically sustainable. The Philippines coastline is longer than that of the United States. While it was possible to predict reasonably confidently that the Japanese would land at Lingayen Gulf, the Gulf is 600 miles long and spans three provinces. There were many more beaches than troops available to defend them. MacArthur's concept of fighting on the beaches meant that the limited combat supplies and war materiel would be taken forward and dispersed at the expense of stocking the depots on the Bataan peninsula and Corregidor with sufficient supplies to maintain 43,000 men and 7,000 men respectively for 180 days. As is so often the case in peacetime, when there is pressure on manpower and equipment it is in the nature of warrior generals to prefer combat and combat support troops to logisticians. Immediately prior to the Japanese attack, Brigadier General Charles C. Drake, the Chief Quartermaster, had less than 1,300 officers and men to provide logistic support to the 100,000 men of the Regular Army, the Philippine Scouts and the Philippine Army—just under 1.3 per cent of the force. At that time, the Quartermaster Corps was also responsible for the complicated operation for military purposes of the extensive motor, rail and water transportation network within the Philippines.[83]

8

SERENITY AND
CONFIDENCE

M eanwhile, internment plans were being refined at MacArthur's Headquarters. In a 25 August 1941 signal sent to the Adjutant General, the number of potential alien enemy and malcontents thought to require internment or restraint had been categorized as: Class A (immediate) 3,330 and Class B (possible internment) 12,843. It was proposed to use both the old and the new Bilibid prisons. A component of the American counter-intelligence machinery was the *niseis*, second generation Japanese immigrants. A prominent *nisei* was Richard Sakakida who, together with Arthur Komori, was sent into Manila in April 1941 to infiltrate the Japanese community. Sakakida's cover story was that he had arrived in Manila as a crew member of an American ship which he had jumped to find employment in Manila. Both *nisei* were controlled from MacArthur's headquarters at Fort Santiago. Sakakida was given a job in the Marsman Trading Company in the complaints department. His role was to observe and identify Japanese nationals suspected of working for Japanese military intelligence in Manila.[1] It did not take Sakakida long to discover that approximately half the Japanese males in Manila were Japanese military reservists[2] and that Japanese Military Intelligence in the Philippines was well prepared for the forthcoming invasion. "They had superbly detailed maps and layouts of the labyrinth of

144

tunnels that the United States had built at Corregidor. They knew the location of every coastal artillery battery and they had in their possession a detailed description of our weapons and firepower."[3]

On 21 October 1941, Kihara reported to Tokyo that the ground for an air base was being leveled in the central Mindanao district. Apparently an underground hangar and oil tanks were being planned but, to the Japanese, the building was not progressing as quickly as might be expected. According to Kihara, large heavy bombers were expected in Mindanao shortly.[4] Much of the Magic traffic out of the Manila Japanese Consulate concerned the movement of shipping. Sutherland recalled having seen reports from the Consul of ship movements. The diplomatic messages that Army signals intercepted in the Purple code were delivered in raw form to the Navy decoding center on Corregidor. Only the Navy had the facilities for decryption and translation and there was no guarantee the Army got all its messages back. "I have had to barter like a rug merchant throughout the war to get the intelligence I have needed from the Navy," complained MacArthur.[5] By the time the diplomatic message of Japan breaking off negotiations with the United States had been decrypted, the news of the attack on Pearl Harbor had been broadcast over Manila commercial radio five hours previously.[6]

On 4 November, the Japanese Consul in Manila reported the arrival of 2–3,000 brown soldiers at the Fort Stotsenburg barracks and that they were "not too friendly with American soldiers." These were probably logistic troops in support of the Army Air Corps.[7] Only two days later, in a signal to Marshall, MacArthur insisted that the presence of colored soldiers would only exacerbate a difficult racial situation. "If white units are not available in the United States, it would be preferable to organize Philippine units with materiel furnished from the United States and Officer Personnel from the United States." In addition, the Japanese Consul Nihro reported further construction work at Tarallo on Miguel Airfield,[8] that the wooden bridges on the highway between Tarallo and Lingayen had been replaced with concrete bridges, and that approximately 200 barracks had been constructed near Tarallo overlooking the Lingayen Gulf. This type of intelligence traffic became a regular feature but it was not all one way. For example, on 5 November, Tokyo instructed Secretary Yuki to conduct an investigation for the Naval General Staff. At each "port of call" he was to enumerate the conditions at airports; the types and number of planes at each; the warships and the machinery belonging to the land forces; and the state of progress being made on all equipment and establishments.[9] During November and December 1940, Japanese military personnel had flown seven missions in commercial aircraft across Luzon, conducting detailed photographic reconnaissance of American and Filipino bases.[10] Small wonder that MacArthur would claim: "Never in military history did an army know so much about the enemy prior to actual engagement."[11]

At the political level in Manila most attention was reserved for the forthcoming elections on 11 November. There was some jitteryness about the risks and threat of war but overall there was an overriding yet irrational conviction that "it won't happen to us." The as yet to be mobilized officers of the Thirty-Second and Thirty-Third Infantry held a party at the Fiesta Pavilion in the Manila Hotel on 25 October, which was followed by one held there by the offshore patrol officers on 7 November. "Many felt that war was still remote . . . and the sense of urgency was lost on many people."[12] An exception to that rule was Brigadier General Vicente Lim, Commanding General of the 41st Division. On 27 November 1941 he had written a letter to his wife who was at the time in the United States.

> War is here now and our people have not felt it yet, because of ignorance. It is rampant in the Filipino mind to think only of how much money is coming in from the United States and the salaries they are going to get. They have not found it out yet that the enemy is on top of us and their lives and property are at stake.[13]

Some leaders within the National Assembly asked Quezon to defer the call-up of conscripts until after the 11 November election so that the men could vote. The matter was referred to MacArthur who rejected it out of hand.[14]

The relationship between MacArthur and Quezon on the one hand and Sayre on the other remained tense. On 21 October, at a dinner to mark the second anniversary of Sayre's arrival in Manila, the High Commissioner spoke of "the whole future of the civilized world (hanging) upon the strength and unity of groups like ourselves."[15] Manuel Roxas was present, as was Admiral Hart, but the President was absent, as was MacArthur. Of the latter's absence, one of Sayre's aides suggested the General "was protecting his 'attitude of messianic aloofness' or he might have thought that Admiral Hart's higher rank would be too noticeable. Or he might not have gone because Quezon had not attended."[16] Whatever the reason, it did not bode well for the strength and unity of the group.

Too much weight was given to MacArthur's infectious optimism and to his assertion that, if the Japanese came, it would not be until April 1942 at the earliest. But arguably, the principal reason why the Japanese threat was not taken seriously was because the Japanese were simply not rated for their martial qualities. If they were unwise enough to take on the might of the accumulating forces in the Philippines it would be no contest. The American correspondent Clark Lee wrote of Hart's ships riding at anchor in Manila Bay: "They certainly are beautiful. When the Japs come down here, they'll be playing in the Big League for the first time in their lives."[17] The Filipinos themselves observed the inability of Japan to truly dominate China without having the remotest comprehension of the enormity of that military task: How could the Japanese get anywhere with "cardboard" tanks and flimsy planes?'[18]

General Claire Chennault, American liaison officer and air adviser to General Chiang Kai Shek, warned that the Japanese pilots in their Mitsubishi Zero fighters were of the highest quality, but he was ignored. Clark Lee had been at Nichols Field watching the Curtess P-40s take off and land: "It was undoubtedly the best pursuit ship in the world, certainly better than anything the Japs could hope to have."[19] There was an assumption that Japanese pilots would have poor eyesight due to the perception of the racial stereotype of the squinting Japanese. The Royal Air Force had informed the Committee of Imperial Defence in March 1920 that: "the Japanese are not apt pilots, probably for the same reason that keeps them indifferent horsemen."[20]

Major General Lewis Brereton, MacArthur's choice to command the Far East Air Force (FEAF), arrived in Manila on 3 November accompanied by his Chief of Staff, Colonel Francis M. Brady. In Brereton's briefcase were two top secret messages.

One was from Marshall giving MacArthur the requisite authority to fight the coming land battle as he saw fit. The other was from Arnold concerning the state of the air assets in the Philippines. Brereton had under his command 8,000 officers and men and more than 300 aircraft including 35 heavy bombers, a greater concentration than anywhere else. Consideration was even being given to the transfer of B-17s from Hawaii to the Philippines. The problem was that less than half of the aircraft in Brereton's FEAF were suitable for combat and the bulk of the equipment required for air defense was still awaiting shipment from the United States.[21] The Arnold memorandum offered the prospect of redressing the FEAF situation with the promise of the requisite shipments over the winter period which had already begun. MacArthur was ecstatic. Now he could see movement; now at last the Philippines was being afforded the priority he had demanded. He jumped up from his desk and hugged the startled Brereton, saying "Lewis, you are as welcome as the flowers in May." "Dick," he said, turning to Sutherland, "they are going to give us everything we have asked for." 4th November was one of MacArthur's most satisfying days.[22] He then gave Brereton "the most concise and clear cut estimate of the situation . . . it seemed that nothing would happen before 1 April 1942."[23]

The excitement carried through to the evening and when he got home MacArthur wanted to share the news of his good fortune and promised reinforcement, perhaps even to gloat. He told Jean to ring Hart, three floors below, to see whether it would be OK for MacArthur to call on him. Hart replied in the affirmative and MacArthur set off, in his pink bathrobe. After boasting about the size of his command, MacArthur said to Hart: "Get yourself a real Fleet, Tommy, then you will belong." Hart listened to the patronizing talk and later wrote that "under the circumstances it was not pleasant." He confided in his wife: "Douglas is, I think, no longer altogether sane—he may not have been for a long time."[24]

Although MacArthur had a clear idea of what Brereton was required to do, he had little grasp of the size of the problem. As was so often the case with his subordinate functional commanders, he gave them the task in anticipation that they would deliver. "There was neither equipment nor money nor manpower organized and available for the immediate 100 per cent implementation of the program required," wrote Brereton in his diary. "It was a question of improvising all along the line."[25] Nichols, and other airfields being upgraded and brought into emergency service at Aparri and Vigan in northern Luzon, and Legaspi in southern Luzon, had virtually no air defense. Clark had some 3-inch and 37mm anti-aircraft guns, but the ammunition for the 3-inch guns was fused for low altitude use, so that aircraft flying above 27,000 feet were immune from their effects.[26] This intelligence was already in the hands of the Japanese. So great was the threat of sabotage that aircraft were parked close together for their physical protection, thus ignoring or accepting the risk of attack from the air. "Conditions were disappointing," wrote Brereton. "The idea of imminent war seemed far removed from the minds of most. Work hours, training schedules, and operating procedure were still based on the good old days of peace conditions in the tropics."[27] Instead of being allowed to tackle the immediate problem of unpreparedness, Brereton was sent off on an 11,500-miles odyssey on the first stage of liaising with prospective allies at Rabaul, Port Moresby, Townsville and Melbourne. A new southern route avoiding Midway and Wake which were in close proximity to the Japanese military had become a pressing requirement. By 10 November, Brereton had put into effect an alert system. On that day, which was immediately prior to his departure on the reconnaissance to Australia, he had a meeting with MacArthur. "I got the impression that his belief in 1 April as the earliest probable date when hostilities might commence had been severely shaken since my earlier conferences with him." The shortage of radar equipment was partly offset by the employment of air watchers posted at strategic points, who had telephone or telegraph contact with their control at Nielson Field. Although seven radar sets would reach the Philippines by the first week in December, only two sets were operational by the time the Japanese attacked.

Since the Navy controlled the decoding systems, urgent intelligence was understandably disseminated by the Chief of Naval Operations. In a signal to Hart dated 24 November, with the requirement that he "inform the senior army officer in your area," the message read:

> Chances of favorable outcome of U.S.-Japanese negotiations are very doubtful. This situation together with statements of Japanese Government and movements of their naval and military forces intimate in our opinion that a surprise aggressive movement in any direction including attack on Philippines or Guam is a possibility.

Addressees were ordered to treat the information with "the utmost secrecy in order not to complicate an already tense situation or precipitate Japanese action."[28]

On 25 November 1941, the Chief of Naval Operations sent a further signal to Hart:

> Preparations are becoming apparent in China, Formosa and Indo China for an early aggressive movement of some character although as

yet there are no clear indications as to its strength or whether it will be directed against the Burma Road, Thailand, Malay Peninsula, Netherlands East Indies or the Philippines.

This message was subsequently extended as though from the President to Sayre to tell Quezon: "I am relying upon the full cooperation of his government and his people. Please impress upon him the desirability of avoiding public pronouncement or action that might make the situation more difficult."[29] On the same day in Washington, the Secretary for War, Henry Stimson, had one of his by now regular meetings with Cordell Hull and Roosevelt. The President opined that the Japanese were likely to initiate a pre-emptive strike as early as 1 December, in which case, what should America do? "The question was how we should maneuver them into the position of firing the first shot without allowing too much danger to ourselves. It was a difficult proposition. Hull laid out his general broad propositions on which the thing should be vested—the freedom of the seas."[30]

On 27 November, the War Department advised the Commanding Generals in the Philippines and Hawaii that negotiations with Japan appeared to have terminated and hostile action was possible at any moment. "If hostilities cannot, repeat cannot, be avoided, the United States desires that Japan commit the first overt act."[31] Reconnaissance was authorized at the discretion of the local commander. MacArthur attended a conference that day with Sayre and Hart (who was in receipt of a "war warning") to discuss the warnings they had separately received and to plan the way forward. Sayre recorded how MacArthur had paced "back and forth . . . smoking a black cigar and assuring Admiral Hart and myself in reassuring terms that there would be no Japanese attack before the spring. Admiral Hart felt otherwise."[32] The signals he had received on 24 and 25 November 1941 were unambiguous and could not be lightly set aside. The day previous, the Japanese generals and admirals assigned to the attack on the Philippines met aboard Vice Admiral Ibo Takahashi's flagship *Ashigara* off Formosa to finalize plans. The following day, the carrier force which was to attack Pearl Harbor sailed from the Kurile Islands. X-Day was still to be determined but it was obviously imminent.[33]

The gloomy news accumulating stimulated Quezon to speak on 27 November of the need to stand "to the last man" with the United States. The next day he demonstrated what he freely admitted was his inconsistency in a talk to the University of the Philippines. He once said there was no place for consistency in public affairs, "only little minds were bedeviled by this."[34] His extemporaneous talks were always susceptible to the influence of the emotion of the occasion. The source of the problem was the ongoing matter of civil defense, which Sayre insisted was the Commonwealth's responsibility and which he believed Quezon had accepted as the Commonwealth's responsibility. In reality, little had been done. Air raid practices were arranged but largely ignored, first aid stations had been built and evacuation plans made but little could be done short of declaring major conurbations to be open towns or cities. In Manila, the water table was so high that shelters could not be dug and, even if there was transport to evacuate the population, where would they go? Quezon declared that "if war breaks out soon and people die here unprotected by the bombs, those men who have stopped me from doing what I should have done ought to be hanged—every one of them on one lamp post."[35] Sayre was both distressed and incensed at what he saw to be Quezon's attempt to shift responsibility for the lack of civil defense preparations. Sayre's position was not helped by Ickes and Mayor Fiorello La Guardia, national director of civil defense in America, declaring Sayre to be the civil defense director in the Philippines. Totally bemused, Sayre wrote to MacArthur, saying "there must be some mistake since I have had neither recent conversation nor correspondence with Mayor La Guardia."[36] Ickes clearly had had his finger in the pie. MacArthur agreed with Sayre's position. "The executive power in the PI for peacetime execution of measures involving extraordinary controls of the civil population are vested in the Commonwealth Government."[37] The fury and consternation in Washington over Quezon's hang them on lamp post speech caused Quezon to reconsider his position and step back from the brink. This was to be his last major confrontation in peacetime.

On 28 November, Sutherland sent orders to Major General Wainwright, Commander North Luzon Force. "It is desired that you take necessary action to insure immediate readiness for any eventuality, but without creating local agitation or more comment than is unavoidable among the civilian population or in your command."[38] Their orders were to "prevent a landing." In the event a landing was made, he was to "attack and destroy the landing force." By a process of elimination, the most probable landing beaches were reduced to an accumulated length of 250 miles. The Navy advised that the influence of the prevailing monsoon meant that the Lamon Bay area could be excluded as a potential landing zone.[39] Only one regiment per division was available to man the beaches and prepare obstacles because the remainder were still under training.

Each of the Philippine Army's ten Field Artillery Regiments was intended to be equipped with 24 75mm guns. In mid November, an audit of equipment revealed there to be only 96 First World War 75mm guns, of which 14 were on wooden wheel mounts, scattered throughout the archipelago. These had originally been 18-pounder guns, rebarreled to fire 75mm ammunition. In addition there were 52 2.95-inch pack howitzers, the 1898 Vickers-Maxim model, designed to be broken down into constituent parts for transportation on mule or horseback. There was therefore a shortfall of 92 guns and the guns that were available were obsolete. The issue of the artillery was therefore prioritized according to task. The leading edge divisions, assigned to guard Lingayen Gulf and, in MacArthur's words, to hold the beaches "at all costs" the 11th and 21st Divisions—were issued with sixteen 75s and eight 2.95s each. The three divisions defending Central and Southern Luzon—the 31st, 41st and 51st Divisions—were each given sixteen 75s and four 2.95s each. Selleck's 71st Division and the 91st Division, which had been moved northward into Luzon as the strategic reserve, were assigned eight 75s each as well as twelve 2.95s for the 71st and eight for the 91st. The 61st and 81st Divisions, in Visayan, were allocated sixteen 75s and twelve ancient 3-inch naval guns. The 101st Division, in Mindanao, was to have four 2.95s.[40] America was preparing to fight her first land battle of the Second World War equipped with the weapons of the First.

The state of the standard infantry weapons and ammunition was no better. Of the mortar bombs for the 3-inch Stokes mortar, 70 per cent were found to be dud.[41] "With adequately trained men, though, and dependable ammunition, these weapons were still effective. But spare parts were missing and many of the machine guns were incomplete."[42] One American officer reflected that "many units went into battle without ever having fired their basic arm."[43] The 11th Division's case was typical of the artillery situation among the rest. Its depleted artillery regiment was not available for the defense of the beaches, coming into action for the first time with only 60 per cent of its manpower as the Division withdrew into Bataan in late December. "The artillery men were poorly trained and contributed little to the support of the infantry when they did begin firing."[44] Subsequently and inexplicably, 24 155mm M1918 Grand Puissance Filloux guns were found in a depot. They were originally intended to protect the coasts of the southern islands but were taken into use as field artillery. Fifty half-tracks mounting the ancient M1897 75mm gun, and intended for the immobilized anti-tank battalions, arrived immediately prior to the outbreak of hostilities. Three new field artillery regiments were accordingly raised. Two were assigned to Wainwright's North Luzon Force and one to Parker's South Luzon Force.[45]

MacArthur had been obliged through force of circumstances to quietly reassess the most likely timing of a Japanese attack. The reality of the situation facing him meant his long-held assertion that there would be no attack before April had simply evaporated. He now thought January likely and confided as much in Clark Lee. If he had taken a macro strategic view of the Far East, he might have guessed that the Japanese had discounted amphibious operations during both January and February because weather conditions in Malaya would be unsuitable for the projected landing operations. By process of simple calculation, therefore, an attack could be anticipated in days rather than weeks. Lunar tide conditions would be best for amphibious operations on or about December 8. Imperial General Headquarters took these factors into account in determining X-Day, which was still to be decided upon.[46] Although MacArthur's subsequent actions and warning orders quite clearly indicated his change of mind, he appeared unable to admit in words that he had been wrong. In public and in his dealings with allies he still rehearsed his "not before April" line.

Hart and MacArthur settled their "who does what" with air patrolling at the end of November. The Navy, with their Catalinas, 32 consolidated PBY flying boats, took responsibility for the south of Luzon and up to Indo Chinese waters, while Brereton's B-17s would patrol the sea towards Formosa.[47] Soon these patrol planes observed large numbers of Japanese warships and transports in the South China Sea, apparently bound in the general direction of Camranh Bay, Indo China. Two B-24s equipped for high altitude photo-reconnaissance were assigned to the Philippines.[48] They had not arrived by 2 December but USAFFE requested the War Department to have them photograph the Pelews (sic) en route. MacArthur promised the Commander in Chief Singapore that as soon as the B-24s arrived, he would "ascertain War Department views with reference Camranh Bay."[49] Hart sent his cruisers southward.

On 29 November, USAFFE Headquarters ordered the Commanding Officer of 200th Coast Artillery to "Assume alert position. Further

information will follow."[50] The coastal artillery guarding the entrance
to Manila and Subic Bays was under the command of Brigadier General George F. Moore. MacArthur's coastal artillery plan was his solution to the absence of any major dependable naval defense. There
were 155 large guns in stock in Manila depots in 1941. Their mounts
were in the process of being poured when war broke out. Within
General Moore's command were four regiments of American, Scout
and Philippine Army regular troops manning three sea coast artillery
units and one anti-aircraft unit. The coastal artillery's vital ground was
the tadpole-shaped island of Corregidor. A rocky island, four miles
long and about half a mile wide at its widest point, it commands the
entrance into Manila Bay, rather like a cork in a bottle. It is twenty-
six miles from Manila, ten miles from Cavite and three miles from
Bataan. There were twenty-three batteries on Corregidor and the
nearby islands which provided interlocking and supportive fire. In
total, there were 56 coastal guns and mortars, thirteen anti-aircraft
batteries totaling 76 guns and ten 60-inch Perry searchlights.[51] Many
of the guns were antiquated. For example, the four 12-inch mortars
at Battery Way have casting dates of 1903. Nevertheless, they would
have been useful in their purpose of denying Manila Bay to enemy
shipping. The problem was that the enemy were not to attempt a
naval assault on the Bay, the *raison d'être* for Moore's command. Two
of his batteries stood out, exposed like bulls eyes in a target, daring to
be hit. The remainder were on disappearing mounts on parapets.
General Moore established his Headquarters in one of the laterals at
the south side of the ventilated Malinta Tunnel, which had been
largely completed before the Japanese invasion. There was a tramline
running the 925 feet length of the 25 feet wide main tunnel. From
the sides of the reinforced walls ran 24 main laterals—13 on the north
side and 11 on the south side. Each lateral was approximately 160 feet
long and 15 feet wide. There were two other sets of laterals, one of
which became a 100-bed hospital and the other MacArthur's headquarters.

A 28 November 1941 signal from Marshall, in response to one of
enthusiastic reassurance sent earlier by MacArthur, recorded how
"The Secretary of War and I were highly pleased to receive your
report that your command is ready for any eventuality."[52] In a letter
of 1 December to Marshall, concerning the anti-aircraft plan, Mac-
Arthur did not neglect the opportunity once again to add words of
reassurance. The question was, who was he trying to reassure? "Army

morale here, among both American and Filipino troops, is high and in spite of many deficiencies [among which were serviceable horse gas masks][53] in our present state of development I have every confidence that we can hold our own."[54] Roosevelt later complained how he had been repeatedly misled by MacArthur as to the real situation in the Philippines. "If I had known the true situation," remarked Roosevelt, "I could have babied the Japanese along quite a lot longer."[55]

By now, American and British intelligence were well aware of Japanese maneuvering but they lacked precise information. On 1 December 1941, Imperial General Headquarters decided that 8 December would be X-Day[56] which, to the Americans, was M-Day. President Roosevelt, never shy of direct involvement in military affairs, particularly naval affairs, sent secret personal instructions to Hart to form a Defensive Information Patrol. The President had never before intervened to such a degree as this, which might suggest that his intentions may have been rather more than intelligence gathering. He was precise in the requirement. Three small vessels were to be chartered and manned and adequately armed to indicate that they were U.S. warships. They were to sail north into the South China Sea and Gulf of Siam and take up positions astride the most likely southerly routes for a Japanese invasion fleet.

One of the three small ships was the two-funneled yacht *Isabel*, commanded by Lieutenant John Walker Payne Junior. The other two were not prepared in time.[57] The skipper was given an alibi, to tell his crew that they were searching for a downed plane. Extra lifeboats were taken aboard. Payne was told that if necessary he was to fight his ship, which was not to fall into Japanese hands. On 5 December, Japanese aircraft detected *Isabel* off Camranh Bay and shadowed her throughout the day, but took no overt action. If Roosevelt was trying to provoke the Japanese, they were not prepared to prejudice their complicated maneuver plan of multiple, concurrent attacks through the precipitate action of neutralizing a small craft doing them no harm. Accordingly, Hart recalled the *Isabel*. Hart was convinced that Roosevelt intended to provoke an incident[58] to justify American intervention through a declaration of war in the event that Japan bypassed American territories and attacked the British and Dutch.[59]

Major Gerald H. Wilkinson worked for a British sugar brokering company in Manila, Theo H. Davies & Company. Wilkinson was married and accompanied by his wife and children. His wife was a granddaughter of the founder of the British Pacific-wide company whose head office was in Honolulu. The sugar brokerage was a cover for Wilkinson, who was really the British Secret Intelligence Service's representative in the Philippines. Willoughby knew of Wilkinson's purpose but was not impressed by the British mixture of commerce with intelligence. Moreover, Willoughby was peeved because the Briton had ignored American law in the Philippines which required enemy agents to register with the authorities! The fact remains that Wilkinson was one of the most effective agents in the region. He would later join MacArthur's staff and be among the few to be evacuated from Corregidor by submarine. On 3 December, he sent an urgent cipher about developments in Indo-China to his equivalent in Honolulu, Harry Dawson, the British Vice Consul there, concluding: "Our considered opinion concludes that Japan envisages early hostilities with Britain and U.S. Japan does not repeat not intend to attack Russia at present but will act in the South. You may inform Chiefs of American Military and Naval Intelligence Honolulu."

The American Army and Navy took no action, but SIS Agent Dawson's boss in Honolulu, the British Consul, John E. Russell, was also President of Theo H. Davies & Co., the company which provided Wilkinson with employment and cover. Russell read Wilkinson's cipher, fully comprehended its meaning and immediately rang the manager of the company's San Francisco office. Russell told the San Francisco manager, C.V. Bennett, to cancel all shipments to the Philippines, to try to turn around any shipments en route, and not to proceed with any more proposed sugar contracts.[60]

At 0530 hours on 2 December, a Japanese reconnaissance aircraft was seen over Clark Field but not challenged. On the following nights, Japanese aircraft were observed by Brereton's Pursuit patrols 50 miles off the Luzon coast, but they veered off once aware they had been detected. One of the two operational radar sets, the one at Iba Field, detected several unidentified aircraft in the Zambales area and Luzon Plain on the nights 5 and 6 December but there was no contact.[61] On 5 December, MacArthur ordered Moore to shoot down the next night intruder.[62] James writes of MacArthur responding to the threat of sabotage rather than to the threat of air attack. MacArthur signaled the Adjutant General to the effect that all the Air Corps stations had been placed on alert status, that the aircraft had been "dispersed" and were under guard. "All airdrome defense stations manned. Guards on installations increased. Counter subversive

activities . . . being organized and have started functioning in a limited manner."[63] MacArthur explained to Marshall that, "the heavy
bombers should be located south of the island of Luzon, where they
are reasonably safe from attack, but from where, through partial
utilization of auxiliary airfields, they can deliver their own blows."[64]
MacArthur's indomitable Chief Engineer, Colonel Hugh J. Casey,
found a more or less ideal site at the Del Monte pineapple plantation
on Mindanao. Here, 500 miles south of Clark, he had none of
Manila's cloying bureaucracy to frustrate him and there was a preponderance of willing and able men to do the work. In two weeks,
Del Monte's airstrip had been converted by a workforce of 1,500 men
into a mile long runway capable of accepting B-17s, well beyond the
range of Japanese aircraft based on Formosa. On 1 December, Mac-
Arthur ordered FEAF to move the 35 B-17s at Clark down to the safe
environment of Mindanao. The redeployment had been recommended to MacArthur by FEAF's Chief of Staff, Colonel Brady.[65] On
4 December, Casey advised Sutherland that, thus far, not one B-17
had arrived at Mindanao. Sutherland rang Brady and, in no uncertain
terms, ordered the B-17s to be moved. "General Brereton did not
want them to go," said Sutherland. "I ordered they be sent down anyway."[66] On 5 December, sixteen of the thirty-five B-17s flew down to
Mindanao. Manchester claims that Brereton was unaware only half
the B-17s had been flown south[67] while MacArthur wrote: "I never
learned why these orders were not promptly implemented."[68] Neither
of these statements is acceptable. Brereton defended his failure to act
as being due to reinforcements destined for Mindanao being shortly
anticipated. That in itself should not have been a compelling reason
for not putting those aircraft already in theater out of harm's way. The
Army Air Corps did appreciate their comfort and a pleasant social
environment, neither of which was on offer at Mindanao. Moreover,
their brother bombardment group, the 27th, planned to hold what
promised to be a memorable party in the Manila Hotel in honor of
Brereton on Sunday evening, the 7th December. The officers of the
19th wanted to be there. Brereton has been described as one of
the foremost party animals in the Air Corps, regarding such events as
being an essential instrument in the maintenance of *esprit de corps*.
All the while, Tokyo pressed the Japanese Consulate in Manila for the
latest intelligence of military and naval strength in the Philippines
prior to the intended attack. The intelligence sent back by Manila was

not always of the best quality. On 27 November 1941, the Office of the Chief of Naval Operations released information gathered by Japanese spies that there were 1,283 military and 26 naval planes on the islands, when in fact there were only 298 military and 43 naval planes at that time. On 29 November, Consul Nihro advised Tokyo that codes for which the office had no continuing use, as well as duplicate copies, had been destroyed. The next day, Nihro advised Tokyo he was unable to decipher their message to him of the 29th because he had destroyed the codes. The pressure of work increased to the degree that Nihro requested Kihara's return to Manila "as soon as possible." Kihara's return had been delayed due to a "providential" cold. Kihara had a key political function to perform following the anticipated Japanese success in the Philippines. On 5 December, Tokyo requested an immediate report on ships in port, as well as on the movements of capital ships.[69]

On 5 December the British Commander in Chief (designate) Far East, Vice Admiral Sir Tom Phillips, arrived to discuss war plans with Admiral Hart. Two Royal Navy capital ships, the battleship *Prince of Wales* and the battle cruiser *Repulse*, were to take up station as the spearhead of a strong British naval force, with reinforcements to follow. The capital ships' carrier, *HMS Indomitable*, had unfortunately run aground and been dry-docked. The emergence of irreconcilable national interests meant that Hart would no longer have to consider his subordination to Phillips. As Marshall informed MacArthur, who had been invited to the first meeting, "strategic direction by the British in the Far East area has been discarded." Coordination was now to be effected "by mutual cooperation." Accordingly, there would be a plethora of allied representatives with whom American commanders would have to cooperate in "a very complicated command system." Marshall then pointedly emphasized: "In such an arrangement, it is therefore of the utmost importance that the local United States Army and Navy commanders should be in complete accord and prepared to lead the way in both the planning and the conduct of operations."[70] After briefing his naval opposite numbers of his war plans *after April 1942*, MacArthur concluded: "Admiral Hart and I operate in the closest cooperation. We are the oldest and dearest friends." Leutze records that although "Hart's staff had trouble keeping their composure; the admiral maintained an impassive visage."[71] When MacArthur hosted earlier meetings with Phillips' predecessor Air Chief Marshal Sir Robert Brooke-Popham, there was an inevitable blaze of publicity. MacArthur liked it, and so did the British enjoy emphasizing their association both with the United States and a hint of a future alliance. Brooke-Popham had a habit of dozing off in the middle of MacArthur's pontifications. Phillips' visit was much more low-key. He was not seen in Manila but instead stayed at the home of Rear Admiral Francis W. Rockwell at Cavite.

Phillips recognized that his capital ships would be exposed if and when he had to take them northward from Singapore to oppose Japanese landings in northern Malaya. Phillips wanted Hart to assign two destroyer divisions for their protection. Agreement was already in place for U.S. destroyers to be based in Singapore if the U.S.A. was to join the war should Britain be attacked by Japan. Although Hart had variously described Phillips as "the best" and "good stuff" they were not, despite being of the same short stature, entirely going to see eye to eye. Here was Hart, who had been goaded so consistently by MacArthur for being the admiral of a small fleet, who had sent his larger ships to the safety of the south, now being asked to detach two destroyer divisions northward. Hart suggested Phillips should take destroyers from Hong Kong, to which Phillips replied that such a course of action was politically unpalatable. Hart ducked and wove in the arguments, which "got rather heated."[72] The Americans did not know the waters to the north and besides, the destroyers were needed to work in cooperation with Hart's cruisers and submarines.

Hart conceded that Destroyer Division 57 at Balikpapan was earmarked to deploy to Singapore on commencement of hostilities but he was not yet prepared to order them to move. On hearing subsequently of the anticipated Japanese amphibious expedition in the Gulf of Siam, USS *Blackhawk* and one destroyer division were ordered to sail from Balikpapan to Batavia and, once sailing westward, "were directed to proceed towards Singapore and placed under the orders of the British CinC."[73] By the time they arrived, HMS *Prince of Wales* and *Repulse* had been lost and Phillips was dead. Even if the American ships had been present during the battle, it is unlikely that they would have prevented these sinkings.

On Saturday, 6 December, Marshall learned through intercepts of Japan's intention that their Washington envoys would hand Hull an ultimatum. Marshall, there and then, wrote out in longhand the urgent information to alert MacArthur and Lieutenant General Walter Short, the Army Commander in Hawaii. "Japanese are presenting at 1:00 p.m. Eastern Standard Time today what amounts to an ultimatum.

Also they are under orders to destroy their code machine immediately. Just what significance the hour set may have we do not know but be on alert accordingly."[74] Communications with the Pacific were down, so this vital information was telephoned through the laborious means of Western Union.[75]

During the course of the party held in his honor at the Manila Hotel—"the best entertainment this side of Minskys"—Brereton had a conversation with Sutherland and Hart's Chief of Staff, Rear Admiral William R. Purnell. It seems that what both officers said to Brereton surprised him. Purnell had said: "It was only a question of days or perhaps hours before the shooting started." Sutherland chipped in, in agreement, adding that the War and Navy Departments believed hostilities might commence at any time. Brereton thereupon told Brady, his Chief of Staff, to place all units on combat alert with effect from Monday 8 December.[76]

At 2:30 a.m. on Monday, 8 December Manila time, a radio operator in Hart's headquarters received a terse transmission from Admiral Husband E. Kimmel's headquarters in Honolulu: "Air raid on Pearl Harbor. This is no drill."[77] Hart's telephone rang just after 3:00 a.m., after which he quickly dressed and rushed off to his operations room. No one bothered to tell the Army. They received their news due to the good fortune of a duty signalman picking up the information from a California radio station. MacArthur's telephone rang at 3:40 a.m. Sutherland told him of the attack on Pearl Harbor, to which he exclaimed, "Pearl Harbor! It should be our strongest point." Sutherland prepared a press release. "The American command here has been alerted and all populations are in readiness for defense." A second version, signed off by MacArthur, concluded "My message is one of serenity and confidence."[78] Shortly after Sutherland's call, Brigadier General Leonard T. Gerow, War Plans, telephoned MacArthur in confirmation of the news from Sutherland. MacArthur was to say later that he formed the "impression that the Japanese had suffered a set-back at Pearl Harbor."[79] What Gerow had told him was that Hawaii had suffered considerable damage and that he would not be surprised "if you get an attack there in the near future."[80]

Whatever the truth was, MacArthur must have seen the writing on the wall. If the Japanese had attacked American Pearl Harbor, they would have no political or military scruples in attacking the Philippines. He was unprepared, caught between two plans, neither of which, independently or collectively, offered any encouraging prospects. James, his principal biographer, wrote how MacArthur had done the best he could with the men, materiel and meager funds at his disposal and that he was the logical choice among the available American generals to build up a Philippine defense force. But he

must bear a large share of the blame for the pitiful situation of the fall of 1941, which would soon lead to military disaster . . . his overconfidence and unjustified optimism as to the abilities of himself, his staff, and the untried Filipino soldiers unfortunately became a contagion which ultimately affected even the War Department and the Joint Army and Navy Board.[81]

9

"ONE OF THE MORE SHOCKING DEFECTS OF THE WAR"

At the outbreak of war, the Rainbow strategy envisaged the Pacific Fleet operating from Pearl Harbor into the Central Pacific, taking the Japanese-held Caroline and Marshall Islands and setting up an advanced base at Truk. Thus, having secured its lines of communication the fleet, through its superiority, would be able to redress any deterioration which might have occurred in the defense of the Philippines. The problem was that the pre-emptive Japanese strike upon Pearl Harbor had, by 10 a.m. on the morning of 7 December Eastern Time, removed from the equation the supporting or avenging capability of the Pacific Fleet. The Japanese had seized the initiative by eliminating the Battle Force of the Pacific Fleet so that it would not interfere in their first-phase Southern operations. The Japanese concept of operations for the Philippines came in three stages: one, decisive aerial battles; two, the seizure of airfields by advance elements; and three, landings by the main ground forces.[1]

The attacking Japanese pilots had concentrated upon Pearl Harbor's Battle Force, sinking three battleships, capsizing one and damaging four others. Among the ships badly damaged were three light cruisers, three destroyers and various smaller vessels. The Army lost 96 planes: the Navy lost 92. Two thousand, two hundred and eighty men died, 1,109 were wounded. The Japanese, by comparison, lost 29 aircraft and 5 midget submarines.[2] Fortunately, the Japanese had not hit the Pearl Harbor repair shops or the oil storage sites, and the carriers were at sea.

When he heard the news of the attack on Pearl Harbor, MacArthur asked his wife for his Bible and read it before going off to the chaotic scenes in his office MacArthur had done well to recognize his need for spiritual comfort. Sayre, who had been awakened at 4 a.m. by his executive assistant, hit the nail on the head when he wrote: "Our entire military strategy had been based on holding Corregidor and some territory on the Bataan peninsula against capture, and waiting for the American main fleet to fight its way to our rescue. We now learned that there was no American fleet which would come."[4] Sayre was not precisely describing MacArthur's intended strategy but rather the strategy which realistically evolved because the key component, the Philippine Army, was insufficiently trained or prepared to deny the beaches of Luzon to an Imperial Japanese Army which had been at war since 1935. Having conceded command of the sea, being fatally unprepared to dominate the impending land battle, the only environment over which the United States retained any prospect of temporary dominance was the air over Luzon and the surrounding sea. Air superiority, no matter how temporary, became a key element to be defended at all costs, even though the Japanese always had a greater preponderance of aircraft with which to face the Americans.

President Quezon was in the executive "Mansion House" in the summer capital of Baguio, recovering from illness, when his telephone rang at between 5 and 6 a.m. His valet told him it was Jorge Vargas calling from Manila. When he heard this, he knew instinctively that the United States was at war with Japan for it was the only reason Vargas would have disturbed him at that hour. He was quite unprepared for the news that Pearl Harbor had been attacked. "You are joking; Pearl Harbor is the best defended naval station in the world. Where did you get that nonsense?" Vargas explained that he had been telephoned by United and Associated Press and their news had been confirmed by MacArthur.[5] Quezon returned to Manila. Before seven o'clock, a female reporter from the *Philippine Herald* was on the line, asking for a statement. "The zero hour has arrived," responded Quezon. "I expect every Filipino—man and woman—to do his duty. We have pledged our honor to stand to the last by the United States and we shall not fail her, happen what may." He summoned a meeting of the Council of State for the next morning.[6]

Brereton, having put the Air Corps on standby, reported to

MacArthur's headquarters at 5 a.m. Sixteen B-17s were at the Del Monte Field at Mindanao but nineteen were still at Clark, possibly unbeknown to MacArthur. The 3rd Pursuit Squadron at Iba Field, where the radar set operated out of a hut, and the 17th at Nichols, each had 18 P-40Es; the 20th at Clark had 18 P-40Bs. The recently arrived 21st and 34th Squadrons, at Nichols and Del Carmen fields respectively, had, again respectively, 18 cobbled-together P-40Es and obsolescent P-35s. There was a number of non-combat aircraft in addition to the twelve Philippine Army Air Corps' P-26s at Batangas.[7]

Allegedly Brereton requested of Sutherland permission to effect offensive action immediately after daybreak.[8] It is at this point that the available individual accounts and war diaries are more often than not at variance with one another. What actually happened has become a celebrated controversy which historians have striven, apparently unsuccessfully, to untangle. That was undoubtedly the aim of individuals desirous of protecting not only their own reputation but also that of MacArthur.

When the Japanese struck at Pearl Harbor, they also struck almost simultaneously at Kota Bharu, Malaya; Singora, Thailand; Singapore; Guam; Hong Kong and Wake Island, but not yet at the Philippines which, nine hours after the attack on Pearl Harbor had still not experienced the anticipated attack. In the meantime, Brigadier General Sutherland had not allowed Major General Brereton in to see MacArthur. On the face of it, this seems difficult to accept but, subsequently, Sutherland routinely denied senior officers access to MacArthur. Only later, when Major General George C. Kenney commanded MacArthur's air assets was Sutherland told by MacArthur to desist. Nonetheless it is strange that MacArthur, who was being visited by a distressed Admiral Hart at the time, did not demand to see and give precise orders to his air commander. Was it true that there was little sign of the Headquarters functioning properly for six hours due to what Manchester suggests as MacArthur's catatonic state? Manchester was not a hostile biographer but he chronicles the recollections of others, who saw MacArthur during the early hours of that fateful morning looking "gray, ill and exhausted." Manchester points out that MacArthur was in good company, for Napoleon at Waterloo had been catatonic also, Washington was in a daze at the Battle of Brandywine and Stonewall Jackson had been far below par at the crucial engagement of White Oak Swamp.[10]

It is possible that MacArthur had suffered an "overload."[11] In the space of a few hours he had to take in the unwelcome news of the attack on Pearl Harbor, a questioning of his credibility, the impending withdrawal of the Asiatic Fleet, Quezon perhaps striving again for neutrality, the problems posed by Brereton and the Air Corps, as well as a mass of similar problems. Hart, who is supposed to have seen him that morning, would not have made any public utterance if he had found MacArthur in a parlous state. He may not have liked MacArthur but, as an officer and a gentleman, he would have known what was right and proper. Besides, he had already confided to his wife his thoughts that MacArthur was unbalanced. Perhaps Sutherland, the man with the private pilot's license and who enjoyed interfering in air matters, denied Brereton access to MacArthur because he feared Brereton might be less restrained in what he said about MacArthur in the future. It is possible, but it is nothing more than conjecture. MacArthur expected loyalty from his subordinates and, more often than not, he reciprocated. The relationship in the inner command sanctum was decidedly masonic by nature if not by actuality.

Some historians have said there is no mystery; that MacArthur would have been fully involved in staff planning. However, the barometer by which the functioning of the staff should be measured is by reference to what the B-17s of the Air Corps were doing. They should either have been ordered to fly north to inflict damage on the Japanese in Formosa or, they should have been ordered south, away from the danger of the first, predictable attack upon Clark Field. But they were doing nothing. Apparently, Sutherland had given Brereton provisional agreement to prepare to attack Formosa and promised in the meantime to secure MacArthur's approval. Brereton's commanders found the provisional nature of the given authority incomprehensible. They regarded the proposed attack on the Japanese forces as the bread and butter, the *raison d'être* of the B-17s. Surely, they thought, the attack upon Pearl Harbor had been an overt action. Brereton recorded how he gave instructions to begin the planning to mount a bombing operation against Takao harbor, Formosa, where warships and transports were assembling, and also to prepare three aircraft for reconnaissance missions over Formosan airfields.[12] The loading of bombs was to await MacArthur's orders, which were not forthcoming until 11 a.m.—too late. In an interview after the war, MacArthur denied Brereton's version of events. He recalled no such recommendation to bomb Formosa ever being made.[13]

However, in an interview Sutherland admitted that Brereton "did propose the bomber attack against Formosa," but he asked "what was the target, where was the field? He didn't know, he had no target data . . . there were 20 fields in Formosa and General Brereton had no notion of what he would attack, and he almost certainly would lose his planes."[14] Whereas the Brereton Diaries did mention Takao harbor as a potential target, it has to be remembered that they were not a contemporaneous record, but written months after the events, parts even after the war. The Far East Air Force Diary was also potentially flawed. What was called *General Brereton's Headquarters Diary 8 Dec 41–24 Feb 42* was a collection of loose-leaf papers, held together by an *acco* fastener. The daily summaries 8–13 December give the year as 1942, with the summaries for 8–10 December corrected in ink. At the beginning of a new year, it is not uncommon to make the mistake of continuing to use the previous year in documents and checks. It is, however, unusual to use the upcoming year in documents ahead of that year. There is no explanation why this error occurred but the FEAF diary tends to corroborate Brereton's account quite closely. The compilers of *The Army Air Forces in World War II* regard the FEAF Diary as representing "a valuable record compiled closer to the events described than any other known source of comparable scope."[15]

Brereton tells how, after his first unsatisfactory 0500 meeting, he returned to his Headquarters at Nielson Field unable to take any offensive action whatsoever. The FEAF Summary of Activities picks up what must have been a second unsuccessful visit to MacArthur at "0715" and at 0900 there is an entry logged as follows: "In response to query from General Brereton a message received from General Sutherland advising planes not authorized to carry bombs at this time."[16] The B-17 pilots were profoundly dismayed by these developments. They wanted to strike at the Japanese in Formosa with everything they had and without delay. The need to avenge for Pearl Harbor was doubtless uppermost in their minds. When Brereton arrived for their briefing, he told them his orders were that they could not attack but could go on reconnaissance bombed up, but bombs and armaments were not to be used unless attacked.[17] Accordingly, three aircraft were prepared for reconnaissance of the Formosan airfields. Those manning the obsolete and obsolescent anti-aircraft guns were under orders not to engage enemy planes unless "the aircraft had dropped an object and that object had hit the ground and exploded."[18] The report by the aircraft warning service of enemy aircraft over Lingayen Gulf heading for Manila then led to all the B-17s at Clark Field being ordered into the air to patrol the sea off Northern Luzon. Two Pursuit Squadrons were scrambled until 54 aircraft were in the air and 36 on standby. The interceptors failed to make contact because the Japanese bombers' target was not Manila but Baguio, Luzon. Thus, by swinging east, no contact was made.[19]

Five hundred Japanese bombers and fighters were assigned to attack U.S. air bases in the Philippines on 8 December 1941. Take-off from various Formosan airfields was scheduled for two hours before dawn so that the striking force would be over their targets at first light in the hope of achieving tactical surprise. At 3 a.m. on the morning of 8 December, a heavy mist blanketed western Formosa but did not affect the east. The airfields of the Imperial Japanese Navy's long-range, land-based 11th Air Fleet were in the west but the Imperial Japanese Army's Fifth Air Group under the Fourteenth Army had its short-range bombers on eastern fields, enabling them to attack on schedule. It was these latter aircraft which had attacked Baguio and the other northern towns at approximately 0925 a.m. while the navy planes assigned to Clark and Iba—it was the radar system which made Iba a strategic target—were fog-bound.

While the Japanese naval pilots impatiently bided their time at Tainan airbase, Formosa, a voice over the loudspeaker system pierced the thick mist. "At 0600 this morning, a Japanese task force succeeded in carrying out a devastating surprise attack against the American forces in the Hawaiian Islands." Pandemonium broke out as ecstatic pilots danced in the gloom around their grounded aircraft until, quite suddenly, the significance of what they had just heard dawned upon them. They became quiet and reflective. Airfield gunners manned their weapons to face the onslaught that must surely come. At 0800 the Japanese intercepted an American broadcast indicating that such an attack was being considered and that the B-17s were expected over Formosa at 1010.[20] The Japanese just sat there, apprehensively, grounded by mist for six hours. They had little of their fighter strength left "since in addition to the attack groups sent against Luzon, we had dispatched planes to provide anti-submarine patrol for the invasion convoys headed for Aparri and Vigan."[21] The mist began to disperse at about 9am and take-off was scheduled for an hour later. An accident which caused a bomber to explode on take-off blocked the runway and led to further delay. Not until 1045 was the strike force of 53 bombers and 45 Zero fighters in the air and set on course for Clark Field.[22]

At 1010 the FEAF daily summary sheets reveal Brereton receiving permission to send reconnaissance aircraft over Formosa. At 1014 (other accounts say 1100) Brereton received a telephone call from MacArthur telling him to hold his bombers until the reconnaissance information had been assessed. MacArthur categorically denied authorizing bomber raids on Formosa despite a radiogram being sent under his name to Marshall on 8 December, telling of a planned attack on Formosa the next day.[23] If the order did come from his Headquarters, and the assumption is that it must have done, why did it take over seven hours to come to a decision vis-à-vis the bombers' deployment? It is possible to suggest that this was an unfortunate ramification of the less than precise habits of a peacetime Headquarters. MacArthur, remote, aloof and rarely present, had delegated to an ambitious Sutherland not simply the detail and routine but also the majority of the policy decisions. Using B-17s to bomb Formosa was part of USAFFE's strategic plan but it would have required MacArthur's ultimate authority. The delay could well have been due to MacArthur being *hors de combat*, Sutherland awaiting a decision and then finally taking that decision on MacArthur's behalf. Again, this is speculation; the truth will never be known.

"Lacking report of reconnaissance, Taiwan (Formosa) would be attacked in late afternoon," read the FEAF log at 1014. This entry is at variance with other contemporary entries. The decision to take offensive action was delegated to Brereton, bombers were ordered to bomb-up on returning from patrol. Clark had not been bombed and, accordingly, the aircraft which as a precaution had taken off that morning returned to base. "Shortly after 1130, all American aircraft in the Philippines, with the exception of one or two planes, were on the ground." At about this time, the plotting board at Nielson Field received reports of a formation of enemy aircraft over northern Luzon.[24] A warning was sent to Clark by teletype and was acknowledged but it never reached Bomber Command.[25] Pursuit Squadrons at outlying fields were scrambled by Interceptor Command. The pilots of 20th Pursuit who had been airborne since 0900 landed and parked up neatly at the fuel lines at Clark to await the ground crew who were at lunch. Most of the fighter pilots headed for the Officers' Club where the bomber pilots were having a quick drink before returning to their aircraft.[26] Fighters from the nearby Del Carmen Field, tasked to provide top cover during refueling at Clark, were unable to take off due to a dust storm. The fighters from Nielson

Field, which had been covering Clark during the morning, had been withdrawn back to their base for reassignment that afternoon to cover Bataan and the western approaches.

Clark was not a difficult airfield to locate. It lies to the east of the 3,800 feet high Mount Arayat and close to the white-painted symmetry of Fort Stotsenburg. The silver of parked aircraft sparkled in the midday sunshine. Saburo Sakai and his squadron of Zeros arrived over Clark in advance of the bombers.

> The sight which met us was unbelievable. Instead of encountering a swarm of American fighters diving at us in attack, we looked down and saw some sixty enemy bombers and fighters neatly parked along the airfield runways . . . the Americans had made no attempt to disperse the planes and increase their safety.

Sakai flew over Clark at 22,000 feet under orders not to attack until the main bomber force arrived. Below him at 1,500 feet he saw the first of four American fighters take off, but they made no attempt to engage the Japanese. Then Sakai saw the bombers approaching from the north at 25,000 feet, two thousand feet higher than the ceiling of the 3-inch anti-aircraft guns. He jettisoned his external fuel tanks, armed his guns and prepared for action.[27]

The drone of aircraft engines brought out people at Clark to look up into the sky. There were 27 planes in 9 tight Vs. "Look at those B-18s," someone said. An elderly crew chief disagreed. "We ain't got but ten left in the whole Philippines. They can't be ours!"[28] The bombers were almost directly overhead at the time the air-raid siren was sounded, "and the bombs began exploding a few seconds thereafter." Anti-aircraft fire fell 2–4,000 feet short and the anti-aircraft gunners reported that their ammunition, the most recent of which had been made in 1932, was over 15 per cent dud. It was about 12:20 p.m. After the first 27 bombers there followed a further 27, and then 34 Zeros strafed the parked aircraft for over an hour.[29] "The place was a shambles," wrote General Jonathan Wainwright, who watched the attack from his office at Fort Stotsenburg, planes were "twisted and burning and sending great pillars of black into the sky. More than half of the new B-17s which had just been flown in were scattered about the place in thousands of pieces."[30]

Meanwhile at approximately 12:30 p.m. a similar formation attacked Iba Field, destroying what was then the only operational radar in the Philippines and accounting for all but two of the P-40s of the 3rd Pursuit Squadron which, having been patrolling all morning, had just returned to base, out of fuel. It had been an exercise in overkill—the assigned resources far exceeded what was required. By mid afternoon, over half of MacArthur's Philippine combat air arm had been destroyed. Only 18 of the 35 bombers survived; the seventeen at Mindanao and one Clark-based aircraft which had been away on reconnaissance. Approximately fifty-five of the seventy-two P-40s were lost as well as many of the older marks. Seven Japanese planes were downed. Fatalities at Clark and Iba were considerably less than at Pearl Harbor—approximately 80.[31]

Despite many hours" advance warning and, unlike Admiral Kimmell at Pearl Harbor, having Magic intercept and decoding means, American air power in the Philippines had been virtually neutralized on the first day of the war. The pilots tended to blame MacArthur for stopping the planned raid against Formosa[32] while one historian is emphatic that "holding the bombers at Clark Field that day was entirely due to Brereton."[33] When Roosevelt heard the news he said, incredulously, "on the ground! on the ground!"[34] When asked at his first wartime press conference on 9 December about the Clark Field disaster, he said he had no new information and moved quickly on to another subject.[35] Less coy was General H. "Hap" Arnold. Ironically the telephone service within the Philippines was execrable but from the Philippines to the United States it was invariably good. Brereton recollected a call from Arnold who seemed "excited and apparently under great strain." "How in hell could an experienced airman like you get caught with your planes on the ground? That's what we sent you there for, to avoid just what happened!"

The conversation was then interrupted by Zeros strafing the field. Brereton looked out of the window and saw his Douglas plane on fire.

"What in the hell is going on there?" demanded Arnold.

"We are having visitors," replied Brereton.

Brereton implored Arnold to defer judgement until a full report could be forthcoming. He explained how he had done everything in his power to get authority to attack Formosa on 8 December but had been relegated to "a strictly defensive attitude" by higher authority.

Brereton went to see MacArthur and asked for his assistance in setting the facts straight. "He was furious," wrote Brereton, "it is the only time in my life I have ever seen him mad." Told to go back, to fight the war and not to worry, Brereton heard MacArthur tell Sutherland to get General Marshall on the phone. In contacting and criticizing Brereton directly, Arnold had cut across the chain of command. Marshall had been one of the foremost proponents for putting B-17s into the Philippines. Usually utterly circumspect in any of his comments, he was to say two weeks later, "I just don't know how MacArthur happened to let his planes get caught on the ground."[36] Criticism vis-à-vis the loss of half the airforce struck a raw nerve with MacArthur. "It has always been my impression," recalled Brereton, "that erroneous reports had upset him and, lacking authentic information, he had been unable to justify the losses to himself or his superiors."[37]

MacArthur followed his call to Marshall with a signal to Arnold. He explained how every possible precaution had been taken within the limited means and time available. The FEAF's losses were due entirely to the overwhelming superiority of the enemy force. "They have been hopelessly outnumbered from the start . . . no item of loss can be properly attributed to neglect or lack of care."[38] Arnold responded in a signal to Brereton. It has a hollow and overly optimistic ring about it but it provided support and encouragement when it was most needed:

> The eyes of the entire world friend and enemy are focused in admiration upon the officers and men of the American Air Forces in the Philippines. The fighting spirit being displayed by you has brought America to its feet as one man. Your heroic success against such extreme odds and discouragement has set the pace that will carry this nation forward to victory. We continue to depend on you. Keep your heads high and your chins up. Your country will not fail you.[39]

The signal to Brereton did not reflect what Arnold thought. He had obviously been "leaned" upon. He was never able to get "the real story of what happened in the Philippines." Brereton's diary did not "give a complete and accurate account" and the story by Sutherland "does not completely clear it up, by any means." In his memoirs, Arnold admitted "that we were surprised and outnumbered, but I had always believed that our airmen would fight it out in the air; they should never have been caught flat footed on the ground. It was a very sad blow to me."[40]

On 27 May 1944, between the time MacArthur departed the Philippines and his return, the historian of the Fifth Air Force contacted General Headquarters South West Pacific Area in order to fill some gaps in the AAC/AAF files. He wanted to communicate with those people who held key positions under General MacArthur at the outbreak of war to ascertain first, the pre-war plans for the employment of FEAF; second, the possible effect of the political status of the Philippines on decisions taken not to assume the initiative against the Japanese after official confirmation of the Pearl Harbor attack had been received; and third, an indication of such orders as may have been issued to the airforce on the morning of 8 December relating to the use of bombers based in Clark Field. The request was returned to its originator with an endorsement of 7 June 1944: "There is no official information in this headquarters bearing upon the questions propounded in basic communication."[41] Many of the records were already missing, but these were times when record-keeping was not an immediate priority.

Although preliminary plans had been drawn up for a B-17 attack on Formosa in the event of war against Japan, they had not been developed. There was no clear vision as to how precisely the B-17s were to be used. It seems that they were a tool, an Army component in the unending competition to outdo the Navy in terms of size and importance. If the Japanese had waited until after April 1942 as MacArthur insisted they would, then more time could have been devoted to the consideration of operations and targets and the infrastructure, notably radar. Air defense and fighter protection would have been in a better position to support the bomber force. MacArthur, Brereton and Sutherland share the blame for the débâcle, but so too must the War Department for having an inflated expectation of what the B-17s could achieve as offensive and defensive weapons. The B-17 was thought likely to deter Japanese aggression in the Pacific but in reality it had the reverse effect. In December 1941, FEAF was not an operational combat force, nor would it be for a number of months. "They were simply a gaggle of planes and crews, without adequate communications, not yet coordinated as a team, and therefore uncertain and awkward in action."[42] Among MacArthur's staff there was clearly no great confidence in the B-17 as a battle-winning asset. Richard Marshall said to Sutherland, "Well, Dick, it doesn't make much difference. If we hadn't lost them on the ground at Clark today, we would have lost them later, in the air or on the ground, and it wouldn't have made any difference at all."[43]

Some of MacArthur's staff may well not have been impressed by the B-17, but to the Japanese they represented a credible threat. The Japanese did not covet the Philippines to the degree that it was vital to their plans, but the archipelago was necessary to secure the eastern approaches to the resource area and to drive the U.S. presence that much further to the east. The goal of the Fourteenth Army was the oil of Borneo and Java to the south. In that respect, the Philippine archipelago provided the stepping stones towards that goal. Since the B-17s represented a threat to the ultimate aim of the Japanese because they could attack the Japanese bases on Formosa, "it was necessary to eliminate this danger . . . until we did this, we could not continue to the south and capture the oil which we needed."[44] The Japanese feared that by the time they appeared over Clark, the B-17s would all have been flown south beyond their range of operations. However,

> the destruction of the American airforce at the beginning of the operation enabled the Japanese to land in force without opposition. After the landings had been made, Japanese air superiority enabled the ground forces to move much more rapidly and effectively than would have been possible had we not had definite air superiority.[45]

Brereton insists that neither MacArthur nor Sutherland ever told him why authority was withheld to attack Formosa immediately following the Japanese attack on Pearl Harbor.

> I have always felt that General MacArthur may possibly have been under orders from Washington not to attack unless attacked. If it was a decision that had been reached in Washington that he was trying to change via radio telephone, this may explain the "strictly defensive" attitude under which we operated that fateful morning. General Mac-Arthur's position was a peculiar one because he occupied a dual role as Marshal of the Philippine Army and Commander of U.S. Forces in the Far East. Owing to the political relationship between the Philippine Commonwealth and the United States it is entirely possible that the Pearl Harbor attack might not have been construed as an overt act against the Philippines.[46]

MacArthur's statement that the overall strategic mission of the Philippine command was to defend the Philippines, not to initiate an outside attack, represented a somewhat parochial view of general war. His most recent orders relating to Rainbow 5 (19 November 1941) required him at the outbreak of war to conduct air raids against those Japanese targets within the operating range of the Philippine airfields. He also harked back to his well-rehearsed routine that everything was geared to readiness by 1 April and, since the Japanese had arrived before his essential reinforcements, all bets were off.[47] But this was the General who had assured the Chief of Staff a week before the Japanese attack, "I have every confidence we can hold our own."[48] It should have been of concern that MacArthur had not regarded the attack on Pearl Harbor as the "first overt act" made by Japan which Washington regarded as being "desirable." As Larrabee said: "MacArthur seems to have assumed that war as it applied to the United States and war as it applied to the Philippines were two different things."[49] In an interview with the historian Morton after the war, MacArthur confirmed that he had had "explicit" orders not to "initiate hostilities against the Japanese." He also made oblique mention of the Philippines" "somewhat indeterminate international position" and that great local hope existed "that the Philippines would not be attacked."[50]

Rear Admiral John D. Bulkeley who, as a young PT boat commander, would take MacArthur from Corregidor to safety, blamed Quezon for preventing offensive action not only by the B-17s but also by his naval craft. It seems unlikely that this young, junior naval officer would have been in an appropriate position to state with any authority that Quezon "was not convinced that the Japanese were actually making war. He was the one who insisted on the three mile limit until the Japs actually dropped their bombs. It was Quezon who put the clamp on things."[51] On the other hand, Eisenhower said that when Quezon called on him in Washington in 1942, he told Eisenhower that:

> when the Japanese attacked Pearl Harbor, MacArthur was convinced for some strange reason that the Philippines would remain neutral and would not be attacked by the Japanese. For that reason, MacArthur refused permission to General Brereton to bomb Japanese bases on Formosa immediately after the attack on Pearl Harbor.[52]

Herbert Ellis, a former commanding officer of 3rd Pursuit Squadron who wrote the foreword to *Doomed at the Start*, addressed the author's complaint that the information available during the short campaign was "inadequate, confusing and contradictory." Ellis sought to explain the causes of the obvious inconsistencies. The main cause was confusion. "Confusion is a given in war. And it doesn't just happen; it is contrived. Once started, it feeds on itself." He then went on to identify deception as another factor. "The ability to deceive and confuse is one of the most effective weapons of war." Deception is a capability available to the enemy and it can equally be used by friendly forces against the enemy and against their own people. Ellis went on to point out how rare it is for any two people to come away from any dramatic incident with the same story. "Finally," he wrote, "there is the terrible destruction of war which transforms the familiar into the unfamiliar, and which in turn causes disorientation."[53]

Much has been written of Sutherland denying Brereton access to MacArthur. Rather more should be made of the fact that MacArthur did not *demand* to see Brereton. But who can say with any certainty that MacArthur did not see Brereton before the attack on Clark Field? Certainly, the relationship between MacArthur and Brereton was curious. It was partly Brereton's fault that the B-17s were caught on the ground. As MacArthur pointed out, the tactical handling of the force was in Brereton's hands, but publicly MacArthur insisted that criticisms of Brereton "do an injustice to this officer."[54] Privately, MacArthur was determined to rid himself of the "bumbling nincompoop" Brereton.[55] MacArthur was rather dismissive and economic in his description of the whole affair. "Our fighters went up to meet them, but our bombers were slow in taking off and our losses were heavy. Our force was simply too small to smash the odds against them."[56] But the buck stopped, as it must, at MacArthur's desk, even though it is remotely possible that he did not know that the B-17s had not gone to safety—for a while—at Del Monte Field. MacArthur was not averse to sacking commanders who appeared to have failed. He sacked General Selleck for apparently lacking offensive spirit on Bataan. But Brereton's men blamed MacArthur for the Clark fiasco and it should be remembered that MacArthur asked for Brereton to join his staff. How much more difficult it is to sack a person whose presence is due to the one who desires his removal.

In an interview given to Clare Boothe Luce in April 1942, Brereton told Mrs. Luce that he had conferred with MacArthur before daylight on 8 December. According to Mrs. Luce's interview notes, MacArthur told Brereton that "there were to be no 'overt acts' on the part of the U.S. forces in the P.I. until the Japs struck the first blow at the Filipino people." When told to "stand by and wait," the Luce record has Brereton leaving, "closer to weeping from sheer rage than he had ever been in his life before." Both men were to deny the early morning meeting and Mrs. Luce, who believed MacArthur's reputation should be safeguarded, never published the details of this interview which were found among the papers of Willoughby, a partisan and sympathetic figure.[57] MacArthur let Brereton go South, as the force of circumstances dictated, but he made no attempt to recall Brereton once equilibrium had been restored.[58]

Of USAFFE's reluctance to bomb Formosa, Morton recalled that, in an interview, "Sutherland states that the diary is all wrong in this connection and that Brereton's explanation is pure fiction."[59] MacArthur denied all knowledge of Brereton's recommendation to bomb Formosa. "Such a suggestion to the Chief of Staff must have been of a most nebulous and superficial character, as there is no record of it at headquarters." MacArthur said if there had been a serious proposal it should have been put to him, but he heard nothing on this subject from Brereton either before or after the Clark Field attack.[60] "Had such a suggestion been made to me, I would have unequivocally disapproved. In my opinion it would have been suicidal as well as in direct defiance of my basic directive."[61] MacArthur may have been correct in his decision not to send the B-17s over Formosa.[62] The Japanese had been warned of a retaliatory strike and that Takao harbor would be a target was easily predictable. The Japanese were not replete with resources to meet incoming B-17s—they had no radar—but there were Zeros available in reserve and a surveillance screen was out between Formosa and Luzon. The American P-40s did not have the range or the oxygen systems to escort the B-17s over their target. The B-17s would have had to rely on bombing from high altitude to provide them with protection. There may have been an assumption that the Zero could not climb to high altitude and, even if it could, that the B-17 would see it off, in which case it is a beneficial exercise to see how the RAF had fared in its earlier high altitude operations with the B-17. The first time the B-17s flew in battle was on 8 July 1941 when three aircraft were assigned the target of the Naval Barracks at Wilhelmshaven. The attack excited much interest, being observed by RAF and USAAC. When two enemy fighters rose to intercept, the B-17s were taken up to 32,000 feet. The enemy fighters lost control at this altitude and aborted the attack but, ominously for the B-17s, "There would have been no defense against the enemy fighters had they successfully closed to attack." All guns and gun mountings had frozen solid. In less than one month the Luftwaffe had solved their altitude problem. On 2 August, over Borkum, two Messerschmitt Me 109s intercepted a B-17 at 32,000 feet and attacked, damaging the solitary aircraft.

This ability of the German fighters now to close an attack at altitude produced serious premonitions in the 90 Squadron crews, who were often helpless due to frozen guns and mountings, and also suffering the disadvantages of intercom failures, engine failures, and severe physical discomfort due to flying at such heights. In addition, there was no tail gun position, leaving the aircraft particularly vulnerable from astern.[63]

The Germans had an information exchange scheme with the Japanese and it is more than likely the Japanese would have known of the B-17's serious shortcomings. Secondary sources reveal that the Mitsubishi A6M2 Reisen Zero fighter did intercept B-17s flying at over 25,000 feet during the campaign in the Philippines. The A6M2 Zero had a service ceiling of 10,000m (32,810 feet).[64] The historian Walter D. Edmonds noted that although the Zero "enjoyed a wide margin of performance" over the B-17 up to 20,000 feet, "At 20,000 feet the margin began to dissipate; and above 25,000 it turned in favor of the B-17."[65] What the navy Zeros over Formosa would have had to do was to meet the incoming B-17s at altitude. Even if they forced them higher, beyond the fighters' ceiling, the prospect of a successful bombing sortie, given the B-17s' limited capacity, became doubtful. Nevertheless, it does seem that on first contact the Zeros would have surprised the B-17s because the American pilots would not have expected to meet fighters at altitude. On Christmas Day 1941 a B-17C and a B-17D flew into Del Monte from Batchelor Field, south of Darwin, with a view to bombing Davao. Intercepted after bomb release, the B-17s were engaged by "ten Japanese fighters including both Zeros and Messerschmitts" for twenty minutes. "Though they had climbed during the fight to 28,000 feet, the Zeros, because of Schaetzel's[66] (American B-17 pilot) dead engine, were able to swarm all over them at that altitude." One crewman in Schaetzel's B-17 was killed and two in the other aircraft were wounded.[67] This curious reference to "Messerschmitts" would appear to reflect not only the prevailing confusion relating to Japanese aircraft production that colored Allied accounts of the air war over the Pacific but also a conviction among some Americans that the Japanese planes that had made the devastatingly accurate bombing attack on Clark could not have done so unless they had been "at least partially manned by white pilots,"[68] i.e. Germans.

On the day of the attack, the High Commission prepared public statements, notified Commonwealth officials and prepared for the defense of the High Commissioner's residence. Sayre wrote how, "on this first day of the war . . . through the tragic blunder of failure to attack we were ignominiously stripped of the planes on which our defense heavily rested." He saw MacArthur that afternoon in his office. The General paced the floor, his face revealing "how grave the situation must be." Something had gone badly wrong. "We supposed that an official investigation would follow. But the war was on then, and minds were immersed in the immediate problems of resistance."[69] The anticipated official inquiry was never held. Although Pearl Harbor was the subject of no fewer than eight investigations, there was never an inquiry into the "other Pearl Harbor," the fiasco at Clark Field. The 1946 Joint Congressional Committee which investigated the Japanese attack on Hawaii declared the Clark attack to be beyond their brief.

As a result of the successful Japanese pre-emptive attacks commencing 7/8 December, the commanding Allied generals and admirals did not fare too well. Admiral Husband E. Kimmel, Commander in Chief Pacific Fleet, and General Walter C. Short, Commander of United States Army forces in Hawaii, were both immediately relieved of command, found guilty of dereliction of duty by a Presidential commission, and never returned to active duty. In Burma, two months later, the British generals Lieutenant General T.J. Hutton and Major General J.G. Smyth were also summarily dismissed. Major General Christopher Maltby, Commander British Forces Hong Kong and Lieutenant General Arthur Percival, British Commander in Malaya had both been taken into Japanese prisoner-of-war camps. Major General Gordon Bennett, commanding general of the 8th Australian Division, escaped from Singapore but, on his return to Australia was greeted with hostility and derision.[70] MacArthur suffered none of this censure after the destruction of FEAF. It is extraordinary that his depiction of this as a second Japanese sneak attack was not challenged more energetically at the time. Politically and militarily he was untouchable. Later, General Claire Chennault wrote: "If I had been caught with my planes on the ground, I could never have looked my fellow officers squarely in the eye.[71] The lightness with which this cardinal military sin was excused by American high command has always seemed to me one of the shocking defects of the war." MacArthur was promoted to the temporary rank of General on 22 December; Sutherland became a Major General and Akin, Marshall and Casey became Brigadier Generals.[72]

10

To Corregidor

The Japanese anticipated the success of their Army and Navy Air Forces but perhaps not quite the speed and completeness of success that was achieved. Before the planes had taken off from Formosa to attack the air facilities on Luzon, three task forces had set sail from Formosa to make a three-pronged landing on Batan Island (not to be confused with Bataan Peninsula) and on the north coast of Luzon. Their limited mission was reflected in their relatively small size, no larger than a regiment and as small as a company. They were to seize short-range fighter bases ready to be used to support the main landings on Luzon. On 9 December, another task force left Palau Island, 550 miles east of Mindanao, to land at Legaspi close to the southwest tip of Luzon while a second task force prepared to seize Davao, the principal port of Mindanao, with a substantial Japanese population.[1] Davao would be used as a springboard from which to attack Borneo. The three-pronged northern task force was at sea 7-10 December, landing on Batan Island on 8 December and on Luzon on 10 December. In a distinct understatement, a Japanese declared it to have been "a miracle that the convoy wasn't spotted."[2] While the Japanese did have Army and Naval Air Forces they were not hidebound by demarkation lines of functions. American air power was largely represented by untrained pilots, which was unfortunate, operating in two distinct and uncoordinated packages, which was inexcusable.

When Secretary Vargas telephoned to tell Quezon that Clark had been bombed and the "whole place is now afire," Quezon asked: "what are the American planes doing?" Vargas did not know, nor was he told to find out. "Up to this day," wrote Quezon, "I never addressed that question again to anybody."[3]

On 10 December, Nichols Field was bombed for the second time and the Navy was singled out for attention in a devastating two-hour attack on Cavite Naval Base. The irony of this attack was that, at Pearl Harbor, which the Japanese were not to occupy, they spared the facilities, whereas Cavite, which would be required for use after the occupation, was obliterated. Hart watched the destruction for as long as he could bear it, resentful of the total absence of Army fighter protection.[4] The Japanese were well aware that the principal opposition they could expect from the Navy would come from submarines, motor torpedo boats and flying boats. With the examples of Pearl Harbor and the loss of the British capital ships in mind, Hart argued that a purely ship-versus-plane argument was pointless. "Amphibious warfare is primarily a matter of ships *and* planes. The ships and planes must be handled and fought together, and that can be successfully done only if all the personnel is continuously trained together, understands each other's problems and speaks each other's language."[5] But this should not detract from the truth of the matter which was summarized by Churchill. "The efficiency of the Japanese in air warfare was at this time greatly underestimated both by ourselves and by the Americans.[6]

The effect of the Cavite attack upon Hart was profound. It was plain that the air war was being lost, "and we shall be blockaded here, for a long time."[7] The large submarine, the *Sealion*, had been sunk, the destroyer *Pillsbury* and minesweeper *Bittern* were damaged, and there had been 500 casualties. He rued the day that he had not sent more vessels southward, which is something he now actioned by clearing Cavite of all non-essential shipping in addition to the allied and neutral merchant ships in Manila Bay. He informed Washington that the air situation had rendered Manila an untenable base.[8]

The Japanese landing at Aparri, at the northern end of Luzon, had been unopposed. The Philippine Army company there withdrew without engaging the two-company-strong Tanaka detachment which, by 1300 hours, 10 December, had taken the airfield. General Wainwright assumed that the main landing would occur in Lingayen Gulf where he had the bulk of his force. These minor landings were never intended to deceive the Americans as to Japan's true intentions, nor were they interpreted as being part of a deception plan.[9] "We did not disperse forces," confirmed General Sutherland, "but waited for what we felt would be the main attack."[10] The route south from Aparri went through the Balete Pass where it was felt a relatively small, dug-in force could hold and delay a substantially larger advancing force. A P-40 pilot detected the 2000-man detachment landing at Vigan at 0513 also on the 10th. It was against the Aparri and Vigan landings that FEAF would launch its last coordinated attack. The first American B-17, flown by Captain Colin Kelly, to be destroyed in air combat was downed returning from an attack on Aparri.

Kelly had taken off in a four-plane sortie from Clark at 0930, 10 December, and headed for Aparri with three 600 lb. bombs on board. Off Aparri, he witnessed the disembarkation of the Tanaka detachment under the covering fire of six small warships further out to sea. Beyond the ships, five miles from shore, Kelly saw what he believed to be a battleship, later presumed to have been the *Haruna* but subsequently found to have been a cruiser.[11] Kelly attacked the large ship. Successful, high-level B-17 attacks against naval targets owed more to luck than judgement. The first of his bombs fell short, the second struck the sea 50 feet from the bow of the ship and the third was claimed to have struck the aft turret. With all bombs dispatched, Kelly turned the B-17 round, on course for Clark. Although it was claimed that several transports had been sunk, only one was damaged and was later able to be beached. "All in all, it was not a very auspicious beginning for U.S. bombing air power but the aircrews had displayed courage and devotion to duty."[13]

Descending to 6000 feet, Kelly encountered Saburo Sakai and nine other Zeros. The Japanese were surprised to encounter an unescorted bomber. Each of the Zeros engaged the B-17, but to little apparent effect. "The airplane's unusual size caused us to misjudge our firing distance ... [its] ... extraordinary speed was another factor," wrote the Japanese pilot. Saburo Sakai with two other Zeros came round for a second pass, attacking from the blind rear. "Pieces of metal flew off in chunks from the bomber's right wing, and then a thin white film sprayed back. It looked like jettisoned gasoline but it might have been smoke." It was smoke, the wing tank was on fire. Kelly was flying a B-17C which, unlike the D series, did not have self-sealing tanks. Out of ammunition, Saburo Sakai watched the other two pilots effect the *coup de grace*, which he nonchalantly photographed with his Leica camera. He saw three men bail out before the aircraft fell through the cloud. When Kelly's bomber emerged from the cloud at approximately 2500 feet, the Clark tower air controllers saw what they believed to be five parachutes. One air crewman, the waist gunner, was decapitated and then Kelly, the last to leave, hit the tail in the slipstream and his parachute never opened. The Japanese pilots were later upset by accounts of their having machine gunned the men on the parachutes. Two of their Zeros were found to have been riddled with bullets from Kelly's B-17.[13]

Kelly's crew had been undoubtedly brave to press home their unsupported attack and it came at a time when a hero figure was needed in order to offset the unending news of doom and gloom. One media report claimed "Kelly had dropped his bomb squarely down the smokestack of the battleship," while according to another, "Kelly, after ordering his crew to bail out, had flown his B-17 right into the warship."[14] MacArthur used the press and public relations opportunity to good effect. In the public relations photograph of the award ceremony of Distinguished Service Crosses, an American (Second Lieutenant Jack D. Dale) and a Filipino (Captain Jesus A. Villamor) stood symbolically side by side. Sometimes truth was not permitted to interfere with the required effect. Kelly's citation read in part, "With his airplane a focal point of fire from strong hostile naval forces, Captain Kelly exhibited a high degree of valor and skill in placing 3 direct hits upon an enemy battleship, resulting in its destruction." At the medal ceremony, held at Fort Santiago, MacArthur said of the posthumous award of a Distinguished Service Cross to Kelly:

> It is my profound sorrow that Colin Kelly is not here. I do not know the dignity of Captain Kelly's birth but I do know the glory of his death. He died unquestioning, uncomplaining, with faith in his heart and victory his end. God has taken him unto himself, a gallant soldier who did his duty.[15]

As late as 10 December, MacArthur sent Marshall a signal which revealed just how out of touch he was with the reality of the moment and with what was possible in the context of grand strategy. He proposed to Marshall that, with the Japanese Army and Navy so heavily committed in the theater, the "most favorable opportunity now exists and immediate attack on Japan from north would not only inflict heavy punishment but would at once relieve pressure from objectives of Jap drive to southward."[16] Stalin was in no position to intervene, with German forces at the gates of Moscow and Leningrad. He was more interested in the Allies opening a second front to support Russia. It was a strange sense of timing for MacArthur now to present himself as a military statesman but there is no doubt that that is precisely how he saw himself. On 13 December he sent Generalissimo Chiang Kai Shek "a message of greeting," telling the Chinese leader, "In sympathy and spirit I have been ranged by your side from the beginning of your epic struggle for freedom."[17] Meanwhile, messages from Washington encouraged him to cling to straws. On 11 December, Marshall told him, "We are making every effort to reach you with air replacements and reinforcements as well as other troops and support. Will communicate detail when safe to do so."[18] Marshall was undoubtedly sincere in his hope that he could find a way to deliver relief to the Philippine garrison and was not simply making cynical promises to keep up the morale of troops he knew could not be saved. He suspected they were doomed but did not give up hope of relief no matter how remote such a prospect must have appeared.

At 5:30 p.m. on 11 December 1941, the status of FEAF's aircraft availability was: at Del Monte, 7 Fortresses in commission, 5 others suitable for low level missions and 4 unsuitable for tactical missions. There were 22 P-40s in commission at Clark and Nichols Field with 6 more, 3 at each airfield, which would become serviceable on the 12th. "That's all we had to stop the Japs with," wrote Brereton.[19] On the 12th, a small Japanese force landed at Legaspi. Only two Philippine divisions had been allocated for the defense of south Luzon, Brigadier General Vicente Lim's 41st Division in the west and Brigadier General Albert M. Jones' 51st Division in the east. So much for MacArthur's concept of defending the whole of the Philippines. On 12 December, he informed Quezon that if the Japanese landed in strength he would move his headquarters to Corregidor, declare Manila an open city and fight it out with the Japanese on the Bataan Peninsula.[20] This represented a shift away from wishful thinking to an acceptance of what the limited land forces at MacArthur's disposal could safely achieve.

Japanese land forces were always inferior in number but they succeeded because they were able to achieve superiority at the point of contact. Before Eisenhower had departed the Philippines he gave a strategic appraisal to Quezon.

> There is one line, and one only, at which the defending force will enjoy a tremendous advantage over any attack by land. That line is the beach. Successful penetration of a defended beach is the most difficult operation in warfare. If an attacking force ever succeeds in lodging itself in a vital area of the Islands, particularly on Luzon, 90 per cent of the prior advantage of the defender will disappear. Behind the protective lines established by such attacking force, more and more strength can be brought in, by echelon, until with superior armaments and with naval and other support, the whole will be strong enough to crush the defending army. The enemy must be repulsed at the Beach.[21]

The Japanese had none of the customized landing craft which were such a feature of Allied landings later in the war. They were, however, a seagoing nation and had adapted Daihatsu wooden, civilian craft to carry up to 120 men at 8-10 knots.[22] By the third week in December, they had launched nine amphibious operations. The six which had been unopposed succeeded while, of the three which were opposed, two ended in defeat and one almost in disaster.[23]

MacArthur's central problem lay in logistics. He did not have the time or resources to support both a beach defense at Lingayen and a citadel-type defense on Bataan and Corregidor. He had to make his choice, and his last best chance was undoubtedly to defeat the major Japanese amphibious landings on the beaches. Lingayen was a raging certainty, while Tayabas Bay, Nasugbu and Batangas Bay were also considered likely landing areas. The occupation of Bataan *ab initio*, with only 180 days' supplies when most optimistic estimates put relief in terms of 2-3 years, was not the wisest of moves. But MacArthur was not without a few aces of his own, namely a substantial number of supporting submarines, and there was the difficulty the Japanese invaders would face in getting established ashore. Nevertheless, on 16 December, he changed the mission of General Wainwright's North Luzon Force. No longer was the line of resistance to be the beach; instead the Force was to hold the enemy north of San Fernando, a town in La Union.[24]

Most forces had been drawn northward, so much so that when the Japanese landed at Legaspi, at the southernmost end of Luzon, the

nearest American and Filipino troops were 150 miles away. The stationmaster's report of the landing to railroad control was allegedly
switched through to USAFFE headquarters and the following conversation is said to have ensued:

STATIONMASTER: "There are four Jap boats in the harbor, sir, and the
   Japs are landing. What shall I do?"
USAFFE OFFICER: "Just hang onto the phone and keep reporting."
STATIONMASTER: "There are about twenty Japs ashore already, sir, and
   more are coming." A pause. "Now there are about three hundred
   Japs outside the station, sir, what am I to do?"
USAFFE OFFICER: "Just sit tight."
STATIONMASTER: "Sir, a few of those Japs with an officer in front, are
   coming over here."
USAFFE OFFICER: "See what they want."
STATIONMASTER: "Those Japs want me to give them a train to take
   them to Manila, sir. What do I do now?"
USAFFE OFFICER: "Tell them the next train leaves a week from Sunday.
   Don't give it to them."
STATIONMASTER, HANGING UP: "Okay, sir."[25]

The influence of Japanese agents was widespread. "They had
agents everywhere," wrote Brereton, who reported that Intelligence
was aware the military telephones were being tapped. "On the second
night that Nichols Field was bombed we found fires and flares marking the field. Philippine Scouts found pro-Japanese Filipinos lighting
one of these flares." Lieutenant Anders, Regimental Intelligence
Officer of the 57th Infantry, Philippine Scouts, observed "a scattering
of flares and fires in the direction of both airfields"[26] (Nielson and
Nichols Fields). In addition, northwest of Clark Field, signal fires
were lit at night, marking the direction of the Field. When he went to
MacArthur's Headquarters, Brereton always varied his route. "My car
was fired upon at least twice over this period."[27]

Japanese air attacks against military facilities continued unabated,
all the time whittling down the strength of FEAF and Navy air. The
potential of the flying boats, Consolidated PBYs, called Catalinas, was
overrated: "They were designed for reconnaissance, for rescues at sea
and for the bombing of unsuspecting or relatively undefended targets."[28] Admiral Hart had 28 lumbering PBYs organized into two
squadrons in Patrol Wing No 10 (Patwing 10). His request to Washington for dive bombers to operate from land was never actioned. On

the 12th, seven Navy PBYs returning to Manila were followed in by Zeros and destroyed on the water.[29] The next day, at Subic Bay, more PBYs were destroyed, thereby halving the former strength of Patrol Wing 10. The impact of these accumulating Navy losses upon Hart was to send even more resources southward so that by 14 December, all that remained of the Asiatic Fleet in Philippine waters were two destroyers, six MTBs, two tenders, three gunboats and twenty-seven submarines. Most of the staff had gone but Hart remained for as long as the submarines could be operated and serviced from Manila.[30]

On Sunday, 14 December, Marshall arranged for Brigadier General Eisenhower to call on him in his War Department office. After a twenty minute introduction, during which the Chief of Staff summarized the naval and military situation in the western Pacific, he abruptly asked Eisenhower, "What should be our general line of action?" "Give me a few hours," replied Eisenhower.[31] The Navy's inability to conduct offensive action meant that surface vessels could not now venture into Philippine waters, from which it was possible to conclude "that the Philippines could not, at that time, be reinforced directly by land and sea forces." Eisenhower reasoned that an operating base should be established in Australia with a view to re-supplying the Philippines using submarines, blockade runners, and possibly even aircraft. Returning to Marshall's office, Eisenhower presented his "bleak conclusions."

> It will be a long time before major reinforcements can go to the Philippines, longer than the Garrison can hold out with any driblet of assistance, if the enemy commits major forces to their reduction. But we must do everything for them that is humanly possible. The people of China, of the Philippines, of the Dutch East Indies will be watching us. They may excuse failure but they will not excuse abandonment. Their trust and friendship are important to us. Our base must be Australia, and we must start at once to expand it and to secure our communications to it. In this last we dare not fail. We must take great risks and spend any amount of money required.

Eisenhower felt that Marshall had given him the task just to confirm the conclusions he had already drawn regarding the situation in the Philippines. "I agree with you," Marshall said, "do your best to save them." Eisenhower's hands were tied by the Europe First policy and by the fact that, as Admiral Kimmel said, the loss of the battleships at

Pearl Harbor had put the Navy on the strategic defensive.[32] General George H. Brett, an Air Corps officer with an enviable reputation as an administrator, was sent to Australia to begin the process of establishing a base there. Roosevelt also authorized Brereton up to $10 million being spent to charter tramp steamers to try to run the blockade of Luzon.[35]

After two out of three B-17s sent on 14 December to disrupt the Legaspi landing failed to return, Brereton obtained MacArthur's permission to relocate his remaining B-17s south of Darwin, Northern Australia. The move was providential for the Del Monte field had its first attack four days later.[34] With FEAF gone, Brereton's continuation in USAFFE made little further point and, on Christmas Eve, he was called into MacArthur's office and told that he was to follow his headquarters to the south. The airman asked to remain on MacArthur's staff, an offer that MacArthur declined. When Brereton rose to leave, MacArthur said to him, "I hope that you will tell the people outside what we have done and protect my reputation as a fighter." Shaking hands, Brereton replied, "General, your reputation will never need any protection."[35]

When the Japanese attacked, there were two regiments of National Guard artillery en route to Manila, aboard a convoy of seven ships escorted by the heavy cruiser *Pensacola* and the submarine chaser *Niagara*. On board the convoy were also aircraft required by the 27th Bombardment Group and large quantities of supplies and ammunition.[36] The troops knew about the convoy which had been dubbed "the victory convoy." The ammunition alone would have raised the combat effectiveness of the forces in theater. On or around 18 December, MacArthur and Hart held a conference in Hart's office to discuss the *Pensacola* Convoy. The President had intervened to say that he wanted no effort spared to get the convoy through to Manila. Hart said he listened to MacArthur's "speeches" about the General's side of the war, apparently uninterested in the Navy situation. "He asked no questions whatever, evinced no curiosity and, as has so often been the case, the interview was quite futile as far as furthering any meeting of minds between us."[37] The convoy arrived off Brisbane on the 22nd so was tantalizingly close, so close that MacArthur urged Hart to use his surface fleet to escort it to the Philippines but, in spite of the President's urgings, it remained there. Given the rate of deterioration in the situation in the Philippines, allowing transit time for the convoy, taking due note of Japanese landings already effected, the question to be answered is, even if the *Pensacola* Convoy had got through unscathed, where could it have been unloaded? Hart obviously did not fancy the risks and feared, like Stark, that he would be reinforcing failure, but the fact is that even the most minor tactical decisions affecting his ships were being taken by the Naval Department in Washington.[38] MacArthur maintained his criticism of Hart to Marshall, and Stimson remained content that the Navy should be blamed for MacArthur's parlous situation. To Stimson's mind, the Navy had become ultra cautious after the trauma of Pearl Harbor. Stimson wrote in his diary: "Hart (in conversation with General MacArthur) took the usual Navy defeatist position and had virtually told MacArthur that the Philippines were doomed instead of doing his best to keep MacArthur's lifeline open."[39] Hart was on the defensive, reluctant to be identified as the scapegoat and aware that (MacArthur) is inclined to cut my throat and perhaps of the Navy in general."[40] The *Pensacola* issue was not the Navy's only cause for concern in Manila at that time. In ten attacks against Japanese surface targets 12-25 December 1941, not one torpedo fired by U.S. submarines successfully detonated against its target. On Christmas Day, Hart sent a signal to MacArthur telling him that he was vacating his command post in Manila and that Rear Admiral Rockwell, Commandant of 16th Naval District would assume full command of the naval coastal frontier and all forces operating in the surrounding water. Rockwell intended to establish his command post on Corregidor. "I expect to be leaving Manila Bay some time this evening to join the naval forces in southern waters."[41] Hart's message put paid to any lingering expectation MacArthur might still have been harboring that somehow the *Pensacola* Convoy would get through. At 2:00 a.m. on 26 December, Hart slipped quietly out of Manila in the submarine *Shark*. After hearing on 24 December of MacArthur's plan to declare Manila an open city, Hart had no option but to leave. In such circumstances it would have been impossible to continue with surface naval operations from Manila and Manila Bay.

Soon after the first Japanese attacks, Sayre had discussed with Hart the evacuation of civilians by sea but was persuaded that, due to Japanese sea and air superiority, the risk in evacuation by ship "was considerably greater than that involved in their remaining in Manila."[42] The High Commissioner's staff now routinely assembled at the Residence, meeting each afternoon before last light. There were one or two rooms which could be effectively blacked out and it was here, after supper, that the staff gathered for games of cards before throwing themselves down, partially dressed, upon mattresses for a fitful night's sleep. The blackout was rigorously enforced in the city. Cars had to have masked headlights and, in the darkness of the silent hours thieves and robbers found easy pickings. Few went out at night for fear of them and of trigger-happy security officials who both challenged and fired at the same time.[43]

Internment was MacArthur's responsibility and it proceeded smoothly soon after the attack on Pearl Harbor. On the first day, 40 per cent of Japanese aliens in Manila and 10 per cent outside, had been interned. On 13 December, the net was widened to include Germans and Italians, their countries having declared war on the United States two days previously.[44] Sayre was responsible for the treatment of enemy aliens who had been interned and for the requisitioning of their property. MacArthur passed on a message from the Treasury Department requiring him to nominate a coordinator of enemy property to act "as a clearing house and record center of all properties in the Philippine Islands."[45] Sayre gave the Treasury short shrift. "Your telegram re enemy property inadequate to meet problems here arising from fact this is theater active operation (sic) and in view present possible blockade.'[46]

In order to deny currency to the Japanese, Sayre and his staff destroyed most of it and the commercial paper in the possession of the Manila banks before the Japanese entered the city on 2 January 1942. The gold and silver were transported over to Corregidor. On 15 December, Roosevelt belatedly allocated $10 million for civilian defense and public relief. Despite their best efforts, the High Commissioner's staff were only able to spend $25,000. The money arrived too late.[47]

It must have been a sobering experience for the pacifist Sayre to find himself involuntarily and inescapably drawn into war. During the First World War he had worked for the YMCA. But now he rose to the occasion. On 13 December he made an emotive radio appeal to America. "Out here on the firing line we have come to grips with reality . . . We are in the fight to stay. War enjoins upon us all action, action, action. Time is of the essence. Come on, America!"[48] Although outwardly optimistic, Sayre realized that there was little hope of America being able to send help to the Philippines. Privately, he wrote to his friend Maynard Hazen in the United States, asking that Hazen look after the education and lives of his children.[49] Publicly, Sayre acted his part, asking Roosevelt to scotch the rumor doing the rounds in Manila, that the United States could not send aid to the Philippines. Naturally, Roosevelt was unable to say so directly, which meant euphemism and circumlocution became the vogue.

Roosevelt reassured Sayre that there would be "no wavering in the determination to support you." In a radio broadcast of 29 December he offered some slim hope of salvation.[50] Earlier, on 24 December, MacArthur's latest poison pill from Marshall had had a sugar coating. The Chief of Staff told MacArthur that in view of operations now ongoing in Luzon, the plans for sending pursuit planes would have to go on hold, but that "every effort permitted by situation in the Pacific is being devoted to this purpose and our fighter and bomber strength will begin to increase rapidly." On 30 December, MacArthur sent Marshall his birthday wishes. "I send heartiest felicitations and reiterate the complete confidence I feel in your professional leadership of the army." Marshall scribbled on the bottom of the message, "Sexton-Smith draft acknowledgment, including any encouraging details possible." There were no encouraging details but Marshall's reply read: "We are leaving no stone unturned to provide you with assistance and the President is giving your affairs his direct and personal attention. The hopes of the entire nation are centered on your struggle."[51] These messages of hope to the civilians and military ultimately led to acute disillusionment and utter despair among both.

Quezon was obviously in a dilemma. Did he owe his first duty to the United States or to his own people? War situations do not provide all inclusive situations and the tension between choosing to support the sovereign state or those who had democratically elected him was a fine line to tread. In an act of faith the National Assembly passed a resolution on 11 December, pledging "support and cooperation of the Filipino people to the Government of the United States in the prosecution of the war." Also at this meeting, Quezon was confirmed as President and Osmeña his deputy. Three days later, the Assembly gave Quezon extraordinary powers to deal with the national emergency.[52]

Unfortunately, Quezon's health kept him in his Mariquina country home overlooking the river, surrounded by mango, papaya, banana and orange trees. His Cabinet traveled to Mariquina daily between 12 and 24 December to meet and discuss the deteriorating situation. On 12 December Quezon met Lieutenant Colonel Sid Huff who told him that MacArthur wanted the President to be at four hours' notice to move to Corregidor. Quezon was "shocked" by the proposal, never imagining for a moment that he would need to take refuge inside the fortress.

Shaken by the message from MacArthur, Quezon told Huff to inform MacArthur that he would see him that evening at the Manila Hotel, arriving at the rear entrance so that no one would be aware of their meeting. On arrival, Quezon noted how calm and composed MacArthur was. What did his message mean, enquired Quezon? MacArthur explained that his hope that Quezon would move to Corregidor was entirely precautionary. If the Japanese were to land in strength at different places, it would make little sense leaving the Army scattered throughout Luzon. In those circumstances he intended to withdraw the Army to Bataan and Corregidor to fight to the end. Not comprehending why he should act as a fugitive, Quezon questioned the need for him to go to Corregidor. After all, he said, the defense of the Philippines was an American responsibility, not his, and he had already placed every Filipino soldier under MacArthur's command. "My own first duty," he continued,

> is to take care of the civilian population and to maintain public order while you are fighting the enemy . . . Were I to go to Corregidor, my people would think I had abandoned them to seek safety under your protection. This I shall never do. I shall stay among my people and suffer the same fate that may befall them.

It seems a reasonable certainty that MacArthur was determined to take Quezon to Corregidor, if only to remove him from contact with the Japanese. Consistency had never been one of Quezon's attributes. MacArthur therefore had to draw upon all his powers of practised persuasion. Unruffled by Quezon's reply, he said: "Mr. President, I expected that answer from such a gallant man as I know you to be." It was not a question of Quezon running away from his countrymen. He reminded the President that they had agreed to declare Manila an open city to spare it being bombed and to protect the civilian population. Quezon noted that MacArthur was not certain that they would have to leave the city but MacArthur reminded the President that his safety was not a personal matter but a matter of great importance to the Government which he headed.

> He asserted that it was his duty to prevent my falling into the enemy's hands. He was also of the opinion that as long as I was free, the occupation of Manila, or even of the Philippines, by the Japanese Army would not have the same significance under international law as if the Government had been captured or surrendered.[53]

Sayre recalled how "reports kept coming in of disaster after disaster." The High Commissioner was also ill at ease with the MacArthur plan to remove to Corregidor. "This seeming abandonment of the people of Manila was distasteful to me and I wondered whether I should not remain and throw in my lot with them."[54] Sayre would go if Quezon agreed and Quezon promised he would reply to MacArthur after a hastily convened meeting of the Council of State the next day. When Quezon asked MacArthur who should accompany him if he should go to Corregidor, the General said that there was little space for additional civilians so there would only be room for those he considered absolutely necessary, including his doctors and his family.[55]

That night, Quezon discussed his predicament with his wife. She persuaded him to look at his duty in a broader context. "The winning of the war is the only question before us. Nothing else matters[56] . . . do as you wish, but my preference is to be with you."[57] Before the Cabinet meeting of 13 December, Quezon asked his children their opinion. They all agreed that they would abide by any decision he made. The Cabinet took the almost unanimous view that the capture of Quezon by the Japanese would mean the overthrow of the Commonwealth Government. The next day, Quezon decided to go to Corregidor, taking with him Vice President Osmeña, General Valdés, Chief Justice Santos and Manuel Roxas. Among those not selected was Jose P. Laurel who enjoyed good relations with the Japanese. After disbanding all the executive departments, the only man left in authority was Quezon's unelected *alter ego*, Jorge Vargas. Quezon asked Laurel to act as Secretary of Justice and "to help Vargas." Laurel fully understood the difficult position he was being put in if the Japanese occupants required or compelled him to take action inimical to the interests and wishes of the Government in Corregidor or of the United States. Recognizing the problem, Quezon sent Vargas to MacArthur for clarification of Laurel's concerns.

Vargas said to MacArthur, "General, I have been commissioned by the Cabinet to ask you for last minute instructions—what to do when the Japanese arrive in Manila. What are we going to do?" For a while, MacArthur considered the question, then, stepping in front of Vargas, he pointed at him and allegedly said: "There is nothing you can do; you have to follow what the Japanese Army of occupation orders you to do. Under international law you must obey the orders of the military occupant. There is only one thing you should not do: take the oath of allegiance to Japan because, if you do, we will shoot you when we come back." Vargas conveyed the message to Quezon who is said to have informed Laurel.[58] If what Vargas is reported to have told Quezon is true, then MacArthur gave those of Quezon's people who were to remain behind virtual *carte blanche*. Unfortunately, Quezon's autobiography is entirely silent on this vexed matter of collaboration while, for his part, MacArthur denied that this meeting with Vargas ever took place, and there were extreme recriminations when the former did return.

Prior to the Japanese entering the city, Vargas represented the President's sole national official left in Manila. A pair of international lawyers pointed out to him that, as an officer of a national government, he was, under international law, liable to arrest but, under the same law, he was immune to arrest if he was a local or municipal official. Vargas told Quezon of the problem, who said over the phone, "George, you are hereby appointed Mayor of the City of Greater Manila."[59]

On 22 December the first of the major Japanese landings forecast by MacArthur occurred. Forty-three thousand one hundred and ten men of General Homma's Fourteenth (Watari) Army disembarked from eighty-five transports in Lingayen Bay. Two days later, seven thousand men landed at Lamon Bay, south of Manila, as the second arm in an enveloping attack, intended to capture Manila in fifty days in order to release substantial numbers of the Fourteenth Army for second-phase duties elsewhere.

The Arcadia Conferences in Washington 22 December—14 January 1942 established the Combined Chiefs of Staff Committee. It was agreed as a "cardinal principle" of the Anglo-American coalition strategy "that only the minimum of force necessary for the safeguarding of vital interests in other theaters should be diverted from operations against Germany." The Navy found some elasticity in its understanding of "vital interest" so as to allow it to reinforce the Pacific but not the Army. In a study which the Army planners submitted on 3rd January, they showed that the Philippines could not be reinforced and that MacArthur's plan for an offensive northward from Australia to Mindanao would represent "an entirely unjustifiable diversion of forces from the principal theater—the Atlantic."[60] Prior to the publication of the War Plans paper, Stimson had been reconciling himself to the probability "we shall . . . all have to go through the agonizing experience of seeing the doomed garrison gradually pulled down while our preparations are not yet completed."[61] When he read the planners' paper he thought it had been worked out "with ruthless severity and some overstatement." Neither he nor Marshall made comment on it. "Everybody knows the chances are against our getting relief to him but there is no use saying so beforehand."[62] But that did not mean Stimson and Marshall did not try.

On 20 December, two officers, Colonel Stephen J. Chamberlin and Lieutenant Colonel Lester J. Whitlock, departed Washington in a B-24 bomber on a circuitous 16,000 mile route to Melbourne, where they arrived on 9 January 1942. Their secret mission (Plan X) was to liaise with the Commanding General, American Forces in Australia who was "authorized to do anything that may be required to get supplies, equipment, arms and ammunition to the United States Army Forces in the Far East."[63] On 18 January, Patrick J. Hurley, a former Secretary of War in the Hoover administration and recently appointed Minister to New Zealand, departed for Australia to provide support to Plan X. Hurley had a reputation as a hustler and his mission was to speed up the work in getting food supplies to MacArthur utilizing small surface vessels. To strengthen his arm he was promoted to Brigadier General in the Reserve Corps.[64]

The other matter of regional significance to be discussed during the Arcadia Conferences was the formation of a combined American, British, Dutch and Australian (ABDA) command. The Dutch were included but not consulted. As Churchill signaled the Lord Privy Seal in London on 28 December 1941: "Question of unity of command in South West Pacific has assumed urgent form. Last night the President urged upon me appointment of a single officer to command Army, Navy and Air Forces of Britain, America and Dutch . . . You will be as much astonished as I was to learn that man President has in mind is General Wavell"[65] (General Sir Archibald Wavell, a British General). This was a shrewd choice of Roosevelt's. The situation in the South West Pacific was dire and therefore so much more important that failure should not reflect adversely upon American command.

On 4 January 1942, Churchill sent a signal to Australia's Prime Minister John Curtin, copied to Wavell, outlining the agreed general strategic policy:

a. To hold Malay Barrier defined as line Malay Peninsula-Sumatra-Java-North Australia, as basic defensive position of ABDA area, and to operate sea, land and air forces in as great depth as possible forward of Barrier to oppose Japanese southward advance.

b. To hold Burma and Australia as essential support positions for the area and Burma as essential to support of China, and to defence of India.

c. To re-establish communications through Dutch East Indies with Luzon and to support Philippine Island garrison.

d. To maintain essential communications within area.[66]

During the afternoon of 22 December, MacArthur sent Sid Huff into the city to buy gifts for Jean and toys for his son. When Huff returned with the presents wrapped in brightly colored Christmas paper, the General said to his wife, "we must pretend it's already Christmas Eve." Jean opened the boxes of presents of scarves, dresses and embroidered blouses, thanked her husband and put her presents in the closet, never to be seen again.[67] The evening of 23 December in the High Commissioner's residence was spent wrapping Christmas packages of cigarettes and toiletries for the Red Cross to deliver to the men on the front line and to the wounded in hospital. The next morning, Sayre took a call from MacArthur. He said the fall of Manila was imminent and that he should leave within four hours for Corregidor with President Quezon. MacArthur promised to join them that evening. The burning of the residue of documents began and the High Commissioner's smart, air-conditioned automobile was run off the dock and sank in the bay. Sayre's quota of staff permitted to go to Corregidor was nine people, together with his wife Betty and his stepson. They took with them all that could be hurriedly thrown into a suitcase. Sayre remained unconvinced as to the wisdom of the move. "There seemed to be little choice between Corregidor and Manila. Manila had no tunnel to resort to; but Corregidor promised to be the center of Japanese attack, where life would be anything but safe or pleasant."[68]

Quezon's separation from his friends proved heartbreaking. He told them to do everything in their power to minimize the suffering of the civilian population and to keep faith in the United States. Turning to Vargas, "my faithful, hardworking, able, honest and public spirited secretary," Quezon gave him his final instructions. Almost in tears, the President said, "God bless you, George, and lead you in the right path. You have my absolute confidence, and I am sure you will not fail me.

Goodbye."[69] The presidential party's departure was delayed due to the Japanese bombing the port area but eventually, in two launches, they set off for SS *Mayon* lying a mile off shore. After some delay in getting up steam, the *Mayon*, carrying Quezon, Sayre, their respective families and staff, sailed for Corregidor. They were greeted there by a 15-gun salute and a regimental guard of honor. As Sayre made his way up to the entrance to the tunnel he saw a sign inviting Americans to go in, and for Filipinos to find shelter elsewhere.[70] "Out of the late afternoon sunlight," wrote Sayre, "we stepped into the dark tunnel, wondering what fate lay in store for us."[71]

In the Manila Hotel, Jean MacArthur prepared for her departure by packing hand luggage and a footlocker. The General's ten thousand volume military library was left behind, and the personal treasures belonging to both families. Jean took a pair of bronze vases, which had been presented to General Arthur MacArthur by the Emperor of Japan, and set them up in the entrance. "There," she said, "maybe when the Japanese see them, they will respect our home."[72] Sid Huff sent little Arthur's tricycle downstairs to be loaded in the cars with the rest of the luggage. Jean had packed in one of the suitcases MacArthur's Field Marshal's baton and his medals and decorations wrapped in a Manila Hotel bath towel.[73] While Jean tended to the last finishing touches, guests were dining below and the SS *Don Esteban* waited close by the hotel for the VIPs to board.

At MacArthur's insistence the stars and stripes had continued to fly each day outside the exposed headquarters building at 1 Calle Victoria. It was a legitimate military target but was never attacked. The sound of many aircraft engines would draw him outside to witness the spectacle. He counted them. "Fifty-five," he said to Huff. He ignored an aide's suggestion that he would be safer inside.[74]

The General had already supplemented his staff by calling upon his friend since 1928, Carlos Romulo, a newspaper editor, to head the Filipino side of his public relations. "I am calling you to active duty," MacArthur said to Romulo. Romulo thanked the General but said he needed time to get his affairs in order. "I'm not asking you, I'm ordering you—report tomorrow morning."[75] MacArthur would christen Major Romulo "the voice of freedom." He drew up the necessary order declaring Manila an open city with effect from 26 December. This process included a meeting with the already interned Japanese Consul-General Nihro to acquaint him with the plan so that the diplomat could convey the information to the Japanese military.[76] As night fell on the 23rd, MacArthur looked around the walls of his office at the military memorabilia representing every step in his long military career. His eyes came to rest upon a red pennant bearing four stars on a pole in the corner of the room. It was the car flag from the days when he had been Chief of Staff of the Army. A four-star General once more, he told his Chief Clerk to pass it to him. Putting the rolled-up pennant under his arm, he turned away, saying to Sutherland, "Well Dick, I guess it's time to go. There isn't anything left to do here."[77]

11

"... Their Freedom Will Be Redeemed"

Having gained air and sea supremacy, and with fighter bases established in Luzon and seaplane bases in the south, Japan was ready for the serious matter of the land campaign. The plan, which involved a major landing at Lingayen Gulf and a lesser one at Lamon Bay, was known to only a few. The fetish of secrecy was at times close to being self-defeating. "Important orders were delivered just before they had to be executed with little time for study and preparation." The Japanese post-operation report went on to observe how all this "proved incentives to errors and confusion, uneasiness and irritation."[1] The process of assembling General Homma's 14th Army had begun in November, but not until 17 December were the various components of the convoy ready to sail, the first at 0900 from Northern Formosa and the last departing Takao at 1700 on the 18th. Ever since Pearl Harbor, Homma had feared intervention by the B-17s from the Philippines but not one was to fly over Formosa where the bulk of the convoy had been assembled. When the seventy-six Army transports and nine Navy transports with their heavy Navy escort cast off, the danger had not abated: it had changed, with the additional threat posed by the 21 submarines of the Asiatic Fleet.

MacArthur and Hart had their final meeting on 22 December, the day the Lingayen force went ashore. The failure of Hart's submarines ensured that an outraged MacArthur would register a justifiable complaint. "What in the world is the matter with your submarines? The Jap ships are coming in here in the Lingayen Gulf, landing, and your people haven't sunk a single solitary ship."[2] For Hart, it was an uncomfortable meeting for he had no defense to offer.

Homma's invasion fleet was seen from Lingayen Bay at 1713 hours, 21 December, by the submarine *Stingray* commanded by Lieutenant Commander Ray Lamb. Ordered by Captain John Wilkes, Comsubs Asiatic Fleet, to press home the attack, *Stingray* spent fourteen and a half hours on the sea bed avoiding detection.[3] After *Stingray* returned to Manila without having fired a single torpedo, Lamb was relieved of his command. When Wilkes received Lamb's contact report, he sent six submarines to Lingayen Gulf with the order to "enter Lingayen Gulf and attack the enemy landing forces."[4] One 5,445-ton transport, *Hayo Maru*, was sent to the shallow bottom by S-38. That was the single success of the submarines.[5] Why did the Navy only have one submarine in Lingayen Gulf at a time when a landing there seemed more than a good bet? There were 14 fleet boats in the vicinity of Lingayen Gulf 20–25 December.[6] If they were not to enter the Gulf, why was it not heavily mined? It had, in fact, not been mined at all.

The Japanese were proficient at detecting the presence of submarines but much less competent in achieving kills.[7] The first operational loss to be announced was that of the *Shark* which disappeared in mid February 1942.[8] Meanwhile, it was becoming patently clear that something was seriously wrong with U.S. torpedoes; countless numbers of which were launched at the fat targets in Lingayen Bay, until the submarines were detected by destroyers. Being forced to lie on the sea bed, no more than 120 feet deep in places, suffering close depth charge attack, affected the psychological balance of some commanders. One said, "you'd better relieve me. I'm afraid my nerves are too bad to take this submarine out again, and I may lose it, through no fault of the crew."[9] Peacetime training and poor upkeep and maintenance were the principal reasons for the failure of Hart's submarines but it is also true that geography was against them. The eastern Asiatic littoral falls away gently, the shallow bottom extending many miles out to sea, strewn with boulders. Unable therefore to dive to a safe depth, they were also unable to move on the bottom or to lie motionless with their motors closed down.[10] Moreover, in the shallow, clear water they could be seen by over-flying aircraft.

In the first weeks of war, the submarines were not in a position to know what degree of latitude they could expect from the attention of the busy, depth-charging destroyers above them. Those who were sent out on these early, preventive missions, however, would have been impressed by the size of the naval force detailed to protect the transports. The Japanese recognized the potential threat the American submarines posed to their communications, which is why they assembled heavy screens of anti-submarine vessels. The Japanese established an outer cordon of ships to prevent any interference with the Lingayen landings. This outer ring comprised two battleships, four heavy cruisers, one light cruiser, two seaplane carriers and supporting destroyers. In close support of the landing force were two light cruisers, sixteen destroyers and a large quantity of torpedo boats, minelayers, minesweepers and patrol craft.[11]

It would not be until 1943 that part of the reason would be discovered why the Navy's Mark XIV torpedoes were dud. The problem lay with the Mark VI magnetic exploder, which ironically Hart had helped develop in 1929.[12] Unlike the contact exploder fitted to the Mark X torpedo, the Mark XIV was detonated by magnetic influence. There was time at the outbreak of war to make confirmatory live tests on the Mark XIV but it was not done, despite the complaints of skippers that the torpedo was either running deep or did not detonate.[13]

General Homma must have felt supremely fortunate to have avoided intervention by both American air and naval forces. He must surely have held no illusion as to the difficulties to be faced in the next phase, a contested amphibious landing across the beaches. The Japanese had an enormous degree of respect for American military capabilities. Moreover, the continuing dictates of secrecy denied Homma the surface bombardment of shore objectives as well as tactical air missions.[14]

The bulk of the forces allocated to the Lingayen landing came from Lieutenant General Yuichi Tsuchibashi's 48th Division. The Division had been formed in Formosa in 1940 and was untried in battle. Two of its three regiments were Formosan. The 48th Division had been reinforced by the 9th Infantry from the 16th Division. The force was modestly motorized and one battalion in each regiment was equipped with bicycles. A further important attachment consisted of between 80–100 light and heavy tanks. In addition to the 48th Division's own Mountain Artillery Regiment issued with the 75mm pack mountain gun there were also other respectable artillery enhancements: eight horse-drawn 75mm guns, sixteen 105mm guns, eight 150mm guns and twenty-four 150mm howitzers. The total landed from Homma's 14th Army between 22–28 December 1941 was a surprisingly small force of 43,110 men which, after the deduction of shipping units (4,633 men) and the Army Air Force (3,621) shrank to a military component of only 34,856.[15] When MacArthur informed the War Department of the Lingayen landing, he described a "major enemy effort in strength estimated at 80,000 to 100,000 men of four to six divisions."[16] When the General surveyed the intelligence estimates on the battle map, he remarked to Sutherland, "what a target this would have been for the submarines."[17]

The day-to-day operational planning of the land battle was in the hands of Major General Richard Sutherland. In 1938, Sutherland had been a captain in Tientsin. Since then, his service on MacArthur's staff had been unbroken. Thus, he had no command experience at battalion, regiment, brigade or division. In command of the hot spot of Northern Luzon was Major General Jonathan Wainwright. Sutherland said: "Wainwright was one of the bravest men I knew. He was a cavalryman of the old school, utterly without personal fear, but strategically and tactically, he wasn't too good."[18] While Sutherland's views of Wainwright are debatable, what is less debatable is the deployment of American and Philippine forces in accordance with the MacArthur Plan. MacArthur's original intention had been that each of the ten Philippine Divisions would fight within the regions where they were raised. The undeniable importance of Northern Luzon, however, meant that two southern divisions—Selleck's 71st from Negros and the 91st from Leyte and Samar—were deployed into reserve in Luzon in support of the divisions of the Northern Luzon Force. The 11th and 21st Divisions were deployed into static defensive positions on Lingayen Gulf, the 31st Division was assigned the Zambales Coast, and the 41st and 51st had a roving commission against secondary landings that might occur at Batangas, Nasugbu and Tayabas Bays. Three divisions remained to defend Visayan and Mindanao. In being drawn northward, therefore, MacArthur's dispositions bore some semblance to Grunert's War Plan Orange–3. But there was one critical difference. Grunert intended to man the most likely invasion beaches with regular forces supported by the Philippine Army once they had been sufficiently trained. The only regular unit in a forward position was the mounted 26th Cavalry.

Thus, the Philippine Division (one American Regiment and Philippine Scouts), two tank battalions and the 4th Marines were not committed on the beaches but were held back in reserve. Their superior training and significantly superior arms and equipment to that in the hands of the Filipino divisions could not tell at the critical time. The concept of the Filipino Army manning the beaches and hurling back an invader who dared to cherish their territory was one which MacArthur had staked his reputation on in selling his plan to Washington. On 27 November, he had been cleared to put his plan—Revised Orange Five—into effect. Even after command of the air and sea had been forfeited, the Plan was kept intact. The option of withdrawing into Bataan remained as a last resort but, to have adopted what MacArthur described as a "defeatist" strategy would have been to the prejudice of his reputation. The majority of MacArthur's staff opposed the Philippine Army First plan which, significantly, had the support of Sutherland and Willoughby.[19] "We didn't win at the beaches because we weren't asked to do so," said a staff officer. "Had we been given the opportunity we would have been victorious."[20]

A study of operations and administration and logistics at this time reveals an alarming number of contradictions and loose ends, one of which concerned the "powerful veteran organization" the 4th Marines who (with Navy personnel) had been "made available to MacArthur through Rockwell for such use as might be profitable."[21] Sutherland tells the lamentable story of how he wanted to use the Marines:

> in the fighting but Colonel W.T. Clemens (Clement), Asiatic Fleet Marine Officer, contended that the Marines were not fit for combat having been stationed in China for too long a period. As a result, I placed them on Corregidor on work details, etc., where I expect I would have assigned them eventually anyhow. I had an awful time with Clemens, but the CO, Colonel Howard, was a swell guy who wanted to see action with his men.[22]

The literature shows, however, that it was Rockwell who gave the Marines their executive orders. Rockwell enjoyed good relations with MacArthur and appeared to have no problems with the 4th Marines being under Army tactical command. Howard, accompanied by Clement, reported for duty to MacArthur who sent Colonel Howard to Sutherland, "who provided him orders to prepare for duty on Corregidor." Howard, realizing the assignment would take the 4th

Marines away from the front, asked that his regiment be allowed to guard the western beaches on Bataan. Sutherland replied that he wanted "the 4th Marines to take over the beach defenses (of Corregidor) as soon as possible."[23] It is not beyond the realms of possibility that MacArthur was unwilling to give the Marines a prominent role in his defense of the Philippines. "Tactical command" did not include administrative command. The Marines and the Navy maintained their own supplies and medical support on Corregidor. The extremely divisive situation therefore arose when the Army was put on half rations and the Navy continued on full rations. Not until February, when Washington confirmed the Navy elements to be under full Army command, was the Navy instantly placed on half rations.[24]

That everything was not entirely ready and provided for could be gleaned from one of the last signals Brereton sent, on 19 December, before leaving for Australia. He asked of the commanding General of the *Hawaiian Air Force*, "information as to maps now available Hawaii of Philippine Islands particularly Luzon." The unavailability of maps for the defenders was one of a number of issues to exasperate Colonel Richard C. Mallonée, artillery "senior instructor" to the 21st Philippine Division. "We had these islands for 40 years, we have been planning the defense of this beach for over 15 years to my knowledge—and yet we have only an inadequate number of inaccurate, out of date maps and not one airplane photo, much less a mosaic."[25]

Mallonée's observations are important. He had previous service in the Philippines from 1926–1929, had served in G3 operations when MacArthur commanded the Philippine Department, and had studied the people and the history of the Philippines. On 6 December, twenty of the regiment's 75mm guns arrived, followed by the other four the next day. Sixteen of the guns were road transportable while the others had wooden wheels, a vestige of horse-drawn days. Each gun came with 200 rounds of ammunition and 100 rounds for each soldier's rifle. At 7 a.m. the next day, when attention was to be turned to introducing the newly-inducted Filipino peasants to their artillery equipment, the news of the attack on Pearl Harbor was broadcast on the radio.

Mallonée recalled how, in his previous G3 appointment, the operations staff had maintained a file indicating positions of individual artillery pieces, their fields of fire, the water depth, channels and any other useful information regarding landing points. The "senior instructor" failed completely in his efforts to persuade the Filipino Divisional Commander, Brigadier General Mateo Capinpin, or the "division instructor," Lieutenant Colonel O'Day, to call for the files. "So after twenty years of continuing and unhurried reconnaissance and study, we were to occupy positions selected during a forty-eight hour trip over 120 kilometers of front by a major of Constabulary and a reserve captain of limited experience."[26] When trucks arrived to deploy to the beaches, the men scrambled aboard in a disorderly mob. Four hours after loading began, the trucks were ready to set off. Mallonée discovered one battalion commander had not loaded the ammunition because of insufficient room on the trucks. When he ordered the trucks to be off-loaded, "I noted that every officer's over-sized bedroll and clothing had been loaded, as well as such unauthorized impedimenta as suitcases, trunk lockers, guitars and boxes of every size and description."[27] After a reassessment of priorities, the 21st Division drove off to war.

The 21st Division's position was at the southern end of Lingayen Gulf, thought to be the most likely landing area, between Lingayen and San Fabian. Mallonée reconnoitered the beach and put his three battalions in direct fire positions. This meant it would be difficult if not impossible to extract the guns but, from Mallonée's point of view, this was the only way to deploy them in view of the lack of training and inadequate communications and transport. Besides, he had sufficient ammunition for less than a full day, after which the guns would be useless. The North Luzon Force orders required a last ditch defense: "We must die in our tracks, falling, not backward but forward, toward the enemy." Mallonée had cause, therefore, to be bemused when Colonel Irwin of USAFFE Operations looked at the 21st's ammunition disposition and "violently announced" that it would be impossible to withdraw the ammunition in time to save it and he would "crucify anyone who lost as much as one round." Mallonée explained to Irwin that there were no plans to withdraw and that anyway it would be physically impossible to withdraw from the beach, in action. "Don't believe everything you hear. As God is my judge, if you leave one round of ammunition behind for the enemy, I'll have your head."[28] This exchange is of interest, showing that as early as 13 December there were some thoughts in the USAFFE of abandoning the beaches.

During the evening 20th–21st, 21st Division was alerted to the presence of between 100 and 120 Japanese transports escorted by warships. From the observation post atop the capitol building at Lingayen, Mallonée could see at first light the enormous Japanese armada in the vicinity of San Fernando, unopposed and well beyond the range of his guns. What caused Mallonée concern was the quietness. "Heartsick and despondent, I felt the impending hand of disaster. Apparently there had been no effort to effect the basic defense plan: no opportunity to attack the enemy convoy. I realized that if we didn't have sufficient air strength to assist us in this critical period, the remainder of our campaign would be under the eyes of Japanese aviators.[29] Not being in contact with the enemy, the 21st Division awaited orders to move north to contest the landings. No such orders were forthcoming.

The static defense of Lingayen Gulf must surely be regarded as among the most lackluster, uninspiring defenses conducted throughout the duration of the Second World War. No effort was made to put together a mobile reserve as a quick reaction force to take the contest to the water line. Lieutenant General Masami Maeda, Chief of Staff of the Fourteenth Army, said that if he had been MacArthur, he would have placed his cavalry and armor north of San Fernando (at La Union on Lingayen Gulf) so that they were in a position to oppose troops coming south from Aparri or swing south to take the disembarking invasion force in the flank.[30] In the event, the American use of their two armored battalions was extremely tentative. Undoubtedly, part of the problem arose through the creation of the Provisional Tank Group (PTG) on 21 November and Brigadier General Weaver's perception that it was "a separate tactical command under the Commanding General, U.S. Forces in the Far East."[31] The 194th battalion was south of Manila with General Parker's Southern Luzon Force. The 192nd meanwhile had remained at Clark but, on 21 December, received a warning order from USAFFE to move northward to support Wainwright's North Luzon Force. Surprisingly, they were not put under Wainwright's command. Company B, moving in advance of the main body, had a special mission to oppose enemy landings which might take place in the area of Agoo. It was planned to re-supply the tanks at Gerona and again at Bauang. When the armor reached Bauang they were refused gas and, by the next morning, Bauang was in Japanese hands.[32]

The landing of the Japanese was not as uncomplicated as it first appeared to Mallonée. It had been the intention to land between San Fernando and Bauang 32 and 24 miles respectively north of Damortis but what they thought was the Agno River was one just to its north and, in consequence, the Japanese undershot the mark. The 48th Division accidentally landed in an undefended sector while the 9th Infantry, which landed where the 48th Division should have done, at Bauang, suffered heavy casualties from the beach defenders. The sea was rough when the first wave of barges went ashore. Homma and Maeda, through their binoculars, saw the barges being smashed onto the beaches and some being overturned. Lieutenant General Masahuru Homma was a stocky man compared with the normally slight Japanese figure. He had learnt his military skills after the British tradition and, while he understood English, he was less confident speaking it. The radios had been soaked in the landing and Homma remained out of communication with his advance troops. "Had the Americans attacked us then," claimed Maeda, "we would have had to surrender."[33] The bad weather delayed the completion of the landing throughout the 22nd, until 30 December 1941.[34]

On the right of 21st Division, along the eastern shore of the Gulf as far north as San Fernando, was 11th Division reinforced by a regiment of the 71st Division. The 11th Division did not have its own integral direct support divisional artillery, that function being provided by a Philippine Scout Battalion, the 86th, equipped with 155mm guns. The 26th Cavalry was held in reserve at Pozorrubio on Route 3. This is on the central plain of Luzon, through which Route 3 runs directly into Manila. The Japanese 9th Infantry had the misfortune to land in the only spot on the Gulf that was manned by Filipinos armed with one .50 caliber and several .30 caliber machine guns. The .50 machine gun accounted for many Japanese but faulty ammunition clogged the firing mechanisms of the .30s. Once the Japanese had established a foothold on the shore, the Filipinos withdrew. Across the length of the landing area the Japanese, representing three infantry regiments, moved relentlessly inland, despite the fact that the bulk of the 14th Army was still aboard with most of its artillery and heavy equipment. Suspecting an imminent counterattack, Homma ordered the convoy to move to the south, to calmer water, to commence landing on the 23rd off Damortis.[35]

The pragmatic company commander of 192nd tank battalion, Captain Donald Hanes, had by now pooled his gas resources to permit a platoon of five tanks to advance towards Agoo. Along the road they

The Manila Hotel *(Manila Hotel)*

MacArthur on his appointment as Field Marshal at the dinner given in his honor on August 24, 1936, at Malacañan Palace. Standing on his left is Eisenhower. *(MacArthur Memorial Archives)*

U.S. High Commissioner Francis B. Sayre making an office call on the newly appointed commander of the Philippine Department, Major General George Grunert. June 7, 1940. *(U.S. Army Military History Institute)*

Right, Lieutenant General MacArthur being congratulated by President Manuel Quezon on his appointment as Commanding General, United States Armed Forces Far East. *(MacArthur Memorial Archives)*

Lieutenant General MacArthur talking with Major General Wainwright, October 10, 1941. *(MacArthur Memorial Archives)*

THE CHIEF OF STAFF IS IN AGREEMENT WITH THE ESTIMATE PRESENTED

HEREWITH AND REQUESTS THAT YOU INFORM THE SENIOR ARMY OFFICER

IN YOUR AREA : CHANCES OF FAVORABLE OUTCOME OF US-JAPANESE$

NEGOTIATIONS ARE VERY DOUBTFUL. THIS SITUATION TOGETHER WITH

STATEMENTS ØQF JAPANESE GOVERNMENT AND MOVENTS OF THEIR NAVAL

AND MILITARY FORCES   INTIMATE IN OUR OPINION THAT A SURPRISE

AGGRESSIVE MOVEMENT IN ANY DIRECTION INCLUDING ATTACK ON

PHILLIPPINES OR GUAM IS A POSSIBILITY , THIS INFORMATION MUST BE

TREATED WITH THE UTMOST SECRECY IN ORDER NOT TO COMPLICATE AN

ALREADY TENSE SITUATION OR PRECIPITATE JAPANESE ACTION

DECLASSIFIED PER JCS LTR OF
20 AUG 75

System

From CHIEF OF NAVAL OPERATIONS	Action	CINCAF CINCPAC COM 11, ETC.	Info										
Precedence		To be acknowledged		Coding Off.					Date 24 Nov 1941				
SECRET	Oper.	Gun.	Supply	Mat.	Int.	Comm.	Asst. Comm.	Flag Sec.	Flag Lieut.	Mar.	Surg	File No.
AFPS—9-9-41—8500. 385,												

One of a number of signals at that time (November 24, 1941) warning of possibility of Japanese attack. *(MacArthur Memorial Archives)*

Air Raid on Clark Air Base, December 8, 1941. Japanese War Art. *(National Archives, Maryland)*

Quezon Family on Corregidor Island, 1942. Zeneida (Nene), Aurora, Manuel, Maria (Baby), Manuel Jr. (Nonong). *(MacArthur Memorial Archives)*

Lateral No. 12 which the Finance Corps (foreground) shared with the Signal Corps. Behind the partition are the code machines and telegraph operators of the Signal Corps. *(U.S. Army Military History Institute)*

券 降 投
SURRENDER CARD

Any Filipino or American soldier and their friends will received special consideration by presenting this card to the Imperial Japanese Forces.

本投降券持參者に對しては特別の考慮を
與へられ度

Surrender card.
(Sayre Papers. Manuscript Division, Library of Congress)

Propaganda dropped by the Japanese on Filipino soldiers, February 2, 1942. *(U.S. Army Military History Institute)*

To Our Sons and Brothers In Bataan

On behalf of the Filipino people, and as the Chairman of a Provisional Philippine Council of State, I urge you to lay down your arms immediately and abandon cooperation with the American Army.

The present war was forced upon Japan by the American Imperialists headed by President Roosevelt who, under the hypocritical claim that they are fighting for democracy, wish to rule and dominate the whole world. America is now master of the Western Hemisphere which is one half of the world and the British Empire which occupies one fourth of the area of the earth is now virtually a colony of the United States. Therefore, America controls three fourths of the world today. And yet, she still craves for the remaining fourth which is the Orient, because her greed for power is insatiable.

Japan will never consent to American domination of the Orient. Once more, she has taken up arms to stem the tide of Occidental Imperialism so that Asia may be preserved for Asiatics and the Philippines for the Filipinos. Furthermore, Premier Tojo of Japan has solemnly promised at the 79th session, of the Imperial Diet held on January 21st, 1942; in which he said in part "Japan will gladly grant the Philippines its independence so long as it cooperates and recognizes Japan's program of establishing a Greater East Asia Co-prosperity Sphere." Are you going to be traitors to the cause of the Oriental Races? Remember that never in the history of mankind has the white people fought for the colored race. Even now the American command always place you in the vanguard while American soldiers stay behind.

Brothers-in-arms! Japan has come to help us realize our ideals and aspirations and establish an economic, cultural and spiritual confederacy of Oriental nations known as the Great East Asia Co-prosperity sphere. Let us shake off the yoke of white domination forever, and find a dignified place for us among this concert of Oriental nations.

JORGE B. VARGAS
Chairman of the Executive Commission,
Provisional Philippine Council of State.

Propaganda leaflet under the name of Jorge B. Vargas. Evidence such as this was brought forward at the time consideration was being given to his trial for collaboration. *(Sayre Papers. Manuscript Division, Library of Congress)*

Captured Japanese photograph of United States soldiers, marines and sailors surrendering to Japanese Forces on Corregidor. *(U.S. Army Military History Institute)*

Admirals Purnell, Hart, Lieutenant General Brett and Major General Lewis Brereton. Java, 1942. *(National Archives, Maryland)*

The fourteen officers and one sergeant who left Bataan and Corregidor on PT boats with General MacArthur, family and amah, March 11, 1942. The Bataan Gang. Clockwise from 12.00: Major General Sutherland, Brigadier General George, Brigadier General Willoughby, Brigadier General Marquat, Captain McMicking, Master Sergeant Rogers, Lieutenant Colonel Diller, Lieutenant Colonel Wilson, Major Morhouse (a doctor brought specially from Bataan), Lieutenant Colonel Huff, Lieutenant Colonel Sherr, Brigadier General Casey, Brigadier General Stivers, Major General Akin. *(MacArthur Memorial Archives)*

encountered a Japanese tank unit. All five of the American tanks were hit: four made it back to Rosario where they were lost in a bombing attack later in the day.[36] By the evening of 22nd the Japanese had captured the defiles leading down into the Luzon Valley, had linked up with the Tanaka Force from Appari, and occupied Damortis and Rosario.[37] The ease of their success caused concern among the less valiant Japanese. Suspecting retribution around the corner, they proposed abandoning an unconsolidated advance in favor of building up a bridgehead. The aggressive element demurred, arguing that the Americans would not risk an offensive in front of the Agno River line. Much more important, therefore, to seize the bridgeheads over the Agno while the initiative still appeared to remain in their hands.[38]

The Philippine infantry, of whom MacArthur had such high but unreasonable hopes, broke at the first appearance of the Japanese and fled in disarray to the rear. This action in Luzon had been reminiscent of the 1917 Battle of Caporetto, albeit on a smaller scale, where the German General Otto von Bülow's Fourteenth Austrian Army, assisted by a phosgene gas attack, swept away a larger Italian force. The lessons arising from the Battle of Caporetto—surprise, objective, mass and economy of force—are principles MacArthur might have orchestrated in the waiting period 8–22 December. The Japanese may well have anticipated a coordinated attack by the four divisions of the North Luzon Force once they had broken out into the Luzon valley but, lack of equipment and transportation, the most basic of training and the absence of communications, meant that such an attack would have been impossible. If the MacArthur Plan was to have any prospect of success, it involved having a full, mobile force of regulars available to contest the beaches. If that were not on offer, the foolhardy attempt to defend the beaches with untrained Filipinos, many of whom had never fired their personal weapon (and two of the three regiments of each division had trained for a month or less), should never have been entered into.

On the 23rd, the Japanese made their main thrust southward down Route 3 towards Manila. Blocking their way south of Sison was Brigadier General Selleck's 71st Division less one battalion. Selleck's temporary appointment as Brigadier General was only made effective on 21 December.[39] The Division suffered during the day from the attention of the planes of the 10th Independent and 16th Bombardment Regiments. It had no anti-aircraft defense. As evening drew in, it promised some respite but, "at this critical time Nip tanks (4th Tank

Regiment) appeared and a rout ensued."[40] The Division's officers were unable to stop the flood of men to the rear. Fortunately, 26th Cavalry had rested and reorganized. They faced up to the armored thrust, permitting the troops that had held to break clean and withdraw to the Agno, proving what Filipino troops, properly trained, equipped and motivated, could achieve. Meanwhile Wainwright, realizing that the position on the beaches had been lost, had already asked USAFFE's permission to withdraw over the Agno River. Permission was granted. Wainwright hoped to consolidate south of the river and, reinforced with the regular U.S. Army Division, counterattack the Japanese. USAFFE instructed him to submit his plans. When asked whether he could include the Philippine Division in his planning assumptions, the eventual answer was "highly improbable."[41]

The 26th had already fought five major battles in as many days and their strength had now fallen to 450. At Binalonan, from 0500 until 1530 on the 24th, they fought a rearguard action to enable General Wainwright to establish the line along the Agno River. "With no antitank weapons the troopers had halted the Japanese armor with fanatical feats of heroism, throwing themselves on tanks, dropping grenades down hatches and firing into the gunports. Then as they fell back from one defensive line to the next, they gave ground grudgingly, and at terrible cost."[42] The addition of the 2nd Formosans into the attack swung the balance in favor of the Japanese and forced the withdrawal of 26th Cavalry in mid afternoon. Wainwright had witnessed this heroic action, the last combat action in the history of American horse cavalry, for he had gone to Binalonan to find Selleck and the 71st Division, but found the 26th Cavalry instead.[43] "Here," wrote Wainwright, "was true cavalry delaying action, fit to make a man's heart sing. Pierce (CO) that day upheld the best traditions of the cavalry service."[44] On the 24th, General Homma and his staff came ashore at Bauang to add momentum: he had been allocated only 30 days in which to take Manila. The previous night, after some 40 hours of procrastination, MacArthur had bowed to the inevitable conclusion that the Philippine Army of which he had expected so much, had broken before the Japanese advance in Northern Luzon. Gavin Long likened MacArthur's performance over this crucial period to that of "an old-time fighter, recalled from retirement and suddenly thrust into the ring against a young and hard hitting opponent whose lightning reflexes left him dazzled."[45]

MacArthur had warned Marshall on 22 December that what he

believed to be "this enormous tactical discrepancy will compel me to operate in delaying action on successive lines through central Luzon plain to final defensive position on Bataan to cover Corregidor."[46] MacArthur made no reference to the failure of the Filipino divisions in the disastrous fighting of 22–23 December. Instead he explained the reverse by saying that "the imminent menace of encirclement by greatly superior numbers forced me to act instantly."[47] On 24 December, the Lamon Bay Force comprising in the main General Morioka's 16th Division of approximately 7,000 men, landed there in three places—Mauban, Atimonan and Siain[48]—covering a front of 30 miles.

MacArthur had already announced his reluctant acceptance of reverting to what was described as WPO-3, War Plan Orange 3, a misnomer but the Americans knew what it meant whereas the Filipinos did not. It meant Bataan and it meant Corregidor, both of which should have been fully stocked to sustain the military for 180 days of combat. Some supplies had gone into Corregidor, which MacArthur had told Marshall in his signal of 22 December, "I intend to hold," but Bataan was virtually devoid of combat supplies and medicines. MacArthur ordered Wainwright to withdraw slowly down the Central Luzon Plain in order to buy the time to allow Parker's South Luzon Force to come up to Bataan and for the logisticians to stock the Peninsula. Wainwright had five successive delaying positions which had been the subject of command post and field training exercises since the late 1920s. "Back in my Stotsenburg days I had gone over the final line (D-5) many times," recalled Mallonée.[49] The aim was to hold each line in sufficient strength to oblige the Japanese to halt and prepare for a formal attack and then to withdraw sequentially at night to the next line before the full attack was launched.

The Japanese 16th Division, designated for the Lamon Bay Landings, had seen service in Manchuria and China, but it was a formation that General Homma did not rate highly. Initially, its intended landing place was the rather obvious Batangas Bay which was almost ideal for beach landing. As the overall Japanese plans developed, the support capability available for the Philippine invasion began to erode and the American offensive capability increased, so it was decided to land at Lamon Bay on the south-east coast rather than the more accessible south-west. There were two basic problems with Lamon Bay. Firstly, and as the U.S. Navy had recognized, the prevailing winds did not favor a winter landing, and secondly, the Tayabas

Mountains lay between the beaches and the Japanese objective of Manila. Fortune favored the Japanese for the artillery of South Luzon Force, two batteries of 86th Field Artillery's 155mm guns and a battalion of sixteen 75mm guns on self-propelled mounts, were all on the west coast at Batangas, Balayan and Nasugbu Bays—on the direct route through to Manila and over favorable terrain. Generals Parker and Jones pleaded with USAFFE Headquarters to switch some of the artillery assets to the east coast—decisions which should have been within the prerogative of local commanders—but their entreaties were consistently rebuffed.[50]

The Lamon Bay Landings are important, not only because they succeeded beyond the wildest dreams of a skeptical Homma but also because one of the prongs of attack, the most northerly at Mauban, was the only landing in the campaign where the Japanese encountered a dug-in and relatively prepared Filipino unit. The outcome of that contact is revealing.

This unit, The First Regular Division, should not be confused with the Philippine Division, which was a U.S. Formation including the Philippine Scouts. The First Regular Division was an original formation of the Philippine Army but it was not inducted into the U.S. Army at the same time as were the other ten Filipino Divisions. It had always been under-strength and its function since its activation on 18 January 1936 seems to have been principally in the field of ceremonial duties. Demands for trained manpower had a devastating effect upon it and when war came, it was deficient in officers and men at all levels. The problem was overcome to some degree when it was discovered that the staff of the Philippine Military Academy had not been assigned war roles. The Academy had closed and Camp John Hay at Baguio was now in Japanese hands. Perhaps one reason the West Point-trained Superintendent Colonel Fidel Segundo had been overlooked for a wartime command was because it was he whose earlier skepticism had so irked and irritated MacArthur. Suddenly, he found himself promoted to Brigadier General, nominated Commanding General of the First Division, tasked to bring it up to establishment with volunteers, train it, and be ready for war within a week.

There were two regiments in the Division, the First Infantry and the Third Infantry. The third regiment (Second Infantry) was never raised. The First Infantry had 20 per cent of its intended strength available at the outbreak of war. The balance had to be made up from volunteers. The Regiments were organized into three battalions, each of three rifle companies and a machine gun company. The war establishment for each regiment was 70 officers and 1,500 men. They were equipped with First World War Enfield rifles which were issued covered in preservative grease. There was also a more general collection of assorted weaponry: Browning automatic rifles, a few Springfield rifles, four 3-inch trench mortars (but no ammunition), a few .30 caliber machine guns and one .50 caliber heavy machine gun (but no ammunition). There was no signal equipment, no engineering or quartermaster supplies, and rationing was subject to local purchase arrangements, the money sometimes having to be loaned by the regimental officers. The division had no artillery and no organic transport. On 19 December 1941, the First Division, for better or for worse, was inducted into U.S. service by Brigadier General Richard Marshall.

While the Third Regiment remained in Manila, the First was deployed during the evening of 20 December to the South Luzon Force, to the area Infanta-Mauban, with a view to relieving elements of the over-stretched 51st Division. While the Regiment prepared its defensive position in the area of Mauban, the Lingayen landings had already taken place and the deterioration in the military situation there had become evident. USAFFE rescinded the order placing the First Regiment under command of South Luzon Force and ordered it northward to come under General Wainwright's command. Fortunately the orders did not percolate down to the First Regiment, now busily digging foxholes in the sand. The soldiers' best efforts to remove the cloying cosmolene from their rifles were frustrated due to there being insufficient solvent. Many were never test-fired. The military engineers who were supposed to construct beach obstacles were unable to do so because the barbed wire and engineering equipment had not arrived.

The necessity of a regiment being required to join the Northern Luzon Force had never gone away and, in anticipation of orders being promulgated during the evening of 23rd, the 51st Division unit designated to take over from the First Regiment ordered its machine guns and supporting infantry to Infanta and Mauban. From 10 p.m. on 23 December, ships began to anchor off Mauban. The 51st Division's infantry withdrew to Atimonau, but it was too late to remove the machine guns. Soon, the unmistakable sounds of disembarkation could be heard in the darkness beyond the pier at Mauban. Five hundred thinly-spread Filipino riflemen, each with 60 rounds of ammunition, prepared themselves to confront an invasion force of 1,000 Japanese soldiers.

In order to achieve surprise, the Japanese came shoreward without preparatory naval bombardment. At 1:30 a.m. on the 24th, when the lead boats were 50–75 meters from the shore, the Filipinos opened fire. It was the Japanese who were surprised and forced to retire under the weight of fire, but the Filipino fire discipline had not been good. A number of machine guns had overheated and seized while the earlier inability to clean many of the Enfields properly had led to their misfiring or bursting their barrels. The next action, Japanese naval gunfire, was predictable and it took casualties among the men crouching in their foxholes. When the naval gunfire lifted, the landing resumed but the Filipinos, some now out of ammunition, found themselves in hand-to-hand fighting with the veteran Japanese. It was not an even contest. When daylight came, aircraft from the seaplane tender *Mizuho* attacked the Filipinos in the line who, with ammunition supplies exhausted, began to pull back.

With the news of the reversion to War Plan Orange also came the news that, effective midday the 24th, General Parker would assume command of the defense of Bataan and would be replaced as commander South Luzon Force by General Jones. The natural instinct of the untrained Filipinos to withdraw was reinforced by the unauthorized order of an American adviser to do so. General Jones heard the news of the First Regiment's withdrawal just as he was about to have his Christmas lunch. Jones was a gung-ho general who believed that the Japanese could be beaten. Going off to investigate, he came across groups of men withdrawing. He reorganized these and sent them back from whence they had come, to hold the Japanese in terrain which favored the defense. Late that Christmas afternoon he encountered the erstwhile defenders at Mauban. Angrily confronting them, he shouted: "Why do you allow these Goddamned bastards to overrun your country?"

The Filipinos replied that they had done their best but the Japanese were better soldiers. Jones then turned on their American adviser: "Just what the hell did you mean by pulling back?"

"We had been ordered by the Commanding General South Luzon Force."

"*I* am the Commanding General South Luzon Force."

To another Filipino officer, Jones said, "This country is yours! I want you to defend every inch of your country. Do not allow the Japanese to overrun your country, so let's go and fight!" Jones ordered the Filipinos to re-embus and, in his own sedan, headed off along the muddy roads to counterattack. Sedan and buses, traveling at different speeds, became separated and Jones did well to turn around and escape being ambushed.

By the 26th, the defense was strengthened with the arrival of two self-propelled artillery pieces and a platoon of four tanks from 194th Tank Battalion. The penny-packeting of these force multipliers was a waste and one of the many lessons to be learned from this campaign. As the tanks moved forward, Japanese anti-tank guns let off four rounds and knocked out the four tanks. The Japanese advanced and the Filipinos began to fall back without first being ordered. The First Infantry was thereupon tasked with holding the mountain pass at Luisiana. Just as the line was about to collapse under the pressure of the next Japanese attack, a fleet of taxi cabs drew up at the rear of First Infantry's position. Out got Major Montgomery McKee who had collected 375 retired Scouts from Fort McKinley and driven towards the sound of guns, to "stiffen the green division." Unfortunately the reinforcements came too late. The First Regiment had been fighting without a break for two days and the positions elsewhere were also crumbling. For many, the long withdrawal to Bataan had begun, while others simply went home. In his summary, Jose wrote:

> The defense of the beaches by the First Infantry was the best that the freshly formed regiment could have done. Lack of reconnaissance, lack of artillery, loss of air support, lack of training of both officers and men, lack of time for preparation and training, and confusion of orders from higher headquarters were among the factors that handicapped the beach defense and subsequent defense lines.[51]

What is extraordinary is that MacArthur thought his plan of putting the Filipinos, unsupported, in the front line would work. Certainly he would have preferred the Japanese to attack in the spring of 1942, but war is not like that. He told Marshall in December 1941 that he was nevertheless ready. The fault lay in his habit of developing ideas and concepts very often without having a clear idea of the difficulties and implications of his broad-brush requirements. He had surrounded himself with sycophantic staff who, because MacArthur said "let's do this," got carried away by his wave of optimism and unrealistic expectations rather than dare to question the feasibility of the great man's requirements.

When MacArthur arrived at Corregidor's North Dock, comprising the Army's three piers—(the Navy's jetty, South Pier, was 500 yards away, on the other side of the narrow waist of the island)—he was met by General Moore who escorted him and his family to Malinta Tunnel. Such dank living quarters were not for MacArthur, who cherished his own space. "Where are your quarters?" he asked Moore. "Topside," replied Moore. "We'll move in there tomorrow morning," said MacArthur. Topside was the upper level of the island as opposed to the self-explanatory Middleside and Bottomside. Moore protested, pointing out that his house was open to air attack. "That's fine," said MacArthur, "just the thing."[52] The strange feature of the officers' quarters on tropical Corregidor was that they had chimneys. In addition, USAFFE took over the long, two-storied headquarters building at Fort Mills. No effort was made to disguise from over-flying aircraft the fact that the building was a working headquarters, readily evident from the staff cars and jeeps parked in front of the building.

The irony of the humiliation that was beginning to be heaped upon MacArthur was that whereas he recognized and felt it, as did the American forces in the Philippines (less so the Filipinos), it was not seen as such in America. To a large degree that was due to the astute Carlos Romulo in MacArthur's public relations office. Reverse followed reverse, and they were largely self-generated because, militarily, MacArthur lacked the feel for what was achievable in modern warfare and what sensible course of action should be adopted. That he was also logistically dyslexic is probably due to a mental malaise and attitude—found among warrior generals—that logistics is not proper soldiering. The analogy is often drawn between "teeth" and "tail," between fighting men and those who sustain them in battle. In truth, the relationship is a lot closer than some would admit. A more appropriate analogy might be "teeth" and "gums," the latter making it possible for the former to be held in place. Perhaps one should not try to suggest what might have happened if the logistic planning in USAFFE had been anything other than dilettantish. Time and space considerations suggest that MacArthur's command was inevitably doomed. But the Japanese undoubtedly faltered and ran out of steam. Who knows what might have been possible if the battling men of Bataan and Corregidor had had food with which to maintain their energy, medicine to treat their illnesses and reliable ammunition with which to hit back at the Japanese?

Some officers in G-3 operations had believed for some time in the merit of contingency stocking Bataan and, at one USAFFE staff meeting it was actually proposed as "a safety measure" but "MacArthur said 'oh no!' He wouldn't even listen to the suggestion. He didn't want any divided thought on it."[53] The task of producing a logistic miracle therefore devolved upon the shoulders of Brigadier General Richard Marshall who was in command of USAFFE (Rear) in Manila. He called in the competent quartermaster, Brigadier General Charles C. Drake and the willing supply chief, Colonel Lewis C. Beebe, to plan the stocking of Bataan and Corregidor. MacArthur had given the North and South Luzon forces until 8 January to withdraw into Bataan while, at the same time, the limited supplies put forward to sustain beach defenses were being systematically overrun by the grateful Japanese or abandoned to Filipino civilians. When Drake and Beebe reported to Marshall on the morning of 23 December, they could see from his face that all was not well. "How do your defense reserves stand at Corregidor?" Marshall asked. Drake replied that there might be some shortages but otherwise the island was reasonably well stocked. "Check up on this and get the (Corregidor) quartermaster to come right over here to Manila and draw his shortages from base depot." Drake replied in the affirmative but, since he had no reason to believe all was not well on the Lingayen front, he asked: "But first, what is it all about?"

"General MacArthur has just made a decision to withdraw all his troops into Bataan," replied Marshall. "You will also stock Bataan. However, no Quartermaster Corps supplies will be moved into Bataan until the shipments to Corregidor are completed."[54] Drake stood there, dumbfounded. On 8 December, he had calculated that it would take two weeks to stock Bataan to sustain 40,000 troops for six months. MacArthur refused Drake's request to begin the preliminary stocking of Bataan, ordering him to stock the depots in the Tarlac area in anticipation of the battle of the beaches at Lingayen. By 22 December, 18,000 tons of supplies had been taken north.[55]

On 8 December, Drake had requisitioned 1,000 civilian trucks for supply purposes, but loaned vehicles were never returned and others were simply commandeered. "The troops had hijacked all the motor transportation on the roads no matter who it belonged to or who was using it."[56] There was therefore no reliable transport available with which to out-load the depots close to Manila. Troops withdrawing south towards Bataan were told to make best use of dumped stocks. Drake recorded how, "since we could not get them to turn over the supplies we asked them to pick up on their retirement into Bataan, the QMC (Quartermaster Corps) saw nothing of what they had. I believe the troops got a lot of it on their way through."[57] As the 26th Cavalry withdrew through the important supply depot of Cabanatuan, Ramsey observed that after being bombed,

> oil drums were exploding and ammunition crates were thundering their contents into the night sky. The flashes pulsed beneath a black cloud-bank that covered the horizon, blotting out the moon . . . A million pounds of provisions destined for our forces had been destroyed, and we pushed on without rest or food while the cinders of our own supplies rained down upon us.[58]

There was also a massive central rice depot in Cabanatuan, with stocks of fifty million bushels, which served the requirements of the civilian population of Manila. This was enough rice to feed the Bataan garrison for five years, but MacArthur threatened to court-martial any soldier who touched it. It was alleged that Quezon applied pressure on the USAFFE to ensure that both rice and sugar could not be moved from the province in which it was bought.[59] But MacArthur has been unreasonably criticized for kowtowing to Philippine political pressure over this.[60] There were many other available sources of adequate supply at Tarlac and closer to Manila, including Fort Stotsenberg which had been evacuated with indecent haste. The difficulty lay in transportation, but those withdrawing had ample facilities for that.

As Mallonée withdrew through Stotsenberg, thirty miles north of Bataan, he was told the base had been abandoned and he could help himself to what he wanted. "Our supply officer had gone there and returned with a black eye, a truckload of canned goods, a case load of butter and a truckload of blankets. He got the black eye from a cavalry officer who accused him of looting and wanted me to have him shot."[61] Operationally, the Philippine Division less 57th Infantry, Philippine Scouts, was ordered into Bataan to prepare defensive positions. The 57th was sent north to cover the withdrawal of the North Luzon Force. At Stotsenberg, the 57th found an inexhaustible supply of clothing and food in addition to 36 Smith and Wesson 45 caliber revolvers from the Provost Marshall's office. "The most valuable acquisition was enough Class C (Combat) Rations to fill two buses . . . They were to be worth the equivalent in gold later in the campaign when food became scarce . . . there was much more that could have been saved. But the timidity of the regimental commander prevented any further exploitation of abandoned supplies."[62] Drake admitted that "the Quartermaster salvaged very few supplies from Stotsenberg," some reports suggest as little as five per cent.[63]

Tarlac is only 70 miles by road from Bataan. Bureaucracy was already being allowed to work against military preparedness. There were 2,000 cases of canned fish and corned beef and stocks of clothing which belonged to Japanese wholesalers. Colonel Lawrence, Chief of Logistics at Tarlac, was threatened with court martial if he proceeded with his intention to confiscate the Japanese stocks on the grounds that it was private property. Similar restrictions were placed on stocks closer to Bataan, causing dismay among the military. One of the most outspoken critics of the hagiographies of the campaign emerging in the U.S.A.,[64] which were published as books at war's end, was Colonel Ernest B. Miller, commander 194 Tank Battalion. His *Bataan Uncensored* told the whole story of incompetence and ineptitude in high places. "Perhaps it was fortunate that, as we bivouacked amid the smoking ruins of Clark Field on that first day of war, we could not see these things that were yet to come—food and material of war sabotaged by that same mismanagement and indecision which had destroyed our air power."[65] Tarlac was the main railhead in the north, groaning with supplies delivered by rail. Mounting air attacks on the railroad led to the progressive abandonment of rail stock by the crews. By 25th December, not one engine was available to bring the stock southward towards Manila and Bataan. There were American military personnel available to run the railroad but allegedly, due to President Quezon's opposition, it was decided the Constabulary would undertake the task instead. However, in an effort to mobilize every capable individual, the majority of the Constabulary troops had been dragooned into the newly-formed 2nd Division in Manila. There was therefore no one to salvage the supplies which could have made a substantial difference in the manner and effectiveness of the defense of Bataan.[66]

As the Northern and Southern Luzon Forces made their converging, fighting withdrawals towards San Fernando, twenty miles north of Manila, where MacArthur intended to "pivot on my left" into Bataan, the logisticians were only too well aware that they had a race against time on their hands. On 28 December MacArthur sent Jones a message, repeated the next day and including Wainwright as an action addressee: "Commence foraging and accumulating rice and other food supplies . . . Commandeer all available commercial transportation not assigned to army for foraging and movement. Conserve all supplies by reducing issues to a minimum."[67] On 28 December, the North Luzon Force had reached the D-4 line to await the next Japanese attack, having held the Agno Line until the night 26–27 December.[68] In the South, the Japanese advanced along two fronts requiring the First Infantry, at 10:00 a.m. on 28 December, to fall back to Los Banos, at the most southerly point of Laguna de Bay close to Route 1, the main road northward to Manila.[69] Reports of MacArthur's action at this period of great danger run contrary to the "hands-off" impression given by Sutherland. Full of nervous energy, he involved himself in the detail of the withdrawal. He allegedly also had time on the 28th to attend to other detail. He put a call through to Jorge Vargas at Malacañang Palace: "George," he said, "I have already received my salary for December but I have not yet taken the 70,000 pesos contingency fund that is due to me."[70]

"What do you want me to do, General?" asked Vargas.

"Can you buy me $35,000 worth of Lepanto (mining) stocks?" said MacArthur.

"We will try, General, we will try," assured Vargas. By then it was too late in the day to contact brokers in New York but Vargas rang the manager of the Philippine National Bank's New York office who bought the stock for MacArthur. As Vargas later explained: "After the war, MacArthur became a millionaire on account of that last minute purchase."[74]

Drake recalled a discussion with Manuel Roxas who told him that Bataan was the worst region in the Philippines for malaria. He said that the Commonwealth had considered establishing a national park there but abandoned the idea because of the inability to eradicate the disease.[75] There was an inadequate supply of anti-malarial prophylaxis in the Philippines whereas there was sufficient food and ammunition to meet the requirements of MacArthur's forces. The trick lay in delivering them in time to Corregidor and Bataan. The routes towards Bataan were becoming congested with the impedimenta of a defeated army and a panic stricken population, while the mountainous peninsula itself was only served by the most primitive of roads. The answer lay in water transport which could out-load stocks from

Manila and from Fort McKinley, which lay on the Pasig River. Manila was, of course, the largest commercial storage center in the Philippines. Rice was purchased from Chinese merchants and other scarce supplies were bought off the ships in the harbor. Arrangements were made with American companies—Armor, Swift and Libby, McNeil and Libby, to take over their stocks of canned meat and fruit.[73]

Colonel Frederick A. Ward, Superintendent of the Army Transport Service, was one of the campaign's unsung heroes. He arranged the assembly of all available tugs, barges and launches, selected those he required and had the rest destroyed. After taking a day to execute the mandatory topping-up of Corregidor's supplies to the requisite level to sustain its planned 10,000 garrison, he turned his attention to Bataan. Barges can only be moved at a pedestrian pace, barely three miles an hour, and the round trip Manila to Bataan is sixty miles. This meant that individual barges were generally only capable of making one trip in the week available before the Japanese occupied Manila. Offloading was also a time-consuming business because Bataan's three small piers could only accept five barges at a time. This is not to say that there were no problems at the Manila end. The Japanese continued to bomb the docks area. Many of the stevedores had fled at the first appearance of Japanese planes, never to return.[74] In response to radio appeals, 200 Americans, Britons and Europeans joined the loyal Filipinos to load the barges, working day and night, for eight days. In that manner, it was possible to send 300 barges carrying 30,000 tons of equipment and combat supplies to Corregidor and Bataan. There had been insufficient time to load anything but a small fraction of the requisite 10,000,000 gallons of gasoline. Gasoline left behind in civilian depots and at Fort McKinley was set on fire by engineers.[75] Finally, the Quartermaster Corps in Manila opened up, for the benefit of *Manileños*, the huge Commissary of supplies that they had neither time nor transport to move.

Once the withdrawal into Bataan had been completed, a head count revealed 15,000 Americans, 65,000 Filipinos and 26,000 refugees—a potential ratio of defender to attacker of approximately 2:1.[76] Some units had heeded instructions to forage and were self-sufficient in rations for 10–25 days, although none of this food was offered up to the Quartermaster for the common good. When the deliberately dispersed stocks were totted up, it was discovered that at normal rates of consumption, instead of the 180-day stocks, there were only 50 days of canned meat and fish, a 40-day supply of canned milk, a 30-day supply of flour and canned vegetables and a 20-day supply of rice. Essentials such as sugar, salt and lard were in short supply while coffee, potatoes, onions, cereals, beverages and fresh and canned fruits were almost totally lacking. The pampered privates of Fort Santiago now had something real to complain about. In reserve, for emergency use, were half a million C rations.[77] From a quantitative point of view, the supply of ammunition appeared to be satisfactory. It had been planned to stock 4 million rounds of .30 caliber ammunition but 16 million rounds were achieved, artillery rounds were available to the planned scale.[78] Unfortunately, a worrying amount was found to be both old and dud.

The reason for the delay in ordering "WPO-3 is in effect" is difficult to fathom but the effect the delay had on the preparation of Bataan is not. On 22 December, General Marshall was still trying to reassure MacArthur that help was on the way, this time 80 B-17s and B-24s via Africa and the Indian Ocean.[79] While this could be argued as a reason for not abandoning the area around the central Luzon airfields, the fact remained that MacArthur still did not have the wherewithal with which to defend the airfields and protect the aircraft. He desperately wanted to believe help was on the way but it was little more than wishful thinking. In Australia field artillery and naval supplies were put aboard two of the fastest ships in the *Pensacola* convoy, the *Holbrook* and the *Bloemfontein*. The ships sailed on 28 December but, with the Japanese already in Borneo, it was self-evident that the route northward had been effectively blocked.[80] However, Marshall persisted in offering MacArthur straws to clutch. "The President has personally directed the Navy to make every effort to support you," he informed MacArthur on the 28th.[81] On the 29th, Roosevelt sent a message of encouragement, but one word in that message gave reasonable cause for concern. "I give to the people of the Philippines my solemn pledge that their freedom will be redeemed . . ." Grammarians understood only too well that something had to be lost in order to be redeemed. When the message was released from Corregidor, the word "redeemed" had been removed from the text[82] and the word "protected" inserted.

To the majority of American survivors, the MacArthur Beach plan, in the manner it was planned and executed, had been "a tragic error." According to General Harold K. Johnson, a Lieutenant in 57th Infantry and future Chief of Staff of the United States Army, it was an error of judgement that should have been corrected earlier than it was. "The supplies that could have been moved in that two week period probably meant the difference between another three or four weeks" delay on Bataan. It wasn't the enemy that licked us; it was disease and absence of food that licked us."[83] And that, unquestionably, was yet another command failure.

The Japanese attacked the Fourth Delaying Line (D-4) on two fronts. Enemy tank regiments forced the 91st Division out of Cabanatuan during the night of 29 December and advanced along Route 5 towards the junction with Route 3, the axis of advance of the Japanese 48th Division. On the 30th, the Japanese forced the 21st Division to yield up Tarlac. Over-eagerness to blow bridges left fifteen tanks abandoned on the wrong side of a bridge at Moncada and, at Zaragoza a battalion had to ford the Zalagot river. They were caught in mid-stream by heavy Japanese fire, losing almost 400 of their strength of 550 men. By 31 December, the remnants of 11th, 21st and 91st Division held the line D-5. The South Luzon Force had to cross the Calumpit bridges in order to pass into Bataan, so depended upon the North Luzon Force holding its position. The Japanese armor, moving close to the junction of Routes 3 and 5 near Plaridel, threatened to turn what had been, to that point, an orderly and well-executed withdrawal, into chaos.[84]

The situation was not helped by continual mission changes emanating from Fort Mills, Corregidor. On 28 December, South Luzon Force was at Tiaong, forty miles southwest of Manila. General Jones was ordered to withdraw immediately to Bataan via Manila. On 29 December, South Luzon Force was ordered to about face and to hold the advance of 16th Division. With the Japanese already in Tiaong, the Force was obliged to dig a new defensive position. On 30 December, Jones was ordered to abandon the recently prepared defensive line and to be over the Calumpit Bridges by 6 a.m. on 1 January 1942. Jones was further ordered by MacArthur to defend the Angat River Line until his entire force had satisfactorily crossed over the bridges and then to blow them. These orders were not relayed to Wainwright who entered Plaridel and ordered Jones to move his troops. Jones, who had been put in command by MacArthur, demurred in a manner appropriate to his nature. Caring little for Jones' attitude, Wainwright entered into an argument which was joined by Brigadier General Stevens, Commander of the 91st Division. The heated debate was ended by the arrival of a messenger to report that the Japanese had entered Baliuag just to the north and that the defenders were now withdrawing southward. Just after 6 a.m. on 1 January 1942, the last of South Luzon Force crossed over the Pampanga River, the reserved demolition "execute" order was personally given by General Wainwright and the Calumpit River Bridges were blown.[85] Consequently, the 11th and 21st Divisions holding the line D-5, were also given the green light to withdraw towards Bataan. Of the 28,000 men who had left the Lingayen Beaches as part of the North Luzon Force, only 16,000 reached Bataan. Some had been killed, others wounded, while a proportion had decided to soldier no more and had gone home. Of the 15,000 men that had withdrawn from Lamon Bay, 14,000 reached Bataan safely. Homma's 14th Army lost 627 killed, 1,282 wounded and 7 missing.[86]

On the morning of 30 December, a small group of soldiers added the finishing touches to a rude dais they had constructed in front of the Malinta Tunnel. The two chairs on it were occupied at 4:30 p.m. by President Manuel Quezon and General MacArthur on the occasion of Quezon's second inauguration, which began with an enthusiastic rendition of "Hail to the Chief" played on a field church organ. It was a strange event, the installation of Quezon for his second term at a time when the partially wrecked Manila was about to be entered by invaders and when the gaunt President was so obviously suffering a terminal illness. Nevertheless, he took the oath of office and told the assembled people of the Filipinos' determination to become independent. His voice was high-pitched, excitable and punctuated by fits of coughing. He thanked MacArthur for "your devotion to our cause, the defense of our country and the safety of our population." MacArthur began his short, one page speech in a barely audible voice. "Never before in all history has there been a more solemn and significant inauguration. An act, symbolical of democratic processes, is placed against the background of a sudden, merciless war." MacArthur was known to be an emotional man but invariably, in the past, he had been able to control his feelings in public. As he concluded his speech: "Through this its gasping agony of travail, through what Winston Churchill calls 'blood, sweat and tears,' from the grim shadow of the Valley of Death, O Merciful God, preserve this noble race," his voice broke and, as he struggled to finish, he wept openly. He turned away, tears flowing down his cheeks.[87] Sayre said a few words and then read a personal message from Roosevelt. Barely had Quezon been sworn in than Roosevelt's recommendation that he be evacuated was considered by an ad hoc war council and then rejected by MacArthur as being too hazardous. On 1 January, Brigadier General Richard Marshall closed the Rear Headquarters in Manila and took his staff to Corregidor. The Japanese entered the city on 2 January and, the next day, Jitaro Kihara arrived from Tokyo to act as the liaison official between the occupation forces and Vargas.[88]

The pursuit of the American forces by the Japanese appears to have been less than energetic. The 16th Division's advance from the south had been delayed by some very effective military engineering but the 48th Division's advance from the north had been influenced by a tension between General Homma and his Chief of Staff, General Maeda as well as by competition between the two Japanese divisions. "I had ordered the 48th Division to send as few troops as possible toward Manila and send its main force toward Bataan," explained Maeda. "However, the objective of Imperial General Headquarters was the capture of Manila, so the 48th Division rushed toward Manila anxious to beat the 16th Division into the city." The aim of the Japanese pincer movement from Lingayen and Lamon Bay was to capture Manila. If the American forces could be destroyed as a consequence of that aim, then it was considered by the Japanese to be a bonus. Designating Manila an open city had little tactical significance for the Japanese, it still had to be occupied. Nevertheless, the Japanese did make some effort to stem the flow of American forces into Bataan. "I ordered air units to bomb the bridges at Calumpit," said Maeda, "but they did not do this. Time, topography, military strength—these three things prevented us from cutting the escape route."[89]

That is a pretty weak justification from any Chief of Staff responsible for the coordination and planning of operations.[90] The two Calumpit Bridges, one road and one rail, spanned the deep, unfordable Pampanga River in an obvious tactical defile. The long tailback of troops, up to ten miles, waiting to cross the bridge presented an aerial target of great magnitude that went begging. The Japanese 48th Division put in an air strike request to Colonel Monjiro Akiyama at 14th Army Headquarters for 5th Air Group to take out the bridges. Akiyama believed that the destruction of the bridges would serve no useful purpose and, as a consequence, no specific orders were issued. Colonel Harry A. Skerry, the engineer responsible for the reserved demolition, was amazed the Japanese had not attacked the bridges "despite the previous almost total destruction of our air force and the resulting enemy air superiority."[91] It had not therefore been a case, as MacArthur alleged, of the Japanese discovering "too late the movements of my forces behind the curtain of the rearguard actions in both the north and south."[92] However, this should not detract from the fact that MacArthur's "side-slip" was very competently executed.

When General Parker arrived at Bataan at 1700 on the 24th to assume command, the only troops deployed there were the Philippine Division, less 57th Infantry and 26th Cavalry, and a provisional air corps regiment. The 14th Engineers of the Philippine Scouts marked out the defensive positions in preparation for the arrival of the 31st Division (26 December) and the 41st (28 December) who commenced the digging of foxholes and erection of wire obstacles.[93] Already, the USAFFE daily press communiqués were exaggerating the situation on the ground and in the air. It was a difficult act to carry off, the reassurance of people at home and those left behind in Manila with information that the fighting man readily recognized as a blatant untruth. The dreadful, contrary influence of the home team's propaganda, on the fighting soldiers' morale went unrecognised. This is a selection of communiqués from the end of December 1941:[94]

21 4:00 p.m. Ground and air commands of the United States Air Forces in the Far East struck back with increasing fury at the invaders, routing enemy patrols in the Vigan and Legaspi Sectors, shooting down at least 5 Japanese planes in the air and at least 25 aircraft on the ground.

22 5:00 p.m. This afternoon, heavy fighting developed including tank combat. Our troops more than held their own. At one point Japanese destroyers and transports were driven off by our heavy guns and that landing was prevented.

1 (Jan) General MacArthur narrowly escaped serious injury in a recent bombing raid in Bataan Province when a large bomb exploded less than ten feet away from him. On a quick inspection trip the General was accompanied only by two orderlies . . . during the raid the orderlies protected the General to the best of their ability providing him with a steel helmet and shielding him with their bodies. A piece of rock struck the General in the shoulder and one faithful orderly was wounded in the hand.

This refers to the first bombing of Corregidor on 29 December 1941. MacArthur was not on an inspection trip but was out in the garden of his cottage with his orderly, Sergeant Domingo Adversario, who was indeed wounded.[95] A bomb destroyed his topside cottage, forcing him to move to another on bottomside about one mile east of Malinta Tunnel. (Beds were available for him and his family but he refused to sleep there.[96] When the air raid sirens sounded, his driver shuttled the family to and from the tunnel.) When Jean rushed out of the kitchen to see if he was all right, he said, "Look what they've done to the garden."[97]

Those communiqués involving himself which he did not actually write were nevertheless seen and approved by MacArthur. "General MacArthur personally checks all publicity reports, and writes many of them himself," said Sutherland, "always with an eye on their effect on the MacArthur legend."[98] Almost without exception, MacArthur's generals had to accept that the good which they did in support of their Caesar would be interred with their bones. There was no prospect of MacArthur sharing any of the available glory with his generals. General Robert L. Eichelberger became best known as the most prominent among those to complain that his place in history had not been properly established.[99] To a somewhat lesser degree, that same sense of exasperation is evident in Sutherland's later writing although it has to be remembered that there was cause for the significant cooling in MacArthur's support for his Chief of Staff due to the latter taking a mistress in Australia.[100] Sutherland observed how MacArthur's dispatches were replete with references to the deity, "but he has no more religion than a goat." He added: "MacArthur, if he thinks he has a weakness or that the public think so, gets his publicity men to play up that angle so that what was once a weakness becomes a strength."[101]

In the first three months of the war, MacArthur or his staff wrote 142 communiqués, 109 of which mentioned one man, MacArthur.[102] They carried brave, exciting, heartwarming, gripping though often imaginary accounts as to how MacArthur's guile, leadership and military genius had continually frustrated the evil intentions of Japan's armed forces. His picture appeared on the cover of *Time* at the end of 1941 and, early in the new year, the effect of these press releases upon the American public served to whip them up into a frenzy of fawning adulation of MacArthur, American hero.

12

"A TIME WHEN
MEN MUST DIE"

The Bataan Peninsula has been likened to a thumb[1] protruding from the mainland of Luzon between Subic and Manila Bay, at the end of which, no more than three miles distant, lies the island of Corregidor. Corregidor is the largest of five islands across the mouth of Manila Bay, though *Islands* is perhaps too grand a term for what is in reality a grouping of rocks. The other four are Caballo, Carabao, El Fraile and La Monja. All but La Monja were heavily defended. Caballo was named Fort Hughes. The post on El Fraile, which was so artificial as to resemble a concrete warship, was called Fort Drum, and the installation on Carabao Island was named Fort Frank. Setting to one side the health consideration, the twenty-five miles long and twenty miles wide peninsula was ideally suited for defensive warfare. There are two dominant features on Bataan, both extinct volcanoes: the 4,222 feet high Mount Natib in the north and the 4,722 feet high Mount Bataan, 14 miles to the south. The mountainous terrain is covered in primary jungle, through which run ravines and watercourses which meander down towards the sea. On the east there is an open, swampy, coastal plain which becomes more hilly and rugged as it progresses southward. There is very little by way of a plain on the west coast since the mountains come down virtually to the sea. Communications were very limited. Route 7, running along the top of the peninsula, had been forfeited by the Americans who had consolidated upon their first defended line and main battle position from Mabatang to Mauban, which was more usually known as the Abucay-Mauban Line or Abucay Line. One road, Route 110, was a loop-road following the line of the coast, although the eastern half was in a better condition than that on the west. There was also an important lateral route connecting to Route 110 at Bagac and Pilar, which ran between the main battle position anchored on Mount Natib and the rear battle position 8 miles to the south and forward of Mount Bataan.

The men had a fortuitously easy withdrawal into Bataan since the Japanese air force failed to press home their attacks on the American-Filipino force, sometimes barely moving along heavily congested roads. MacArthur deployed two Corps on the Abucay Line, side by side, down the length of the peninsula; General Parker's 25,000-strong II Corps comprising four Philippine Army Divisions and 57th Infantry of the Philippine Scouts of the U.S. Philippine Division on the right, and General Wainwright's 22,500-strong I Corps of three Philippine Army Divisions on the left.[2] To the rear of the two Corps was the Service Command Area under Brigadier General Allen C. McBride. MacArthur commanded the battle from the Corregidor office he shared with Sutherland in Lateral 3 in the Malinta Tunnel but had established a forward headquarters on Bataan commanded by his chief logistician and Deputy Chief of Staff, Brigadier General R.J. Marshall. On 7 January MacArthur radioed the War Department. "I am on my main battle line awaiting general attack."[3]

Meanwhile, troops worked hard to improve the main battle position and to continue with the preparation of the rear position. It was hard work in the enervating heat, so not the best of times to put the men on half rations, even "temporarily." According to Mallonée, half rations "was the principal cause of the ultimate surrender—the most important single factor of the campaign, not even excluding the destruction of our air force." It comprised 3.7 ounces of rice, 1.8 ounces of sugar, 1.2 ounces of canned milk, 2.44 ounces of canned fish, salmon or sardines, and tomatoes when available, rationed to one can for ten men.[4] Nevertheless, the men's morale was good, fortified by the knowledge that the period of constant withdrawal was at an end and now at last they could face their enemy. The jungle canopy served to neutralize Japan's air superiority and observation capabilities, which initially were directed almost entirely at Corregidor.

The pre-existing plans for the defense of Bataan had the Main Battle Position where the present Rear Battle Position was in preparation, with a second line further to the south in depth. The German successes in Europe in 1940, based on mobility and air power, led to the adoption of forward defense in order to permit greater dispersion and flexibility—also the Rear Position was not ready. There was only a selective learning of lessons from the Germans for a study of their campaign in Greece would have revealed what Wolfe had proved to Montcalm at Quebec in 1759: that men could invariably overcome the handicaps imposed by uncompromising terrain. The false assumption was made that the upper slopes of Mount Natib were "unassailable to a force of any consequence."[5] The key to turning the defenses of the Abucay Line was a four-mile swathe of undefended, rugged territory running the length of the inter-Corps boundary.

Having secured Manila, Homma now turned his attention to the military forces he had by-passed in pursuit of his primary mission. Neither side had remotely accurate intelligence as to the size and condition of their opponents. Despite having lost 48th Division, required for follow-on operations in Java and replaced by the inexperienced but reinforced 65th Brigade of six battalions, Homma was quietly confident that the battle for Bataan would not be difficult. His G2 intelligence staff told him there were only 25,000 disorganized troops on the peninsula, when in fact there were more than three times that number. Homma's plan was to attack each of the Corps' areas before developing the main thrust down the eastern side, aimed at reaching Mariveles.

The 65th Brigade was commanded by Lieutenant General Akira Nara who had graduated from U.S. Army Infantry School in 1927. He had no illusions as to his 6,500 officers and men who were "absolutely unfit for combat." Its original mission was to act as a garrison unit once the major opposition had been crushed. According to Olson, the men were conscripts and had only one month's training.[6] In fact, they were reservists and had thorough military training compared to the men of the new Philippine divisions.

The Battle of Bataan began on 9 January, with the 65th Brigade advancing under covering fire. In the eastern sector, the Japanese believed the American line to have been a few miles forward of where it actually was. When the attack therefore attained its maximum momentum, it was still well short of its intended target and vulnerable to American retaliatory artillery fire, which took a heavy toll of the advancing Japanese. As they came down the middle of the road in columns of four, 75mm and 155mm shells rained down. All the observation spots along the road had been accurately surveyed and hence the American fire was devastating. As soon as each engagement finished, those among the Japanese who were able, picked themselves up and continued the advance to the next position. "The Fil-American spotters could not believe that they could have such a 'Turkey Shoot,' but relentlessly engaged the persistent formations."[8] What should have been the concurrent attack in the western sector also went badly. The going proved to be so difficult that the attackers did not close-up to the defended localities until the 19th. On or about 10 January, Emperor Hirohito decided to issue an Imperial Rescript commemorating the dead of the Philippine Campaign. General Sugi-yama, Chief of Staff at General Staff Headquarters, informed General Homma of the Emperor's desire and told him that Bataan should be taken as soon as possible. "Naturally," said General Maeda, "this caused him to proceed with his pursuit tactics and deprived him of even more caution."[8]

MacArthur, arriving at the Tunnel each morning at 8am, seemed a man burdened by trouble. According to Romulo he looked like a "tired hawk."[10] No longer was his uniform immaculately pressed; his hair was long, and his face had lost its freshness through having been washed and shaved in salt water. Only his shoes retained the customary sparkle. He became convinced in his own mind that the Roosevelt administration and George Marshall had decided to sacrifice him, in part because of dissatisfaction with his performance. But that was far from the truth, and even Ickes had gone on record as saying that MacArthur had given "an excellent account of himself in the Philippines . . . despite the long established military opinion that we could not hold on to them in the event of war with Japan."[10] MacArthur never aired his anti-Washington grievances in public but apologists such as the sycophantic Courtney Whitney no doubt represented his feelings when he wrote: "Not only were no large reinforcements sent to the Philippines but, more important, the administration never intended to send them and concealed the fact that they would not be sent."[11] The administration had consistently endorsed the Europe First strategy but that is not to say that no efforts were made to reinforce the Philippines. The problem was that they were frustrated by

unexpectedly competent Japanese armed forces. Despite all of Mac-
Arthur's aspirations to be recognized as a strategic analyst, he seemed
unable to grasp this truth.

Marshall and Eisenhower could do little other than sympathetically
humor MacArthur and attribute his lack of realism to his unenviable
position. Marshall assured MacArthur that he invariably submitted to
the President MacArthur's grand strategies,[12] which Eisenhower suggested were more suitable for "plebes at West Point than for real
war." MacArthur believed Eisenhower to be responsible for delaying
reinforcements. Eisenhower, for his part, privately believed that with
more care and determination many of the planes could have been
saved, and he also wondered in private why MacArthur had not
"made a better showing at the beaches." But MacArthur enjoyed the
devoted support of the American public and, although Eisenhower
regarded him "as big a baby as ever," Washington had to be seen to be
supportive of him.[13] After the war, a reporter asked MacArthur
whether he truly believed help had been on its way to relieve his command. "By God, I did believe it . . . I went over those messages since
to see how I could have gotten that impression. And, do you
know—those messages didn't say yes, but they didn't say no. They are
full of meanings which could be interpreted two ways. I see now that
I may have deluded myself."[14] Certainly the administration dodged
the difficult task of putting to MacArthur Stimson's view that there is
a time when men must die.[15] It was to Stimson particularly that Mac-
Arthur sent messages of a "most harassing and agonizing character."[16]
"I stood in Washington," wrote Stimson, "helpless to reinforce and defend the Philippines and had to simply watch their glorious but hopeless defense."[17] Churchill had no such qualms or need for subtlety
when he signaled the Governor and Commander British Forces in
Hong Kong as they fought the Japanese.

> The enemy should be compelled to expend the utmost life and equip-
> ment. There must be vigorous fighting in the inner defences and, if
> need be, from house to house. Every day that you are able to maintain
> your resistance you help the allied cause all over the world and by a
> prolonged resistance you and your men can win the lasting honour
> which we are sure will be your due.[18]

Hong Kong fell on Christmas Day.

While it is true that he was to a large degree responsible for the predicament in which his family, the Quezons and those under his command found themselves, it is also true that MacArthur was let down by Washington. As Eisenhower, no great fan of him at this time, acknowledged:

> Much of the blame for the overwhelming of the Philippines should be placed squarely on us Americans at home. For months before Pearl Harbor and Clark Field, we had been trying to fool ourselves that war was far away. When the first Japanese bombs fell on the planes parked a few miles from Manila, our ships at sea were carrying troops *away* from, not *to* the city soon to be the enemy's target.[19]

In his office on Corregidor, MacArthur would stride up and down considering his position or alternatively would sit on the corner of his desk, one foot resting on a drawer. Here was a man who seriously worried how others would assess his military reputation. "His need for external confirmation of his own value had always been a vital factor in his behavior," suggested Carol Petillo.[20] Never at any previous time in his life had MacArthur been so uncertain as to his future. He pestered the sick President Quezon to agree to employ him on the same terms, in the same rank of Field Marshal, after the war. His acceptance of a large financial reward from Quezon at this time may well just be a reflection of his sense of vulnerability but it also struck an ethically dubious note.[21] In his Executive Order No 1, issued on 3 January 1942, Quezon eulogized MacArthur's Military Mission, which stood "as the outpost of victory of individual freedom and liberty over slavery and tyranny in the mighty struggle that engulfs the world. Win or lose, live or die, no men have ever carried a heavier burden or weightier responsibility with greater resolution and determination." For their "distinguished service" between 15 November 1935 and 30 December 1941, the President of the impoverished and occupied archipelago awarded MacArthur half a million dollars, Sutherland $75,000, Richard Marshall $45,000 and Huff $20,000.[22] With the exception of Sutherland, none of the recipients went public to announce their windfall. Schaller suggests that MacArthur may have justified this extremely generous award as a typical example of the reciprocal obligation and bonding which was such a feature of Philippine culture, and thus not a bribe to encourage him to work more diligently to obtain American assistance.[23] When Quezon visited Eisenhower in Washington, for example, he made an offer of

$60,000 in recognition of Eisenhower's contribution in the 1930s to the Commonwealth, which Eisenhower politely declined.[24] In 1935, the Adjutant General had authorized MacArthur to accept any amount of money from the Philippine Government, and that authority was never rescinded. But Quezon's award also covered the period July–December 1941, when MacArthur resumed active service as a member of the U.S. Army, so questions vis-à-vis the legality of the award do arise. Army regulations forbade and forbid army personnel accepting "a substantial loan or gift or any emolument." It seems that President Roosevelt, Stimson and Ickes were aware of the award but only the latter uttered any comment or complaint—characteristically, in his diary. Larrabee rehearses many of the unanswered questions raised by a transaction that was "appallingly improper"[25] and which, if ever it had been made public, would have proved very damaging to the individuals concerned.

> Did MacArthur actually believe there was no impropriety? Would he have answered, if asked, that he acted as a Philippine and not an American officer? Why did Roosevelt and Stimson allow it? Did they feel they had an angry and unruly general on their hands who needed pacifying? How much effect was there on MacArthur's subsequent favoring of Quezon's departure to Australia? What was the role of Manuel Roxas, who countersigned the order as Philippine treasurer and later received much needed support from MacArthur in his campaign to become Quezon's successor?[26]

As MacArthur advanced in seniority, increasingly he became the victim of his own ego and sense of infallibility, to the degree that he could not accept that it was human to err or to fail. His performance on Corregidor showed that his physical courage remained undiminished but, as the historian Thaddeus Holt observed, "it was his moral courage that was defective." He became a reclusive and remote man whose own reflections on his inadequacy and failure made him so uncomfortable in the presence of his own troops that he eschewed their company.

One of the tasks given to two *nisei*, "sprung" from internment, together with a former legal counsel from the Japanese Consulate whom they had recruited, was to listen to Clark Field's air traffic. Signals Intelligence monitored voice communication between the planes to determine their targets. As soon as targets became known, the units involved were alerted.[27] Very often Corregidor was the target and the siren was accordingly activated. Personnel out in the open in the vicinity of Malinta Tunnel would flow in two streams towards the protection offered by the tunnel. The sirens had the reverse effect on Douglas MacArthur who, accompanied by an aide, would go against the incoming flood of personnel and walk about in the open to watch the incoming bombers, stick in hand, corn cob pipe in his mouth and his soft Field Marshal's hat upon his head. MacArthur's coolness under fire impressed Sayre.

> His quixotic defiance of the enemy was not an exhibition of Renaissance Italian bravado, but the subtle application of psychology. It was intended as a deliberate act of leadership. To dare the bombs in a sally to the open is a commander's bitter privilege. *Noblesse oblige.* The men liked it. The subtle corrosion of panic or fatigue, or the feeling of just being fed-up, can only be arrested by the intervention of a true commander.[28]

MacArthur's display of bravado deeply worried Quezon. MacArthur laughed off these concerns: "Oh, you know, the Japs haven't yet fabricated the bomb with my name on it." Then he addressed the old man's concerns seriously: "Of course," he said, "I understand what you mean, and I know I have no right to gamble with my life but it is absolutely necessary that at the right time a commander takes chances because of the effect all down the line, for when they see the man at the top risking his life, the man at the bottom says, 'I guess if that old man can take it, I can too.' "[29]

Where people stood on this question of MacArthur's bravery depended where they sat. Chynoweth wrote how "he (MacArthur) never visited his troops and his tactical judgement was nil. He was the poorest judge of subordinates that I ever knew yet he achieved greatness."[30] Lieutenant Ramsey of the 26th Cavalry recorded how on Bataan

> the commander's absence began to be felt. Though the Filipino soldiers clung to their devotion to MacArthur, the Americans more and more began deriding him. As ammunition and food ran out, and as the weeks passed with none of the promised relief, they made up derisive songs and jokes about the general, whom they called "Dugout Doug."[31]

They sang "Dugout Doug" to the tune of "The Battle Hymn of the Republic." One verse went:

> Dougout Doug MacArthur lies ashakin' on the Rock
> Safe from all the bombers and from any sudden shock
> Dugout Doug is eating of the best food on Bataan
> And his troops go starving on . . .[32]

One stanza of cruel doggerel, attributed to the war correspondent Frank Hewlett, summed up for some the situation from their point of view:

> We're the battling bastards of Bataan:
> No mama, no papa, no Uncle Sam,
> No aunts, no uncles, no nephews, no nieces,
> No rifles, no planes, or artillery pieces
> And nobody gives a damn.[33]

MacArthur was invariably well informed of events going on around him. Once he had been given the unjust sobriquet Dugout Doug, it was something that followed him throughout the Pacific War. At no time did he acknowledge hearing it but, in Tokyo after the war, he was in conversation with Major Faubion Bowers when the discussion focused upon undeserved rumors which hurt generals. "Once they start talking," said MacArthur, "everybody believes them, and you've got to change your tack. Take that story in the Philippines . . ." "Which one?" enquired Bowers. "You know the one," said MacArthur. Later, Bowers wrote: "He wouldn't repeat the phrase Dugout Doug and it was only later in context that I remembered it."[34]

In attempting to find the balance of truth as to how precisely MacArthur's men regarded MacArthur, his principal biographer, James, draws on the official Army history: "Among American officers, to many of whom he was already a legend, his reputation placed him on a lofty eminence with the great captains of history." James admits, however, that MacArthur's stature among the Americans on Bataan never matched that of Wainwright, of whom it could not honestly be said that he was a great captain of history. Nevertheless, MacArthur did retain his old mystique among his men, who half hoped that somehow he would save them from looming defeat by pulling off an eleventh hour miracle.[35]

Word came through from MacArthur's Forward HQ on Bataan that his presence was needed "to stimulate sagging morale."[36] On the evening of 9th January, he informed Wainwright and Parker that he would be visiting their Corps areas and that they should assemble their key people to meet him. At dawn on the 10th he made the relatively safe five minute journey in a torpedo boat from Corregidor to Mariveles where a Ford sedan drove him up the east road to Balanga to make rendezvous with General Parker and his II Corps officers. Reinforcements from the States were coming, he told them. Then he was off to the Abucay Line, where he met the officers of 57th Infantry in the church at Abucay. Moving westward, MacArthur visited Wainwright. En route, his party was delayed by heavy Japanese artillery fire. Ordering his officers to take shelter off the road, MacArthur remained in the center of it. Urged by Sutherland to take cover, MacArthur replied: "There is no Jap shell with MacArthur's name on it."[37] At the 31st Division, MacArthur told the officers: "Help is definitely on the way. We must hold out until it arrives."[45] MacArthur congratulated Wainwright on the withdrawal and inquired about his 155mm guns. Wainwright offered to show the USAFFE commander the two which were closest. MacArthur responded jovially: "Jonathan, I don't want to *see* them, I want to *hear* them."[38] After being away all day, MacArthur and Sutherland returned to Corregidor where MacArthur assured Quezon that morale was high and he believed he could hold Homma off "for several months without outside help."[39] That was MacArthur's sole visit to Bataan. He never returned.

Sutherland later claimed that he noted the extent of 1 Corps' exposed right flank on Mount Natib and told Wainwright to close it.[40] Sutherland was none too happy about the troop deployments in general. As he explained to historian Morton, he felt the enemy "would attack down the center of the peninsula over the roughest terrain and not along the coast where the roads were located."[41] He said he told both Corps commanders to strengthen their interior flanks, instructions which were followed on 11 January by orders to do so, so that contact between the two Corps "be actual and physical." According to Sutherland, he told Wainwright "to defend heavily the right part of his line. I also told II Corps to do the same. As it turned out, the Japs did attack on the inside of the line and penetrated the II Corps line on its extreme left flank thus leading directly to the defeat of our forces on Bataan."[42] On 12 January, Brigadier General R.J. Marshall, commander of USAFFE Forward HQ and USAFFE Deputy Chief of

Staff, visited Wainwright and discussed the gap between the two Corps. Apparently Wainwright did not see it as a problem, telling Marshall that "he thought the center of our position was too difficult terrain for the major attack."[43]

MacArthur wrote in his memoirs how his men were approaching exhaustion and how he saw them "slowly wasting away," but "how they would cheer when they saw my battered, and much reviled in America, 'scrambled egg' cap. They would gather round and pat me on the back and 'Mabuhay Macarsar' me."[44] He described their grins as "that ghastly skeleton-like grin of the dying," and how they roared in unison: "We are the battling bastards of Bataan—no papa, no mama, no Uncle Sam." This period gives rise to some of the most emotional writing in MacArthur's memoirs: ". . . around their necks, as we buried them, would be a string with its dangling crucifix. They were filthy, and they were lousy, and they stank. And I loved them."[45] Sadly, this was mostly fabrication. He certainly saw little of the combat on Luzon or Bataan. There were Filipino troops on Corregidor, but it was not in MacArthur's nature to attend burial ceremonies.

The men on Bataan suffered far more than those on Corregidor who enjoyed a ration three or four times greater and could eat in relative safety.[46] The Navy was still on full rations. Corregidor was stocked to support 10,000 men for six months and those levels were achieved before the stocking of Bataan was allowed to begin. The population on Corregidor and its satellite forts on 24 January was approximately 9,000. On that day, MacArthur ordered the Bataan depots to forfeit food stocks to allow Corregidor to support an increase in strength to 20,000. Doubtless he envisaged reinforcing Corregidor from Bataan. It would have been simpler and kinder to have ironed out the inequities in the ration scales that existed between Bataan and Corregidor. In view of the manning levels, it would not have made a great deal of difference, but at least it would have been seen to be fair. It proved to be an unnecessary storm in a teacup because, over the next few weeks, the bulk of the rations removed from Bataan were returned. Bataan had a haunting effect upon MacArthur for the rest of his life. He had his C-54 airplane christened *Bataan*, the name emblazoned across its nose. In later years, the mere mention of the word could bring tears to his eyes.

On 10 January, MacArthur received an invitation to surrender from Homma. "You are well aware that you are doomed. The end is near. The question is how long you will be able to resist. You have already cut rations by half. I appreciate the fighting spirit of yourself and your troops who have been fighting with courage. Your prestige and honor have been upheld."[47] MacArthur ignored the "epistle." Later, the surrender demand was repeated with an appeal directly targeted at the "dear Filipino soldiers," "cornered to doom" printed on the back. "General MacArthur has stupidly refused our proposal and continues futile struggle at the cost of your precious lives . . . There is still one way left for you. That is to give up all your weapons at once and surrender to the Japanese force before it is too late, then we shall fully protect you."[48] MacArthur wrote: "Every foxhole on Bataan rocked with ridicule that night."[49] Nevertheless, he contacted the War Department, advising that something had to be done about the "deadly effectiveness" of the propaganda: "I am not in a position here to combat it."[50] He also sent a letter to all unit commanders which had the primary purpose of expressing his displeasure "at continuous reports stating that troops are tired and need relief." The letter also deprecated "most severely loose talk tending to aggrandize the potentialities of the enemy." Commanding Officers were directed "to deal harshly with every man who spreads such enemy propaganda, and especially enjoins upon all officers that demeanor of confidence, self reliance and assurance which is the birthright of all cultured gentlemen and the special trademark of the Army Officer."[51]

The previous day, January 15th, MacArthur had sent his unit commanders a letter for dissemination to their subordinates.

Help is on the way from the United States. Thousands of troops and hundreds of planes are being dispatched. The exact time of arrival of reinforcements is unknown as they will have to fight their way through Japanese attempts against them. It is imperative that our troops hold until these reinforcements arrive. No further retreat is possible. We have more troops in Bataan than the Japanese have thrown against us; our supplies are ample; a determined defense will defeat the enemy's attack. It is a question now of courage and of determination. Men who run will merely be destroyed but men who fight will save themselves and their country. I call upon every soldier in Bataan to fight in his assigned position, resisting every attack. This is the only road to salvation. If we fight we will win; if we retreat we will be destroyed. MacArthur.[52]

This was based upon what he had been told by Marshall in his message of 13 January. It might appear gullible or even naïve to pass these words on but MacArthur, unaccustomed to failure, seemed content to clutch at any straw that might protect his reputation. Many of the officers by now could see what MacArthur could not, but many of the men still took the view that if MacArthur said it, it must be right. In his message, Marshall had admitted that he did not know when help would come, and that reinforcements would have to fight their way through, but he emphasized that they were coming. Roosevelt reiterated that pledge in his 30 January message to Quezon.

Why was Washington disseminating untruths? The Philippine Campaign was the first-ever land conflict between America and Japan. An early capitulation would have had a profound effect upon subsequent campaigns and upon the American psyche. The Philippine garrison had to be kept fighting for as long as possible in order to exact an irreplaceable toll from Japan's limited resources of combat manpower. This approach raises profound moral and ethical questions, but war is hell and only victory matters; pity the decision-makers. The day before the fall of Bataan, Stimson wrote in his diary of suggestions "that we should not order a fight to the bitter end because that would mean the Japanese would massacre everyone there. McCloy, Eisenhower and I, in thinking it over, agreed that . . . even if such a bitter end had to be, it would be probably better for the cause of the country in the end than would surrender."[58] When questioning whether it would not have been better to have been honest at the outset, one can only look at the people involved, the information they had and their record for integrity. Eisenhower was among those associated with the pretense, and that is a strong argument in favour of it.

Supplies were stretched. On Corregidor, anti-aircraft ammunition had already been so restricted that only token fire against incoming aircraft was now possible. The Philippine Scouts' (PS) 57th Infantry, one of the best trained and equipped units in the battle, became fully engaged in Nara's probing attack into II Corps' area on 11 January 1942. Hordes of Japanese surged from the cane fields to storm the trenches. Of the mortar bombs which fell among the advancing Japanese, two out of every five failed to detonate. This was symptomatic of problems with ammunition across the board. Also,

> The gross failure of the War Department to ship ammunition for weapons that had been in the hands of the Philippine Division since early 1941 was inexplicable and handicapped all of the combat units of the Division throughout the campaign. The inability of the men to fire the

60mm mortar was to be particularly frustrating later in the campaign when the fighting was at close range in the jungle.

Two thousand rounds of 81mm mortar ammunition arrived by submarine in January but there is no indication that a single round reached the combat units.[54] The total amount delivered by submarines was 53 tons of food (sufficient for one meal for two thirds of the men on Bataan), 3,500 rounds of 3 inch anti-aircraft ammunition, 37 tons of .50 caliber ammunition, one million rounds of .30 caliber ammunition and approximately 30,000 gallons of diesel oil. It hardly seemed worthwhile, but Marshall justified the risk and cost on the grounds of the effect on morale that even the arrival of occasional small shipments could have upon the defenders.[55]

MacArthur's friend the diplomat Pat Hurley arrived in Australia in February fired with the task given to him of running the Japanese blockade of Luzon but soon encountered the reality that "not only were few ships available at any price, but the risks discouraged most sea captains who could be found.[56] Hurley quickly understood why the American military commanders in Australia had been unsuccessful. "We did not have the ships, the air force or ground forces to make the operation successful. We were out-shipped, out-planed, out-manned, and out-gunned by the Japanese from the beginning."[57] Despite the availability of unlimited funds, only six ships set out from Australia, of which three got through—one to Mindanao and two to Cebu. Here in the southern Philippines, 10,000 tons of supplies were offloaded, of which only 1,000 tons reached the garrison, since it was very hard to find the small inshore coasters to take the supplies to Bataan and Corregidor under cover of darkness.

Yet, as MacArthur said, the Japanese had not established an impenetrable blockade around Corregidor and Bataan. Aircraft and ships could come and go, and did. Aircraft continued to operate from Corregidor's landing strip. It was in this manner that the British intelligence agent, Major Gerald Wilkinson, was flown to Australia. The two *Time Life* representatives on Corregidor were evacuated south on a small steamer, but it was the small inter-island boat *SS Legaspi* which showed what could be done given even measures of determination, resourcefulness and bravery.

The *Legaspi* had been stranded in Manila Bay by the war, and Manuel Quezon sent for the skipper, Captain Lino Conejero, to ask him to risk his ship and the lives of his crew to run the Japanese blockade. Quezon's predictable offer of a considerable reward was declined. Roxas communicated with the Governors of the Visayan provinces and told them of the *Legaspi* mission and asked them to contribute what they could for the starving troops on Corregidor and Bataan. *Legaspi* set out and within a week returned to Corregidor at night. The Japanese were aware of its movements, their batteries at Cavite bombarding the jetty while the 14,500 sacks of rice, eggs, chickens, sugar and salt from Capiz were unloaded. Hollow-eyed and unshaven, the Captain and his mate came ashore for further orders. While they were being interviewed by Romulo, MacArthur came into the lateral. "I'm decorating you both," he said. So overcome was the Captain that he had a choking attack. It had been a great morale booster. "Amazing, the importance four dry fish or half a dozen tiny cookies can assume in a man's life," wrote Romulo."[58] *Legaspi* was sent back for a repeat voyage, this time to the American military at Panay, who had no shortage of food. When Captain Conejero reported to Chynoweth there, the Americans suspected a trick, for it was known that the Japanese were also short of food. Conejero was subjected to intense interrogation, and it was not until the Captain spoke of his meeting with MacArthur that Chynoweth knew what he was saying was true. "General MacArthur spoke to me as though I were his son and said that I was risking my life for my country. When I left MacArthur, he was crying like a baby." "I knew," wrote Chynoweth, "that General MacArthur would use such language and could have been that emotional."[59] *Legaspi* was loaded and returned for another successful voyage to Corregidor. Shortly afterwards, a message arrived at Chynoweth's Command Post from General Sharp, 250 miles away at Mindanao, "Who authorized you to load it *(Legaspi)* with food? Why are you anxious to help the enemy of your country by sending them supplies and letting their boats load on your island?" Relations between Chynoweth and Sharp were not the best. "Somebody needs psychiatric treatment," wrote Chynoweth. He signaled back to Sharp's Headquarters that he believed their codes had been compromised and would disregard further messages unless confirmatory evidence was forthcoming. Sutherland urged Chynoweth to continue to support the *Legaspi* voyages because every landing represented 4–5 days of food for Bataan. On 21 February, the *Legaspi* arrived at Panay once more and reloaded to return on her final voyage. En route she was intercepted by a Japanese gunboat off the island of Mindoro and run onto the rocks. Captain Conejero ordered his crew to take to the hills and torched the *Legaspi*.[60] As Romulo remarked, "the *Legaspi*, and other little boats that ran the blockade, survived long enough to prove it could be done,"[61] but there were too few small ships. Ten of the inter-island steamers were sunk or scuttled by their crews as the Japanese tightened the blockade. Seven thousand tons of food, petroleum and other supplies were thereby lost.[62]

Out on the Abucay Line, Nara concentrated his main effort on the enemy's right flank which offered the best "going," down Route 110 to Mariveles. His force was to fight through Abucay to Balanga, from where the main force would continue down the main eastern road while a smaller force advanced from Bagac in the west. Astride this road, where there was little cover and gently rolling terrain, was 57th Infantry (PS). On their immediate left was Brigadier General Vicente Lim's 41st Division (PA). Lim's division had had no enemy contact up to this point in the campaign and had a length of front which might normally be thought commensurate with an operational division. On the left of the 41st was Brigadier General Jones' 51st Division (PA) which had suffered severe losses in the Battle of Luzon, not so much through battle casualties as through desertion, so it reached Bataan as only a token force. There was no prospect of 51st Division defending adequately the 5,000 yards of front it had been allotted on the heights above the gorge of the shallow Balantay River.[63] On the left of 51st Division was the "impenetrable gap," so wide that they were not in contact with I Corps' right flank.

Shortly before midnight on 12 January, Nara made a determined attack, supported by artillery, on 57th Infantry's position. It was forced to give ground, but reinforcements were rushed in and by 19 January the Japanese were back virtually at the point from which the battle had begun one week previously. A position therefore, which had been held earlier by three under-strength battalions, was occupied by eight under-strength battalions at the end of the battle. Parker had been ordered by MacArthur to "use the entire force if necessary" to restore the status quo.[64] During the course of the Battle of Abucay, the Japanese had made probing attacks on II Corps' left flank, held by Jones' 51st Division. The Japanese drove a wedge between 41st and 51st Divisions and occupied the south bank of the Balantay River while still attempting to find a way through to the left of 51st Division to turn Parker's left flank. The Corps commander, having committed all his reserves, was now in a fix. The Staff at USAFFE were not surprised to hear of the threat building up on the Corps' inner flanks but, realizing the danger, released the Philippine Division (less 57th Infantry) from their reserve and Wainwright's 31st Division (PA). Reinforced, Parker decided to counterattack and set aside the objections of Jones, who insisted the 51st Division was not up to it. At first the attack succeeded, but Nara had recognized that the inner flank was the key to unlock the position and had therefore anticipated Parker's action. Squeezed from three directions, the hapless 51st Division gave way and fled the field. Fearing for their own security by exposing their flanks, the Japanese did not follow-up and it was this failure of the Japanese to exploit their advantage which temporarily saved the II Corps line. There still remained the gap where the 51st Division had been. If Nara could attack southward, through the hole, and then swing eastward, he could roll up the whole of II Corps into Manila Bay. Wainwright's I Corps position would be untenable and he too would be forced to withdraw. The viability of the whole line rested upon a counterattack planned for the morning of 17 January to repair the damage created by the disappearance of 51st Division. That task was assigned to an American regiment, the 31st Infantry, supported by 45th Infantry (PS). The counterattacking force fought bravely against an enemy with mortars and grenade dischargers and effectively supported by artillery and aircraft. By 22 January the counterattack force had failed in its mission to plug the gap in II Corps' line, and was worn out.

Meanwhile, all had been relatively quiet on I Corps' front. The west was much more difficult terrain in which to fight conventionally. It "was practically all wooded and almost totally uninhabited."[65] The coast road was much inferior to that on the east coast and petered out into a series of trails at the *barrio* of Moron. The defensive position was anchored on the coast at Mauban and, compared with II Corps, had few infantrymen in the line. The 31st Division (PA) was assigned to beach defense and the 91st Division (PA) was held back in Corps Reserve. Wainwright's Corps was bolstered by the addition of the tired and disorganized 26th Cavalry (PS). There were no replacement horses and very little fodder. Accordingly, the cavalry was reorganized into a motorized squadron of riflemen and a mechanized unit equipped with scout cars and bren gun carriers taken earlier from a ship in the harbor destined for Hong Kong. The Canadians to whom they had been consigned had, in January 1942, no use for them, since they were prisoners of war. The cavalry's horses were destined to supplement the rations with fresh meat.

Homma viewed with concern Nara's lack of progress against II Corps. He accordingly relieved Nara of responsibility for I Corps' area, creating instead a new, 5,000-strong detachment from the 16th Division under the command of Major General Naoki Kimura, under control of 14th Army.[66] After securing Moron and getting through the outpost lines, Kimura attacked Wainwright's main defensive line on 19 January. In the close country Kimura was able to infiltrate Wainwright's line and resisted all attempts to oust him by the Corps, which had already forfeited its reserves to II Corps. Coming through the east flank gap on 21 January, behind I Corps' forward positions, a Japanese battalion managed to block the only lateral road capable of taking heavy traffic. By chance, Wainwright was passing nearby and, commandeering a platoon, attacked the road block but to no avail. A composite infantry and cavalry force was called in to remove the impediment but, despite energetically attacking through 22–23 January, the Japanese could not be moved. By 24 January, this road block had caused a severe shortage of ammunition and rations in I Corps' area. Sutherland visited both Corps commanders on 22 January and both recommended withdrawal to the shorter, stronger position along the Bagac-Orion Line. On 22 January, the orders were accordingly passed. "Hostile penetration through the center of the Main Battle Position makes the further defense of this position inadvisable. The I and II Philippine Corps will withdraw under cover of darkness, beginning 23 January 1942, to the Reserve Battle Position. The withdrawal will be completed on the morning of and prior to daylight 26 January 1942."[67]

By this time there had been many citations sent in by units of brave acts by their individuals. Some were short on detail. HQ USAFFE sent out a signal message to all commanders: "A statement that the individual to whom the award of a decoration is recommended has been heroic or gallant in action is not sufficient."[68]

MacArthur reassured Marshall by cabling him that the Bagac-Orion Line had been personally selected and prepared by him "and it is strong . . . With its occupation all maneuvering possibilities will cease. I intend to fight it out to complete destruction."[69] I Corps fell back with little difficulty but had to abandon much of its artillery; the withdrawal of II Corps was, however, not a text book operation. By

244 MacArthur and Defeat in the Philippines

26 January, the new line had been occupied. The defenders had withdrawn as far south as they sensibly could. Their backs were now up against the sea.

MacArthur did not blame himself for the need to withdraw from the Abucay Line. He wrote of the Japanese in his *Reminiscences*, that "nearly 100,000 replacements kept their original strength intact . . . (and) . . . At a critical moment, 150 guns of heavy caliber came in one shipment from Hong Kong."[70] In the last analysis, "It was Japan's ability to continually bring in fresh forces and America's inability to do so that finally settled the issue."[71] *Reminiscences* was published in the mid-1960s when it was known that Kimura's strength had been approximately 6,000 and Nara's 6,651 compared with the American-Filipino opening strength on Bataan and Corregidor of 90,000. By 24 January, Nara's 65th Brigade had suffered 1,472 combat casualties and had, according to its commander, "reached the extreme stages of exhaustion."[72]

The seriousness of the situation on Bataan was now apparent to many of the defenders. The defeat of America's armed forces, short of a miracle, appeared inevitable. MacArthur radioed to Washington on 23 January that: "My losses during the campaign have been heavy and are mounting. They now approximate 35% of my entire force and some divisions have registered as high as 60%." Yet on 25 January, when the enforced withdrawal from the Abucay Line began, MacArthur radioed Marshall: "Our counterattack on the right was a smashing success. Our powerful artillery concentrations of one five fives was deadly. Our infantry found the enemy completely disorganized in this area; he left hundreds of dead on the field and quantities of supplies and equipment."[73] Four days later, on the Bagac-Orion Line, MacArthur again radioed Marshall:

> Under the cover of darkness I broke contact with the enemy and without the loss of a man or an ounce of material am now firmly established on my main battle position. The execution of the movement would have done credit to the best troops in the world.[74]

Roosevelt responded: "Congratulations on the magnificent stand that you and your men are making. We are watching with pride and understanding, and are thinking of you on your birthday."[75] King George VI wrote how: "The magnificent resistance of the forces under your command to the heavy and repeated attacks of an enemy much superior in numbers has filled your allies in the British Empire with profound admiration." Stimson said: "We all think of you. Everyone of us is inspired to greater efforts by the heroic and skilful fight which you and your men are making." General Pershing, who wanted his son to join MacArthur on Corregidor, wrote: "Heartiest congratulations to you and the brave members of your command for the splendid fight you are making." All these messages were a source of great pride to MacArthur. They were carefully recorded in his memoirs, concluding with some words from General Marshall:

> The magnificent fight of American and Filipino soldiers under your dynamic leadership already has become an epic of this war and an inspiration to the nation. The successes of your troops and your name headline the news of the day. You are rendering a service of incalculable value to the country. The Japanese Army you are holding in check is prevented from reinforcing the enemy's attacks to the southward which gives us the fighting chance to build up the concentration necessary to break through his widely over-extended operations. May the good Lord watch over you and your devoted men.[76]

The sum total of P-40s to have survived the Philippine Campaign thus far was the seven aircraft on Bataan. Their commander, Brigadier General George, had an open authority to use these aircraft at any opportune moment. Towards the end of January there were rumors of heavy concentrations of aircraft at Nichols and Nielson Fields and also of flying boats near the Manila Yacht Club. On 27 January there was a full moon and this was taken as the opportunity to give the Japanese a night to remember. At last light, the aircraft were prepared and bombed up. Unfortunately one aircraft was lost on take-off, but the others divided into two sorties to attack the Japanese fields. They came in low, under the mist, first dropping fragmentation bombs then returning to machine gun the neat line of Zeros and type 97 dive bombers. Between 14 and 37 planes were claimed to have been hit and burned, 300 Japanese killed or wounded and fuel stocks destroyed. For the defenders of Bataan it had been a most satisfactory night.[77]

There was a meeting between General Homma and General Kimura on 14 January 1942. Homma was aware of the great success General Yamashita had enjoyed in Malaya by landing behind the British lines and had already ordered landing barges to be moved from

Lingayen to Olongapo. At the time of this pivotal meeting, the Japanese were facing sturdy resistance on the east coast and a stalemate on the west coast. Apparently Homma did not order Kimura to conduct amphibious operations in his enemy's rear areas but Kimura could see that if landings succeeded, he could unhinge the Bagac end of the Rear Battle Position and cause commotion and panic among the less well trained defenders in the Service Command. Unfortunately for the Japanese, they did not have the manpower to make anything more than token forays into the Rear Areas—no more than two battalions were employed on a number of thrusts into the fingers of land running into the sea on the southwest coast of Bataan. Nevertheless, the threat posed by these operations had results far beyond the size of the force employed. That they did not achieve more was due "to chance, poor seamanship and the lack of adequate maps and charts."[78]

The one hundred square miles encompassed by the Service Command was divided into an East and West Sector. The eastern sector was under the command of Major General Guillermo B. Francisco, commanding general of the reinforced 2nd Division (PA). The western sector was commanded by Brigadier General Clyde A. Selleck who only had his HQ, service troops and a depleted battalion of artillery under command with which to defend the ten miles of western coast from Caibobo Point southward to Mariveles, whose defense was a naval responsibility. Selleck had the agreement of Commander Francis J. Bridget that if the western sector was threatened, a reserve would be supplied from Mariveles. Commander Bridget commanded the Provisional Naval Battalion, an ad hoc unit comprising 150 of Bridget's ground crewmen from Patwing 10, 80 sailors from the Cavite Naval Ammunition Depot, 120 sailors from Cavite, Mariveles and Olongapo and 130 men from the submarine tender *Canopus*, which was disguised as a burnt out derelict. In addition, there were approximately 120 marines who were assigned to the anti-aircraft defense of Mariveles. Only this latter group had any knowledge of field craft and, generally, the handling of personal weapons. ". . . Perhaps two thirds of the sailors knew which end of the rifle should be presented to the enemy, and even practised on a target range, but field training was generally a closed book to them,"[79] wrote Bridget. The *Canopus* with its comprehensive workshops prided itself on being able to respond to any challenge, and they were called upon to dye the sailors' whites so that they looked less conspicuous in the jungle. They had no dye, so used coffee which made white cotton "a sickly mustard bright yellow."[80] Other components in Selleck's indifferently armed, dressed and equipped rear area Security Force were some Philippine Constabulary and the planeless airmen of 3rd, 20th, 21st and 34th Pursuit Squadrons.[81]

The 2nd Battalion, 20th Japanese Infantry, embarked at Moron on the night of 22 January to effect a landing at Caibobo Point, in Selleck's sector. It was not long before the landing barges became separated by strong tides and the heavy swell. A USN MTB, PT34, commanded by Lt. John D. Bulkeley, encountered one isolated barge which he sank, and then another that was similarly dispatched, but Bulkeley was unaware that he had encountered isolated components of a larger landing force that had unintentionally divided into two dispersed groups. The groups landed seven miles apart at the heavily timbered Longoskawayan and Quinauan Points. They achieved tactical surprise, "but only at the expense of their own utter, though temporary bewilderment."[82]

The 300-strong group which landed at Longoskawayan, though disorientated, did what was militarily smart and headed for the high ground, Mt. Pucot, which overlooked Mariveles. A Navy lookout raised the alarm and, after a firefight with a mixed force of Chemical Company soldiers, airmen of the 3rd Pursuit Squadron and elements of the Provisional Naval Battalion, the Japanese were forced from the peak. The Americans were unaccustomed to the Japanese habit of fighting at night and were totally unprepared for the successful counterattack launched shortly after last light. The Japanese also had things to learn. A diary taken from a Japanese revealed how a "new type of suicide squad" dressed in bright coffee colored uniforms had been observed. The observer noted that "whenever these apparitions reached an open space, they would attempt to draw Japanese fire by sitting down, talking loudly and lighting cigarettes." On 24 January the Naval Battalion drove the Japanese back to where they had landed, but the Marines among them recognized that to shift them would require a comprehensively supported infantry battalion.

The 600-strong group which came ashore at Quinauan Point was unopposed, despite the beach being covered by .50 caliber machine guns manned by personnel of 34th Pursuit Squadron. Selleck sent the 3rd Battalion of 1st Philippine Constabulary to throw the Japanese back into the sea. By the time the Battalion arrived the Japanese were well entrenched, requiring a stronger force to shift them. Armor was requested but it was deployed on the Abucay Line to facilitate the break-clean there and none was available. MacArthur personally decided that Selleck was to lead the attack on Quinauan, which was launched on 24 January, unsuccessfully. Richard Marshall had under-estimated the number of Japanese who had come ashore and con-cluded that new leadership was required. Selleck was already regarded with undeserved suspicion after his division fled the field in northern Luzon, and the failure at Quinauan Point seemed to confirm this. On 24 January, Colonel Clinton Pierce, the impressive CO of 26th Cav-alry (PS), presented himself to Selleck with the information that he was to take over command of the Western Sector. This was Selleck's first intimation of USAFFE's intentions. On 25 January, Selleck was demoted to Colonel[83] and on 30 January, Pierce was promoted to Brigadier General.[84]

Wainwright, who had seen at first hand how his Corps' position on the Abucay Line had been completely undermined by a Japanese battalion-level roadblock on his rear boundary, was determined that there should be no repetition. USAFFE had augmented Bridget's sailors in their resumed attack on Longoskawayan Point on 25th Janu-ary but to no avail. The 26th was spent on planning and preparation, essentially to coordinate firepower. In direct support and in support were 2.95-inch mountain howitzers, Marine 81mm mortars, the Scout 75mm guns and Corregidor's Battery Geary—eight 12-inch mortars firing 670 pound projectiles at a range of 12,000 yards. Geary's mortars had been adjusted the previous day by an observer on Mount Pucot. At 0700 on 27 January, the fire mission began and 200 men of the provisional battalion advanced in a skirmish line. The 12-inch mortars proved devastating. "We were terrified," wrote a Japanese soldier who faced the first hostile heavy-caliber American coast artillery fire since the Civil War. "We could not see where the big shells or bombs were coming from; they seemed to be falling from the sky. Before I was wounded, my head was going round and round, and I did not know what to do. Some of my companions jumped off the cliff to escape the covering fire." Unfortunately, insufficient Japa-nese took this course of action to be of assistance to the Ameri-cans. When the supporting fire lifted, the Japanese reoccupied their trenches and effectively engaged the sailors at close range. The Navy was withdrawn and replaced by regular troops sent by Wainwright from the Corps reserve. On 29 January the Scouts, supported by the minesweeper *Quail* out of Mariveles and the four remaining P-40s, put in a comprehensive attack upon the Japanese shoreline position. By dusk, all but a few stragglers had been eliminated, at a cost to the naval battalion of 11 killed and 26 wounded, and a similar number of Scouts. There was an attempt to reinforce the Japanese at Quinauan Point on 27 January and again on 2 February, but these were dealt with by the Scouts.[85] Opposition finally ceased there on 7 February. The failure of the Japanese amphibious incursions meant that they were not repeated, but Wainwright was still worried by the possibility.

The majority of the 90,000 American and Filipino troops were in position on their new defense line by 26 January. The defended front had shortened, there were no gaps, and there was only half the territory there had been to defend when on the Abucay Line, but Wainwright was unhappy. On 27 January he sent a memorandum to MacArthur suggesting that both Corps withdraw further south so as to further shorten the front and length of coast to be defended.[86] Wainwright's tactical thinking was not held in great regard in Lateral 3 in Corregidor's Malinta Tunnel. Sutherland wrote: "The plan was completely unsound and on this occasion General MacArthur sent him one of the most blistering letters I have ever seen the General write."[87] In fact, the letter is quite mild and encouraging:

> Were we to withdraw to such a line now it would not only invite immediate overwhelming enemy attack but would completely collapse the morale of our own force. Sooner or later we must fight to the finish . . . Once again I repeat, I am aware of the enormous difficulties that face you and am proud, indeed, of the magnificent efforts you have made. There is nothing finer in history. Let's continue and preserve the fair fame that we have so fairly won.[88]

MacArthur asked Marshall to ensure that the glorious service of Bataan's defenders be "duly recorded by their countrymen," for "no troops have ever done so much with so little." He requested that in the event of his death, Sutherland be appointed his successor because, "of all my general officers he has the most comprehensive grasp of the situation."[89] The hard-drinking, soldier's soldier Wainwright, known to his peers as Skinny, would therefore have been overlooked. Sutherland did not rate him. "On several occasions it was necessary for me to get him to change his tactical plans and his troop deployments. He made incorrect estimates and sometimes drew up plans which were unsound."[90] MacArthur was now less certain that there was "no Japanese shell with his name on it." "They will never take me alive, Sid," he said melodramatically to Huff. He carried his father's small Derringer and asked Huff to find "a couple of bullets for it." He later admitted to Frazier Hunt that he fully expected to be killed.

> I would never have surrendered. If necessary I would have sought the end in some final charge. I suppose the law of averages was against my lasting much longer under any circumstances. I would probably have been killed in a bombing raid or by artillery fire. And Jean and the boy might have been destroyed in some final general debacle.[91]

Jean refused to accept Marshall's offer of a submarine to rescue her. She said to Doña Aurora, "We have drunk from the same cup, we three shall stay together." Jean wrote her answer on a piece of paper which she had delivered to her husband. MacArthur came out of the Tunnel and talked earnestly to her, and people who knew what was going on saw the little Tennessee lady persistently shaking her head. MacArthur returned to the tunnel and drafted a cable to Marshall saying that his family preferred to stay on the island and "share the rigors of war with me."[92] In his response of 14 February, Marshall gently chided MacArthur, pointing to the desirability of taking a broader view.

> I think it very important that you have in mind the possibility that some later situation might require duty from you that would compel separation from them under circumstances of greatly increased peril. While I intend no interference in your freedom of action and decision in this matter I am anxious that you do not overlook this particular possibility of poignant embarrassment to you personally.[93]

The desirability and feasibility of extricating MacArthur from Corregidor was at that moment a subject of discussion in Washington.

13

"I Will Bring You in Triumph on the Points of My Bayonets to Manila"

By the time the Filipino-American forces had withdrawn from the Main to the Rear Battle position, the politicians left behind in Manila had had over three weeks in which to adjust to the requirements of the Japanese, who had entered the city on 2 January 1942. The next day, leaflets were distributed among the Manileños explaining that "the purpose of the Japanese expedition is nothing but to emancipate you from the oppressive domination of the U.S., letting you establish 'the Philippines for the Filipinos' as a member of the Co-Prosperity Sphere of Greater East Asia and making you enjoy your own prosperity and culture."[1] Homma advised those leaders left behind to organize themselves quickly and establish working arrangements between themselves and the Japanese. For a number of days, the pre-war Commonwealth leaders debated and argued over their collective response to the Japanese directive.[2] Vargas, who was unelected but nominated as Quezon's representative, was accepted by the Japanese as the leader of the Filipino group, even though the lawyer Jose Yulo, formerly Speaker of the National Assembly, was the most senior elected official left in Manila. Vargas suited the Japanese. He was already in post, he had a sound reputation as an administrator, he knew the ropes and he was trusted by Quezon. There was, however, no question of him becoming the President of the Republic they intended to set up. He was the locum who would be used to prepare the way as directed by the many "requests" he would receive from Jitaro Kihara.[3]

The elected officials were content for Vargas to represent Filipino interests because he had already dealt with the Japanese and, as an un-elected official, was not a representative of the people. Initially, the Japanese wanted Quezon to return to resume the Presidency and to help, in Homma's words, "to drive out the evil influence and powers of the United States of America and to establish 'Asia for the Asiatics, the Philippines for the Filipinos . . . the fate of 17 million Filipinos rests in your hands. Now is the time to act, to cooperate with the Imperial forces and to push onward the realization of your ideals.' "[4] Vargas reported to the Japanese that the telephone cable between Manila and Corregidor had been severed and that Quezon was effectively out of contact. Vargas was accordingly ordered to form a government.

Over the next few days, the number of politicians involved in the debate to determine the best way forward increased. At first there were six, then seven, and finally thirty-two. The majority wanted to persuade the Japanese to accept the Commonwealth Government. They were aware of the warning not to take an oath of allegiance and they did not wish to assume responsibility for pacifying the provinces. There were others in the group who were pro-Japanese and prepared to acquiesce in all the Japanese asked in exchange for the promise of a Republic. Ultimately, a compromise was reached whereby the Japanese would be asked to recognize the Commonwealth Government and to agree to the election of a provisional President and Vice-President. But the Japanese Chief of Staff Maeda would not abide the continuance of the Commonwealth. As far as he was concerned, since it had been underpinned by American sovereignty, it had ceased to be of significance once that had effectively disappeared from the archipelago. Maeda told the assembled politicians that they had two choices: "a government of iron backed by military force" or a puppet government.[5] Neither course offered Vargas any freedom of action but a puppet government did offer the prospect of limiting the influence of other individuals in the group who were either strongly pro-Japanese or who might wield power "for profit and political vengeance."[6] Comprehensively intimidated they descended into fine detail of legal argument which would lead ultimately towards collaboration. To ensure Vargas' compliance, Kihara was provided with an office in Malacañan Palace. He was henceforth known among Filipino politicians as the Rasputin of the Malacañan Palace.

The puppets were guided and steered towards forming a provisional Commonwealth Council of State, namely the Philippine Executive Commission, with Vargas nominated as the Chairman. In words laden with humility and subservience, they informed Homma that:

In compliance with his advice, and having in mind the great ideals, the freedom and happiness of our country, we are ready to obey to the best of our ability and within the means at our disposal the order issued by the Imperial Japanese Forces for the maintenance of peace and order and the promotion of well-being of our people under the Japanese military administration.[7]

It might have seemed that they had traded a hegemony of limited duration for one which could be indefinite, but such cynicism was to be dispelled by a speech made by Premier Hideki Tojo to the Diet on 21 January 1942, in which he promised "the honor of independence" to the Philippines if they cooperated with the Japanese to form the Greater East Asia Co-Prosperity Sphere. Vargas welcomed the Tojo statement and then justified collaborating with the Japanese at the end of January in a pragmatic and realistic broadcast to the Filipino people:

Our crops have to be harvested, our roads and bridges reconstructed, and our lines of communications restored; our gainful occupations have to be resumed and our industry rehabilitated. This we cannot accomplish under a reign of lawlessness and unless we cooperate fully with the Japanese Military Administration. And the sooner we salvage what is left of our possessions, the less suffering there will be at the end . . .[8]

Approximately 75 per cent of the pre-war Philippine Senate and 30 per cent of the House had succumbed to Japanese persuasion and accepted positions in the puppet regime.[9]

The knowledge that the majority of the fighting men on Bataan, and by implication the majority of the casualties, were Filipinos, placed a crushing burden upon President Quezon. His health so deteriorated in the hot, humid tunnel that from 26 January he found shelter in a tent at the rear of the hospital, just outside. When the bombers came overhead, he would be wheeled back into the shelter of the tunnel. Quezon had two problems. First, he was sick, and second, he had little to do other than contemplate his situation and that of his country-men. He had clung to the hope that relief would be on hand before Bataan and Corregidor were forced to surrender.[10] Manuel Quezon II remembered MacArthur's reassurance—the constant promise of 400 aircraft on the way.[11] Now he had his doubts, doubts which he aired to MacArthur. What brought matters to a head was a radio broadcast from Tokyo on 28 January which "gleefully announced that a new gov-ernment had been established in the Philippines." The impact upon the Americans close to Quezon "was very bad." High Commissioner Sayre recommended that Quezon repudiate the action, but this the President declined to do. Quezon knew the people involved and that "they could be depended upon under any and all circumstances to commit no act of disloyalty, either to America, to the Philippines, or to me, the head of their government."[12] Besides, he was hardly in a strong position to threaten anyone.

He settled down to write a long letter to MacArthur. Quezon admitted to MacArthur his fear of the effect Tokyo's broadcast would have on the outside world and asked that the content of his letter "be given the widest possible publicity." MacArthur had it relayed to the War Department, fully aware that it would find its way to the Presi-dent's desk—which was Quezon's intention. "Now we are fighting by her (America's) side under your command despite overwhelming odds. But, it seems to me questionable whether any government has the right to demand loyalty from its citizens beyond its willingness or ability to render actual protection. This war is not of our making . . ."[13] Stimson spent a large part of 29 January trying to frame a suitable response to Quezon's detailed letter. "Eisenhower made a very good draft which Marshall and I worked over and finally got one which is the best we can do," wrote the Secretary of State in his diary.[14] Once approved by the President, it was transmitted to Corregidor.

Its message was much the same as had gone before. It emphasized "the magnificent resistance of the defenders of Bataan in contributing definitely toward assuring the completeness of our final victory in the Far East." No promises were made as to when relief would arrive, but "every ship at our disposal is bringing to the South West Pacific the forces that will ultimately smash the invader and free your coun-try." What was meant was that the military assistance was being directed towards Australia, not the Philippines. It offered hope where in reality there was none. In a memo scribbled on 22 January, Eisenhower had written: "We've got to go to Europe and fight, and we've got to quit wasting resources all over the world—and still worse— wasting time."[15] Quezon appreciated the human sympathy and understanding contained in Roosevelt's message, addressed personally to him, but he wrote: "I confess that my grave concern for the welfare and security of my people and the incalculable loss of life on the part of our soldiers was not put at rest." Quezon expressed his continuing misgivings to MacArthur, who promised: "I will bring you in triumph on the points of my bayonets to Manila."[16]

Rumors as to the attitude of Filipinos under Japanese domination, particularly the Manileños, continued around and within the hearing of Quezon. By spring, Bulkeley estimated that approximately 80 per cent of Filipinos were anti-American or neutral and only 20 per cent pro. These veiled criticisms around him caused Quezon great pain. He doubted that his continued presence on Corregidor served any useful purpose and, with his declining health, he thought that perhaps he might serve his country and America better if he returned to Manila and allowed himself to become a prisoner of war. But then something happened to reassure him that there was merit in his remaining on Corregidor. Three Japanese bombers dropped propaganda leaflets over Corregidor and Bataan, targeted at the Filipinos, urging them to surrender. Quezon was quick to repudiate this so-called "Ticket to Armistice" in a proclamation by radio, warning his people against listening to Japanese propaganda which was "designed to lead them to believe a large group of Filipino leaders was disloyal to America."[17] MacArthur had no defense against the anti-American propaganda weapon and confided his concern in a message to Marshall, with particular reference to an article in *Tribune Manila* of 24 January in which the old revolutionary General Aguinaldo, prompted by Homma, proposed lending "our wholehearted cooperation to Japan." Marshall's recommendation was that the propaganda agencies would compare and contrast Aguinaldo with Quezon, "with the purpose of exciting admiration for the latter and contempt for the former."[18]

On the practical side, the War Department toyed with the idea of sending Brigadier General Theodore Roosevelt[19] to Mindanao, where MacArthur hoped to organize guerrilla activities. Roosevelt was meant to manage a propaganda campaign from there, but MacArthur was unenthusiastic and the idea was dropped. On 6 February,

Manila Radio broadcast an open letter from Aguinaldo to MacArthur recommending "that you pay due consideration to humanity and stop this useless fighting against the Japanese Army and thereby avoid wanton loss of life and property not only to Filipinos but to the Americans as well."[20] The Filipinos did develop their own, effective, counter-propaganda scheme to combat that of the Japanese. They took as their symbol of Japanese barbarity *Erlinda of Bataan*, a young woman discovered by Filipino soldiers who had been raped and killed by the Japanese. MacArthur may have been at a loss as to how to combat propaganda, but he had few equals in generating his own.

During the frequent periods of disengagement, the men turned to the radio to discover what was happening, both in their particular world in the Philippines and elsewhere. A San Francisco station, KGEI, broadcast a "Freedom for the Philippines" program to which most of the men listened.[21] From San Francisco they heard that the crippling raid on Pearl Harbor had not been so crippling after all and that the relief Armada had now assembled in Australian waters— ships "as far as the eye could see." The Japanese propaganda service, broadcasting in English from Manila, had the true measure of the situation. Its theme song was *I'm waiting for ships that never come in.* The Bataan defenders reserved the depths of their indignation for Carlos Romulo's *Voice of Freedom* broadcasting from Corregidor: "propaganda so thick it served no purpose except to disgust us and incite mistrust."[22] Colonel LeGrande A. Diller, Head of USAFFE Public Relations, and Romulo himself crafted the public releases under the guidance of MacArthur.[23] This MacArthur-centric propaganda told the story as the General wanted it to be rather than how it was. The press in the U.S.A. dutifully peddled the drama of the siege as embodied in MacArthur's dispatches, telling of good progress in what was then virtually the only area where there was armed conflict between America and her enemies. Roosevelt remained deeply sensitive[24] to the anti-Roosevelt press and did not want to question MacArthur's claims for fear of providing it with ammunition.

Lieutenant Malcolm Champlin, USN, was the naval liaison officer in Wainwright's headquarters. He was both shocked and offended as he glanced through the dispatches which arrived from HQ USAFFE. There was one among MacArthur's communiqués to the United States in which he claimed to have been in Bataan's front line 48 hours earlier. He knew MacArthur had been only once to Bataan, on 10 January, and had never returned. "To Champlin it seemed an unforgivable breach of an officer's code and honor to lie in such a manner."[25]

What MacArthur was authorizing for release proved to be irresistible copy for editors crying out for news of American boys succeeding in battle. There was, in Washington, a Coordinator of Information, whose job was to collect and catalogue copy from the national newspapers. MacArthur was among those sent the writings. A slice of these fawning reports—27 January 1942 to 7 February—reveals the grave misrepresentation by the newspapers.

27 January 1942. A special article on the front page of the *Washington Post* read:

> To an American soldier who spent his sixty-second birthday shaming the prophets of disaster . . . There was no way yet for millions of humble Americans to tell General MacArthur fighting his last ditch fight in the bamboo jungles of Bataan of the hope and pride he has fanned to flame in their hearts. They could not bridge the thousands of sea miles to the far off Philippines with the message that his own inflexible courage has strengthened the will of every man and woman and child back home.

Utah's Senator Thomas said:

> Seldom in all history has a military leader faced such insuperable odds. Never has a commander of his troops met such a situation with greater and cooler courage, never with more resourcefulness of brilliant action. Man for man and gun for gun the U.S. troops have proved their superiority over the Japanese.

The day's clips were rounded off with a leading editorial from the *Philadelphia Record*:

> Douglas MacArthur celebrated his 62nd birthday yesterday by proving anew that he is one of the greatest fighting generals of this war or other war. This is the kind of history which your children will tell your grandchildren, which will go down in the schoolbooks alongside Valley Forge, Yorktown, Gettysburg and Chateau Thierry. To wish Douglas MacArthur a happy birthday is superfluous. He won it.

30 January 1942. The *Philadelphia Record* began MacArthur's life story on the 29th. The paper told how, "As a soldier, MacArthur's

fighting brilliance inspired all who knew him." They retold the 1918 story when an officer asked a doughboy where he might find MacArthur. "Do you know him when you see him?" inquired the officer. "Hell, sir, everyone knows MacArthur, replied the doughboy."

MacArthur sent Roosevelt birthday wishes: "Today, January 30, your birth anniversary, smoke begrimed men covered with the murk of battle, rise from the foxholes of Bataan and the batteries of Corregidor, to pray reverently that God may bless immeasurably the President of the United States."[26] It was a curious message bearing in mind that MacArthur could not abide Roosevelt, but it was intended for a wider audience. So impressed was Texas' Lee O'Daniel by the birthday greeting that he sent Roosevelt a telegram suggesting that, "In view of the daring, heroic and almost miraculous defense of Luzon Island . . . you advise him on this your birthday that hereafter all American citizens will refer to the island as 'MacArthur Island.' "[27] The editor of the *Baltimore Sun* lauded MacArthur's birthday greeting:

1 February 1942. General MacArthur is not only a professional soldier. He is something in the nature of a military genius with the capacity to foresee contingencies and take the best use of resources at his disposal to accomplish the end in view but like all men of genius his capacities do not exhaust themselves in a single field. He has, we may be sure, a sense of the dramatic. He has some conception of that high romance which lifts the soldiers' calling to a level where on occasions ethereal lights play upon it.

2 February 1942. Associated Press Newspapers commented how "almost every day jolts Japanese with unpleasant new reminder of the strength of General MacArthur's Gibraltar." Apparently, the town fathers of Mikado, Michigan were studying a proposal to change its name to honor General MacArthur. The *New York Herald Tribune* carried half a page of photographs taken during MacArthur's military career.

In February 1942 Representative Luther Johnson of Texas proposed in the House that Conduit Road should now become MacArthur Road. A movement to honor MacArthur was sweeping Congress and the country. Representative Jennings offered a Bill to change the name of the TVA Douglas Dam to Douglas MacArthur Dam. Representative Thomas proposed giving MacArthur the Congressional Medal of Honor.[28]

On 2 February, MacArthur sent a signal to Marshall concerning the possible evacuation of President Quezon and his family from Corregidor. In his reply, Marshall said that the President and his advisers felt that when military considerations no longer called for Quezon's presence, his evacuation would be desirable. While Quezon was on Corregidor he, and indeed MacArthur, remained a beacon of hope for the Filipino forces in Bataan. On the other hand, there was the consideration of Quezon's unpredictability and that he might insist on returning to Manila. For the time being, Quezon was inclined to listen to MacArthur who had told him that rather than re-install him in Malacañan Palace, the Japanese were more likely to slit his throat. Moreover, MacArthur had told Quezon that if he turned himself over to the Japanese his motive might be misinterpreted. Quezon retorted that he was not interested in other people's opinions, but that was not entirely true and his mind turned to alternative courses of action.

On 4 February, the submarine *Trout* out of Honolulu and bound for Java became one of the few boats to breach the Japanese blockade. During the night, 2,750 rounds of 3-inch anti-aircraft ammunition which had served as ballast, were offloaded and replaced by $10 million in gold bullion from the Philippine Treasury vault on Corregidor. Lieutenant Colonel Warren J. Clear, an intelligence officer who had been sent to the Far East in July 1941, was ordered to leave Corregidor in the *Trout*. Clear had worked with British intelligence operatives in Singapore before arriving in Manila two days before the attack on Pearl Harbor. Before Clear left, MacArthur questioned him closely as to how the War Department had intended to support operations in the Philippines. Clear told how Roosevelt's closest advisers had said that the President's position was that "England and Russia had priority in all things and would continue to receive such priority." MacArthur had never been informed of the decisions arising from the Arcadia Conferences and is said to have replied: "Never before in history was so large and gallant an army written off so callously." This exchange was overheard by Quezon.[29]

On 4 February, Marshall again[30] formally raised the question of MacArthur leaving if Bataan were to fall because, "under these conditions the need for your services there (Corregidor) might be less pressing than at other points in the Far East." Marshall sought from MacArthur his views on two courses of action: that he either proceed initially to Mindanao to stimulate guerrilla operations there and in Visayan or, he proceed south (presumably to Australia) without stopping at Mindanao. MacArthur's response the next day ignored Marshall's options because, "from my present point of vantage I can see the whole strategy of the Pacific perhaps clearer than anyone else." He proposed "A sea threat (which) would immediately relieve the pressure on the south and is the only way that pressure can be relieved."[31] Marshall explained that the Navy, crippled at Pearl Harbor, did not have the ships. The plan of strategic defense had the limited objective of containing the advance of the Japanese and securing the areas the Allies would need from which to retaliate once the requisite force structure had been built up.[32]

Quezon remained in an agitated state, a rumbling volcano liable to erupt at any moment. The officers around him, rather like seismologists, kept a watchful eye on him. On one occasion, MacArthur overheard the radio in Quezon's tent telling the listeners of the bountiful supply of war materials flowing from America's industrial heart into Europe. Quietly, MacArthur summoned the Spanish-speaking Willoughby to go and see Quezon to draw some of the sting that the broadcast would have generated. Willoughby found an apoplectic Quezon in the company of his wife Doña Aurora and his Swiss physician, Dr. Trepp.

> For thirty years I have worked and hoped for my people. Now they burn and die for a flag that could not protect them. By God and all the Saints, I cannot stand this constant reference to England, and to Europe . . . I am here and my people are here under the heels of a conqueror. Where are the planes that this shameless one is boasting of? *Que demonio!* How typical of America to writhe in anguish at the fate of a distant cousin, Europe, while a daughter, the Philippines, is being raped in the back room![33]

Now his agonized yet fertile mind identified a new solution: "I would ask the President of the United States to authorize me to issue a public manifesto asking the Government of the United States to grant immediate, complete and absolute independence to the Philippines; that the neutralization of the Philippines be agreed at once by the United States and the Imperial Japanese Government."[34] Quezon envisaged both the American and Japanese Armies being withdrawn, the Philippine Army demobilized and expatriate non-combatants repatriated. When Quezon delivered this plan to his Cabinet, both Vice President Osmeña and Roxas expressed their reservations as to the effect the proposal would have upon President Roosevelt. Quezon explained to them my "misgivings as to the ability of our forces to prolong their resistance with so little food and so much dysentery and malaria—a resistance that might be weakened by their knowledge that the civilian population had accepted 'independence' at the hands of the Japanese."[35] The Cabinet thereupon "unanimously" agreed to a radiogram being sent to Roosevelt, for not to have agreed would have resulted in Quezon's resignation.[36]

Independently, however, Roxas and Osmeña spoke to Carlos Romulo. Roxas told Romulo of Quezon's intentions, "but I tell you, Carlitos, surrender is the worst thing that can happen to the Filipinos. It will brand us as cowards who prefer comfort to freedom. We will be humiliated all over the world, and everything Bataan has meant to us will be lost." Romulo struggled to find words to express his feelings but could only say, "he is a sick man." Shortly afterwards, Romulo was sent for by Vice President Osmeña. Osmeña said that when Quezon returned to Manila, "we will take a submarine and set up our Government in exile in Washington." Romulo confirmed his support but said he wanted to talk to the President, once he had made his evening broadcast to the Philippines. Romulo tells in his memoirs how it was a "blockbuster" of a broadcast. "I was desperate and pulled no punches." He told his listeners how the Filipinos were fighting as never before, "determined to hold on and keep faith in America." He hinted that certain Filipinos were beginning to get cold feet, but that was not true of the fighters, who were going to fight Japan to the end, to the last man."[37] No sooner had he finished the broadcast than he was told President Quezon wanted to see him.

When Romulo entered Quezon's tent he could see he was extremely angry. What was he trying to do? Romulo said he was expressing the views of the Filipinos fighting in Bataan. In a spirited defense of his decision, Quezon said to Romulo, "I tell you our boys are dying. Our country is being destroyed. Do you expect me to continue this sacrifice? The fight between the United States and Japan is not our fight. I want to stop this murder. I want to go back to Manila to try to protect the Filipinos, our people, our own people, Romulo, not America."

Romulo replied to the effect that America was fighting for ideals which were shared ideals, to which Quezon angrily responded: "What good are ideals to boys who are dying? Don't you realize, Romulo, that every single drop of blood shed by every Filipino boy there on Bataan is on my conscience, that it is I, their President, who sent them there?"[38] Romulo left to seek out MacArthur to tell him of the crisis. MacArthur refused to influence Quezon. "I have my own views Carlos but I think Manuel is entitled to his. He wants to correspond with the President of the United States in this matter, and I have promised to transmit anything he has to say."[39]

The war had served to push Sayre into adopting a less dominant role on Corregidor. His attempt to pressurize Quezon to condemn the collaborators who Quezon indignantly insisted were not quislings, did nothing for the relationship between the two men. Dufault suggests that Sayre did not comprehend the depth of Quezon's emotions or the web of obligations which bonded Philippine society.[40] But when MacArthur showed Sayre Quezon's draft message to Roosevelt, Sayre said that if aid should not be forthcoming, the sound course to follow would be "immediate independence and neutralization." As the local ranking constitutional expert, Sayre argued that the Tydings-McDuffie Act had provided for neutralization and, moreover, he agreed with Quezon that Americans and Filipinos were dying because of American unpreparedness.[41] MacArthur's reaction to Quezon's message, although less frank, was nonetheless considered worse by Stimson because "it went more than half way towards supporting Quezon's position."

Some observers suggest that Quezon raised the issue for effect and for the impact it would have on Washington, but the evidence does suggest that he was in earnest. Others suggest that MacArthur gave his qualified backing to shock Washington; about that, judgement must be reserved. Friend, for example, suggests that the General saw a way in which he could use Quezon's proposed surrender to save his own declining reputation.[42] MacArthur's long military estimate of the situation, which went as a postscript to Quezon's appeal to Washington, meant it was sent in two parts over two days. MacArthur told Washington that his troops had sustained 50 per cent casualties. "The temper of the Filipinos is one of almost violent resentment against the United States. Every one of them expected help, and when it has not been forthcoming, they believe they have been betrayed in favor of others." Undoubtedly, this was a shared opinion. MacArthur went on to wonder "whether the plan of President Quezon might offer the best possible solution of what is about to be a disastrous debacle . . . please instruct me."

On the 9th, when the complete text was to hand, Stimson recognized the absurdity of Quezon's proposition. The Japanese were in occupation in his capital, intent upon making the Philippines a component of their Greater Co-Prosperity Sphere. Possession being nine tenths of the law, they were not going to march away from a prize in the process of being won at great cost. Stimson thought Quezon's plan took "no account of what the war was for or what the well known characteristics of Japan towards conquered people were." Worse, thought Stimson, was MacArthur's somber picture of the military situation and his partial support of Quezon's plan.[43]

Marshall and Eisenhower had begun drafting a response to Quezon's plan, which they redrafted after hearing Stimson's opinion. Marshall and Stimson had an appointment with Roosevelt at 10:30 a.m. that morning and at the White House. Stimson presented his views of a situation he described as "ghastly in its responsibility and significance." When he had finished, Roosevelt declared, "we can't do this at all." There had been unanimous agreement that the Philippines *belonged* to the United States and was as much theirs as Britain's and the Netherlands' colonies were theirs. In subsequent correspondence, Roosevelt told Quezon bluntly, "You have no authority to communicate with the Japanese Government without the express permission of the United States Government."[44] What was being acted out in the White House was not a subject of purely military significance; the political implications presented the President with one of the most serious challenges thus far in the war. Admirals King and Stark were called to the White House that afternoon to add their views. Marshall was much impressed by Roosevelt's firm and resolute grasp of the situation. "I immediately discarded everything in my mind I had held to his discredit . . . Roosevelt said we won't neutralize. I decided he was a great man."[45] By four o'clock, the reply was drawn up and then dispatched to MacArthur in two parts. The first, drafted by Eisenhower and Stimson, was for MacArthur and the second part, drafted by Stimson, was for Quezon. Both went under the President's signature.[46]

MacArthur read the President's emphatic denial of "the possibility of this Government's agreement to the political aspects of President Quezon's proposal." Washington was addressing and chiding MacArthur but also had the shaming of Quezon in mind when authorizing MacArthur to "arrange for the capitulation of the Filipino elements of the defending force," while insisting that "American Forces will continue to keep our flag flying in the Philippines so long as there remains any possibility of resistance."[47] The message was clear. America's garrison in the Philippines was expected to fight to the finish. Stimson reflected that "To give the order was a matter of duty, but it was in its loyal execution that the true glory would be found."[48] Quezon, in his message to Washington, had mentioned Japan's promise of independence for the Philippines and it was this point that Washington focused on: "I only have to refer you to the present condition of Korea, Manchukuo, North China, Indo-China and all other countries which have fallen under the brutal sway of the Japanese Government . . . is it . . . possible for any reasonable person to rely upon Japanese offer(s) or promise(s)?" The message went on to say how "we shall not relax our efforts until the forces which we are now marshaling outside the Philippine Islands return to the Philippines and drive the last remnant of the invaders from your soil," Signed Franklin D. Roosevelt.[49]

When Quezon was handed Roosevelt's reply, he was sitting in his wheelchair in the tent by the entrance to Malinta Tunnel. As he read it, so did his rage grow. He got out of his chair and stomped around inside the small tent, decrying Roosevelt's grasp of global war strategy. In the text of his message, Roosevelt had admitted that reinforcements would not arrive in time to save the Philippines. "Who is in the best position, Roosevelt or myself, to judge what is best for my people?" He fell back into his chair in an exhausted state and dictated his resignation as President of the Commonwealth. At a Cabinet meeting an hour later, Osmeña and Roxas attempted to get Quezon to change his mind but it appeared that the greater the pressure they applied, the greater his resolve to return to Manila. They could either come with him, he said, or they could remain on Corregidor. Osmeña decided not to press the issue but rather to wait until an opportunity arose for him to talk privately with Quezon.

Very early on the morning of 11 February, Osmeña rose from his cot to make a visit to the latrine. As he passed the President's cot, he heard Quezon coughing. Quezon, recognizing Osmeña, called him into his alcove and invited him to sit down by the bedside. They reminisced about old times and Osmeña was struck by the depths of Quezon's depression. His old friend then took this chance to discuss Quezon's proposed resignation and return to Manila. Osmeña suggested that if Quezon went ahead and made what he argued was a serious mistake, then history might well regard him as a traitor and coward. What of his wife and teenage daughters? continued Osmeña. There were reports from Manila that Japanese soldiers had raped women and girls. Did he want those he loved to be taken hostage so that the Japanese would force Quezon to do as ordered? After listening without interruption, Quezon said resignedly, "*Compadre,* perhaps you are right. I shall think it over."[50]

The suggestion that his Filipinos might be permitted to surrender, or the thought that this is what he was proposing, may have been anathema to MacArthur. Nevertheless, the Marshall/Eisenhower draft to him was heavily laced with rebuke. The terms used in the radiogram emphasized Washington's control of events, a Washington that was not going to be dictated to.

> The duty and necessity of resisting Japanese aggression to the last transcends any other obligation in the Philippines. I particularly request that you proceed rapidly to the organization of your forces and defenses so as to make your resistance as effective as circumstances will permit and as prolonged as humanly possible.[51]

MacArthur bridled at the suggestion he had any other intention than "fighting (on) my present battle position in Bataan to destruction . . . I have not the slightest intention . . . of surrendering or capitulating the Filipino elements of my command." The implication behind this, that he, and his family, were going to die on Corregidor, rang alarm bells. Unlike Eisenhower, Marshall believed that MacArthur should be rescued because, despite his well advertised idiosyncrasies, he was the most suitable Army General to pick up the pieces in the Far East. Politically, the administration was also coming under increasing pressure from the Republicans to rescue MacArthur.

Neither America nor Japan would accede to Quezon's rather fanciful idea of neutralization because that was not in the interests of either of the belligerent states. Quezon explained his change of mind: "When I realized that he (Roosevelt) was big enough to assume and place the burden of the defense of my country upon the sacrifice and heroism of his own people alone, I swore to myself and to the God of my ancestors that as long as I lived I would stand by America regardless of the consequences to my people and to myself."[52] With both MacArthur and Quezon back on board, plans in Washington went ahead to remove both from Corregidor, beginning with the latter.

Meanwhile, in Washington, there was a Republican influenced proposal to nominate a Commander in Chief of all the armies of the United States. There was a meeting on 12 February where the idea was put to Stimson by General Benedict Crowell. Stimson demurred, arguing that there should be no one "between the President and the Commander of different task forces," believing the Chief of Staff played the necessary coordinating role.[53] But Crowell's approach had been the opening round in a wider strategy, for that evening at a Lincoln dinner the defeated 1940 Republican candidate for the presidency, Wendell L. Willkie, spoke of

> the one man in all our forces who has learned from first hand, contemporary experience the value and the proper use of the Army, Navy and Air Forces fighting together toward one end: the man who on Bataan Peninsula has accomplished what was regarded as impossible by his brilliant tactical sense; the man who also alone has given his fellow countrymen confidence and hope in the conduct of this war—General Douglas MacArthur. Bring Douglas MacArthur home . . . put him in supreme command of our armed forces under the President.[54]

Senator Arthur Vandenberg, Republican of Michigan, heavily criticized Roosevelt for rescuing the British and Russians yet leaving MacArthur to fight alone. Vandenberg threatened that if MacArthur got out alive, "I think he will be my candidate for President in 1944."[55] It was left to the military analyst Hanson W. Baldwin to put his finger on the central problem: evacuation of MacArthur might precipitate the collapse of his command.[56]

However, it was the Quezon and Sayre families who were to go first. The problem was that it was not possible to evacuate both families in the *Swordfish*, the next submarine due to call at Corregidor. Since the plan was to take the Quezon party initially only as far as Capiz, it was agreed that they should go first. Back in Washington, Eisenhower took over War Plans from Gerow on 16 February. As he left, Gerow said to him, "Well, I got Pearl Harbor on the book, lost the Philippine Islands, Singapore, Sumatra and all the NEI north of the barrier. Let's see what you can do."[57] On 18 February, Vargas put further pressure on Washington by sending, on behalf of the Council of State, a wire prepared by the Japanese military administration. It was a request from the Filipino people to President Roosevelt to order a cessation of hostilities in order to avoid the loss of further Filipino lives as well as those of USAFFE troops who lacked suitable arms and ammunition.[58] As Laurel later explained, "What the Japanese military authorities wanted had to be done. Consul Kihara received the military orders and instructions for

Mr. Vargas. We were made to send cables to President Roosevelt and President Quezon and a manifesto to the fighting Filipinos in Bataan and Corregidor. To save ourselves and avoid retaliatory measures from the Japanese, all these things had to be done."[59]

The decision to evacuate the Quezons brought to a head the delicate matter of the rewards due to MacArthur and his staff. On 14 February the Chase National Bank was ordered by cable to transfer funds from the Philippine account to the designated individuals, including MacArthur's $500,000. The transfer would take four days to effect and, in the interim, the equivalent in Philippine Treasury Certificates was placed in a footlocker and handed by Roxas to Huff, acting as MacArthur's agent, as collateral. On 18 February, Quezon cabled Chase to inquire whether the transaction had gone through.[60] MacArthur had no immediate relatives other than his wife and son who, presumably, unless the family had a change of heart, were all going to "share the fate of the garrison." Why, therefore, this placing of a substantial sum of money in America? Schaller makes the controversial suggestion that MacArthur's behavior indicates his intention not to share the fate of his garrison.[61]

On 20 February, the day the Quezons were to leave Corregidor, MacArthur was awarded the Distinguished Service Star of the Philippines. The citation concluded: "The record of General MacArthur's service is interwoven forever in the history of the Philippines and is one of the greatest heritages of the Filipino people." Signed Manuel Quezon. Cars were forbidden to move through the tunnel that night as the Quezons left for the jetty. The last car to arrive carried MacArthur and Sutherland who got out and supported[62] President Quezon on either side. According to Romulo, as he saw his President in the moonlight, "he looked like the ghost of the old Quezon." Before boarding the small navy tender alongside the jetty, which would take the party out to *Swordfish* in the deeper water of the Bay, MacArthur took the frail, gravely ill old man in his arms. "Manuel," said MacArthur, "you will see it through. You are the father of your country and God will preserve you." It was an emotional moment for two emotional men. That day, Quezon had written a testimonial for MacArthur. "I am leaving you with a weeping heart, for you and I have not only been friends and comrades, we have been more than brothers . . . I am leaving my own boys, the Filipino soldiers, under your care." Quezon slipped from his bony finger the signet ring which he used to seal letters of state and placed it on MacArthur's finger. "When they find your body," said Quezon close to tears, "I want them to know that you fought for my country."[63]

The *Swordfish* was skippered by Lieutenant Chester (Chet) Smith, a deceptively mild, conservative officer. His orders were to proceed, on the surface, only at night and lie hidden underwater by day. On arrival at Panay, a code signal was to be sent: "precious package arrived." Smith wrote how Quezon "wore pajamas the whole trip. Quezon's two little girls and Mrs. Quezon were seasick and miserable. But the son, Manuel, had a ball."[64] According to the son, Smith found the chance of sinking a Japanese freighter too tempting to let pass by. He attacked the ship and was depth-charged for his troubles, with the result that half the air-conditioning plant was put out of commission.[65]

In his autobiography, Quezon recounts his wish "that the seat of the Philippine Government should be transferred to the free territory of the Islands, at first in Visayan."[66] His thinking seems to have been at variance with Washington's and Chynoweth's, who thought Quezon merely intended to break his journey in Panay before moving on immediately to Australia and the United States. Chynoweth signaled MacArthur: "We met Mr. Quezon and he came ashore here. He was advised to remain on board for secrecy, but would have none of it." Chynoweth wrote in his memoirs how Quezon was determined to go ashore to make speeches and to remain on Panay.[67] The *Swordfish* was ordered to return to Corregidor to collect High Commissioner Sayre, his family and three others. However, there had already been a heated exchange of signals with Washington, Sayre insisting that his staff, which he had taken to Corregidor, should leave with him. So as well as taking off the three Sayres, *Swordfish* also took eight members of the High Commissioner's staff and two others, a total of thirteen. The code-breakers, who were intended to leave Corregidor for Australia, were left behind in favor of the civilian administrators.[68] In Sayre's possession was a footlocker consigned to Riggs National Bank, Washington—MacArthur's bank. The letter to the manager explained that the locker contained "valuable records and documents from my personal files. It is requested that you hold the trunk for me in your safe deposit vault to be withdrawn by me or by Major General R.K. Sutherland."[69] Sayre and his party left Corregidor on 23 February 1942. "When you next see daylight," said MacArthur, "it will be an altogether different kind of world."[70] Romulo wrote in his diary, "they are leaving us one by one."[71]

14

"I SHALL RETURN"

Concurrent with the Japanese initiatives which had culminated in the Battle of the Points, there were two Japanese attacks upon the very recently occupied reserve battle position, the Orion-Bagac Line. The amount of territory to be defended by what was now somewhat less than 90,000 men had been halved, but their combat effectiveness had also been much eroded. The new front line running to the south of the lateral road was much shorter than the previous one and the inner flanks of the two Corps were this time in contact. Parker's Corps held approximately 15,000 yards of front and Wainwright's Corps about 13,000 yards. The inter-Corps boundary was the Pantingan River flowing generally northward from the Mariveles Peaks. The new position was dominated by Mount Samat which afforded a good view over the battle lines to the front. The "going" in General Parker's II Corps' area on the right was better than that in Wainwright's I Corps area, covered as it was in primary jungle. "Nowhere on Bataan," wrote Morton "was the terrain less suitable for military operations."[1] Apart from one small sector, the entire line was held by Filipino troops, who had learnt their military skills the hard way—under fire. But they never had a proper grounding in the art of war, founded upon progressive training. According to one diarist,

> they had not what seems to me now to be utterly requisite in the training of all combat units in war—a thorough toughening process

through extended and realistic maneuvers ... we lost men in the
Philippines when they used the half squat, semi-crouching method
common in peacetime maneuvers and training, as they approach the
enemy.[2]

Individual skills were also understandably found wanting. The Japanese had observed and reacted to the tendency among Filipino machine gunners not to fire in bursts but continuously until the weapon seized.

Homma's intention of attacking the Filipino-American line immediately, before his opponents had become properly established, meant Nara's 65th Brigade and the Kimura Detachment attacked Parker's and Wainwright's Corps respectively without the benefit of supporting artillery fire. Immediately following the withdrawal from the Abucay Line, Parker's Corps had been in a state of disarray due to USAFFE's last-minute orders to constitute a reserve. There had been a large gap in the line but, by 27 January when Nara attacked, it had been closed. The finding of a battle map supposedly showing outposts where in fact the main line of resistance lay, caused an early setback to Homma's plans against II Corps. Try as Nara might, his sterling efforts against the "outposts" were consistently repelled. After losing an entire regiment, Nara paused to reorganize his Brigade with a view to resuming the attack on 8 February, that is until being ordered by Homma to disengage and withdraw.

Kimura spent the period 26–29 January pressing and testing Wainwright's I Corps line to find its weak link. On the night 28–29 January they found it in 1st Division's area. The divisional personnel, who had lost much of their equipment, were still preoccupied with the preparation of their own defenses and were unable to resist the infiltration of the 1,000 men of Colonel Yoshioka's 20th Infantry. The staff of 1st Division knew they had Japanese in their rear area but assumed their strength to be small and limited to a number of fighting patrols. The "door" the Japanese had used to infiltrate 1st Division's area had now been firmly closed behind them. Yoshioka's immediate problem lay in exercising control over his unit in the barely penetrable jungle. Unintentionally, the Japanese force divided, one company going into an area known as The Little Pocket and the remainder into The Big Pocket. Wainwright went forward daily, growing more concerned as the true strength of Yoshioka's force became evident from the increasing number of casualties.[3] His leadership was inspirational. He "liked to get into a pair of jumpers and take a rifle right up into the front defense areas. The troops were very fond of him and the fact he was there sometimes, bossing them about and fighting with them, meant a lot."[4] Wainwright set the standard for other officers, many of whom copied his style and this, together with the presence of Scouts, did so much to steady the line. The General invariably had a case of Scotch whisky in his command car, from which he would occasionally pour a dram for officers he encountered along the way.[5] The manner in which Wainwright took risks amazed his naval liaison officer, Lieutenant Champlin. Following another dangerous encounter, Champlin asked him why. "Think it over for a minute," said Wainwright.

> What have we got to offer these men? Can I give them more food? No. We haven't any more food. Can I give them ammunition? No. That is also beginning to run low. Can I send them supplies, equipment, medicines, or tanks? No. Everything has practically gone. But we *can* give them morale, and that is all I have left to give them. That is why I visit the front every day. Now do you understand, son, why it is important for me to sit on sandbags in the line of fire while the rest of you seek shelter?[6]

Wainwright's response to the threat posed by the Japanese in the Pockets increased by the day but, by 5 February, the close quarters fighting had achieved little except casualties on both sides. However, by now the Japanese were suffering severely. The temperature during the day reached 95°F and plummeted at night. It was the dry season and there was no water in the streams. The Japanese attempted to air supply their exposed contingent but only served to supplement the rations of the grateful Filipinos. At 0900 on 7 February, deliberate attacks were launched against the Pockets, and by 9 February the Japanese in the Little Pocket had been annihilated. This left the divisional commander, General Jones, free to concentrate all his effort on the Big Pocket. Whilst Jones was in the process of planning a decisive offensive, Colonel Yoshioka was ordered by Homma to withdraw his weary force. When the Filipinos entered the Big Pocket on 12 February, all they found were 300 dead Japanese, 150 graves and a large quantity of equipment. Yoshioka was making his way northward with his wounded to rejoin the Japanese lines, reaching safety after a march of four days through the American lines. Of the 1,000 men he had taken into the Pockets, only 377 came out. Yoshioka's 20th Infantry had begun the Bataan campaign with a strength of 2,690 men. His

First and Second Battalions had been virtually annihilated at the Battle of the Points and, by mid February, it was estimated that the Regiment's strength was no more than 650 men, the majority of whom were sick or wounded.[7]

Attrition of this magnitude meant that Homma was unable to sustain the land offensive against Bataan without reinforcement. There were only three effective Japanese battalions left in the Philippines. Homma would later claim that his forces were in such bad shape that: "If the USAFFE took the counter offensive, I thought they could walk to Manila without encountering much resistance on our part."[8] Perhaps, but what would his opponents have done when they got there and how would they remain there without command of the air and sea? The best the American Filipino Army could hope to achieve was to hold out for as long as possible in anticipation that, in Mallonée's words, "something would throw a cog into the enemy machine and start it unexpectedly in reverse. Holding out meant the maximum conservation of effort, and that did not allow for offensive action, with its wastage of personnel and material."[9] But the fact was, Homma's 14th Army had lost 2,725 men killed in action, 4,049 wounded and 250 missing. Between 10–12,000 men were sick with malaria, beriberi and dysentery.[10]

A staff meeting was held at San Fernando, 8 February, to discuss options. Homma's senior operations officer argued for the aggressive resumption of the offensive along the east rather than the west coast. Chief of Staff Maeda believed there to be no need for an offensive at all since the Americans and Filipinos would eventually be starved into submission. Listening to both arguments, Homma decided upon a compromise. Although there may have been some merit in Maeda's proposal, it would have led to an inglorious and hollow victory. Already having failed to achieve his mission in time and with the forces made available to him, Homma faced up to the embarrassment of asking Tokyo for reinforcements. In the meantime, he ordered the survivors to rest, to train and to tighten the blockade around Bataan and Corregidor. From this point in mid February until the end of March, other than occasional, intermittent gunfire, offensive military activity ceased on the Bataan front.

Morale had soared among the Filipino-American forces. The Filipinos had made an incalculable contribution to the victory. "This was not a defensive battle where the Japanese threw themselves upon entrenched Filipinos. Rather, it was the offensive spirit, firepower, and ability of the Filipinos which destroyed the Japanese."[11] It had been a victory achieved against great adversity. The need for reliable mortars had become increasingly evident. "Even the old Stokes mortar with good ammo would have been of great value," wrote the 11th Infantry's Colonel Townsend. The problem was that the First World War ammunition had deteriorated throughout its long period of storage in the Philippines. During one phase of the Battle of the Pockets, only 14 rounds out of 70 fired actually detonated. Later, "we used up our last 22 rounds and got 5 bursts. No wonder the Japs once set up a captured Stokes mortar between the lines and scoffingly draped it with flowers."[12] Unexploded shells were found within yards of Japanese machine gun posts and in enemy trenches.[13] The hand grenades were of the same First World War vintage. "Our grenades were all 1918 jobbers and if two out of ten went off, we'd be lucky."[14]

Food shortages had an obviously debilitating influence upon combat effectiveness. On 2 March, against the protests of both Wainwright and Parker, MacArthur further reduced Bataan's basic ration to three eighths of a regular ration.[15] The men became more inventive than even their Quartermaster, who regularly inflated unit ration strengths. Supplements to the daily ration were to be found in the sea, on the farms and in the jungle. Colonel Mallonée wrote of having had *carabao* or water buffalo on a number of occasions, "not issued but killed on the line and 'procured.' By the same method we had *calesa* pony once and mule twice. I can recommend mule . . . The pony was tougher but better flavored than the *carabao*. Iguana was fair."[16] One officer thought monkey was all right, until the animal's hands turned up on his plate. There is another record of American soldiers fleeing the dining table when the Filipino cook brought in roast monkey. "It had looked like roast baby, too much for them to stomach."[17] Some Filipinos risked death by smuggling luxury goods to the troops, but the rewards were high—as much as $200 for a carton of cigarettes. Payday was still held regularly but there was little on which to spend their money, which is why gambling stakes were so high.[18] The disparity between American and Scouts' pay on the one hand and the Filipino military on the other led to MacArthur's request to Washington for equal pay for all. However, Corregidor fell before any progress had been made in that direction.[19]

It is a perennial and generally correct observation of the infantry that support troops in rear areas eat better than them. This was true of Bataan, but the meals on the submarine tender USS *Canopus* anchored at Mariveles were in a class of their own. Ice cream was regularly available on board right up to the fall of Bataan. It was not just the choice and quality of food that made an invitation so cherished: the drinking water was refrigerated, there were shower baths and bunks with freshly laundered sheets. One day, Les Tenney of the 192nd Tank Battalion was in Mariveles and asked a *Canopus* crew member who was interested in Japanese war souvenirs, the price of an invitation. Tenney was soon driving off to the Pilar-Bagac road, where he had been involved in a fight with some Japanese. He quickly found a flag of the rising sun and a sniper's rifle, enough to negotiate dinner for himself and his friend. "The first night, [of a number] we had roast beef, all the trimmings and chocolate cake with ice cream."[20] Officers ate even better. At a thank you dinner following the Battle of the Points, Captain Mills of 57th Infantry described the occasion:

> Waiters in white jackets, a beautiful table cloth, real silver, wine goblets filled with wine, the whole works. The menu—Roast Turkey, Ham, mixed vegetables, salad, white bread, butter, and the dessert of all things, ice cream. After dinner came after dinner drinks and fine cigars. I felt at the time I was surely in the wrong branch of service. I stuffed myself so much that I was sick for three days.[21]

Fodder for the cavalry's horses had also been exhausted. On being told, Wainwright said: "Horsemeat ain't so bad. Captain, you will begin killing the horses at once. Joseph Conrad (his own personal charger) is the horse that you will kill first." So saying, he went up to his trailer with tears in his eyes. Wainwright and Champlin had just returned from visiting the front. One battalion they had found to be riddled with malaria and dysentery. The dead stood propped up in their foxholes, their faces pointing northward and their personal weapons in lifeless hands in an attempt to persuade reconnoitering Japanese that the position was still strongly held. The corpses were covered in bloated flies feeding off the feces close to the foxholes.[22] "A life long characteristic of many of the *barrio* Filipinos," wrote engineer Colonel Skerry, "seemed to be to relieve his bowels when and where he chose. To scramble out of a foxhole at night and run for the platoon latrine in the inky jungle darkness with dysentery and diarrhoea dogging at his heels required a lot more training in field discipline than the average Filipino was granted the time to acquire."[23]

That the Japanese so often engaged in night operations was good cause to keep troops in their foxholes, waiting patiently for the reassuring first light of the new day. The Japanese were not averse to the wearing of uniforms taken from dead Americans or setting off fire-crackers behind Filipino lines just to keep them on edge.[24] On some occasions during the build-up for a night attack, the defenders could hear the sound of approaching drums, a device used by the Japanese to maintain their line as they advanced through the jungle. On other occasions, Japanese radio vans would broadcast "homely" American music. Another ruse at night would be a voice in the darkness calling, "Joe, come here and help me." The Filipinos and Americans got the measure of that trick by interrogating the "casualty" beyond his com-petence in English. The propaganda leaflets produced by the Japa-nese proved to be ineffective. "They weren't at all convincing. I doubt whether a single one of them was ever used for the purpose it was intended for, though I know they were used for other purposes."[25]

During the extended lull in the fighting on Bataan, the fit men were engaged on field engineering projects to strengthen their defenses so as to be better able to receive the inevitably reinvigorated and reinforced Japanese. However, on 18 February, the USAFFE surgeon general's report revealed only 55 per cent of Bataan's troops categorized as combat efficient due to debilities such as "malaria, dysentery and general malnutrition." The two field hospitals were reporting 500–700 daily admissions of malaria victims, and only inad-equate stocks of quinine. This being the dry, hot season, great pres-sure was placed on the supplies of drinking water. Men crazed for water ignored the risks involved in drinking from stagnant pools.[26] According to a report by Wainwright, by 12 March at least three quar-ters of his command was incapacitated for one reason or another.

Although Bataan was able to take advantage of a lull before the continuation of the storm, the same was not true of Corregidor. The Japanese had used their air power over Bataan for scouting and bomb-ing but the jungle canopy provided welcome cover. The American-Filipino forces took sensible precautions not to raise dust and to site cookhouses well to the rear. On Corregidor, however, there was pre-cious little camouflage and cover for the 11,500 people on the 1,735 acre island. Although the USAFFE Headquarters staff and those in the immediate vicinity of the Malinta Tunnel could take advantage of the protection it provided, the majority of Corregidor's garrison, the coastal artillery and the 4th Marines were extremely vulnerable and exposed to enemy bombing and artillery fire.

Twin-engined Japanese bombers would follow the early morning appearance of the photo reconnaissance plane, flying over the defended islands in tight V-formation, invariably at 160 miles an hour and at 20,000 feet. What anti-aircraft ammunition was still available on Corregidor was used sparingly against the daily parade of bombers, although it had a tendency to detonate beneath them. Once the ritual pass had been made over the island, the air armada divided into task forces to attack their designated batteries and other targets. The Japanese would sometimes launch sneak attacks on moonlit evenings, in the hope of catching the defenses unaware. Alternatively, the bombers would also come over when there was broken cloud in the sky so that although they could be heard, they could only be seen intermittently. The execrable weather that routinely affected the archipelago was now earnestly sought after and welcomed by the defenders of Corregidor for the respite it provided from enemy bombing.[27] Enemy artillery fire, however, was not unduly affected by the weather since it had registered its targets. From 26 January, an artillery unit of four 105mm guns and two howitzers, the Kondo Detachment, had been established on the shore close to Ternate, Cavite. Every day for a month the Japanese gunners bombarded the island, firing only in the morning when the sun was behind them. In order that the guns should not be pinpointed by Corregidor's defenders seeing their flash or smoke, the Japanese sent up smoke rings to coincide with their firing.

The effect of the shelling and bombing was devastating since the targets were often surrounded by concrete or rocky ground. The fixed batteries on Corregidor had been originally established to engage warships whose guns had relatively flat trajectories, not bombers. Carlos Romulo told how he had left the Malinta Tunnel after the all-clear had been given when he encountered a grown man, a Private Hamby, "bawling like a child." Sympathetic and curious to discover what was so distressing the man, Romulo eventually coaxed out of him the reason for his distressed state. "It seems he had just been out on hospital detail and had pulled a man's leg out of a rubbish heap that ten minutes before had been a battery. It came away in his hand—a flesh and blood human leg. He was standing, staring at it, when something moved under the rubbish. He dug up the rest of the man. It was his best pal—the fellow Hamby had enlisted with back in the States. What was left of the boy gripped Hamby's hand. 'Keep 'em flying, feller!' he said. Then he died."[28] The man had been fortunate for inside the hospital lateral there were some men who had lost all four limbs. They were known as "basket cases."

On the face of it, the capability to strike back was extremely limited, but it is surprising what determined, angry men are capable of achieving. HQ USAFFE ordered a sortie to find and destroy the Kondo Detachment at Ternate. First, there had to be a photo-reconnaissance mission, but the P-40s were unable to carry the bulky camera. There was still an airworthy Stearman biplane trainer available, in which the Air Corps mechanics installed the camera. The pilot of the unarmed plane was Captain Jesus S. Villamor who had been awarded the Distinguished Service Cross at the same ceremony that Captain Colin Kelly received his posthumous award. Villamor took off from Bataan on 9 February with the six available P-40s as escort. There was no opposition over the target and Villamor's photographer took 110 pictures before they turned back towards Bataan. On the return leg, the Americans were jumped by six Zeros, but all were shot down for the loss of one P-40.[29] Once the photographs had been developed, "the batteries on Corregidor succeeded in landing some mortal blows on the enemy positions at Ternate."[30] If that were true, the Japanese soon recovered and, during the week 15–20 February, the intense artillery fire caused more damage than all the air bombing to date.[31]

The fighter action was fought out over Manila Bay watched by troops on Bataan and Corregidor. This small victory provided a fillip to morale which overall was surprisingly resilient, but there then followed three events which had the opposite effect. There were officers who never accepted the sincerity of MacArthur's promises that help would come, but there were many more who put their trust entirely in his hands, hoping that he knew something they did not and was going to pull a rabbit out of the hat. Success on Bataan, however temporary, had been a welcome boost to morale, as had the erroneous report that Homma had committed *hara kiri* to atone for his failure—in MacArthur's Manila Hotel apartment, of all places. The news of the fall of Singapore on 15 February, however, brought the conduct and the momentum of the war into realistic focus. "A stunned silence greeted the radio announcement. It could not be possible, but it was. The chain of our relief was broken," wrote Mallonée. "I still had unfaltering faith in the leadership of MacArthur, despite the widespread criticism of his staff, and the political entanglements which many times seemed to warp his military judgement."[32]

Java, Sumatra and Borneo fell and on 22 February, George Washington's birthday, the Japanese entered Timor. That same day, Americans throughout the world had been alerted to expect an important presidential broadcast. Roosevelt had no keener radio audience than the embattled troops of Bataan and Corregidor, but the message they received was not the one they wanted. In his fireside speech, the President explained to his global audience the nature of this "new kind of war" and defended his "Europe first" policy. The Philippines warranted only a passing mention. All the unrealistic hopes simply evaporated. The Philippines would in time be redeemed but, for those in the firing line there was no hope of relief. "The curtain had rung down," wrote Mallonée, "and it was only a matter of time."[33]

The third event was the departure of MacArthur from the Philippines. A contributory factor tilting the balance of decision in favor of this arose through a rift between Britain and Australia. Australia's Prime Minister John Curtin, leader of an untried Labor government comprising few men of vision and acutely worried by the approach of the Japanese juggernaut—"They're coming south" was an alarmist cry of the time—demanded of Churchill the return of three Australian divisions. Since the divisions were already fully committed, one in North Africa fighting Rommel's Afrika Corps, that was an impossible demand upon which to deliver immediately.[34] But with the American-British-Dutch-Australian Alliance (ABDA), Churchill and Roosevelt came to a new "spheres of responsibility" agreement, under which Britain agreed to take responsibility for the defense of India and Burma, and America the Pacific. This meant Australia would transfer her traditional dependence for defense upon the United Kingdom to the United States. Australia's Labor Prime Minister convened a Cabinet meeting for Saturday, 21 February 1942, at which it was agreed to give up the demand to repatriate the Australian divisions on condition that an American general was nominated supreme commander of the theater and American forces would be predominant in the new command.

In Marshall's view and despite the potential for a rift with the Navy, MacArthur was self-selecting as the new supreme commander in Australia. Churchill was of the same opinion as Marshall and Roosevelt was aware of Churchill's view. Churchill had been in a similar predicament in May 1940 to that in which Roosevelt now found himself, when he had sent an order to General Lord Gort, the Commander of the British Expeditionary Force at Dunkirk in France:

" . . . we shall send you an order to return to England with such officers as you may choose at the moment when we deem your command
so reduced that it can be handed over to a corps commander . . . On
political grounds it would be a needless triumph to the enemy to capture you."[35] The fate of MacArthur and his garrison had been a topic
of discussion as early as December 1941 when Churchill was visiting
the White House. As Churchill explained:

> I learned from the President and Mr. Stimson of the approaching fate
> of General MacArthur and the American garrison at Corregidor. I
> thought it right to show them the way in which we had dealt with the
> position of a Commander in Chief whose force was reduced to a small
> fraction of his original command. The President and Mr. Stimson both
> read the telegram with profound attention, and I was struck by the
> impression it seemed to make to them. A little later in the day Mr.
> Stimson came back and asked for a copy of it, which I immediately
> gave him. It may be (for I do not know) that this influenced them in the
> right direction which they took in ordering General MacArthur to hand
> over his command to one of his subordinate generals.[36]

The Americans on Bataan and Corregidor adopted a very philo-
sophical attitude to their situation. Their real concern was that the
Japanese and the people back home, being unacquainted with the
conditions and circumstances under which the fight had been fought,
would not understand why the Americans had failed; why they had
been defeated. The Filipinos were not possessed of the same sensitivity. One Julio Luz, broadcasting over KZRH Manila, stressed that
he was not propagandizing for Japan or the Japanese when he read
out parts of Roosevelt's speech. Luz said that Bataan was doomed and
a waste of Filipino youth. In the face of the frank admission of President Roosevelt, he emphasized, it was "plain murder" to compel the
Filipinos in Bataan to continue fighting. Luz concluded:

> For General MacArthur cannot hope to know America's ability to help
> our troops better than President Roosevelt himself, and the President
> having said what he frankly admitted in his speech, the General should
> forget his pride and think of the American and Filipino soldiers whose
> lives he is throwing away in Bataan.[40]

The aviator Captain Villamor remarked that he would not be surprised to find a large number of Filipinos believing Japanese propaganda and becoming hostile to the Allied cause. "It really isn't so

much the collapse of the Philippine defenses that has hurt the Filipinos; rather they were hurt because the resources of the United
States, in which they had such great hopes, never came through."[38]
But the Filipino military had not responded to the Japanese propaganda leaflets by voting with their feet because their own Field Marshal, "Macarsar," had stayed with them, sharing in their adversity.

On 22 February, MacArthur informed the War Department that
"There are indications that the enemy has been so badly mauled during the Bataan fighting that he is unable to set up with his present
forces the attack necessary to destroy me."[39] Uppermost in Mac-
Arthur's mind, however, would have been a signal from Marshall the
day before, seeking his views on an idea to move MacArthur from
Corregidor to Mindanao where it was thought he might be better
placed to organize resistance against the Japanese. Clark Lee, the
Associated Press representative, saw MacArthur on the 22nd and was
shocked by his appearance. He looked ill and "drained of the confidence he had always shown." All Lee could discover from Mac-
Arthur's staff was that the General had received an important signal
from Washington.[40] In fact, he had received another on 21 February,
from Brigadier General Patrick J. Hurley in Melbourne:

> For the safe conduct of great reinforcements and material to the South
> West Pacific Area, it is logical and essential that the supreme command
> in the South West Pacific should be given to an American . . . This
> should be done as promptly as possible.[41]

Eisenhower undoubtedly agreed with the sentiment but did not
believe MacArthur to be the man for Australia. He wrote in his diary:
"I'm dubious about the whole thing. He (MacArthur) is doing a good
job where he is, but I'm doubtful that he'd do so well in complicated
situations . . . If brought out, public opinion will force him into a position where his love of the limelight may ruin him."[42] Eisenhower's
was a minority view. Hull, Stimson and Marshall recommended Mac-
Arthur's removal from the Philippines. There was a general consensus
that the only way to get MacArthur off Corregidor was by way of a
direct order from his Commander in Chief, President Roosevelt.
Hurley told General Wavell, commander of the disintegrated ABDA
command, how it would "be necessary for the President to definitely
order MacArthur to relinquish command and proceed elsewhere and
that even if such orders were issued, MacArthur might feel that he

had destroyed himself by leaving his beleaguered command . . . his transfer from Corregidor will have to be effected in a way that cannot possibly compromise his honor or his record as a soldier."[43]

Pressure had mounted in Washington to order MacArthur out of the Philippines. At one press conference, the President was asked whether there was any friction with MacArthur over Washington's inability to reinforce him. Roosevelt's reply was evasive to the point of incoherence: "I wouldn't do any—well, I wouldn't—I am trying to take a leaf out of my notebook. I think it would be well for others to do it. I—not knowing enough about it—I try not to speculate myself." On another occasion, a reporter asked: "Mr. President would you care to comment on the agitation to have General MacArthur ordered out of the Philippines and given overall command?"[44] (meaning overall command of America's armed forces and not simply those in the South Pacific). "No, I don't think so," replied the President. "I think that is just one of 'them' things they talk about without very much knowledge of the situation."[45] Roosevelt fully realized that over a period of time Bataan and Corregidor were certain to fall. He had great reluctance to order the captain to leave the sinking ship and to abandon his men, not least because of the racial overtones involved. But then, he could not hand to the Japanese the propaganda victory that the death or capture of MacArthur would generate. If that were to happen, he would be handing the Republicans a stick with which to beat him. Despite the heart-searching, there was only one course of action and accordingly, on 22 February, MacArthur was ordered by his President to leave Corregidor for Australia with a one-week break in between in Mindanao where he was to determine the feasibility of a prolonged defense of the island.

> With reference to the rapidly approaching reorganization of the ABDA area and also to the rather favorable report on the situation in Bataan in your number 341 as well as your number 344 regarding the build up of resources in Mindanao: the President directs that you make arrangements to leave Fort Mills and proceed to Mindanao. You are directed to make this change as quickly as possible. The President desires that in Mindanao you take such measures as will insure a prolonged defense of that region.[46]

The radiogram of the presidential order, drafted by Roosevelt, Stimson and Marshall, began to arrive in the Malinta Comcen at 11:23 a.m., 23 February and, after decoding, was handed to MacArthur at 12:30 p.m.

Huff was present in MacArthur's office at the time, packing the foot-locker that Sayre would take with him that night in the *Swordfish*. When Huff looked up and saw MacArthur's face, he was aware that something dramatic had happened. He asked Huff in an unusually harsh tone where Jean was. Huff told him she was in another lateral. MacArthur left with Sutherland, found Jean, and together the three of them walked the short distance to the MacArthurs' cottage where they stayed for some time.[47] Sutherland was the first to leave, to call a staff meeting inside Malinta. When MacArthur arrived, he read to those staff present the presidential order. He then explained his dilemma to those in his office: if he defied the President he would face a court mar-tial and yet, if he obeyed, he would be deserting his men. In his mem-oirs he wrote how his "first reaction was to try to avoid the latter part of the order even to the extent of resigning my commission and joining the Bataan force as a simple volunteer."[48] The possibility of his rejecting the President's order was resisted by "Dick Sutherland and my entire Staff[49] (who) would have none of it."[50] The staff were set the task of looking for some hidden significance in the proposal to remove MacArthur by reviewing all cables received from Washington since Christmas Eve. As a result of that review, the staff's interpretation was reinforced, "that the concentration of men, arms and transport which they believed was being massed in Australia would enable me (MacArthur) almost at once to return at the head of an effec-tive rescue mission."[51] What MacArthur discovered on his arrival in Australia—the almost total absence of resources—was among the bit-terest of his military experiences.

MacArthur sent Marshall a message agreeing in principle to his departure but asking that he be allowed to determine "the psychologi-cal time to leave" because, "if done too soon and too abruptly, it may result in a sudden major collapse." A submarine had been made avail-able but he was known not to be at ease in confined spaces. Instead, he proposed the use of a submarine and then a surface craft to Min-danao, followed by a flight of B-24s or B-17s on to Australia. He thought the time required to make the transportation arrangements would allow the psychological and physical adjustments to be made on Corregidor.[52] Eisenhower wrote in his diary on 24 February, "MacArthur says, in effect, 'Not now.' I think he is right."[53] Roosevelt agreed to MacArthur's request that the timing be left to him. On 26 February, MacArthur proposed that 15 March would be about right.

Admiral Hart had already left Asian waters. On New Year's Day

1942, an American submarine had arrived at the Java port of Soura-baya, bringing Hart to take up the appointment as Commander Naval Forces ABDA (Abdafloat). Hart was never able to consolidate his command and some formed the opinion that he believed the defense of the Dutch East Indies[54] was a lost cause, while a number of his subordinates felt that a colonial cause was not one the Americans should be defending. Friction between Dutch and Americans had rumbled on from the inception of Abdafloat. The Dutch resented the American command as represented by Hart. The Dutch East Indies was, after all, the homeland of many of those serving out there in the Navy. The Dutch Ambassador in Washington had argued persistently for Hart to be replaced by a Dutchman and would eventually have his way. Hart left Java for the United States on 16 February for reasons of "ill health." It was too late to be able to form a cohesive combined fleet. There was not, for example, a common system of flag signaling, but that was unimportant compared to overall command and control difficulties and Japanese superiority in tactics, firepower and speed. Among the ships lost in the Battle of Java Sea on 27 February 1942 and its aftermath were the Dutch cruisers *De Ruyter* and *Java*, *HMS Exeter* of River Plate fame, *HMAS Perth* and Hart's former flagship *USS Houston*.[55] Churchill wrote of ABDA:

> It was staffed in strict proportion to the claims of the different Powers, and all in triplicate for the Army, Navy and Air. There were elaborate arguments about whether as a compromise, a Dutch admiral might command the naval forces; how all was to be arranged with the Americans and the British; where the Australians came in and so forth. Hardly had all this been agreed for the five Powers and the three Services when the whole vast area concerned was conquered by the Japanese, and the combined fleet of the Allies was sunk in the forlorn battle of the Java Sea.[56]

Marshall had already given Major General George Brett, the army commander in Australia, the warning order to be prepared to supply aircraft for MacArthur's use. On 1 March, MacArthur had Chief Clerk Rogers type a message to Brett, one which seems to emphasize MacArthur's dislike of flying. "You have probably surmised purpose of mission [he had]. Request detail best pilots and that best available planes be placed in top condition for trip. B-24s if available otherwise B-17s. Ferry mission only. Desire if possible initial landing on return to be south of combat zone. Anticipate call for arrival about 15."[57] On that same day, Lieutenant John D. Bulkeley USN had taken Mac-Arthur, Jean and Huff on a thirty minute familiarization trip in his PT-boat in the waters close to Corregidor. Commander of Motor Torpedo Boat Squadron Three, Bulkeley was:

> a swashbuckling pirate in modern dress. He wore a long, unruly beard and carried two ominous looking pistols at his side. His eyes were bloodshot and red-rimmed from staring out on his nightly missions and from lack of sleep. His nervous energy was tremendous and the supply of it never seemed to give out. He walked with a cocksure gait and one could always count on him to raise particular hell with any Jap who crossed his path. Highstrung, temperamental and gallant, Bulkeley was one of the most colorful figures in the Philippine Campaign.[58]

Small wonder that MacArthur liked him. He epitomized all MacArthur had sought to be back in the Rainbow days.

It was Sutherland and not MacArthur who selected the list of passengers.[59] Although MacArthur was authorized by Marshall to take with him only his family and Sutherland, a list evolved which included thirteen army officers, one enlisted man, two naval officers, Jean, her son and his amah. When precisely all the individuals were told they were to leave is not known, but Captain Joseph R. McMicking heard on 1 March. There has been a debate as to whether it was fair and reasonable for MacArthur to take the bulk of his staff with him. Rogers provides the most coherent justification:

> Had he left Sutherland with (Richard) Marshall and the remainder of Headquarters USAFFE, Wainwright would have been overshadowed by a staff that remained loyal to MacArthur. MacArthur, on his part, would have arrived in Australia, tired sick and dispirited, to be confronted by surly subordinates. It would have taken him a year or more to put together a replacement comparable with the USAFFE group, if he could have done it at all. As it was, MacArthur arrived in Melbourne almost without losing his stride and he was able to set immediately to work. Of the two areas, Australia needed MacArthur more than Corregidor needed him. By the same token, MacArthur had greater need of his staff than did Wainwright.[60]

Meanwhile, life continued on Corregidor and Bataan in its own particular, monotonous and dangerous way. "There were so many things to leave one sick at heart on Bataan and on Corregidor," wrote Romulo.

In the tunnel there was never any cleanliness or any rest. Bedbugs by night, flies by day, and always the bombings, the vibration of the planes thrumming one's nerves, and the incessant hunger. I used to sit before my desk in headquarters and think wearily, what the hell! What am I sticking it out for.

Nevertheless, the work of keeping the outside world informed continued in its own creative way. The communiqué of 3 March 1942 may well have been crafted by a bored and frustrated MacArthur sitting at his desk in the command lateral in Malinta Tunnel.

When the hordes of the north swept down on the south like wolves the legend of Japanese military superiority had preceded them. The legend was built around the emotional fanaticism of the Samurai which was believed to inspire soldiers to accomplish the impossible. Furthermore, the dual character of the Emperor as man and God was an added stimulant. The initial successes of the enemy seemed to bear out the legend but the legend is now shattered. The superiority of the Japanese military machine has been reduced in the crucible of war. Physical clashes of the front line fighters tell the story. Filipinos and Americans shoulder to shoulder and greatly outnumbered have stopped and thrown back the Japanese infantry. The Japanese soldier emerges from the shattered legend as a man with feet of clay.[61]

On 4 March the General then set about dictating to Diller and Romulo the uplifting news of the miracle of Subic Bay. "In a sudden air surprise we swept Subic Bay, destroying many vessels," dictated MacArthur. "We lost no planes by enemy action." Diller and Romulo looked at one another in disbelief. There were no American bombers in the Philippines, just the four remaining P-40s and the 3,000 air corps personnel to look after them. MacArthur continued his dictation: "Thousands were drowned from the transports we sank. The enemy is getting a foretaste of what America will do when she becomes fully armed and does not have to fight with completely overwhelming odds against her."[62] Apparently the Japanese ships had been preparing to land "heavy forces" in Subic Bay when surprised by P-40s modified with a bomb rack so as to carry a 500 lb. bomb. The quartet of P-40s had sunk "seven Japanese transports, innumerable motor launches and other small craft, and thousands of Japanese soldiers had gone down in its waters." Two days after the stunning victory of Subic Bay, MacArthur dictated another report. "The enemy's activities have been completely dislocated by the bloody defeat administered at Subic Bay two days ago. His reactions are weak and defensive."[63] Was MacArthur attempting to paint a picture that, prior to his departure it was the Americans dictating terms to the Japanese and not vice versa? It was another example of blatant dishonesty upon which the newspapers ardently fed but which so depressed the weary combatants. The official record indicates that one of the four P-40s was shot down and the remaining three crashed on landing on Bataan. "Apparently," two transports had been sunk and other small boats had been damaged, but the Joint Army and Navy Assessment Committee did not confirm the sinking of any vessels.[64]

Romulo kept a file of excerpts from radiograms from the Coordinator Office of Information pertaining to any news of MacArthur. The *Kansas City Star* of 8 March suggested "MacArthur is following the principles laid down by Danton, organizer of victory in the French Revolution when he exclaimed: 'To vanquish and crush them, what is necessary—to dare, to dare again and always to dare.'" On the same day, the War Department was said to have announced that the success of the Subic Bay air raid attack by General Douglas MacArthur's tiny air force was believed to have dislocated Japanese plans for an immediate renewal of the offensive against the Philippines. As an aside, and to indicate the poor standard of press objectivity, there is a reference in the *Los Angeles Times* of 8 March, of "Japs fooled into occupying undefended city (Manila) while wily General consolidated Bataan positions." There is also a press summary of the same date: "MacArthur's stand in Philippines, judged by every military standard, has inflicted grievous defeat on attackers who have failed to reach objectives, suffered heavy losses and are now dangerously behind schedule."[65]

As the time of departure drew near, it became apparent from the increased Japanese naval activity around Bataan and Corregidor that Japan knew of Roosevelt's intentions. They could hardly have overlooked the crescendo of Stateside voices calling for the rescue of MacArthur. The submarine *Permit* would not arrive at Corregidor until 13 March. MacArthur had announced somewhat dramatically to his staff in the know, "We go with the fall of the moon; we go during the Ides of March."[66] The increased enemy naval activity and the success rate of submarines moving to and from Corregidor should have made him wait for the *Permit*, but MacArthur had been persuaded by Bulkeley of the feasibility of leaving aboard one of the four remaining

PT-boats, all of which were accordingly assigned to the mission. Bulkeley had already drawn up contingency plans for these, to make landfall in China if the deterioration in the situation in and around Manila so dictated. The nearest part of the Chinese coast under Chiang Kai Shek's control, and to Mindanao, were roughly the same distance from Corregidor—five hundred miles—so all he required to do was to spin his original plan around through 180 degrees and plot a course for Mindanao via Cagayan. MacArthur declared the revised time of departure to be at sunset, Wednesday 11 March. He would later send an immodest radiogram to Marshall: "This hazardous trip by a commanding general and key members of his staff through enemy controlled territory undoubtedly is unique in military annals."[67]

Undoubtedly his vanity, his sense of the dramatic and his claustrophobia steered him towards the PT-boat option but he also found comfort from having subordinates around him whom he knew and could trust. He was ill at ease among newcomers and loath to entrust his and his family's lives to people of unknown and unproven performance. MacArthur knew and respected Bulkeley who had reported to him on a daily basis over a three month period. It was MacArthur who had championed the potential of PT-boats, but had had little success in converting the Navy. A mission such as this, successfully completed, would, in his world of unending competition with the Navy, have been one in the eye for the junior service. He had said to Romulo, "I'm taking a patrol boat, and if the Japs go after me we'll fight it out."[68] Clearly a PT-boat appealed to his combative spirit. Another factor was that the size of his party exceeded that which would fit into a submarine.[69]

The question of change of command required careful consideration for the implications vis-à-vis a future surrender were of inestimable importance. The problem that would face a number of the residual commanders is that they represented armed forces with little experience of surrender. MacArthur had begun the consideration of the reorganization of his command on 4 March but it was not until the evening of 9 March that Wainwright was called to Corregidor to be let into the secret.[70] When he arrived, Wainwright was met by Sutherland who told him MacArthur was leaving for Australia via Mindanao the next evening. MacArthur had decided that he would not relinquish command of the Philippines but would exercise that command through his G-4, Colonel Beebe, who would be promoted and designated Deputy Chief of Staff USAFFE. The appointment of a logistician to be his factotum reveals that MacArthur saw the function of the Corregidor headquarters as overseeing matters of combat supplies and materiel. His retention of ultimate command probably had nothing to do with his predilection for empire building but all to do with his sensitivity towards those being left behind. If they were still within his command, it could be argued that they had not been abandoned.

In his Malinta office, Sutherland explained to Wainwright how MacArthur intended to divide the Theater into four separate field commands. The Visayan-Mindanao force would be split, the former coming under the command of Brigadier General Bradford G. Chynoweth and Mindanao remaining under the command of General Sharp. Since Chynoweth was Sharp's junior, the division of responsibilities was not as precise as probably intended, and this was to cause problems. General Moore was to remain in command of the Harbor defenses and to fulfil the function of Corregidor garrison commander, A new force, Luzon Force, which might more appropriately have been described Bataan Force, would come under the command of General Wainwright. General Jones would be promoted and assume command of Wainwright's I Corps. No immediate promotion was on offer to Wainwright. After explaining MacArthur's intentions to Wainwright, both generals walked across to MacArthur's cottage.[71]

MacArthur greeted Wainwright and invited him to take a seat on the porch. MacArthur began:

> Jonathan, I want you to understand my position very plainly. I am leaving for Australia pursuant to repeated orders of the President. Things have reached such a point that I must comply with these orders or get out of the Army. I want you to make it known throughout all elements of your command that I'm leaving over my repeated protests.

After Wainwright had responded in the affirmative, MacArthur continued: "If I get through to Australia, you know I'll come back as soon as I can with as much as I can. In the meantime you've got to hold." Wainwright added that the holding of Bataan was the intention and that of course MacArthur would get through, to which MacArthur added, "and back." Perhaps Wainwright realized more clearly than MacArthur that even if he did come back, it would not be in time to prevent the tragedy in the Philippines being played out to its inevitable conclusion. MacArthur's principal concern in handing over command was that, as a cavalryman, Wainwright did not seem to comprehend the importance of defense in depth. "The defense of Bataan must be deep," he told Wainwright, "and be sure to give them everything you've got with your artillery." They stood up to shake hands. MacArthur had presents for Wainwright, a box of Quezon's cigars and two jars of shaving cream. "Goodbye Jonathan," said MacArthur. "When I get back, if you're still in Bataan, I'll make you a lieutenant general." "I'll be on Bataan if I am alive," said Wainwright.[72]

In all the commotion, MacArthur failed to discuss or clear his command intentions with General George Marshall. Not knowing that MacArthur still proposed to exercise command over the Philippines from Australia, Marshall did what to him seemed obvious—he gave Wainwright his third star and, with it, command of the Philippines. Washington had therefore put into Wainwright's hands the ultimate authority to surrender all the field commands on the archipelago. The Japanese, highly experienced in the nuances of warfare, realized this and could and did threaten to execute all prisoners unless Wainwright ordered total surrender in the Philippines, including the 40,000 troops in Mindanao and Visayan. Thus, any prospect of establishing an armed resistance in the south evaporated.

On 11 March, Carlos Romulo received a message to meet Sutherland in Quezon's former tent by the tunnel entrance. There, Sutherland told Romulo that MacArthur was leaving that night. "I'm afraid this means a slump in morale," replied Romulo. "It shouldn't," said Sutherland crisply. "No one knows our needs and the situation here better than General MacArthur." Romulo wandered off, deep in thought, until arrested by a hand on his shoulder. "Carlos, I want to talk with you." It was MacArthur. He explained to Romulo his situation. "Bataan can stand," he said, "but if any crisis comes, and I am needed here, I am coming back, alone if necessary." Romulo was then given the choice, to go to Australia with MacArthur or to stay on Corregidor and continue to run the Voice of Freedom. Romulo said he would stay, and MacArthur charged him with the maintenance of morale. "Go to Bataan," he urged. "Talk to the boys for me. Tell them that I had to do this and that they are to believe me when I say it is for the best. Tell them that my heart is with them, Carlos." Then MacArthur spoke to Romulo realistically, telling him that if Bataan should fall and Corregidor prove untenable, he would see that a plane was sent to take Romulo out.[73]

Master Sergeant Paul P. Rogers was Sutherland's stenographer and typist, the chief clerk of USAFFE and the most junior of those selected to leave that night. As he sat at his desk, going through the pretense of work, letters were left on his desk, always without comment. These he picked up and put in his barracks bag. Then Colonel Seals came along and said, "Rogers, I hear you know someone who can deliver letters. Will you see he gets this one?" Another letter to the family back home joined the others in the bag. Then Richard Marshall came to his desk and said, "Rogers, it is time to go." Looking neither to his left nor right, he left Lateral 3 and the west entrance of Malinta Tunnel to a jeep that took the group to their assigned patrol boat, PT-35. One by one the boats took on their designated personnel at the dispersed pick-up points until the final boat, Bulkeley's PT-41 prepared to take on board MacArthur and his family, Sutherland, Huff and the doctor, Major Charles H. Morhouse.[79] MacArthur exercised his prerogative to board last. He stood on the North Dock, looking up to the dark rock face of Corregidor, his battered, braided hat held above his head. While the guns barked out diversionary fire and Philippine Q-ships sought to mislead the Imperial Japanese Navy, MacArthur replaced his cap, stepped aboard PT-41 and said, "You may cast off Buck when you are ready." The four boats made rendezvous at 8 p.m. and followed a minelayer through the gap in the minefield. At 9:15 p.m., the three-shaft, 4050 horsepower engines were opened up full throttle and, adopting a diamond pattern, four distinct white wakes stabbed forward into the inky darkness of the night.[75]

After an eventful and uncomfortable voyage, all four PT-boats reached Mindanao and eventually, on Tuesday 17 March 1942, MacArthur, his family and staff landed at Batchelor Field, 45 miles south of Darwin. On Friday, 20 March 1942, MacArthur arrived at Adelaide railway station.[76] Aware that the press were likely to be present, he had jotted down a few words on an envelope. He was in Australia, he told them, to "organize the American offensive against Japan, a primary object of which is the relief of the Philippines. I came through and I shall return."[77] Those last three words became the source of, often heated, debate. The Office of War Information asked MacArthur to rephrase the three words to "*we* shall return." MacArthur refused, arguing that he was making it *his* own solemn promise to the Filipino people. He said in his memoirs that

The phrase "I shall return" seemed a promise of magic to the Filipinos. It lit a flame that became a symbol which focused the nation's indomitable will and at whose shrine it finally attained victory and, once again, found freedom. It was scraped in the sand of beaches, it was daubed on the walls of *barrios*, it was stamped on the mail, it was whispered in the cloisters of the church. It became the battle cry of a great underground swell that no Japanese bayonet could still.[78]

Despite all the doubts, all the errors of judgement, all the professional lapses, MacArthur was able to weave the old magic among the Filipino people to whom he became virtually a god-like figure. His popularity had declined before the war but he glamorized what had happened on Bataan and Corregidor and his promise to return provided a compelling psychological image.

Partly to counter enemy propaganda, which labeled MacArthur "a deserter," "coward," and "a fleeing general," and partly because the country had an overwhelming need for a hero, Marshall proposed to Roosevelt that MacArthur be awarded the Medal of Honor. Marshall shrugged off the objection of Eisenhower and the rather obvious observation that MacArthur had not taken part in front-line armed conflict. But then neither had Lindbergh, who was awarded the Medal of Honor for crossing the Atlantic in 1927. Roosevelt agreed and Marshall wrote the citation:

> For conspicuous leadership in preparing the Philippine Islands to resist conquest, for gallantry and intrepidity above and beyond the call of duty in action against invading Japanese forces, and for the heroic conduct of defensive and offensive operations on the Bataan Peninsula. He mobilized, trained and led an army which has received world acclaim for its gallant defense against a tremendous superiority of enemy forces in men and arms. His utter disregard of personal danger under heavy fire and aerial bombardment, his calm judgement in each crisis inspired his troops, galvanized the resistance of the Filipino people, and confirmed the faith of the American public in their armed forces.[79]

Of this award, which meant so much to MacArthur, he wrote but one sentence in his memoirs: "I was awarded the Medal of Honor for my role in the Philippines, but the road back looked long and difficult."[80]

15

EPILOGUE

The stunning and rapid success of Japan's armed forces in SE Asia overall meant that reserves and forces now surplus to requirements could be targeted for the second offensive against the Fil-American defenses in the Philippines. A General Headquarters' shake-up of 14th Army resulted in Chief of Staff General Maeda and other senior staff officers being relieved. From the end of February, individual reinforcements restored the strength and vitality of 65th Brigade and 16th Division. The 4th Division from Shanghai was added to the Japanese order of battle, but it was only 11,000-strong and, according to Homma, the worst equipped division in the Japanese Army. On 26 February, the day prior to the arrival of the first troops of the 4th Division, a 4,000-strong detachment of the 21st Division under General Kameichiro Nagano arrived in the Philippines. An artillery headquarters came from Hong Kong to command and control the massive influx of artillery and, on 16 March, two heavy air bombardment regiments augmented by Naval air units arrived at Clark from Malaya. By Friday, 3 April—Good Friday—the reinvigorated and reinforced Japanese forces were ready for the last phase of their operations in Manila Bay.[5]

Only after Wainwright's assumption of command of United States Forces in the Philippines (U.S.FIP) from MacArthur and his direct appeal to Marshall for food, vitamin concentrates and medicine, did the Army Chief of Staff first become aware of the number of troops in the Philippines. Marshall refused to believe there could be 90,000 men on Bataan alone and sought clarification.[2] The clarification made things worse, for Wainwright reported 110,000 men on Bataan and Corregidor. On 28 March, he warned Marshall that there were sufficient supplies to last only until 15 April, and that was a "one third ration, poorly balanced and very deficient in vitamins." MacArthur, who had seen copies of this correspondence, ungraciously told Marshall that, before he left, there had been sufficient food to last until 1 May, but suggested that the disparity might be due to the fact that the "vigor of application of conservation may have been relaxed" since his departure.[3] Notwithstanding the dire food situation and acute sickness, MacArthur repudiated any suggestion of surrender. "If food fails," he told Wainwright, "you will prepare and execute an attack upon the enemy."[4] On 21 March, Wainwright established his Headquarters in Malinta Tunnel, appointing the artillery commander, Major General Edward Postell King Jr., to command the troops on Bataan.

The morale of the Filipinos, who comprised over three quarters of the defenders of Bataan, was shattered by the eventual release of the news that MacArthur was not on Corregidor but in Australia. Americans in Filipino units, such as Mallonée, sought to explain the military rationale for such a development:

> But despite the build-up, despite our explanation to the Filipino officers and men of the more important command and of the value of having their military god at the controls of the machine that would relieve us, despite everything, it was sad news, and the Filipino reaction was as expected. Not outwardly. They gave lip service—but the heart went out of them.[5]

They had done their best and were now at a virtual standstill.

The Japanese Good Friday offensive—the equivalent of approximately three infantry divisions supported by considerable air and artillery assets—struck a hammer blow into the right flank held by Parker's II Corps. Weakened by hunger, the men in the line broke, withdrawing to the rear in disorder. King sought to fill the gap with reserves but, by Easter Sunday, 6 April, the Japanese had seized

Mount Samat, dominating both Corps positions. A counter attack was launched on 6 April but, lacking energy and enthusiasm, it was swatted contemptuously aside by the strong Japanese forces. King urgently sought a staff check as to how many in his command remained combat effective—defined as anyone able to carry his personal weapon one hundred yards without the need for rest and still be able to shoot. The staff response was 15 per cent, but only in those units which remained cohesive.[6]

On 7 April the Japanese maintained pressure against II Corps, thus exposing the flank of I Corps. Wainwright ordered King to deploy I Corps eastward to relieve II Corps. King told Wainwright that, given the men's condition, that could not be achieved. After a telephone conversation between Wainwright, King and Jones, Wainwright left the tactical decision to the man on the ground. King accordingly ordered the withdrawal of I Corps. He told Wainwright the fall of Bataan was imminent. Wainwright reiterated the President's and MacArthur's orders that there was to be no surrender, although he must have realized that surrender was the only means of avoiding a massacre. It was King who, in a classic display of moral courage looked reality in the face and prepared his men for surrender and himself for court martial. "So King shouldered the responsibility alone. For the rest of that terrible day and night, King and Wainwright played out a charade: Wainwright pretended not to know what King was doing and King avoided putting him in the position of knowing until it was a *fait accompli*."[7]

Timing was of the essence. The two Field Hospitals were coming within the range of Japanese Field Artillery, yet King still had to destroy arms, ammunition and stocks on Bataan. On the afternoon of 8 April, orders went out to the subordinate commanders. "You will make plans, to be communicated to company commanders only, and be prepared to destroy within one hour after receipt by radio or other means of the word CRASH, all tanks and combat vehicles, arms, ammunition, gas and radios, reserving sufficient trucks to close to rear echelons as soon as accomplished."[8]

Earlier that week, MacArthur, in his comfortable Melbourne Headquarters, passed final contingency orders to Wainwright. His plan when "food or ammunition failed," for the men he had not seen in three months, had "contemplated an ostentatious artillery preparation on the left by the I Corps as a feint, a sudden surprise attack on the right by II Corps, taking the enemy's Subic Bay (Olongapo) position in reverse, then a frontal attack by the I Corps." MacArthur suggested that, if the plan worked, the supplies seized would enable the fight to continue and, if it failed, his forces would take to the Zambales Mountains, from where they would commence guerrilla operations.[9] In yet another of his meaningless, personal commitment statements, MacArthur told Marshall, "I would be very glad to rejoin the command temporarily and take charge of this movement."[10] On the evening of 7 April, eighty per cent of the force was disabled by malaria, of whom seventy five per cent also had dysentery. After having spent three months on half rations and less, they were down to 15 ounces of watery rice a day per man.[11] At about 10:30 p.m., Wainwright dutifully ordered King to implement the MacArthur Plan to attack, an order which King duly ignored. Instead, he decided to surrender at 6 a.m. the next morning. Shortly after, Bataan was shaken by an ominous, massive earthquake. At an Orders Group held at midnight, King told his staff of his decision. One officer present recorded how all present had wept when they heard what their commander had had to say. The next morning, King surrendered to the Japanese more men than had ever previously been given up by any single American General. In a letter to the historian Louis Morton, King explained that, "I did not receive a direct order not to surrender but I did receive an order wholly inconsistent with surrender."[12]

On 9 April, Wainwright signaled MacArthur telling how at 6 a.m. that morning, General King,

> without my knowledge or approval sent a flag of truce to the Japanese commander. The minute I heard of it I disapproved of his action and directed that there would be no surrender. I was informed it was too late to make any change, that the action had already been taken. Physical exhaustion and sickness due to a long period of insufficient food is the real cause of this terrible disaster. When I get word what terms have been arranged I will advise you.[13]

MacArthur canceled his appointments for the day and, sitting at his desk with tears in his eyes, wrote Bataan's eulogy:

> The Bataan force went out as it would have wished, fighting to the end in its flickering, forlorn hope. No army has done so much with so little, and nothing became it more than its last hour of trial and agony. To the weeping mothers of its dead, I can only say that the sacrifice and halo

of Jesus of Nazareth has descended upon their sons and that God will take them unto Himself.[14]

As the time drew nearer for Wainwright to do with Corregidor what King would have to do for Bataan, he made it clear in a signal to MacArthur on 4 May that: "It has never been and is not my intention to reflect upon General King as the decision which he was forced to make required unusual courage and strength of character."[15] As King went forward to meet General Nagano, he must have felt as General Lee did seventy-seven years earlier at Appomatox. "Then there is nothing left to do but to go and see General Grant and I would rather die a thousand deaths."[16]

On 10 April, Wainwright received a message from Roosevelt; it had come via MacArthur's Melbourne office for the General's concurrence, but was not forwarded from there immediately. In it the President rescinded the "no surrender" order and left "to your best judgement [Wainwright's] any decisions affecting the future of the Bataan garrison."[17] Wainwright bore MacArthur no hard feelings throughout the course of the war except for this one instance, when he had sat on an instruction of immense importance to Wainwright's command.[18]

After the surrender of Bataan, the prisoners had to march 55–60 miles from their collection areas at Cabcaben and Mariveles to the railway junction at San Fernando, detraining at Capas for a hike of a further 6 miles to Camp O'Donnell. They did not eat for the first 2–3 days because there was no food available. The U.S. Army Center for Military History has estimated that, as a consequence, up to 650 Americans and 5–10,000 Filipinos died on what would become known as the Bataan Death March. The Japanese were particularly cruel to the Filipinos, whom they regarded as white men's lackeys. In the first 6–7 weeks, more than 1,600 Americans and 16,000 Filipinos died at Camp O'Donnell. Only 43 per cent of the American men who surrendered on Bataan were eventually to return home. And the survivors' ordeal did not end when they arrived back home. "We had been given up, surrendered; we were marked as cowards . . . There were no banners to welcome us home, no parades to march in, no speeches, and no acknowledgement of any kind. Our folks at home had so many heroes; they were busy welcoming winners, not losers."[26]

Homma had expected no more than 40,000 men to surrender on Bataan but, after the head counts were completed, he found he had an additional logistical dependency of over 100,000—more men

than he had under his command, for whom, also, there was insufficient food and medical supplies. It was several months later that
MacArthur first heard details of the death march and prison camp
atrocities. He immediately prepared a press release but Washington
intervened to prevent its circulation. "Perhaps the Administration,"
he wrote, "which was committed to a Europe-first effort, feared
American public opinion would demand a greater reaction against
Japan, but whatever the cause, here was the sinister beginning of the
'managed news' concept by those in power."[20] However accurate the
first part of his assessment, it seems strange that MacArthur should
protest at the management of news since it was something he had
been doing for years and would continue to do.

The Bataan surrender as good as ended effective American resistance in the Philippines but, for as long as Corregidor and the three
lesser, fortified islands across Manila Bay remained in American
hands, the Japanese were unable to develop Manila Harbor to support and consolidate their position in the archipelago and to the
south. Any hope Homma may have had that Corregidor would be
surrendered with Bataan was short-lived. Homma's men, however,
had to be rested, re-equipped and trained in the skills of amphibious
assault landings before it could be attacked. It was a time-consuming
business but, concurrently, Japanese artillery was brought forward to
positions on the Mariveles Mountains and along the coast, near to
Cabcaben, only two and a half miles from Corregidor. The purpose of
the artillery, supported by air attacks, was to neutralize the defended
positions on Corregidor prior to the amphibious landing. Japanese
preparatory efforts were dogged by the continuing problems of shortage of rations and now, in mid April, a malaria epidemic spread
throughout their order of battle. One regiment from the 4th Division,
which had been selected to conduct the amphibious operations,[21] had
only 250 men fit for training. But after the providential arrival of quinine tablets, Homma set 5 May as X-Day, the day of attack.

There were a number of intelligence personnel and cryptoanalysts
on Corregidor whose skills were so important to the war effort that
their capture had to be avoided at all costs. MacArthur sent two
Catalina flying boats to supplement the "milk run" of a four-seater
passenger plane which shuttled between Corregidor and Del Monte,
Mindanao. Over half of the precious seats were allocated to nurses
but, according to the *nisei* Richard Sakakida, a seat on the "milk run"
was also allocated to him. Sakakida wrote how he could anticipate

difficulties as a prisoner of the Japanese but arguably less serious than the beheading which certainly awaited Clarence Yamagata, the Japanese-American employed by the Japanese Consulate in Manila whom he had recruited as legal adviser. In an extraordinary gesture of generosity, Sakakida gave up his seat to Yamagata. Sakakida's superior could not believe what he was hearing. "The concept of *on*, or moral obligation, was too complex for me to explain to him," wrote Sakakida.[22]

MacArthur used his time in Melbourne to plan and to contemplate. Bataan played on his mind. He had the telephone operators in the HQ respond to incoming calls, "Hello, this is Bataan." When Jean was invited to launch a Royal Australian Navy warship, her husband suggested it be named *HMAS Bataan*.[23] It was a difficult time for MacArthur's staff. General Brett, who had sent unsuitable aircraft to Mindanao to bring MacArthur to Australia and who infuriated MacArthur with his "no can do" attitude, was under orders to leave.[24] MacArthur "was short, sharp and frequently insulting to those he felt had failed him in the Philippines, showing especially his contempt for the Navy and Air Force," recalled one correspondent. Brett put his commander's irascibility down to his "suffering a feeling of guilt in having left his men at the most critical moment of their hopeless fight."[25] However, there were new people whose "good opinion he courted" but, as so often had been the case, his yearning to be loved came out as bathos "and was greeted with ridicule."[26] While he found time to ingratiate himself with his new-found Australian hosts, he no longer had any requirement for Manuel Quezon. Just prior to sailing to join his government in exile in the U.S.A., MacArthur and Prime Minister Curtin called on Quezon in his cabin. Quezon asked MacArthur: "Tell me the frank truth. Can you liberate my country and free my people?" "I intend to do just that," replied MacArthur. "And when I stand at the gates of Manila, I want the President of the Commonwealth at my right hand and the Prime Minister of Australia at my left."[27] Both leaders died before the end of the war: Quezon on 1 August, 1944.

The siege of Corregidor would last for 27 days. Significant damage was caused to the carefully prepared beach defenses by the mass Japanese artillery. The anti-aircraft guns were neutralized and the sea coast artillery was virtually put out of action. "One day's shelling," said one officer, "did more damage than all the bombing put together." Towards the end of the program, Corregidor had been turned into a desolate landscape, "a moving picture version of No Man's Land in World War I."[28] The effect of living under this continuous fire was seen not only in the steadily rising number of casualties but also in the haggard faces of men whose food was rationed and water restricted to one canteen a day. The intensity of Japanese artillery fire from Bataan reached its peak on 4 May when 16,000 shells were fired over a 24 hour period, mostly upon the north shore.

The Japanese landed in two waves, each of battalion strength, commencing at 2300 on 5 May between Cavalry Point and North Point. The 4th Marines had been hard-pressed to provide adequate cover over the entire length of the beaches. Although the regiment had a strength of 4,000 only one third were Marines, the remainder being make-weight Army and Navy reinforcements of varying quality. The North Shore from Malinta Hill to the tip of the island was the defended area of Company A, 4th Marines, so that the Japanese landing point was defended by just one platoon. The available fire of the defenders took a terrible toll of the attackers detected out in the open sea. Of the 2,000 men in the two battalions comprising the landing force, only 800 men reached the shore but, by applying their concentrated force against the lightly held line of defense, they were able to unhinge the American position. During the early hours of the morning of the 6th, the 4th Marines committed their reserves to block the Japanese advancing on Malinta Hill. An American counterattack failed and, when the battle was finely balanced, the Japanese introduced their trump cards, three light tanks which swung the balance in favor of the Japanese.[29] One of the three tanks was an M3 Stuart, captured on Bataan.

At 1000 hours on 6 May, General Wainwright decided to surrender. He had lost between 6–800 men and Japanese artillery had already begun a new fire program in preparation for another landing elsewhere that night. But there were no more than 800 Japanese combatants on the island to Wainwright's 10,000.[30] However, Wainwright had no weapons with which to take out the Japanese armor and he already had his hospital crammed with a thousand casualties. Orders were given for the broadcast of a surrender message over the "Voice of Freedom" and for the destruction of all weapons over .45 caliber.[31] At noon, the Stars and Stripes was hauled down and burned, to be replaced by a white flag. In the communications lateral, a radio message went out to General Sharp on Mindanao, placing all remaining American troops not on the four defended islands under his command and instructing him to take his orders from General MacArthur forthwith. The decision to surrender had been delegated to Wainwright by the President and, after he had set the procedure in motion, he told President Roosevelt and General MacArthur of his decision to "go to meet the Japanese Commander." Wainwright wrote of his "broken heart and head bowed in sadness but not in shame" and asked that the nation be told "that my troops and I have accomplished all that is humanly possible and that we have upheld the best tradition of the United States and its Army."[32]

Homma had heard reports of the white flag over Corregidor but had not heard the broadcasts. There was a plan, however, that if the Americans were to surrender, then Wainwright was to be brought to meet Homma on Bataan. It was for that purpose that Colonel Nakayama, who had taken part in the Bataan surrender, had been sent to Corregidor. The meeting between Wainwright and Homma at Cabcaben, Bataan, began at 1700 hours but immediately became beset by difficulties. Homma refused to accept Wainwright's offer of surrender unless it included all American and Philippine troops on the archipelago. Wainwright responded to the effect that he commanded only the harbor defense troops. Homma insisted Wainwright also surrender the Visayan-Mindanao Force. "I was recently relieved of the command over American forces in the southern islands. General Sharp is now in command. He comes directly under General MacArthur." Angrily, Homma said to Wainwright: "Since you are not in supreme command, I see no further necessity for my presence here." His preparedness to leave, there and then, threw the American negotiators into a turmoil and, after some hurried discussion, Wainwright changed his position. "In face of the fact that further bloodshed in the Philippines is unnecessary and futile, I will assume command of the entire American forces in the Philippines at the risk of serious reprimand by my government following the war." Unimpressed, Homma responded: "You have denied your authority and your momentary decision may be regretted by your men. I advise you to return to Corregidor and think this matter over."[33]

Homma departed, leaving the American delegation with Nakayama. There followed more "animated conversation in a muted tone," followed by what one Japanese observer described as "a desperate, sorrowful plea." Wainwright proposed surrendering the entire American forces in the Philippines to General Homma, unconditionally. The Corregidor garrison had been ordered to lay down their arms.

Wainwright proposed meeting General Homma and he would also send a staff officer to Mindanao to tell General Sharp to comply with Homma's demands. Nakayama considered the proposal and said: "I shall go with you to Corregidor and safely turn you over to the commanding officer there. Stay for the night and first thing tomorrow, go to General Homma with a new surrender and an understanding to contact other U.S. forces in the Philippines."[34]

On the morning of 7th, Wainwright ordered Colonel Jesse T. Traywick, his operations officer, to Mindanao with orders for General Sharp to surrender and to tell MacArthur of developments. In his letter, Wainwright had written: ". . . let me reemphasize, that there must be on your part no thought of disregarding these instructions. Failure to fully and honestly carry them out can have only the most disastrous results." Wainwright's underlying fear was that the Japanese might turn upon and massacre the disarmed garrison of Corregidor. However, there is no evidence to support this. At 1700 hours, Wainwright was taken by his captors to radio station KZRH in Manila where he was subjected to the humiliation of broadcasting the surrender instructions to Sharp and to detachment commanders in Northern Luzon. His husky, emotional voice sounded so unlike him that people who knew Wainwright thought the broadcast to have been bogus. A commercial radio in San Francisco received and re-transmitted the broadcast to the War Department. Marshall telephoned Roosevelt. "With reference to General Wainwright's supposed broadcast from Manila, Mrs. Wainwright and her boy heard it and are absolutely certain it was not Wainwright's voice. You have probably read General MacArthur's radio from Australia in which he states his doubt as to it being Wainwright."[35] Wainwright was no longer as his relatives and friends knew him. General Drake, who saw him after the surrender, wrote how he was "a very sick man both mentally and physically. When he joined us at the POW camp at Tarlac on June 9th 1942, he was in a very bad shape and we despaired of his ultimate recovery."[36]

In his Melbourne office on 6 May, MacArthur handed to Carlos Romulo a statement written in his own handwriting: "Corregidor has fallen."[37] He said nothing. He was prepared for the fall of Corregidor more than for that of Bataan. The obituary had been prepared and merely awaited the inevitable promulgation. He told reporters:

Corregidor needs no comment from me. It has sounded its own story at the mouth of its guns. It has scrolled its own epitaph on enemy tablets.

But through the bloody haze of its last reverberating shot, I shall always
seem to see a vision of grim, gaunt, ghastly men, still unafraid.[38]

MacArthur sent Sharp a signal to the effect that the "orders emanating from General Wainwright have no validity. If possible, separate
your force into small elements and initiate guerilla operations. You, of
course, have full authority to make any decisions that [the] immediate
emergency may demand." When it transpired that Wainwright's
broadcast had been authentic, MacArthur advised the War Department: "I believe Wainwright has temporarily become unbalanced and
his condition renders him susceptible of enemy use."[39]

When Traywick arrived in Mindanao, General Sharp had to balance MacArthur's orders and allegations against the instructions
given by Wainwright: "You will surrender all troops under your command to the Japanese officers."[40] On 10 May, convinced that the
threat to the Corregidor garrison was genuine, he issued orders to his
subordinate commanders to surrender. Although the situation in the
southern islands had not deteriorated to the point where surrender
was inevitable, the apparent threat posed to the lives of comrades in
arms allowed Sharp to feel he had no option but to surrender. However, these were not views shared by Chynoweth on Cebu and
Colonel Albert F. Christie commanding the Panay garrison. Neither
liked nor trusted Sharp. "He was," wrote Chynoweth, "devoid of
resilience and unfit for the stress of war. In crisis, he panicked . . ."[41]
Chynoweth stalled, believing that Sharp and Wainwright might
be acting under duress without MacArthur's authority. Eventually,
Chynoweth obeyed Sharp and capitulated on 16 May, followed two
days later by the surrender of the Panay garrison. "When Sharp's
messenger reached me with orders," recalled Chynoweth in 1949,

we were told that General MacArthur had authorized Sharp to use his
own judgement. Later, General Sharp never gave me the slightest suggestion of the fact that General MacArthur had wanted us to continue
in action. Our belief that MacArthur had agreed to our surrender is all
that made us obey the order.[42]

By 9 June, formal resistance on the islands had ceased. Homma, who
had been expected to achieve this in two months, was recalled to
Japan in disgrace, until taken to Manila at the end of the war to stand

trial before a military court for war crimes. He was executed by firing squad on 3 March 1946.[43]

The military and political executives in Washington had lived through the death throes of their men in the Philippines in a state of considerable anxiety and no doubt a sizeable degree of guilt, none more so than Marshall. The Chief of Staff decided he would recommend Wainwright for the award of the Medal of Honor. Wainwright had been more in the thick of combat than had MacArthur, and the award was supported by three separate citations from the field— unlike MacArthur's which had been written by Marshall in Washington, based on evidence supplied by Sutherland. Roosevelt admitted that the award of the Medal of Honor to MacArthur was "pure yielding to Congressional and public opinion."[44] Two years later, when asked to sign a special citation for the medal, the President could not recall what act of heroism had justified the award. Ickes and Assistant Secretary for War John J. McCloy argued that MacArthur had not been entitled to the Congressional Medal of Honor because he had "not been on the field of battle in the fight for Bataan Peninsula, but had stayed under cover." Ickes suspected MacArthur had begun his campaign for the presidency.[45] All these belated critical comments came from men who were no friends of MacArthur.

Marshall sought MacArthur's recommendation of the award of the Medal of Honor to Wainwright, but was met by a flat negative. MacArthur had not forgiven Wainwright for the surrender order sent to Sharp, nor did he appreciate his own totally impractical idea of a Subic Bay offensive being rejected. MacArthur became convinced that the excesses of the Bataan Death March and subsequent imprisonment could have been avoided if the troops had broken out to the north and established guerilla bases in the mountains. Not only did MacArthur declare the field citations to be untrue, but also insisted that those who wrote them did not know the facts, that Wainwright's performance fell far short of the required standard and, if he were to receive the Medal of Honor, it would constitute an injustice to those who had done more but had gone unrewarded. Marshall was horrified at MacArthur's animosity towards Wainwright, and he discussed the subject with Stimson, who supported the idea of honoring Wainwright. But MacArthur's strong hostility threatened an undesirable public airing of the matter and, on the advice of General Joseph T. McNarney, both men allowed it to rest. Several months later, in the presence of Secretary Stimson, a representative from MacArthur's Australia Headquarters made a number of derogatory observations of Wainwright. Stimson inquired whether the visitor was speaking on behalf of MacArthur, but was not convinced by the denial.[46] Wainwright was consigned to a prisoner of war camp in Manchuria and, at war's end, witnessed the signing of the Japanese capitulation aboard *USS Missouri* and flew on to Manila to be there for Yamashita's surrender. Later that year President Truman presented him with the Medal of Honor[47] on the White House lawn.

After Truman fired MacArthur in 1951 during the Korean War, the General addressed Congress. As a kind gesture, the War Department invited his former artillery commander on Bataan, the retired General King, to come to Washington to hear MacArthur's address. King, like Wainwright, was a staunch defender of MacArthur, a man who could seemingly do no wrong. After the speech, King approached MacArthur to introduce himself, but MacArthur affected not to know him. King wrote an account of this meeting to his friend and wartime colleague, Brigadier General Clifford Bluemel: "There was no recognition in his eye. I believe he does not like to be reminded of Bataan."[48] King had been a true American hero whose moral courage and sense of duty ensured that thousands of lives were saved and yet, he was treated even more shabbily than Wainwright. In *Ramparts of the Pacific*, Hallet Abend made a telling point.

> In 1940 there was a great deal of derisive comment in this country over the way the British politicians and the British press treated the disastrous rout from Norway and the historical withdrawal from Dunkirk. We made fun of them openly in 1941 when again they boasted over their splendid accomplishments of "masterly retreats" from Greece and from Crete. In the first month of our war against Japan, we, too tasted the bitter flavor of defeat, and we, too tried to fool ourselves just as the British had done . . . we lost Manila to the Japanese invaders, and that was the greatest defeat we had met from any foreign foe since the British captured and burned Washington during the war of 1812.[49]

The U.S.A., Great Britain, France and Russia all suffered heavy defeat in the first years of the war. The Germans and Japanese were well prepared adversaries. Roosevelt had summarized the situation in a 30 January 1942 message to Quezon: "The gaps existing in our offensive armaments are those that are to be expected when peace-loving countries such as the United States and the Philippines suddenly find themselves attacked by an autocratic power which has spent years in preparation for armed conflict."[50]

Not all observers were taken in by the apparently glorious defense of Bataan and Corregidor. James Reston declared the defense of Bataan to have been "overplayed and commercialized." "It is natural and desirable," he wrote,

> that we should play up the activities of our generals and especially a general of the caliber of MacArthur. But in the interests of a well-informed public opinion and in justice to General MacArthur it is essential that we maintain some semblance of proportion. The defense of Bataan and the siege of Corregidor were comparable in this war to the siege of Tobruk, and they did not compare in importance to the defense of Malta. Yet who can tell the name of the commander who held Tobruk or the leader of the men at Malta?[51]

The chief official Australian historian suggested that the defense of the Philippines had not been impressive. "It cost a far stronger Japanese army as many days of actual combat to take Malaya and Singapore as it cost Homma to take Bataan and Corregidor."[52] Unamused by MacArthur's posing and grandstanding in Australia, Roosevelt commented that MacArthur seemed to have forgotten that his record in Manila had not been dissimilar to that of Admiral Kimmel and General Short, who both faced courts martial. In fact, MacArthur had much less excuse to be surprised by the Japanese attack than either of the two Pearl Harbor commanders. Roosevelt believed MacArthur's defense of Luzon to have been "criminal" rather than heroic, "more a rout than military achievement."[53]

There is a combination of reasons why MacArthur avoided censure for displaying poor qualities of generalship: he maintained the support of the Philippine Government and the Philippine people; his removal by the Democratic Roosevelt might have generated an unwanted political backlash at a difficult time; the Philippines was so much further distant than Hawaii, tending to emphasize the impression of a lonely hero defending America and what she stood for; finally, MacArthur endeavored to ensure there was no obvious, suitable officer available to replace him. His removal of General Grunert illustrates this latter point. There was then the marketing of MacArthur, a phenomenon far in advance of its time. MacArthur held on to his position in a public relations exercise founded upon the public's hunger for a hero and his management of the media, which allowed the creation of a questionable image of this Far Eastern Alamo manned by plucky, outnumbered heroes facing up to overwhelming odds. What bonded this package together was MacArthur's undoubted gift for words that were inspirational and uplifting, his presence and charisma, and on occasions, that rare ability not only to talk nonsense with confidence but also to get away with it.

When the Japanese struck the Philippines, MacArthur was in his early sixties. He was a distant, remote, suspicious and brooding man whose ego set him apart from others in the Services. He found companionship among Manila's indigenous wealthy, which served to exacerbate his loss of touch. He was at heart and in his performance a nineteenth-century imperial warrior. For all his posturing as an expert on Far Eastern affairs, he grossly underestimated the capabilities of the Japanese—"not even second class"—and overestimated the abilities of the Filipinos, whom he believed to be more than a match for the Japanese. But the Philippines in 1941 presented no clearly defined political or military options.[54] MacArthur's disastrous forward defense and the consequent logistical hiatus were heavily influenced by local political considerations reinforced by a military rationale to hold Clark Field after the arrival of the B-17s. His decision to hold back his first team in reserve is most probably due to his concerns the Japanese development of air landing and airborne capabilities.[55] This would explain why those 4th Marines, permanently based on Corregidor, experienced only 13 hours of combat during the entire campaign. It may well have been in MacArthur's mind that he needed high-quality troops there to defend his headquarters against a possible Japanese airborne assault. When he returned to take Corregidor, he did so with an airborne *coup de main*. MacArthur was not alone in his fallibility in the Philippines. It was inexcusable for the Navy to have begun the war without having properly tested their torpedoes, just as it was inexcusable for MacArthur not to have been more positive in the development of joint plans. MacArthur believed Hart and the Navy to be defeatist and therefore saw the Philippines' salvation as being in his and the Army's hands. Ultimately the Philippines were lost because the U.S. had insufficient trained and equipped forces there to save it and could not get through with reinforcements. MacArthur made monstrous blunders but it was not all his fault; he had a lot of help. In the final analysis, the Philippine garrison was probably doomed by the pre-emptive strike against Pearl Harbor, inadequacies on the air side and the loss of the air forces in the Philippines. "Probably" is the key word because circumstances do strongly suggest that the only "unknown" was the time it would take for the Americans and Filipinos to be defeated. However, the Japanese campaign in the Philippines was not proficiently executed and Homma consistently had fewer troops available to him than the defending MacArthur. If the American campaign had been fought with more imagination, flair, foresight and planning, then a whole new raft of possibilities might have arisen. The Scouts showed what trained and motivated Filipinos could do. There is no question of the new divisions achieving anywhere near a comparable standard in the limited time available. But it is arguable that a general with the ability and talent to train an indigenous army, Stilwell for example, might have achieved a different result.

Defenders of MacArthur such as Willoughby insisted that the defense of the Philippines was a decisive factor towards ultimate victory because of the image of courage that it created and also because it disrupted the Japanese schedule of quick victories. The dogged defense of the Philippines meant that "the Japanese never managed to detach enough men, planes, ships and materiel to nail down Guadalcanal. Nor did they succeed in mopping up New Guinea or seizing a foothold in Australia."[56] It is true that the sturdy defense of the archipelago did dispel the aura of Japanese invincibility but the reason why the already outnumbered Japanese labored so long to beat MacArthur was the withdrawal of the 48th Division at a crucial juncture in the battle and the further burden that placed upon those who remained. It had been a Japanese intelligence failure which resulted in Homma having insufficient troops with which to achieve his mission quickly but, as is evident from the redeployment of the 48th Division to the higher priority East Indies, resistance in the Philippines was not allowed to disrupt the Japanese timetable. Japanese victories elsewhere meant men and resources became available to achieve eventual victory in the Philippines. The Japanese were under no illusions that, as far as occupation was concerned, Australia was a continent too big and too far.

James, his principal biographer, described MacArthur's return as his redemption, but revenge also loomed large. Today it is difficult to conceive the impact and significance of this defeat upon the United

States. When the news of the Death March did become public, the demand and expectation for vengeance swept the United States. When it came, the American invasion force was larger than that which went into Normandy. Given the defeat of Germany, it might have been possible for Japan to have reached an accommodation short of unconditional surrender, but the Death March closed off that option. His "return" was MacArthur's obsession. He maintained a fanatic insistence on conquering all of the Philippines in 1945 in what transpired to be a needless effort that cost thousands of lives and untold damage.[57] Manila was destroyed in order to be saved: for every Japanese defender, ten Manileños died—the majority to American firepower.[58]

MacArthur was too set in his ways, and the only truth he grasped was the truth as he saw it, dutifully supported by his dedicated staff. Self delusion remained an unwelcome feature throughout the remainder of this campaign and also into Korea. However, there is no denying that he arrived in Australia a better soldier. The period spent in Australia consolidating before striking back was also invaluable. From here he initiated eighty-seven amphibious landings, isolating the Japanese and cutting their lines of communication in his progress towards comprehensive victory.[59] His escape from Corregidor had not been a reflection upon his courage: as a soldier, he was obliged to obey the President's orders. And yet there was much else that he did manage to avoid in the way of retribution. Other generals were called to account for their shortcomings in these first months of the Pacific War, but he never was. As Eisenhower wrote in his diary: "Poor Wainwright! He did the fighting in the Philippine Islands, another got such glory as the public could find in the operation. General MacArthur's tirades, to which TJ[60] and I so often listened in Manila, would now sound silly to the public as they then did to us. But he's a hero! Yah."[61]

NOTES

1: GRAND STRATEGIES

1. Due to the International Date Line, 7 December at Pearl Harbor was 8 December in Manila.
2. John Hay was born in Salem, Indiana and President McKinley came from Ohio.
3. These casualty figures are unusual as the ratio of killed to wounded is the opposite to that which might normally be expected.
4. Originally named Dewey Boulevard, it became Roxas Boulevard.
5. The construction of the buildings was the responsibility of William Parsens who stayed in the Philippines 1905–1914.
6. Beth Day Romulo. The Manila Hotel. (Manila, 1987) 3.
7. Stanley Karnow. In Our Image. (New York, 1989), 211.
8. Beth Day Romulo. 25.
9. Leonard Wood Papers. Manuscript Division. Library of Congress, entries PTO 13 and 29 August 1924.
10. Brian McAllister Linn. Guardian of Empire-The U.S. Army and the Pacific, 1902–1940 (University of North Carolina Press, 1997). 65.
11. Linn, 253.
12. This destabilising influence became more serious as war approached. In 1931, for example, the 31st Infantry lost 587 of its 1,336 men.
13. Ian Hamilton, Lieutenant General, *A Staff Officer's Scrap Book,* Volume 2 (London, 1907).
14. Douglas MacArthur, *Reminiscences,* (London, 1964), 30.
15. Tanaka (1863–1929) was allegedly the author of a document subsequently

found to be a hoax, the "Tanaka Memorial," an outline for Japanese conquest. He fought in both the Sino-Japanese and Russo-Japanese Wars, was twice war minister and became prime minister. The significance of 1906 was its proximity to the unequal 1905 Treaty of Portsmouth. Tanaka did visit the Philippines and was unimpressed by its defense potential. He believed the two main problems that would face Japanese invaders would be mosquitoes and the weather. The first real Japanese strategy to target the Philippines was a vague document in 1918. It became fine-tuned from 1920 onward.

16. Japan's attempt to secure a declaration of racial equality at the Paris Peace Conference was rebuffed by the western powers. Roosevelt did, however, oppose and modify the web of San Francisco ordinance and California immigration law. Japan and the U.S. signed a series of notes (the Gentleman's Agreement) in which Japan agreed to forbid the immigration of laborers to mainland U.S.A., but students, businessmen and white collar workers could still immigrate.

17. James, Vol. I. 41.

18. William Manchester, *American Caesar*, (New York, 1978), 19.

19. MacArthur, *Reminiscences*. 31.

20. Richard Overy with Andrew Wheatcroft, *The Road to War*, (London, 1989), 234.

21. D. Borg and O. Shumpei (eds), *Pearl Harbor as History: Japanese-American Relations 1931–1941,* (New York, 1973), 235.

22. MacArthur, *Reminiscences,* p.85.

23. Ibid.

24. Shunsuke Tsurumi, *An Intellectual History of Wartime Japan 1931–1945,* (London 1986) pp. 37–38.

25. The passage in March 1934 of the Tydings-McDuffie Act provided for Philippine independence after an interval of twelve years. With money supply tight stateside, the fortification of a state soon to be independent could not be considered a priority.

26. Francis L. Loewenheim, Harold D. Langley and Manfred Jones (eds), *Roosevelt and Churchill. Their Secret Wartime Coorespondence.* (London 1975) 155.

27. Overy and Wheatcroft, 249.

28. Ibid., 257.

2: EARLY DAYS

1. John J. Pershing Papers. Manuscript Division. Library of Congress.

2. "I won my 'A' (for sporting achievement), became First Captain of the Corps, and to my amazement recorded the highest scholastic record in

twenty-five years" due to "my having, perhaps a somewhat clearer perspective of events . . ." MacArthur *Reminiscences*, 27.

3. D. Clayton James. The Years of MacArthur, Volume 1, 1880–1941 (London, 1970). 39.
4. The rank was abolished after his retirement and not reintroduced until the First World War. *Reminiscences*. 35.
5. However, the Roman Catholic church held strong reservations vis-à-vis MacArthur's active role in Masonic orders.
6. Beth Day Romulo. *The Manila Hotel*, (Manila, 1987), 39.
7. MacArthur. *Reminiscences*. 29.
8. MacArthur, *Reminiscences*. 29.
9. John Gunther. *Inside Asia*, (New York and London, 1942), 12.
10. Washington Army Barracks was renamed Fort McNair in 1948 in honor of General Leslie McNair, commander of U.S. ground forces, killed in Normandy.
11. *Reminiscences*. 36.
12. Leonard Wood Diary. Manuscript Division. Library of Congress. Letter MacArthur to Wood, 7 and 15 May 1914. Perret 70.
13. Jack Sweetman. *The Landing at Vera Cruz: 1914* (Annapolis, 1968) 184. James, Vol. 1. 121. Perret 71.
14. *Reminiscences*. 42.
15. James, Vol. 1. 126.
16. John Hersey. *Men on Bataan* (New York, 1942), 110. Perret 77.
17. James, Vol. 1. 157.
18. Hunt, 74–76. Manchester, 105.
19. MacArthur. *Reminiscences*. 70. Manchester. 106.
20. Awarded retrospectively when, as Army Chief of Staff, he reintroduced the Purple Heart.
21. Frazier Hunt. The Untold Story of Douglas MacArthur (New York, 1954) 97. Manchester. 125.
22. His permanent rank was confirmed in January 1920.
23. James, Vol. 1, 288.
24. Karnow, 262.
25. Carrol Morris Petillo. *Douglas MacArthur. The Philippine Years* (Indiana University Press, 1981) 123.
26. Donald Smythe. *Guerrilla Warrior* (New York, 1973) 123; Perret, 127.
27. Louise and Pinky had a lot in common. When she was young, Pinky had been good-natured, happy, fun loving, and she was always resolutely determined. As if to signify her acceptance of her daughter-in-law and her now-assumed responsibility for her loving son, she handed over to Louise her prized possession, the scrap book she had diligently collected of every morsel of published information about her darling son. Manchester, 143,

wrote of Pinky being "invalided" at the time of the marriage. Perret, 126, mentions her having had a heart attack in November 1921 from which she was obviously still feeling the effects at the time of the marriage.

28. Michael Schaller. *Douglas MacArthur. The Far Eastern General* (New York, 1989) 11. Perret, 126. Petillo, 141. James, Vol. 1, 323.

29. Robert Considine. *It's All News to Me* (New York, 1956) 342. Perret, 127.

30. Wood had been one of Arthur MacArthur's subordinates in the Philippines.

31. Unlike F.D. Roosevelt, MacArthur had not yet become a Mason.

32. James, Vol. 1, 320.

33. Leonard Wood Papers. Manuscript Division, Library of Congress, entry 26 February 1924.

34. James, Vol. 1, 303.

35. Of this group of islands, there are only 460 with a surface area larger than one square mile and only 11 exceed 1,000 square miles. These 11 larger islands comprise 94 percent of the land area of the archipelago.

36. Karnow. 264.

37. Ibid.

38. JANPC to JB. *The Defense of the Philippine Islands 13 Apr 1922.* National Archives, RG 165. JB Policy Defense of the Philippines— Effect of New Treaties 17 May 1922. RG 165. Linn 171.

39. Linn. Preface xiii.

40. Ickes Diary, 25 September 1943. Harold E. Ickes Papers. Manuscript Division, Library of Congress; Perret, 132. Entered as a record albeit from a hostile source.

41. James, Vol. 1, 304, quoting from the Pershing Papers.

42. Leonard Wood Papers. Manuscript Division, Library of Congress. Entries 9 May 1924 and 13 June 1924.

43. *New York Times,* 23 September 1924.

44. Perret, 135.

3: A WHIFF OF POLITICS

1. *Reminiscences,* 87.

2. Report on the Defense of the Philippine Islands by Major General William Lassiter, 21 August 1928. National Archives. WPD General Correspondence 3251. RG 165.

3. In the early twentieth century, the U.S. Army talked about itself as divided into coastal defense forces and mobile troops.

4. Later MacArthur amended Lassiter's plan because, and according to Brigadier General George S. Simonds "he considered a Mobile Force of three divisions the minimum necessary to put this plan for the defense of the Philippine Islands into effect." Memo for COS by Brigadier Gen-

eral George S. Simonds, Assistant Chief of Staff. National Archives. WPD 3251-3. February 18, 1929.

5. Lassiter to Summerall, COS War Department. Basic Plan Orange. September 24, 1928. National Archives 3251-1. RG 165.

6. *Reminiscences*, 88.

7. Perret 141, Moseley memoir, *One Soldier's Journey*, Vol. 2, and appendix "Historical Notes," George Van Horn Moseley Papers. Manuscript Division, Library of Congress.

8. Douglas MacArthur to Stimson, 7 February 1929. Stimson Papers, Yale University Library.

9. Petillo, pp. 147–148.

10. *New York Times*, 21 April 1929.

11. *Reminiscences*, 89.

12. Speech given in Manila Hotel, 18 September 1930.

13. James, Vol. 1, 347.

14. Eric Larrabee. *Commander in Chief Franklin Delano Roosevelt, His Lieutenants and Their War* (New York, 1987) 310.

15. Pratt retired in the summer of 1933, at which point it became apparent that the MacArthur-Pratt agreement had not been universally accepted. James, Vol. 1, 370.

16. War Department Press Release, 9 January 1931.

17. Memo for Army Chief of Staff. National Archives, RG 165 dated 21 April 1922. Henry G. Gole, *War Planning at the U.S. Army War College, 1934–1940*, footnote 46, p. 155. PhD Paper. Military History Institute.

18. Karnow, 268.

19. The conflict between MacArthur and Collins arose through their different perceptions of Defense priorities. MacArthur was intent upon investing in and supporting personnel, whereas Collins, an admirer of Mitchell, regarded modernization of equipment to be the first priority, particularly armor and aircraft.

20. Harold L. Ickes, *The Secret Diary of Harold L. Ickes*, Vol. 1, "The First Thousand Days 1933–36," (New York, 1952,), 71. Larrabee, 310.

21. Letters Dern to Roosevelt, 14 July 1933 and Roosevelt to Dern, 28 July 1933. Franklin D. Roosevelt Library, Hyde Park.

22. Larrabee, 310.

23. *Reminiscences*, 92.

24. Ibid, 93.

25. According to James, Vol. 1, 388, there was a band of approximately 200 Communists posing as veterans, who took their orders from a bankrupt Detroit contractor and recent convert to Communism.

26. Dwight D. Eisenhower. *At Ease: Stories I Tell to Friends* (New York, 1967) 213.

27. Bradford Grethen Chynoweth. *Bellamy Park*, (New York, 1975), 138.

28. Ibid.
29. Bonner Fellers to Admiral Kimmel, 6 March 1967. Box 3. RG 44a. MacArthur Memorial Archives. There was bound to be conflict throughout the duration of MacArthur's relations with Roosevelt. Not only were they each significant figures of their time and in that sense rivals, but MacArthur would always be a subordinate. He could therefore be ordered by his political boss to leave Corregidor, and see his Theater play second fiddle to Europe and to have his authority in that Theater challenged by Nimitz, the interloper from the Navy.
30. Rexford G. Tugwell. *The Democratic Roosevelt* (New York, 1957) 349.
31. Eisenhower, *At Ease*, 215.
32. *Reminiscences,* 93.
33. Ibid, 216.
34. James, Vol. 1, 381.
35. Perret, 154.
36. James, Vol. 1, 401.
37. My italics. To interpret this statement as corroboration that MacArthur did receive orders not to cross the Anacostia Bridge is misconstrued. What Eisenhower is saying is that he chose not to hear the instructions, otherwise the foregoing makes little sense.
38. Eisenhower, *At Ease*, pp. 217–218.
39. Which is not really true. His mutineers in the Philippines did not riot and, while it is possible he may have become involved in civilian disorder in the Philippines, it is unlikely that there were many.
40. *New York Times,* 29 July 1932.
41. Stanley L. Falk recognized that MacArthur "was probably best known for his controversial action in suppressing the 1932 Bonus March, but he made his major contribution in vigorously fighting off reductions in the military budget and in opposing other attempts to reduce the size and quality of the army.
42. James, Vol. 1, 413.
43. Karnow, 268.
44. James, Vol. 1. Footnote 37 to Chapter XIV. Robert G. Sherill, "Drew Pearson: An Interview," *Nation,* CCIX (7 July 1969) 15.
45. *Reminiscences,* 99.
46. Ibid, 101.
47. Perret, 173. Hersey, 162.
48. *Reminiscences,* 101.
49. Ibid, 101.
69. Ickes Diary, 27 July 1933. Harold E. Ickes Papers. Manuscript Division, Library of Congress.
50. Petillo, 168.
51. Ricardo Trota Jose, *The Philippine Army 1935–1942,* (Manila, 1992), 24.

52. Manuel Quezon. *The Good Fight* (New York, 1944) 155.

53. Petillo, 169.

54. Ickes Diary, 9 October 1939. Ickes Papers. As told by Roosevelt.

55. President Roosevelt Press Conference, 12 December 1934.

56. James, Vol. 1, 480.

57. Petillo, 170. Perret, 188. MacArthur's salary as Chief of Staff was $7,500.

58. Beth Day Romulo, 43.

59. Ibid, 44.

60. Interview James/Eisenhower. James, Vol. 1, 506.

61. Ibid.

62. *Reminiscences*, 102.

63. Dwight D. Eisenhower Diary. Undated. 1935–1938. Dwight D. Eisenhower Presidential Library.

64. Dern to Roosevelt. 17 July 1935. Franklin D. Roosevelt Library, Hyde Park, New York.

65. Roosevelt to Dern. 18 July 1935. Franklin D. Roosevelt Library, Hyde Park, New York.

66. The others were MacArthur's aide Captain Thomas Jefferson Davis and MacArthur's personal physician Major Howard J. Hutter. Hutter had a number of medical tasks including the development of health and hygiene plans for the Philippine Army and to provide medical support for Pinky. It is curious that while MacArthur always had a personal physician in close proximity (one, Colonel Roger O. Egeberg, wrote a book, *The General, MacArthur and the Man he called "Doc"*) he seems to have eschewed intrusive medical attention. He also had a fear of hospitals. If he knew a film had a hospital scene in it he would not watch it. One doctor who saw him after his final admission into Walter Read found not a scratch on his body, not even an inoculation scar. One of the reasons he wore baggy trousers is because, for the best part of 40 years, he carried two untreated hernias the size of grapefruit. "I will never understand how such an outstandingly intelligent and physically courageous individual could have refused treatment of such easily correctable medical conditions for so long. As William Manchester described him, 'He was a thundering paradox of a man.' "* (*Norman M. Scott Jr. MD, FACP in letter to author dated 19 August 1997).

67. James, Vol. 1, 493.

68. Dwight D. Eisenhower. *At Ease*, 223.

4: PLANS

1. Henry G. Gole, PhD dissertation. Military History Institute. 5.

2. Ibid. 9.

3. Paul Kennedy, *The War Plans of the Great Powers, 1880–1914*, (London,

1979), 46. Adolf Carlson, *Joint U.S. Army-Navy War Planning on the Eve of the First World War: Its Origin and Its Legacy*. Letort Paper (Carlisle, 1998), 15.

4. Edward S. Miller, *War Plan Orange. The U.S. Strategy to Defeat Japan 1897–1945*, (Annapolis, 1991), 2.
5. Ibid. However, in general, Congress would not enact a War Plan. Congress enacts laws, not war plans, which are more the responsibility of the executive.
6. The Army's and Navy's Planning Staff at this time were very small—the former approximately 12–13. They could not function effectively without the active support of their War Colleges.
7. Gole, 156.
8. Carlson, 17.
9. Gole, 152.
10. Gerald E. Wheeler, "National Policy Planning Between the World Wars: Conflicts between Ends and Means," *Naval War College Review* (February, 1969) pp. 54–69. Gole, 158.
11. Admiral Thomas C. Hart, *Supplementary of Narrative*. Prepared in Op-29-13 by Admiral Hart, Winter 1946–47, Naval History Institute, Washington DC.
12. Memorandum Brigadier General Embick to CG Philippine Department, 19 April 1933. WPD 3251–15. Watson, 415.
13. Mark S. Watson. *Chief of Staff Pre War Plans and Preparations*, (Washington, 1950) 415. Letter Booth to General Kilbourne (ACOS WPD). Among other comments was the disadvantage of too early an occupation of the Bataan Peninsula. WPD 3251-17. National Archives. Washington.]
14. Watson, 415.
15. Major General Frank Parker to COS, 28 February 1935. 3251-27. National Archives. Washington.
16. Bonner Fellers Papers. MacArthur to Bonner Fellers, 1 June 1939, MacArthur Memorial Archives.
17. L. Siguion Reyna. *Problems of National Defense*, 25 May 1935. Manuel L. Quezon Papers, National Library, Manila. Jose. 31.
18. Jose, 30.
19. Jose, 34.
20. Jose, 33.
21. Philippine Commonwealth. Office of the Military Adviser. Report on National Defense (Manila 1936) 24. Jose, 37.
22. James, Vol. 1, 495.
23. Quezon Speech, 26 October 1935. Manuel Quezon Papers, National Library, Manila. Jose, 39.
24. James, Vol. 1, 496.

25. MacArthur to Dern, 20 August 1935. Secretary of War Records. RG 107. National Archives Washington. James, Vol. 1, 498.
26. James, Vol. 1, 499.
27. Ibid.
28. Theodore Friend. *Between Two Empires. The Ordeal of the Philippines 1929–1946.* (Yale, 1965), 185. James, Vol. 1, pp. 499–500.
29. Schaller, 32.
30. Friend, 184.
31. Courtney Whitney. *MacArthur. His Rendezvous with History,* (New York, 1955), 5.
32. Beth Day Romulo, pp. 88–89.
33. Frederick S. Marquardt, *Before Bataan and After,* (Indianapolis, 1943), 233. Jose, 41.
34. Eisenhower, *At Ease,* 220. James, Vol. 1, 494–5. MacArthur, *Reminiscences,* 103.
35. Perret, 193.
36. Beth Day Romulo, pp. 65–66.
37. Gunther, 312.
38. Jose, 42.
39. Karnow, 271.
40. Karnow, 272.
41. Jose, 47.
42. These were: War Plans Division—Brigadier General Lim; Intelligence, Operations and Training—Colonel Fidel Segundo; Personnel and Supply—Colonel Rafael L. Garcia.
43. Robert Ferrell (ed), *The Eisenhower Diaries,* (New York, 1981), pp. 19–20.
44. Jose, 55.
45. Ferrell, 18.
46. James, Vol. 1, pp. 500–501
47. Jose, 58–59.
48. Vorin E. Whan (ed), *A Soldier Speaks.* Public Papers and Speeches of General of the Army Douglas MacArthur, (New York, 1965), 79–95.
49. Interview Eisenhower/James (see footnote 30), James, Vol. 1, 690.
50. Francis Burton Harrison, *Origins of the Philippine Republic: Extracts from the Diaries and Records of Francis Burton Harrison,* (New York, 1974), entry 24 August 1936. Jose, 63.
51. Ferrell, 21.
52. Ferrell, 16.
53. Embick to Chief of Staff, 2 December 1935. WPD 3389–29. National Archives Washington.
54. Eventually a number of training weapons were released from War Department reserve stocks, on loan to the Philippines.

55. Ferrell, pp. 10–15.
56. William Hoge (Robertson Interview) 64. U.S. Army Military History Institute, Carlisle, Pa.
57. Ferrell, pp. 19–20.
58. Ferrell, 22.
59. Whan, 84.
60. Box 1, RG1, MacArthur Memorial Archives.
61. In a dispatch from Manila by Randall Gould, dateline 29 February 1940, MacArthur was quoted as having said: "The riches and potentialities of these islands have been greatly exaggerated. Malcolm's very sound estimate puts their total value at only six billion dollars. We hear much of gold output, for example, yet this amounts even now to only $40,000,000 a year, of which probably not more than 12 per cent is profit. There is but a modest amount of iron, the output now being largely taken by Japan; there is no high class coal, no gasoline, magnificent forests but almost wholly soft woods. As to agriculture, the sugar industry is important now because of the American market, there is no rubber or cotton, the hemp is of course the best in the world, coconut output is declining in importance because of competitive products. All in all its economic value would not warrant a major war."
62. Whan, 80.
63. Hugh A. Drum Papers. Box 21. 23 July 1936. American Army Historical Institute, Carlisle.
64. Ibid.
65. Whan, 101.
66. Ibid.
67. Whan, pp. 104–105.
68. In his 1908 book entitled *The Valor of Ignorance*, Homer Lea predicted a Japanese invasion over the shores of Lingayen Gulf.
69. Jose, 97.
70. "Captain Bonner E. Fellers Defense Theory as Applied to PI," *Herald*, 18 January 1937.
71. Whan, 107.
72. Robert Aura Smith, *Our Future in Asia*, (New York, 1940), 125.
73. Interrogation of Major Kotoshi Doba, Fifth Air Force. GHQ Far East Command. G-2 Historical Section, Army Historical Institute.
74. Drum to MacArthur. Hugh S. Drum Papers. Box 21. 4 September 1936. American Army Historical Institute, Carlisle.
75. Dern to MacArthur. Box 1. RG1. 11 June 1936. MacArthur Memorial Archives.
76. Petillo, 189.
77. Harold E. Fey, "Militarizing the Philippines," *The Nation*, CXLII (10 June 1936), pp. 736–7.

78. Harold E. Fey, *Philippine Magazine,* (August 1936), 382. Jose, 72.

79. Schaller, 36.

80. Friend, 191.

81. Hunt, 184.

82. Friend, 190.

83. MacArthur's response to editor *Times-Dispatch*, Richmond, 11 February 1938, Perret 203–204.

84. Hunt, 185. James, Vol. 1, pp. 512–513. Schaller, 37.

85. Harold E. Ickes Papers. Diary entry 20 January 1937. Library of Congress, Washington.

5: TO BUILD AN ARMY

1. Robert Considine, *MacArthur the Magnificent,* (New York, 1942), 10.

2. Beth Day Romulo, 53.

3. Dwight D. Eisenhower, *At Ease Stories I Tell to Friends,* 228. MacArthur's workrate increased substantially after Pearl Harbor and was maintained at a very high level.

4. Teodoro A. Agoncillo, *The Vargas-Laurel Collaboration Case,* (Manila, 1984), 6.

5. Agoncillo, pp. 6–7, Beth Day Romulo, pp. 52–53. Alfredo B. Saulo, *Let George Do It*. A Biography of Jorge B. Vargas, (University of Philippines Press, 1992), 7.

6. Beth Day Romulo, 53.

7. Perret, 200, based upon *Notes of an Interview with General MacArthur Aboard the* President Coolidge. MacArthur Memorial Archives.

8. Smith, 127.

9 Lt. Col. Robert M. Carswell. "Philippine National Defense," Coast Artillery Journal (March–April 1941), 125, Tribune (3 June 1937). Jose 75.

10. Smith, 127.

11. Eisenhower to Ord, 1 September 1937, RG 1, MacArthur Memorial Archives.

12. Eisenhower to MacArthur, 13 October 1937, RG 1, MacArthur Memorial Archives.

13. Account of Dorothy Fellers (1975). Bonner Fellers Papers, Box 5, Folder 16, RG 44a, MacArthur Memorial Archives. Hunt 192–193.

14. Ibid.

15. *Herald,* 19 January 1937, Jose 98.

16. James, Vol. 1, 518.

17. Quezon to Roosevelt, 20 August 1937, Box 4, RG 44A, MacArthur Memorial Archives.

18. Chief of Staff Malin Craig to MacArthur, 6 August 1937, Bonner Fellers Papers, Box 3, RG 44a.

320 NOTES

19. Military History Institute. USAWC, 5-1939-6/1, Orange. Discussion following student presentation. Collins joined the faculty after graduation. Gole 156. General Collins was Army Chief of Staff when MacArthur was relieved in 1951.
20. James, Vol. 1, 522.
21. MacArthur to Malin Craig, 10 September 1937, MacArthur Memorial Archives.
22. The letter may not have been sent. The reference here is a draft letter in the Bonner Fellers Papers.
23. Malin Craig to Stephen Early, 3 August 1937. DM 201, MacArthur Memorial Archives.
24. Burnett to MacArthur, 13 October 1937, RG 1, MacArthur Memorial Archives.
25. James, Vol. 1, 523.
26. Ickes" Diary, 30 January 1937. Harold E. Ickes Papers, Manuscript Division, Library of Congress.
27. Holbrook was succeeded in February 1938 by Major General John H. Hughes.
28. MacArthur to McNutt, 29 January 1938, Francis B. Sayre Papers, Manuscript Division, Library of Congress.
29. RG 10, 24 November 1937, MacArthur Memorial Archives.
30. Eisenhower, *At Ease*, 218–220.
31. Farrell, 25.
32. Ord to Eisenhower, 18 July 1937. Dwight D. Eisenhower Presidential Library, Abilene, Kansas.
33. Farrell, 26.
34. Eisenhower, *At Ease*, 225.
35. Ibid.
36. Perret, 214.
37. Eisenhower, 226.
38. Sid Huff, *My Fifteen Years with General MacArthur,* (New York, 1964), 23.
39. Manchester, 196.
40. James C. Hasdorff, "Jerry Lee. Founding Father of the Philippine Air Force," *Aerospace Historian,* Vol. 20, Winter/December 1973, No 4, pp. 208–214.
41. Based on interviews Lee/Hasdorff and Gallacher quoted in Perret, 220.
42. Eisenhower, *At Ease*, 227–228.
43. Jose, 104.
44. Eisenhower, *At Ease*, 227–228.
45. The Army at this time had a strength of 118,000 and a budget of only $300 million.
46. Eisenhower, *At Ease*, 229.

47. Schaller, 40.
48. Eisenhower, *At Ease,* 231.
49. Beth Day Romulo, 69. Beth could have heard this from husband Carlos.
50. Box 1, RG 1, MacArthur Memorial Archives.
51. MacArthur to Early, 14 July 1939. Franklin D. Roosevelt Papers. Franklin D. Roosevelt Library.
52. Jose, 120.
53. Vicente Lim, *To Inspire and to Lead. The Letters of Gen Vicente Lim 1938–1942,* (Manila, 1980), 56.
54. Jose, 122.
55. James, Vol. 1, 537.
56. Jose, 126.
57. New York *Herald Tribune* (30 August 1939), Jose 128.
58. Smith, 133.
59. Huff, 27–28.
60. Jose, 85 and 111.
61. Jose, 84.
62. Hugh Parker/Burg interview as in Perret 219.
63. Military History Institute, USAWC, 5-1939-4, the Philippine Department, Tab 1, 1–2, Gole 155.
64. Ibid. Tab 3, 1–2. Gole 156.
65. Steinberg, 15.
66. Jose, 127.
67. F.B. Sayre, *Glad Adventure,* (New York, 1957), 194.
68. Friend, 195.
69. Sayre, 181.
70. Washington had, however, taken a number of initiatives which aligned her sympathetically with Great Britain, namely Lend-Lease, Bases for Destroyers and support with Atlantic convoys.
71. National Outlook (September 1939), Jose 127.

6: RELATIVE VALUES

1. Sayre, 182.
2. David Vawter Dufault. Francis B. Sayre and the Commonwealth of the Philippines, 1936–1942, (University of Oregon PhD, 1972) 316.
3. Hull to Grew, 8 May 1940 and quoted in Dufault. 323.
4. Leutze, 163.
5. Ibid.
6. Sayre, 184.
7. Sayre, 189.
8. Memorandum of conversation Quezon/Sayre, 8 January 1940, Manuscript Division, Library of Congress.

9. According to Hirohito's Deputy Chief of the General Staff, Lieutenant
   General Torashiro Kawagoe, "The Plan was in its sixth year (of ten) and
   a menace to Japan's ambitions. The Japanese had to intervene before it
   was too late." *Reminiscences,* pp. 111–112, Manchester, 198.

10. Memorandum of Conversation Quezon / Sayre, 8 January 1940.

11. Interview Theodore Friend and E.D. Hester (economic adviser at the
    High Commissioner's Office), 1 March 1958, Friend 194.

12. Philippines *Herald,* 26 January 1940.

13. *Herald,* 27 January 1940, Jose 144.

14. Anonymous memo to Sayre, 21 February 1941, Box 9, Manuscript Divi-
    sion, Library of Congress.

15. Jose, 145.

16. Hart to Sayre, 30 Dec 1940, referring to a Feb 1940 conversation between
    Hart and Quezon, Box 4, Manuscript Division, Library of Congress.

17. Leutze, 162–163.

18. Leutze, 163.

19. Emmanuel Raymond Lewis, *Seacoast Fortifications of United States,*
    (Annapolis, 1979) pp. 140–141. *Bulletin* (18 May 1940), *Philippine Maga-*
    zine (March 1940 and June 1940). Jose 153.

20. Memorandum of conversation between Sayre and Quezon, 28 February
    1940. Box 9, Francis B. Sayre Papers, Manuscript Division, Library of
    Congress.

21. *Philippine Magazine,* (May 1940) 165. Jose 149.

22. Sayre to Roosevelt, 23 January 1940. Box 7, Francis B. Sayre Papers,
    Manuscript Division, Library of Congress.

23. Colonel Fidel V. Segundo Diary, 26 March 1940, Jose 149.

24. Craig to Grunert, 24 June 1939. Grunert Papers, U.S. Army Military
    History Institute.

25. Hart's Supplementary of Narrative. Prepared in Op-29-B 1946–47,
    Naval History Institute.

26. Leutze, 160.

27. U.S. Military Operations are defined at three levels: tactical, opera-
    tional, and strategic.

28. Louis Morton, *The War in the Pacific. Strategy and Command: The*
    First Two Years, (Washington, 1962), 68.

29. S. De Jesus to Adjutant General, Philippine Army, 25 August 1937,
    MacArthur Memorial Archives. Ord to MacArthur, 30 October 1937,
    MacArthur Memorial Archives. Perret 200.

30. Military History Institute, 5-1938 22, 88–89.

31. Japanese Secret Intelligence Services, Part 1. Prepared by Australian
    Military Forces. AL 1352, IWM p52 and referred to in Peter Elphick,
    Far Eastern File. The Intelligence War in the Far East 1930–1945,
    (London, 1997), 285.

32. Wayne S. Kirosaki, *A Spy in Their Midst. The World War II Struggle of a Japanese-American Hero,* (New York, 1995), 60.
33. Smith, 138.
34. James, Vol. 1, 516.
35. Steinberg, 23.
36. Kihara left Manila prior to the Japanese invasion but returned the day after the fall of Manila with a "bulging portfolio of instructions." He "maintained a warm, amiable relationship with Vargas"—Alfredo B. Saulo, *Let George Do It: A Biography of Jorge B. Vargas,* (Quezon City, 1992), 123. Kihara became known as the Rasputin of the Malacañan Palace.
37. Interview at Greenhills Residence of Manual Quezon Jr, 22 August 1997.
38. Elphick, 286.
39. John Toland, *But Not in Shame,* (New York, 1961). Elphick, 287.
40. Jose, 151.
41. Manchester, 198.
42. Sayre, 198.
43. Sayre, 199.
44. Dufault, 268, quoting Salisbury to Hull, "President Quezon's Attitude towards Democracy, 24 July 1940."
45. Leutze, 164.
46. Sayre, 189.
47. Sayre to Marshall, Baguio, 19 April 1941. Grunert Papers, Army Military History Institute.
48. Admiral Thomas C. Hart, Supplementary of Narrative. Prepared in Op-29-B. (1946–47) U.S. Naval History Institute.
49. Admiral Thomas C. Hart, Narrative of Events, Asiatic Fleet leading up to war. 8 Dec 1941–15 Feb 1942. U.S. Navy Historical Institute.
50. Military Mission Journal, June 1940. Entry 26 June 1940. RG1 MacArthur Memorial Archives.
51. Watson, 416.
52. Grunert to Marshall, 1 Sep 1940. Grunert Papers, U.S. Army Military History Institute.
53. Mark S. Watson. Chief of Staff Pre War Plans and Preparations (Washington D.C., 1950), 419.
54. James, Vol. I, 551.
55. Memorandum for General MacArthur re Department plans, 19 August 1940. Grunert Papers, U.S. Army Military History Institute.
56. It was a restricted control. Filipinos could only be tried before entirely Filipino courts. As Grunert observed, "conviction, to say the least, was improbable." Some officers, however, were dismissed after courts were established in 1938.
57. Memorandum for General MacArthur re Department plans, 19 August 1940. Grunert Papers, U.S. Army Military History Institute.

58. There is little doubt whom the Axis powers had in mind when each pledged support to any signatory "attacked by a power at present not involved in the European war or in the Sino-Japanese conflict."

59. James, Vol. I, 552.

60. Sayre, 208.

61. MacArthur to Sayre, 5 April 1940. Box 5, F.B. Sayre Papers, Manuscript Division, Library of Congress.

62. Ibid, 17 October 1940.

63. Sayre to MacArthur, 17 October 1940, Ibid.

64. MacArthur to Sayre, 17 October 1940, Ibid.

65. Sayre, 209.

66. Perret, 232.

67. MacArthur to Early, 21 March 1941. OF 400. F.D. Roosevelt Library.

68. Early to MacArthur, 14 April 1941. MacArthur Memorial Archives.

69. Watson to MacArthur, 15 April 1941. MacArthur Memorial Archives and SF 400 F.D. Roosevelt Library.

70. Dufault, 364.

71. WPD 3251.47, 13 October 1941. National Archives.

72. Sayre to Roosevelt, 23 April 1941. Box 7, Francis B. Sayre Papers. Manuscript Division, Library of Congress.

73. Stimson to Roosevelt, 29 March 1941. WPD 3251–44. National Archives. Stimson's request, which reinforced earlier approaches by Marshall, was approved by Roosevelt the same day.

74. Memorandum of Conference, Quezon and MacArthur, 15 May 1941. Quezon Papers. Philippine National Library, Manila. Jose, 182.

75. Jose, 182.

76. Watson, 425.

77. Marshall to Grunert, 29 May 1941. WPD 3251.41. National Archives.

78. Memorandum Gerow to Marshall, 29 May 1941. WPD 3251.49. National Archives.

79. Gerow to Marshall, 6 June 1941. WPD 3251.50. National Archives.

80. Leonard Mosley, *Marshall, Hero of Our Times,* (New York, 1982), 484.

81. Petillo, 197.

82. Marshall to MacArthur, 20 June 1941. WPD 3251.50. National Archives.

83. Japan had closed the northern frontier prior to the invasion through a Non-Aggression and Neutrality Pact. Germany's invasion of Russia provided further reassurance.

84. James, Vol. I, 587.

85. Hart Narrative of Events. U.S. Naval Historical Institute.

86. Grunert to Marshall, 23 July 1941. Box 1, The George Grunert Papers. U.S. Army Military History Institute.

87. *Philippine Herald,* 21 July 1941. General Grunert Birthday Supplement.

88. Jose, 191. James, Vol. I, 589.
89. Manchester, 211.
90. Based on the memoirs of Marshall Green's Pacific Encounters and an account by Bob Fearey, both private secretaries to Ambassador Grew and as recorded in Denis Warner's "Could Pearl Harbor Have Been Averted?" International Herald Tribune, (8 December 1998).
91. Edward J. Drea, *MacArthur's Ultra. Codebreaking and the War Against Japan, 1942–1945,* (University Press of Kansas, 1992), 10. It seems strange that there was no machine allocated to Pearl Harbor. In 1941, Washington believed Hawaii to be reasonably secure and was not prepared to risk the security of the system by distributing it to commands who, in their opinion, did not need to have the information. From the end of July 1941 to early December, not one Japanese diplomatic intercept reached Admiral Kimmel's Pacific Fleet Headquarters.
92. James, Vol. I, 590.
93. *The "Magic" Background of Pearl Harbor,* Vol. 2, 12 May 1941–6 August 1941, pp. 84–85.
94. The report is at WPD 4402-1, National Archives.
95. Morton, *Strategy,* 87.
96. James, Vol. I, pp. 578–9. Morton, *Strategy,* 88–89.
97. Morton, *Strategy,* 88.
98. Ruth Hampton to Sayre, 27 July 1941. Jose, 192.
99. MacArthur, *Reminiscences,* 109.

7: INTERNAL CONFLICTS

1. Manchester, 211.
2. Rogers, 50. Whatever was said, and John Hersey, (*Men on Bataan,* (New York, 1943), 19, suggests: "By God, it was destiny that sent me here," while in Courtney Whitneys's *MacArthur: His Rendezvous with History,* (New York, 1956), 8, it is: "Destiny, by the grace of God, sometimes plays queer pranks with men's lives," and in Francis Trevelyan Miller's *General Douglas MacArthur, Soldier Statesman,* (Philadelphia, 1951), 191, it is: "I am here by the grace of God. This is my destiny." The common denominator was "destiny."
3. Manchester, 211. James, Vol. 1, 591.
4. Ibid.
5. Grunert to Colonel W.C. Koenig, 11 August 1941. The George Grunert Papers, U.S. Army History Institute.
6. Grunert to General James G. Harbord, 6 October 1941. The George Grunert Papers, U.S. Army History Institute.
7. MacArthur to Marshall, 7 October 1941. Army Military History Institute.

8. James, 593.
9. Personal File, 13 September 1941. MacArthur Memorial Archives.
10. Ibid., 23 September 1941.
11. Larrabee, 334.
12. Drea, 11.
13. Marshall to MacArthur, 30 September 1941. MacArthur Memorial Archives.
14. Clark Lee and Richard Henschel, *Douglas MacArthur,* (New York, 1952), pp. 180, 188. This statement is not entirely correct. Akin went on to become Chief Signal Officer of the Army. Chamberlin took over 5th Army. Kenney, Kinkaid and Krueger all became 4-stars. George Decker in 6th Army became Chief of Staff of the Army. Eisenhower became a 5-star and President of the United States. Larrabee, 333.
20. *The U.S. Army in World War II. The Fall of the Philippines,* 12 November 1946. Box 2. Interview of Dr. Morton, Pacific WDSS with Lieutenant General Richard K. Sutherland (Ret). U.S. Army Military History Institute. The later evidence is to the contrary. On Leyte, MacArthur became his own Chief of Staff after Sutherland became ineffective. Kenney's diaries maintain that strategy was worked out between MacArthur, Kinkaid, Krueger and Kenney. The staff was left to fill in the details. With Hollandia, it was Fellers who brought the idea to MacArthur's attention behind the back of Chamberlin. MacArthur did change plans as was evident of Hansa Bay/Wewak area to Hollandia in the spring of 1944. It was a spur of the moment decision by MacArthur to go for the assault on the Admiralties.
16. *Time,* 4 February 1941.
17. Beth Day Romulo, pp. 95–97. Wilfred Sheed, *Clare Boothe Luce,* (New York, 1982), 87. Perret, 235–236. This account is a synthesis of these references.
18. Dufault, 396.
19. Vincent Sheean, *Between the Thunder and the Sun,* (New York, 1943), 376.
20. Ibid., 374.
21. Perret, 236.
22. Clare Boothe Luce Papers. Manuscript Division, Library of Congress.
23. Sheed. Foreword, John J. Beck, *MacArthur and Wainwright,* (Albuquerque, 1974) x, Gunther 26, Manchester 19.
24. Perret, 236.
25. Attributed to the baseball player Wee Willie Keeler.
26. Manchester 184, Hersey 82, Perret 236.
27. MacArthur to Clare Boothe Luce. Letter dated 20 August 1941. MacArthur Memorial Archives.
28. Ralph G. Martin, *Henry and Clare,* (New York, 1990), 209. Perret, 237.

29. Stephen Shadegg, *Clare Boothe Luce: A Biography*, (New York, 1970), pp. 128–130.
30. Clare Boothe, "MacArthur of the Far East," *Life*, (6 December 1941).
31. Henry L. Stimson and McGeorge Bundy, *On Active Service in Peace and War*, (New York, 1947), pp. 388–9.
32. Stimson, *On Active Service*, 395.
33. G2 Annex, Philippine Department, Plan Orange 1940 Revision, RG 165, National Archives. Jose, 177.
34. *Reminiscences*, 109.
35. Mosley. 485.
36. Ibid.
37. WPD 325 1–60 dated 3 October 1941. National Archives. Signed but not used.
38. Owen Thetford. Aircraft of the Royal Air Force since 1918. Ninth Edition (London, 1995) pp 68–69.
39. W.F. Craven etc.
40. Samuel Eliot Morison, *The Rising Sun in the Pacific*, (Boston, 1948), pp. 164–165.
41. Saburo Hayashi, *Kogun. The Japanese Army in the Pacific War*. (Quantico, 1959), pp. 29–33. Based upon Saburo Hayashi's *Taiheiyo Senso Rikusen Gaishi*, (Tokyo, 1951).
42. Sayre to Roosevelt, 15 September 1941. Box 7, Francis B. Sayre Papers, Manuscript Division, Library of Congress.
43. Roosevelt to Quezon, 26 September 1941. Francis B. Sayre Papers, Manuscript Division, Library of Congress.
44. Vice President Henry L. Wallace, Secretary of State Cordell Hull, Secretary of War Henry L. Stimson, Secretary of Navy Frank Knox, Secretary of the Interior Harold Ickes, Army Chief of Staff George Marshall, Army War Plans Brigadier General Leonard Gerow (Eisenhower arrived at War Plans Division in December 1941 where he took over the Pacific and Far East Section), Chief of Naval Operations Admiral Ernest King (replaced Admiral Harold "Betty" Stark in December 1941), Naval War Plans Rear Admiral Richmond Kelly Turner, President's Chief of Staff Admiral William D. Leahy.
45. Hart, Narrative of Events, 8 December 1941–15 February 1942. U.S. Naval History Institute.
46. WPD 3251-60 dated 3 October 1941. National Archives.
47. MacArthur to Adjutant General, RG-2, "15 September—6 October 1941." MacArthur Memorial Archives.
48. Admiral Hart. Supplementary of Narrative. The War Plans. U.S. Navy History Institute.
49. Rogers, 71.
50. Hart to Stark. Private Correspondence. U.S. Navy History Institute.

51. "WW." Undated Position Paper on Civilian Defense Measures. Box 8. Francis B. Sayre Papers. Manuscript Division, Library of Congress.
52. Hart Diary, 22 September 1941. Thomas Hart Papers. Naval Historical Center.
53. Admiral Hart. Supplementary of Narrative. War Plans. U.S. Navy History Institute.
54. Hart to Stark, 20 November 1941. Private Correspondence. U.S. Navy History Institute.
55. MacArthur to Hart, 16 October 1941. MacArthur Personal File, 7 October–7 November 1941.
56. Hart to MacArthur, 23 October 1941.
57. MacArthur to Hart, 7 November 1941.
58. WPD 3251-61 dated 13 October 1941. National Archives.
59. James, Vol. II, 20.
60. Pogue, 185. Marshall to Robert Ward Johnson, 1 November 1942. Sexton Collection.
61. Hart to Stark. Private Correspondence. U.S. Navy History Institute.
62. Frank O. Hough et al, "Pearl Harbor to Guadalcanal," *History of U.S. Marine Corps Operations in World War II,* Vol. I, (Washington ndg), 156.
63. J. Michael Miller, *Shanghai to Corregidor: Marines in the Fall of the Philippines.* Marine Corps History Center, 1997. James S. Santelli, *A Brief History of the 4th Marines.* Historical Division, HQ U.S. Marine Corps (Washington D.C., 1970), pp. 21–22.
64. MacArthur to Marshall, 30 august 1941. RG-2, 26 Jul 41–12 Sep 41. MacArthur Memorial Archives.
65. Ibid. and letter RG2 dated 28 October 1941.
66. MacArthur to Grunert, 7 September 1941. RG-2. USAFFE. MacArthur Personal File, 26 July 41–12 Sept 41. MacArthur Memorial Archives.
67. Rogers, 9.
68. Eric Morris, *Corregidor. The Nightmare in the Philippines,* (London, 1982), 8.
69. Three American National Guard Artillery Battalions, among others, were en route on the Pensacola Convoy (a convoy escorted by the heavy cruiser *USS Pensacola*).
70. Jose, 195.
71. Based on H.W. Tarkington, *There Were Others.* Box 5. *The U.S. Army in WWII.* "The Fall of the Philippines." Louis Morton Papers. U.S. Army Military History Institute.
72. James, Vol. I, 603.
73. The War Diary of General Clyde Selleck, Commanding General 71st Division, USAFFE. *The Battle for Northern Luzon. The initial phase of the Battle of Bataan.* Historical Conservation Society, (Manila, 1985).
74. James, Vol. I, pp. 600–601.

75. The War Diary of General Clyde Selleck, 9.
76. Eisenhower, *At Ease*, 247.
77. 11 September 1941.
78. Memorandum for the Record, 10 October 1941. MacArthur's Papers. MacArthur Memorial Archives.
79. Karl C. Dod, *United States Army in World War II*. "The Corps of Engineers: The War Against Japan," (Washington D.C., 1966), 60.
80. Lewis H. Brereton, *The Brereton Diaries*, (New York, 1946), pp. 17–19.
81. Marshall to MacArthur, 9 September 1941. MacArthur Memorial Archives.
82. Alvin P. Stauffer, *The United States Army in World War II*. "The Quartermaster Corps: Operations in the War against Japan, (Washington D.C., 1956), pp. 3–4.
83. Stauffer, pp. 6–7.

8: SERENITY AND CONFIDENCE

1. Kiyosaki, *A Spy in their Midst*, pp. 53–58.
2. Ibid., 62.
3. Ibid., 63.
4. *The Magic Background of Pearl Harbor*, Vol. 3, 115.
5. Henry C. Clausen and Bruce Lee, *Pearl Harbor: Final Judgement*, (New York, 1992), pp. 141–142.
6. George R. Thompson et al, *United States in World War II: The Technical Services: The Signal Corps: The Test (December 1941–July 1943)*, (Washington D.C., 1957), pp. 10–15 (describes Philippines warning system). Drea, 12.
7. The Army Air Corps received the additional support during summer and fall of two truck companies and two light maintenance companies (Staeffer, p7).
8. Preliminary research failed to relate either Tarallo or Miguel Airfield to the ground. They may have been Japanese code names yet other Philippine names in the same transmission had not been altered.
9. *The Magic Background to Pearl Harbor*, Vol. 3, pp. 114–115.
10. D. Clayton Jaymes, "The Other Pearl Harbor," *Military History Quarterly*, (Winter 1995).
11. Kiyosaki, 19.
12. Jose, pp. 206–207.
13. Vicente Lim, *To Inspire and to Lead*, 98.
14. Jose, 207. *Bulletin*, 1 November 1941.
15. Sayre speech, 21 October 1941. Sayre Papers, Box 16, Manuscript Division, Library of Congress. *New York Times*, 23 October 1941.
16. Dufault, pp. 403–404.

17. James, Vol. I, 616.
18. Pedro Picornell, *The Remedios Hospital 1942–1945*. Unpublished Paper.
19. James, Vol. 1, 616.
20. Gole, 158.
21. Craven and Cate, 176.
22. Brereton, pp. 18–19, Pogue II 188, Manchester 220.
23. Brereton Diaries, 19. Following organization on 9 March 1942, the Army Air Corps became the Army Air Force.
24. Leutze, 218.
25. Brereton, 22.
26. James, Vol. I, 612.
27. Brereton, 21.
28. RG 2, Box 3. MacArthur Memorial Archive.
29. Roosevelt to Sayre, 25 November 1941. Box 7, Francis B. Sayre Papers. Manuscript Division, Library of Congress.
30. Charles A. Beard, *President Roosevelt and the Coming of War, 1941,* (Yale, 1948).
31. Morton, 71.
32. Sayre, 221.
33. James, Vol. I, pp. 615–616.
34. Memorandum of conversation, Quezon and Buss. Box 9, Francis B. Sayre Papers. Manuscript Division, Library of Congress.
35. Quezon speech at University of the Philippines, 28 November 1941. Box 7, Francis B. Sayre Papers. Manuscript Division, Library of Congress.
36. Sayre to MacArthur, 27 November 1941. Box 2, RG 2. MacArthur Memorial Archives.
37. MacArthur to Sayre, 28 November 1941. Box 2, RG 2. MacArthur Memorial Archives.
38. Sutherland to Wainwright, 28 November 1941. Box 2, RG 2. MacArthur Memorial Archives.
39. James, Vol. I, pp. 603–604. Lamon Bay became a major Japanese landing area.
40. The artillery destined for the Mindanao/Visayan force was lost on 17 December when *SS Corregidor* blew up in a minefield at the entrance to Manila Bay. John Gordon, "The Best Arm We Had," *Field Artillery Journal,* (November–December 1984).
41. James, Vol. I, 601.
42. Jose, 205.
43. James, Vol. I, 601.
44. Ibid.
45. Gordon, *The Best Arm We Had.*

46. Coox's (tr) of Saburo Hayashi, pp. 33–34.
47. James, Vol. I, 615.
48. Adjutant General for MacArthur, 26 November 1941. MacArthur Memorial Archives.
49. MacArthur to CinC Singapore, 2 December 1941. MacArthur Memorial Archives.
50. USAFFE to CO 200th Coast Arty. MacArthur Memorial Archives.
51. Alfonso J. Aluit, *Corregidor,* (Manila, 1949), 11,
52. James, Vol. I, 609.
53. Adjutant General from MacArthur, 27 November 1941. Box 2, RG 2. MacArthur Memorial Archives.
54. MacArthur to Marshall, 1 December 1941. Box 2, RG 2. MacArthur Memorial Archives.
55. Michael Schaller, General Douglas MacArthur and the Politics of the Pacific War in Günther Bischof and Robert L. Dupont (eds), The Pacific War Revisited (Baton Rouge, 1997), 24. This was unlikely to have been a substantive declaration but rather the defensive statement of a leader found to have been unprepared.
56. Coox's (tr) of Saburo Hayashi, 33.
57. Leutze, 224.
58. On 4 August 1964, President Lyndon B. Johnson ordered strikes against North Vietnamese ports in retaliation for an alleged attack on U.S. destroyers operating in the Gulf of Tonkin.
59. Elphick, pp. 291–292.
60. Wilkinson detail based upon a synthesis of information in Elphick, pp. 293–295.
61. Craven and Cate, 191. James, Vol. I, 618.
62. USAFFE to Commander Harbor Defenses, 5 December 1941. MacArthur Memorial Archives.
63. MacArthur to Adjutant General, 5 December 1941. MacArthur Memorial Archives.
64. MacArthur to Marshall. Letter of 29 November 1941. MacArthur Memorial Archives.
65. Brady to MacArthur. Proposed Installations and Facilities for FEAF. 21 November 1941. MacArthur Memorial Archives
66. Interview Morton/Sutherland. Morton Papers. Military History Institute.
67. Manchester, 221.
68. *Reminiscences,* 113.
69. *Magic,* Vol. IV, 17 October 1941–7 December 1941, pp. 118–119, 141.
70. Marshall to MacArthur. RG 2. 5 December 1941. MacArthur Memorial Archives.
71. Leutze, 225.

72. Leutze, 225.
73. Hart. Narrative of Events. 34–36.
74. Radio Marshall to MacArthur, 7 December 1941. MacArthur Memorial Archives. The signal was dispatched at 12:05 p.m., 7 December, Washington time and would have arrived in Manila 01:30 a.m., 8 December.
75. John Toland, *The Rising Sun,* (New York, 1970), 197.
76. Brereton Diaries, pp. 37–38. Morton, *Fall of the Philippines,* 73.
77. Morton, *The Fall of the Philippines,* 79.
78. Papers of Richard K. Sutherland. Box 1, RG-30. MacArthur Memorial Archives.
79. *Reminiscences,* 117.
80. Manchester, 230.
81. James, Vol. I, 609.

9: "ONE OF THE MORE SHOCKING DEFECTS OF THE WAR"

1. Hayashi, 36.
2. Morton, *The Fall of the Philippines,* pp. 78–79.
3. *Reminiscences,* 117.
4. Sayre, 223.
5. Manuel Quezon, *The Good Fight,* pp. 181–182.
6. Quezon, *The Good Fight,* 185 and 187.
7. Craven and Cate, 203.
8. Ibid., 204.
9. Quoted in Costello, 24.
10. Manchester, pp. 230–231.
11. Manchester, 231.
12. Brereton Diaries, pp. 38–39.
13. *New York Times,* 27 September 1946.
14. Interview Morton and Sutherland. Morton Papers. Military History Institute.
15. Craven and Cate, 206.
16. Ibid., 207.
17. Craven and Cate, Footnote 31, p 687.
18. Stanley Weintraub, *Long Day's Journey into War: 7 December 1941,* (New York, 1991), 345.
19. Craven and Cate.
20. Ibid., Footnote 30, 687.
21. Weintraub, 453. Quoting Koichi Shimada.
22. Saburo Sakai, *Samurai. Flying the Zero in WWII with Japan's Fighter Ace,* (New York, 1963), pp. 50–51.

23. James, Vol. II, 8.
24. Craven and Cate, pp. 208–209.
25. Ibid., 210.
26. Morris, 84.
27. Saburo Sakai, pp. 50–51.
28. Morris, 87.
29. James, Vol. II, 3. Wainwright, however, said that the attack was over in 15 minutes.
30. Jonathan Wainwright, *General Wainwright's Story*, (New York, 1946), pp. 22–23.
31. Craven and Cate, 213. James, Vol. II, 4.
32. James, Vol. II, pp. 5–6.
33. Craven and Cate, 205. Quoted in Walter D. Edmonds.
34. John Gunther, *Roosevelt in Retrospect*, (New York, 1950), 324.
35. James, Vol. II, 6.
36. Pogue II, 234.
37. Brereton Diaries, 50.
38. MacArthur to Arnold, 10 December 1941. RG 2, Box 1, MacArthur Memorial Archives.
39. Brereton Diaries, 52.
40. H.H. Arnold, *Global Mission*, (London, 1951), 164.
41. Craven and Cate. Footnote 29, 687.
42. Rogers, 98.
43. Rogers, 99.
44. Interrogation of Colonel Monjuro Akiyama of Third Department (Army Organisation), Imperial General Headquarters. G-2 Hist Div. GHQ Far East Command. Transcript in Army Historical Institute.
45. Ibid.
46. Brereton Diaries, 39.
47. Hanson W. Baldwin, *Great Mistakes of the War*, (New York, 1950), 70.
48. MacArthur to Marshall, 1 December 1941. RG-2, MacArthur Memorial Archives.
49. Larrabee, 317.
50. Morton interview with MacArthur, 8 February 1954. Morton Papers. Military History Institute. James Vol. II, 11.
51. Interview James/Bulkeley, 2 July 1971. James, Vol. II, 15.
52. C.L. Sulzberger, *A Long Row of Candles Memoirs and Diaries (1934–1954)*, (New York, 1969), 672.
53. Bartsch. Foreword by Herbert Ellis.
54. *Reminiscences*, 120.
55. Lee and Henschel, 139.
56. Ibid., 117.

57. Interview, Mrs. Henry R. Luce with Major General Lewis Brereton, April 1942. Willoughby Papers. Center for Military History. James, Vol. II, pp. 830–831. Costello, 23.
58. Brereton ultimately commanded the First Allied Airborne Army in Europe in the ill-fated Operation Market Garden, September 1944.
59. Interview General Sutherland by Morton. Morton Papers. Military History Institute.
60. *Reminiscences,* 120.
61. Morton interview with MacArthur, 8 February 1954. Morton Papers. Military History Institute. James Vol. II, 11.
62. This is, however, a relatively balanced argument. It could be said that any offensive action taken against the Japanese at this stage of the war might have considerably altered their analysis about the feasibility of diverting resources from homeland defense to the conquest of the resource area.
63. Paul, *Sing High,* pp. 17–18.
64. René J. Francillon, *Japanese Aircraft of the Pacific War,* (London, 1970).
65. Walter D. Edmonds, *They Fought With What They Had: The Story of the Army Air Forces in the Southwest Pacific, 1941–1942,* (Boston, 1951), 331.
66. Curiously the other pilot's name was Mueller. Cursory inquiry reveals there to have been no specific policy of sending American servicemen of German origin to the Pacific. It just appears that there was a disproportionately large number engaged in the Pacific War as opposed to Europe.
67. Edmonds, 186–188. Christopher Shores and Brian Cull with Yasuho Izawa, "Bloody Shambles: The First Comprehensive Account of Air Operations Over South East Asia December 1941–April 1942," Volume One: *The Drift to War to the Fall of Singapore,* (London, 1992), pp. 195–196. According to Shores' account, the attacking Zeros were A6Ms from the 3rd Kokutai (attached to the 21st Flotilla).
68. MacArthur to Adjutant General, 9 December 1941. MacArthur Memorial Archives.
69. Sayre, 223.
70. Duncan Anderson, "Douglas MacArthur and the Fall of the Philippines, 1941–1942," in Brian Bond (ed), *Fallen Stars,* (London, 1991), 164.
71. Claire L. Chennault, *Way of a Fighter: The Memoirs of Claire Lee Chennault,* (New York, 1949), 124. Manchester, 232.
72. James, Vol. II. Footnote 14, 831. Rogers, 100.

10: TO CORREGIDOR

1. Morton, *Fall of the Philippines,* 98.
2. Ibid., 103.

3. Quezon, *The Good Fight*, 189.
4. Leutze, 233.
5. Gilbert Cant, *America's Navy in World War II*, (New York, 1943), 87.
6. Winston S. Churchill, *The Second World War: The Grand Alliance*, (Boston, 1951), 619.
7. Leutze, 233.
8. Leutze, 234.
9. Morton, *The Fall of the Philippines*, 98.
10. Interview Morton/Sutherland, 12 November 1946. Morton, 121.
11. Edward Jablonski, *Flying Fortress*, (U.S.A., 1965), 56.
12. John H. Mitchell, "The First Bombing Mission of the Army Air Corps in WWII," *AAHS Journal*, Vol. 34, No 1, Spring 89.
13. Saburo Sakai, pp. 54–56.
14. Mitchell, *The First Bombing Mission of the Army Air Corps*.
15. USAFFE Daily Communiques. 22 January 1942. U.S. Military History Institute. General Marshall wrote to Captain Kelly's widow on 18 December expressing his "deepest sympathy" on the loss of her husband whilst "having struck a fatal blow and left an heritage of valor." Larry I. Bland (ed), *The Papers of George Catlett Marshall*, Vol. 3, "The Right Man for the Job," 7 December 1941–31 May 1943, (Baltimore and London, 1991). The Army Air Forces Chief, quoted in the *New York Times* of 19 December 1941, was of the opinion that Kelly's "feat will live in the history of the Army Air Forces, because he and his crew proved that the most powerful naval vessels afloat cannot operate with impunity within the range of our bombers and the flaming courage of our airmen."
16. MacArthur to Marshall, 10 December 1941. Box 2, MacArthur Memorial Archives.
17. MacArthur to Generalissimo Chiang Kai Shek, 13 December 1941. MacArthur Memorial Archives.
18. Marshall to MacArthur, 11 December 1941. Box 2, RG 2, MacArthur Memorial Archives.
19. Brereton, 51.
20. Gavin Long, *MacArthur—as Military Commander*, (London, 1969).
21. Eisenhower, *At Ease*, pp. 246–7.
22. Morison, pp. 165–166.
23. Duncan Anderson. Unopposed: Patani, Singora (8 December), Guam, Vigan, Appari (10 December), Legaspi (12 December). Opposed: Kotabharu (8 December), Wake (12 December), Hong Kong (17 December).
24. Morton, 122.
25. Clark Lee, *They Call it Pacific*, (New York, 1943), 73. Interview Clark Lee/Morton, April 1951. Morton, 110.
26. John E. Olson, *Anywhere—Anytime. The History of the 57th Infantry (PS)*.

27. Brereton, 51.
28. Cant. 84.
29. Morison, 173.
30. Ibid., 97.
31. Dwight D. Eisenhower, *Crusade in Europe,* (New York, 1948), 19.
32. Manchester, pp. 275–6.
33. Beck, 34. Pogue II, 242. Manchester, 276.
34. James, Vol. II, 16.
35. Brereton, pp. 61–62.
36. Morton, Fall of the Philippines, 145.
37. Hart. Memorandum on last two interviews with General MacArthur, 23 December 1941. Hart Papers.
38. Leutze, 239.
39. Leutze, 240.
40. Ibid.
41. Commander in Chief U.S. Asiatic Fleet to Commanding General U.S. Army Forces in the Far East. Move of Command Post of Commander in Chief, U.S. Asiatic Fleet. 25 December 1941. MacArthur Memorial Archives.
42. Sayre, 224.
43. Morton, 116.
44. Morton, 119.
45. Treasury Department to Commanding General USAFFE, 17 December 1941. MacArthur Memorial Archives.
46. Sayre to Treasury Department, 19 December 1941. MacArthur Memorial Archives.
47. Dufault, 417.
48. Sayre, *Glad Adventure,* 225.
49. Dufault, 418.
50. Ibid.
51. Marshall to MacArthur, 24 December 1941. MacArthur to Marshall, 30 December 1941. MacArthur Memorial Archives.
52. Agoncillo, 9.
53. Quezon, pp. 196–198.
54. Sayre, 225.
55. Quezon, 198.
56. Steinberg, 31.
57. Agoncillo, 11.
58. Steinberg, pp. 32–33. Agoncillo, 13. Friend, pp. 211–212.
59. Saulo, pp. 98–99.
60. Morton, *Strategy,* pp. 158–159 and 187. Memorandum Gerow for Chief of Staff, 3 January 1942. Relief of the Philippines. WPD 4639-3. Library of Congress.

61. Stimson Diary, 2 January 1942. Yale. Friend, 209.
62. Stimson Diary, 5 January 1942. Friend, 210.
63. Directive from the Secretary of War to Adjutant General, G-4/33861 under cover of CGS 18136–161 dated 19 December 1941, to General Brett and signed by Deputy Chief of Staff General Moore. Lester J. Whitlock Papers. Army Historical Institute.
64. Beck, pp. 72–3.
65. Churchill to Lord Privy Seal, 28 December 1941. Chartwell 20/50. The Prime Minister's "Grey Telegrams," December 15, 1941 to January 17, 1942. Grey No 141. Churchill Archives, Cambridge.
66. Churchill to Curtin, 4 January 1942. Grey No 209. Ibid.
67. Beth Day Romulo, 105.
68. Sayre, pp. 226–228.
69. Agoncillo, pp. 13–14.
72. Manchester, 250.
73 Beth Day Romulo, pp. 105–106.
74. Manchester, 239.
75. Carlos Romulo, *I Saw the Fall of the Philippines*, (Garden City, 1942), 28.
76. Agoncillo, 14.
77. Rogers, 119.
70. Interview Manuel Quezon II and author, 20 August 1997.
71. Sayre, 229.

11: ". . . THEIR FREEDOM WILL BE REDEEMED"

1. Morton, *The Fall of the Philippines*, 123.
2. Leutze, pp. 242–243.
3. Clay Blair, *Silent Victory. The U.S. Submarine War Against Japan*, (Philadelphia, 1975), 147.
4. Blair, 147.
5. Blair, 148.
6. Blair, 159.
7. Statement of Rear Admiral John Wilkes. Morison, 166.
8. Cant, 105.
9. Leutze, 242.
10. Cant, 105.
11. Morton, 126.
12. Leutze, 241.
13. Blair, 160.
14. Morison, 166.
15. Morton, pp. 125–126.
16. MacArthur to AGWAR, 22 December 1941, RG-2, MacArthur Memorial Archives.

17. Beck, 32.
18. Louis Morton Papers, 12 November 1946. Box 2. Interview Morton/ Sutherland. Military History Institute.
19. James, Vol. II, 28.
20. Rogers, 116.
21. Leutze, 242.
22. Louis Morton Papers. 12 November 1946. Box 2. Interview Morton/ Sutherland. Military History Institute.
23. J. Michael Miller, 20.
24. Hunt, 196.
25. The Richard C. Mallonée Papers, p. 85. Military History Institute.
26. Richard C. Mallonée, *The Naked Flagpole,* (San Rafael, 1980), 20.
27. Mallonée, *Naked Flagpole,* 22.
28. Mallonée, Ibid., pp. 29–30.
29. Mallonée, *Naked Flagpole,* 32.
30. GHQ FEC G-2 Historical Section. Interrogation of Maeda, 10 May 1947, NYK Building Tokyo. Military History Institute.
31. Brigadier General James R.N. Weaver. Report of Operations of the Provisional Tank Group, United States Forces in the Far East, 1941–1942.
32. Bruce Jacobs, *The Evolution of Tank Units in the pre-WWII National Guard and the Defense of Bataan.* Mil Coll & Hist 38 (Fall 1986), 128.
33. This assertion that the Japanese would have had to surrender is unlikely since it is contrary to their military code which was rigorously observed at the beginning of the war. An American attack at this juncture, however, would have made the Japanese position tenuous.
34. Maeda interrogation, 10 May 1947.
35. Morton, 131.
36. Jacobs, 129. Morton, 134. Morton says this action involved Company C.
37. Morton, 136.
38. Morton, 133.
39. Message MacArthur to AG, 21 December 1941. MacArthur Memorial Archives.
40. War Diary of General Clyde Selleck, 15.
41. Jonathan M. Wainwright, *General Wainwright's Story,* 36.
42. Edwin Price Ramsey and Stephen J. Rivele, *Lieutenant Ramsey's War. From Horse Soldier to Guerilla Commander,* (New York, 1990), 53.
43. Morton, 138.
44. Wainwright, 39.
45. Long, 67.
46. MacArthur to Marshall, 22 December 1941. Box 2, MacArthur Memorial Archives.
47. James, Vol. II, 28.
48. Morton, 139.

49. Mallonée, 36.
50. ·Morton, 141.
51. The details of the defense at Mauban are taken from Ricardo Jose's *Beach Defense: The First Regular Division at Mauban, December 23–26, 1941.* Bulletin of the American Historical Collection (Apr–Jun, 1989), pp. 7–24.
52. Steinberg, 30. Beck, 24–25. Manchester, 252. MacArthur also allocated cottages to Quezon and Sayre but they were soon abandoned as being too dangerous.
53. Colonel Collier, quoted in James, Vol. II, 28.
54. John W. Whitman, "Decision that Starved an Army," *Army Logistician,* (Mar–Apr 1995), pp. 36–39.
55. Anderson, 178.
56. Drake's comments on Morton's draft *Fall of the Philippines.* Box 2, page 2. Military History Institute.
57. Ibid.
58. Ramsey and Rivele, 53.
59. James, Vol. II, 33.
60. Anderson, 178.
61. Mallonée, 61.
62. Olson, 48. Olson was F.D. Roosevelt's son-in-law.
63. Drake—comments on the Morton draft, 2.
64. On 23 December 1941, for example, the House of Representatives congratulated MacArthur on "the magnificent fight you are making" and concluded, "We are proud of the glorious struggle you are waging against the enemies not only of our country but the enemies of our Christian civilization." Box 2. MacArthur Memorial Archives.
65. Ernest B. Miller, *Bataan Uncensored,* (Long Prairie, 1949), 75.
66. Stauffer, 11. James, Vol. II, 32.
67. MacArthur to Commanding General South Luzon Force, 28 December 1941, and MacArthur to Commanding General North Luzon Force and South Luzon Force, 29 December 1941. Box 2, MacArthur Memorial Archives.
68. Morton, 178.
69. Morton, 195.
70. The 70,000 pesos contingency fund was a sum of money which had been available to the Governor General and which was included in the emoluments negotiated with Quezon at the time of MacArthur's recruitment.
71. Interview Agoncillo/Vargas, 16 February 1979. Agoncillo, 8. Lepanto was a mining endeavor.
72. Drake comments on Morton draft, p3. Military History Institute.
73. Stauffer, 9.
74 Stauffer, 13.
75. Stauffer, 13. Additional gasoline in 55 gallon drums was taken into

Bataan under cover of darkness from some 100 loaded barges anchored between Corregidor and Bataan.

76. These figures are Morton's (p.367). They are 10,000 less than the numbers declared by General Wainwright immediately prior to the fall of Bataan. Please refer to Footnote No 2 to Chapter 15. In a book written by a Colonel Ongapuco, he gives the Bataan strength at 3 April 1942 as 11,796 Americans, 66,000 Filipinos (77,796) which is close to Morton's figure. Wainwright's figure of 90,000 seems too high but not if the 26,000 refugees are included. USAFFE did feed the majority. A number of civilians brought their own food stock and some brought their own transportation. Most lived in the mountains and jungles, in the rear, thus facing the same problems of hunger, hygiene and disease as the others. Many were relatives of officers and soldiers so the military was somewhat obliged to feed or otherwise take care of them. The U.S. National Archives have many of the strength reports of the all-American units, the last of which went out from Corregidor on the last two Catalinas to fly in and out in May 1942. The Philippine Army records were burned during the surrender apart from those captured by the Japanese and ultimately lost at the time of their defeat in 1945.

77. Stauffer, 13. James, Vol. II, 35.
78. Whitman, *Decision that Starved an Army*, 39.
79. Alfred D. Chandler (ed), *The Papers of Dwight David Eisenhower*, (Baltimore, 1970), 21.
80. Morton, 154.
81. Marshall to MacArthur, 27 December 1941. MacArthur Memorial Archives.
82. *New York Times*, 29 and 30 December 1941.
83. James, interview with Johnson. James, Vol. II, 37.
84. James, Vol. II, 43.
85. Anderson, pp. 176–177. The blowing of the bridges was delayed momentarily to allow time for a platoon of demolition engineers to appear from the south.
86. Morton, 230. Rogers, 117.
87. Re-inauguration of Manuel Quezon, 30 December 1941. RG-2, Box 2, MacArthur Memorial Archives. Manchester, 259. Peret, 262. Huff, 41. Sayre, 234. Quezon, 327–28.
88. Agoncillo, 16.
89. Maeda interrogation, 10 May 1947.
90. Maeda was later sacked as Chief of Staff. He gave two reasons for this. First, he opposed the attack on Bataan, preferring to isolate it and, second, he was seen as being too soft—e.g. in his failure to occupy Philippine Government buildings and General MacArthur's Headquarters in the Manila Hotel.

91. Morton, *Fall of the Philippines,* 210.
92. MacArthur, *Reminiscences,* 125.
93. Morton, 166.
94. Military History Institute, Carlisle Barracks.
95. Rogers, 129. Manchester, 255.
96. Beck, 48.
97. Huff, 43. Manchester, 255.
98. Sutherland, interview with Morton, 12 November 1946. Box 2, Military History Institute, 21.
99. See, for example, Jay Luvaas (ed), *Dear Miss Em: General Eichelberger's War in the Pacific, 1942–1945,* (Westport, 1972).
100. Sutherland had an affair in Australia, ignoring MacArthur's order to desist.
101. Sutherland, interview with Morton, 21.
102. Anderson, 184.

12: "A TIME WHEN MEN MUST DIE"

1. Morton, 245. James II, 46.
2. The North Luzon Force therefore became I Corps under Wainwright and the South Luzon Force II Corps under Parker.
3. Morton, 247.
4. Mallonée, 84.
5. H.K. Johnson, "Defense Along the Abucay Line," *Military Review* 28, (February 1949), 44.
6. Olson, 62.
7. Olson, 65.
8. Interrogation of General Maeda.
9. Manchester, 247.
10. Ickes Papers, 14 and 21 December 1942.
11. Courtney Whitney, *MacArthur: His Rendezvous With History,* (New York, 1956), 27.
12. Marshall to MacArthur, 8 February 1942. RG-2, Folder 1, COS, Radios dealing with Plans and Policies Nov 41–Feb 42. MacArthur Memorial Archives.
13. Ferrell (ed), *Eisenhower Diaries,* pp. 43–44 and 46–47.
14. Horsey, 257. Lee and Henschel, 151. Manchester, pp. 273–4.
15. Elting E. Morison, *Turmoil and Tradition: A Study of the Life and Times of Henry L. Stimson,* (Boston, 1960), 550
16. Diary entry, 2 January 1942. Stimson Papers.
17. Stimson and Bundy, 601.
18. Churchill to CinC and Governor Hong Kong, 21 December 1941. Grey Signal No 36. Churchill Archives, Cambridge.

19. Eisenhower, *At Ease,* 247.

20. Petillo, 204.

21. No doubt, MacArthur justified the award as having been part of his contract on appointment and related to defense expenditures. $^{46}/_{100}$ths of $8 million a year for ten years is $368,000 plus loss of salary and expenses of $33,000 a year, 1942–1945 $132,000, a total of $500,000.

22. RG-1, Box 3, Folio 8, "Exec Order #1." MacArthur Memorial Archives.

23. Schaller, 59.

24. Memorandum for the Record, 20 June 1942. Dwight D. Eisenhower Papers. Dwight D. Eisenhower Presidential Library, Abilene, Kansas. Perret, 272.

25. Larrabee, 315.

26. Carol Petillo, "Douglas MacArthur and Manuel Quezon," *Pacific Historical Review,* (February 1979), pp. 107–17. Larrabee, 315.

27. Kiyosaki, 89.

28. C.A. Willoughby and J. Chamberlain, *MacArthur 1941–1951,* (London, 1956), pp. 37 and 43.

29. Quezon, *The Good Fight,* 245.

30. Chynoweth, 194.

31. Ramsey and Rivele, 61.

32. Miller, 193–194. This song made its first appearance in February 1942.

33. Toland, 310.

34. Hanson W. Baldwin, *Great Mistakes of the War,* (New York, 1949), 73. Manchester, 267.

35. James, II, 68.

36. Manchester, 266.

37. Beck, 67.

38. Morton, 274. Manchester, 266. Beck, 67.

39. Manchester, 266.

40. James, II, 53.

41. Interview Sutherland/Morton, 14 November 1946. In Morton, 274.

42. Interview Sutherland/Morton, 12 November 1946. Box 2. Morton Papers. U.S. Army Military History Unit.

43. Morton, 274

44. MacArthur's personal file has many resolutions drawn up by Filipino units, signed by all members, pledging undying loyalty and everything else to MacArthur. "Mabuhay Macarsar" is a form of greeting meaning "Long life MacArthur," or something similar.

45. MacArthur, *Reminiscences,* pp. 135–6.

46. James, II, 64.

47. HQ USAFFE to AGWAR, 27 January 1942. RG-2, Box 2, Folder 4, 23 Jan 42–11 Apr 42. MacArthur Memorial Archives. MacArthur, *Reminiscences,* pp. 129–130.

48. Ibid.
49. MacArthur, *Reminiscences*, 130.
50. Manchester, 269.
51. HQ USAFFE, 16 January 1942. RG-2, Box 2, Folder 3. MacArthur Personal File, 25 Dec 41–22 Jan 42. MacArthur Memorial Archives.
52. HQ USAFFE, 15 January 1942. RG-2, Box 2, Folder 3. MacArthur Personal File, 25 Dec 41–22 Jan 42. MacArthur Memorial Archives.
53. Stimson Diaries, 8 April 1942.
54. Olson, 69. Olson would not have been aware of the degree of pressure which the lend lease program was placing on shipping and ammunition.
55. Morton, pp. 399–400.
56. Pogue, 245.
57. Don Lohbeck, *Patrick J. Hurley,* (Chicago, 1956), 164. Pogue, 246.
58. Romulo, *I Saw the Fall of the Philippines,* 104.
59. Chynoweth, pp. 226–7.
60. Whitman, 407.
61. Romulo, 104.
62. Morton, 396.
63. Morton, 251.
64. MacArthur to Commanding General Second Corps, 15 January 1942. MacArthur Memorial Archives.
65. Morton, 248.
66. Morton, 280–281.
67. HQ USAFFE Field Order No 9, 22 January 1942.
68. HQ USAFFE, 24 January 1942. MacArthur Memorial Archives.
69. Manchester, 268. Morton, 295. RG-2 13.2, Folder 4. Mac Personal 23 Jan-11 Apr 42. MacArthur Memorial Archives.
70. *Reminiscences*, 132.
71. *Reminiscences*, 133.
72. Morton, 295.
73. Radio MacArthur to Marshall 25 January 1942. Quoted in Whitman, 246.
74. Radio MacArthur to Marshall, 27 January 1942. Quoted in Whitman, 246. Beck, 75. RG-2, Box 2, Folder 6, "Opns. Radios to War Dept," 8 Dec 41–23 Feb 42. MacArthur Memorial Archives.
75. Beck, 78.
76. *Reminiscences*, pp. 133–134.
77. John W. Whitman, *Bataan Our Last Ditch,* (New York, 1990), pp. 247–8.
78. Morton, 300.
79. Frank O. Hough et al, 176. From Bridget Rept; Capt E.L. Sackett USN, *History of the USS Canopus*, 28 Apr 47, NHD, 8.
80. Morton, 303.
81. Morton, 299.

82. Morton, 301.
83. Official Army Register, 1947. Morton, 305.
84. Morton, 305.
85. Frank O. Hough et al, pp. 179–180. Morton, pp. 303–324.
86. Wainwright to MacArthur, 27 January 1942. RG-2, Box 3. Chief of Staff Radios and Letters dealing with Plans and Policies. MacArthur Memorial Archives.
87. Interview Sutherland/Morton, 12 November 1946. Box 2, Morton Papers. Military History Institute.
88. MacArthur to Wainwright, 28 January 1942. RG-2, Box 3. MacArthur Memorial Archives.
89. James, 57.
90. Interview Sutherland/Morton, 12 November 1946. Box 2, Morton Papers. Military History Institute.
91. Huff, 8. Manchester, 285.
92. Manchester, 285.
93. Marshall to MacArthur, 14 February 1942. MacArthur Memorial Archives.

13: "I WILL BRING YOU IN TRIUMPH ON THE POINTS OF MY BAYONETS TO MANILA"

1. Saulo, 109.
2. Salvador P. Lopez, *Elpidio Quirino. The Judgement of History,* (Manila, 1990), pp. 36–37.
3. Agoncillo, 37.
4. Official Gazette, Philippine Executive Commission, Vol. I, No 1, pp. 16–17. Saulo, 110.
5. Friend, 214.
6. Friend, 216.
7. Documents on the Japanese occupation of the Philippines, with notes by Mauro Garcia, (Manila: Philippine Historical Association, 1965), pp. 18–24. Saulo, 117.
8. Vargas broadcast over Station KZRH, Manila, 31 January 1942. Friend, 216. RG-2, Box 2. MacArthur Memorial Archives.
9. James II, 92.
10. Manchester, pp. 278–9.
11. Interview author/Manuel Quezon II, 20 August 1997.
12. Quezon, 255–6.
13. Quezon, 259. Beck, 80.
14. Stimson Diary, 29 January 1942.
15. James II, 84.
16. Quezon, 261–4.
17. Beck, 82.

18. Ibid.

19. Roosevelt was the eldest son of President Theodore Roosevelt who had been Governor General of the Philippines 1932–1933.

20. Aguinaldo to MacArthur. Radio broadcast of 1 February 1942. RG-2, Box 3, MacArthur Memorial Archives. Quezon refers to this broadcast as having been made on 6 February 1942, which is probably correct. See Quezon, p.265.

21. Morton, 385.

22. Mallonée, 108.

23. James II, 90.

24. Schaller, 61.

25. Morris, 349.

26. Beck, 84.

27. Ibid.

28. Chronological extract of first excerpts taken from radiograms by Co-ordinator of Information, Washington, 26 February 1942 for period 27 January—24 February 1942. MacArthur Memorial Archives.

29. Beck, 89–90. Based upon interviews Beck/Clear 8 July and 10 September 1968.

30. The issue was first raised on 13 January 1942.

31. MacArthur to Marshall, 4 February 1942. RG-30, Box 1, Folder 9. Suth Secret File Corresp USAFFE. MacArthur Memorial Archives.

32. Pogue, 246. Marshall to MacArthur, 8 February 1942. RG-30, Box 1, Folder 9. Sutherland Secret File Corresp. USAFFE. MacArthur Memorial Archives.

33. Willoughby and Chamberlain, *MacArthur 1941–1951*, pp. 55–56. Manchester, 279. Beck, 93.

34. Quezon, 269.

35. Quezon, 270.

36. Dufault, 436.

37. Carlos Romulo, *I Walked With Heroes*, (New York, 1961), 220.

38. Romulo, pp. 220–221.

39. Romulo, 222.

40. Dufault, 433.

41. Teodoro Agoncillo, *The Fateful Years. Japan's Adventure in the Philippines, 1941–1945*, Volume 1, (Quezon City, 1965), pp. 259–60.

42. Friend, pp. 220–221.

43. Stimson Diary, 9 February 1942.

44. Super secret file of Philippine situation. WD Records Br AGO. Historical Records Section. WD CSA/381 Philippines (2–17–42) (sent 11 February 1942).

45. Pogue. Interview with Marshall, 14 November 1956, 248.

46. Friend, 221.

47. Roosevelt to MacArthur and Roosevelt to Quezon, 10 February 1942. RG-2, Box 3, Folder 1. COS, Radios Dealing with Plans and Policies. MacArthur Memorial Archives.

48. Stimson Diary, 9 February 1942. Stimson and Bundy, *On Active Service*, 404.

49. Roosevelt to Quezon, 10 February 1942. RG-2, Box 3, Folder 1. MacArthur Memorial Archives.

50. James K. Eyre, *The Roosevelt MacArthur Conflict*, (Chambersbury, Pen, 1950), pp. 42–43.

51. Roosevelt to MacArthur, 10 February 1942. RG-2, Box 3, Folder 1. MacArthur Memorial Archives.

52. Quezon, 275.

53. Stimson Diary, 12 February 1942.

54. *New York Times*, 13 February 1942, as quoted in Beck, 111.

55. Arthur H. Vandenberg Jr (ed), *The Private Papers of Senator Vandenberg*, (Boston, 1952), 76. Schaller, 61.

56. *New York Times*, 14 February 1942, as quoted in Beck, 114.

57. Ferrell, 148.

58. Saulo, 123.

59. Steinberg, 43.

60. Rogers, pp. 166–168.

61. Schaller, 61.

62. Carlos Romulo, *I Saw the Fall of the Philippines*, pp. 116–117.

63. Beck, 116.

64. Clay Blair, 174.

65. Interview author/Manuel Quezon II, Manila, 20 August 1997.

66. Quezon, 277.

67. Chynoweth, 239.

68. Sayre's debate with Hart, which drew Presidential intervention, was well advanced by 14 February when Hart told Sayre that "accommodations are insufficient for your staff. Must limit your party to total of four, I must not unduly crowd submarine officers, and must evacuate additional naval personnel much needed in other theaters of war." Sayre Papers, Folder 4. Manuscript Division, Library of Congress.

69. Sayre advised MacArthur on 17 April 1942 that the trunk had been safely deposited with the bank.

70. Sayre, 241.

71. Romulo, *I Saw the Fall of the Philippines*, 117.

14: "I SHALL RETURN"

1. Morton, 326.

2. Hill, pp. 6–7.

3. Morton, pp. 336–340.
4. Hill, pp. 16–17.
5. Whitman, 362.
6. Morris, 329. Eric Morris' oral interview tapes are held by the Imperial War Museum, London.
7. Morton, 345.
8. James, II, 61.
9. Mallonée, 103.
10. Whitman, 377.
11. Whitman, 371.
12. D. Clayton James, *South to Bataan, North to Mukden: The Prison Diary of Brigadier General W.E. Brougher,* (Georgia, 1971), pp. 25–26. Whitman, 365. James II, 59.
13. Whitman, 367.
14. Pfc. Robert Brown quoted in Donald Knox, *Death March. The Survivors of Bataan,* (San Diego, 1981), 76.
15. James II, 62.
16. Mallonée, 85.
17. Carl E. Engelhart, *Trapped on Corregidor.* Unpublished manuscript. Military History Institute, Carlisle. 26.
18. Hill, pp. 22–23.
19. To alleviate the Philippine Army/Scouts pay discrepancy, Quezon issued an executive order whilst in Corregidor to equalize the pay, but it never came into effect.
20. Lester I. Tenney, *My Hitch in Hell. The Bataan Death March,* (Washington, 1995), 30. When Bataan surrendered in April, the *Canopus* was scuttled midway between the peninsula and Corregidor.
21. Mills to Whitman, quoted in Whitman, 415.
22. Morris, pp. 351–2.
23. Whitman, 394.
24. Hill, pp. 33–35.
25. Ibid.
26. James II, 63.
27. Morris, pp. 335–336.
28. Romulo, *I Saw the Fall of the Philippines,* 80.
29. Whitman, pp. 376–7.
30. Aluit, 42.
31. James II, 71. Nevertheless, these early bombardments of Corregidor were slight in comparison with that endured from mid-March until the fall of Corregidor. On 15 March, 240mm howitzers were added to the inventory of bombarding artillery.
32. Mallonée, 109.
33. Ibid.

34. In January 1942, the 6th, 7th and 9th Australian Divisions were in the Middle East. The 8th Division had been lost in Malaya. The slow withdrawal of the 6th and 7th Divisions began in January 1942 and the 9th remained and fought at El Alamein. From December 1941 to late June 1942, there were no experienced formations in Australia.

35. Winston S. Churchill, *The Second World War. Their Finest Hour*, (Boston, 1949), pp. 107–108.

36. Ibid., 108.

37. Memo. Romulo to Sutherland, 26 February 1942. Propaganda File. MacArthur Memorial Archives.

38. James II, 91.

39. MacArthur to Marshall. Radiogram 341. 22 February 1942. Philippine Islands, January to May 1942. F.D. Roosevelt Library.

40. Beck, 119.

41. Beck, 121.

42. Ferrell, 49. Morton, pp. 359–60. Larrabee, 321.

43. Wavell, who was MacArthur's superior commander, sent MacArthur a personal message on 25 February: "My inability to maintain the area or assist your gallant defense is a matter of deep regret." MacArthur Memorial Archives. Beck, 122.

44. A Washington Democratic Congressman had introduced a Bill which would make MacArthur the supreme commander of America's Armed Forces.

45. Manchester, pp. 286–287.

46. Marshall to MacArthur. DTG Washington DC 0144 Feb 23, 42. RG-2 13.2 Folder 4. MacArthur Personal, 23 Jan—11 Apr 42. MacArthur Memorial Archives.

47. Huff, 50.

48. MacArthur, *Reminiscences,* 140.

49. Reference in the literature to MacArthur calling a staff meeting to air his innermost thinking and then reference here to the views of his "entire staff" appear to attribute to MacArthur a democratic sensitivity which he did not possess. What he meant by reference to his "Staff" can be found in Rogers, 186. 'Staff' was used very loosely by MacArthur, here and elsewhere. It never referred to the collectivity of the Officers assigned to him and acting formally as a body. No such staff meetings were held, especially for top secret strategic problems."

50. Ibid.

51. Ibid.

52. Beck, 127.

53. Ferrell, 49.

54. The Netherlands East Indies (NEI) was the common contemporary description of the Dutch East Indies.

55. David Thomas, *Battle of the Java Sea,* (London, 1968).

56. Winston S. Churchill, *The Second World War. The Hinge of Fate,* (Boston, 1950), pp. 132–133.

57. Ibid. Reference here to "south of combat zone" refers to the attacks made by the Japanese on 19 February 1942, and subsequently, on the Darwin area.

58. Malcolm M. Champlin. Unpublished account of Champlin's experiences in the Philippines including biography of Rear Admiral John D. Bulkeley USN. 7 December 1965. Office of Information, Internal Relations Division, Naval History Division. pp. 70–71. Beck, 135.

59 Rogers, 189.

60. Ibid.

61. RG-2 13.3 Communiqués. MacArthur Memorial Archives.

62. Romulo, *I Saw the Fall of the Philippines,* pp. 133–134. MacArthur's news was divided into two communiqués released on 4 and 5 March respectively. The communiqué of 4 March reads: "In a sudden air surprise we swept Subic Bay destroying many vessels including one of 12,000 tons, one of 8,000 tons and two motor launches of 100 tons each. Many smaller craft were damaged and large fires started on the docks of Grande Island and Olongapo followed by many heavy explosions." This communiqué is supported by a report of HQ 5th Interceptor Command dated 2 March 1942. Why had it taken two days to be released? The inkling of deception is in the 5 March communiqué. It claimed thousands of Japanese drowned. One of the ships said to have been sunk was towing barges but the report from Headquarters 5th Interceptor Command makes no mention of troops having been aboard. The claim that thousands of Japanese were drowned must have been added at superior headquarters. Source: MacArthur Memorial Archives.

63. Romulo, *I Saw the Fall of the Philippines,* pp. 133–134. RG-2 13.3. F Communiques. MacArthur Memorial Archives.

64. Craven and Cate, 405, and Footnote 6, p. 714.

65. Excerpts from Radiograms from Coordinator Office of Information, Washington DC, pertaining to General Douglas MacArthur, 9 March 1942. MacArthur Memorial Archives.

66. Manchester, 290.

67. Beck, 132.

68. Romulo, *I Saw the Fall of the Philippines,* 141.

69. In fact, *in extremis,* room could have been made available. On 3 May 1942, immediately prior to the fall of Corregidor, eleven Army nurses, one Navy nurse, a Navy wife, six Army and six Navy officers set off from Corregidor in a small boat in the early evening. Approximately 4½ miles to the north of Corregidor, "a big dark object rose up out of the water in

front of us." It was the submarine *USS Spearfish.* Lucy Wilson Jopling, *Warrior in White,* (San Antonio, 1990).

70. Morton, 360.
71. Morton, pp. 360–361.
72. Wainwright, *General Wainwright's Story,* pp. 2–4.
73. Romulo, *I Saw the Fall of the Philippines,* pp. 136–139. MacArthur was as good as his word. Romulo left Corregidor on a J2F Duck Seaplane, the *Candy Clipper.*
74. Rogers, pp. 188–189.
75. Manchester, 295.
76. MacArthur's "I shall return" message was relayed to the world from Adelaide but it is unclear where it was first delivered—Batchelor Field, Alice Springs or Adelaide.
77. In *Reminiscences,* MacArthur said he gave these words to reporters at Batchelor Field. That may be so, but he repeated them at Adelaide and it was as a result of the Adelaide Statement that "I shall return" became newsworthy.
78. MacArthur, *Reminiscences,* 145.
79. Telegram Marshall to Sutherland, 23 March 1942. MacArthur Memorial Archives. Marshall wrote: "The President has this date approved the award of a Medal of Honor for General Douglas MacArthur. You will furnish him with the medal." MacArthur received the award at a dinner given by Prime Minister Curtin on 26 March 1942.
85. MacArthur, *Reminiscences,* 147.

15: EPILOGUE

1. Morton, pp. 411–414.
2. Rad Marshall to Wainwright, No 1280, 31 Mar 42, OPD 320.2 Phil (3.31.42) and quoted in Morton, 401. In addition to the original 90,000 there were 26,000 refugees. The Bataan Campaign appears to have ended with roughly the same number of Fil-American combatants with which it began. It is curious that Morton, the official historian of the Philippine campaign, a brilliant historian who wrote an outstanding history, should not answer but leave in the air this most important question of military strength. As a matter of routine, the strength and casualty returns should have been transmitted to Washington by MacArthur's Adjutant General. There are strength returns into MacArthur's Headquarters but it seems that nothing was collated and transmitted on to Washington. MacArthur sent detailed strength returns to Washington immediately prior to the outbreak of war. For example, on 29 November he sent the precise strength of the air component in the Philippines and, on 1 December he sent the strength figures of the anti-aircraft

component. An unmailed letter dated 5 December 1941 was found in the National Archives, in which Marshall thanked MacArthur for keeping him up to date on all the U.S. and Philippine forces under his command. What is strange is the apparent total absence of any consolidated strength return. On 22 December 1941, MacArthur informs Washington of the Japanese landing on Luzon and tells how he had about 40,000 trained troops in partially equipped units at his disposal on Luzon. On 2 January 1942, MacArthur says he has about 7,000 American troops in the Philippines excluding the air component. On 20 January, MacArthur advises Washington he has approximately 20,000 troops on Mindanao, 1,000 in Zamboanga and 8,000 in the Visayas. On 23 January he tells how he has lost 35 per cent of his force and by 8 February he declared all units to be at half strength. While MacArthur *may* have been coy as to the number of troops at his disposal it does not answer the question why there is apparently nothing in Washington's message traffic asking MacArthur how many men he had in his Theater. The conflict in the Philippines was the only active theater at the time and it cannot be the case that the staff's attention was distracted. Shortly after the outbreak of war, MacArthur supported Quezon's executive order raising the pay of Filipino soldiers to be on a par with the Americans. There is therefore a budgetary consideration for which accurate numbers would have been a prerequisite. Perhaps the information does exist somewhere but not in either Sutherland's or MacArthur's records. Source of information: MacArthur Memorial Archives correspondence of 9 February 1999.

3. Morton, 402.
4. Ibid.
5. Mallonée, 110.
6. Thaddeus Holt, "King of Bataan." *Military History Quarterly,* Vol. 7 No 2, (Winter, 1994), 35.
7. Holt, 36.
9. The Filipino Brigadier General Lim had suggested a counterattack plan in February or March but MacArthur disapproved it.
10. MacArthur, *Reminiscences,* 146.
11. Bob Wacker, "The Battling Bastards of Bataan." *The Retired Officer Magazine,* (March, 1992), pp. 41–43 and p.45.
12. King to Morton, 6 January 1949. Louis Morton Papers. Military History Institute. King was awarded an oak leaf cluster to his First World War Distinguished Service Medal. The citation read: "He co-ordinated the employment of all field artillery units in the defense of the Bataan Peninsula, and the allocation of available munitions. The effectiveness of his planning and supervision was demonstrated by the superior performance of the artillery units throughout the operation."
13. Morton, 463.

14. Whitney, pp. 57–58.
15. Wainwright, *General Wainwright's Story*, 83.
16. Triumph in the Philippines. Combat History Division. G-1, U.S. Army Forces, Western Pacific, 203. Morton, 464.
17. James, Vol. II, 147.
18. Ibid.
19. Tenney, xvi.
20. MacArthur, *Reminiscences*, 147.
21. Morton, 524.
22. Sakakida, 91. However, the order for the evacuation of personnel has Yamagata's name on it, not Sakakida's. The list originated in Australia not the Philippines and therefore raises a question vis-à-vis Sakakida's account.
23. Manchester, 331. *HMAS Bataan,* a Tribal Class destroyer, was launched by Jean MacArthur on 15 January 1944.
24. When Kenney arrived, he sacked almost everybody, got his planes operational and was monitoring raids on Rabaul in a matter of weeks.
25. Manchester, 331.
26. Manchester, 334.
27. MacArthur, *Reminiscences,* 160.
28. Morton, 536.
29. Morton, pp. 545–6.
30. The Japanese strength is based on a Japanese estimate.
31. Morton, 561.
32. Wainwright, *General Wainwright's Story,* pp. 122–23.
33. Uno Kazumaro, *Corregidor: Isle of Delusion,* 25. Japanese Tactical Material (Shanghai, 1943). Box 8. Morton Papers. Military History Institute.
34. Uno, 26.
35. Larry I. Bland and Sharon Ritenour Stevens (eds), *The Papers of George Catlett Marshall*. "The Right Man for the Job." December 7, 1941–May 31, 1943, Vol. 3, (Baltimore and London, 1991), pp. 192–193.
36. Drake to Morton. Comments on the Fall of the Philippines. Military History Institute.
37. Romulo, *I Saw the Fall of the Philippines,* 193.
38. Manchester, 335.
39. James II, 149.
40. Wainwright to Sharp in H.W. Tarkington, *There Were Others*. Military History Institute, 434.
41. Chynoweth, pp. 278–9.
42. Chynoweth to Morton, 10 March 1949. Morton Papers. Military History Institute.
43. Manchester, 574.

44. Sidney Fine, *Frank Murphy. The Washington Years,* (Ann Arbor, 1984), 216.
45. Schaller, pp. 63–64.
46. Stimson Diary, 8 September 1942 and 28 February 1943. Pogue, 259. James II, pp. 150–151.
47. Truman disliked MacArthur whom he regarded as an egotist and whom he blamed for the collapse of the Philippines by virtue of having deserted his men.
48. Holt, *King of Bataan,* 42.
49. Hallet Abend, *Ramparts of the Pacific,* (New York, 1942), 189.
50. Roosevelt to Quezon, 30 January 1942. RG-2, 13–2, Folder 4. Mac-Arthur Personal 23 Jan–11 Apr 42. MacArthur Memorial Archives.
51. James Reston, *Prelude to Victory,* (New York, 1942), pp. 116–117.
52. Long, 83.
53. Schaller, pp. 24–25.
54. But the Philippines rarely presented the relevant Administration with uncomplicated choices: there always seemed to be an embuggerance factor present. In the beginning, America was heavily criticized for annexing the Philippines after the Spanish-American War. It had been an operation with the intention of keeping the Spanish fleet from reinforcing the Caribbean and others out. These "others" were Germany. Consider therefore the consequences had Germany annexed the Philippines. After her defeat in 1918, which country would have been the beneficiary of this part of Germany's colonial empire? Japan.
55. German *Fallschirmjägerausbilder* trained Japanese parachutists before the war. In China, air mobile forces had used gliders extensively for the mounting of surprise operations. MacArthur would have noted the success of air mobile and parachute troops in France and Belgium in June 1940 and again in Crete, May–June 1941. The Japanese used airborne troops to seize objectives in Celebes, Timor and Sumatra.
56. Willoughby and Chamberlain, *MacArthur,* pp. 2–3. James II, 151. Long, 83.
57. Interestingly, MacArthur had a similar attitude towards parts of the East Indies. He insisted on needless operations against remaining Japanese forces in those islands during the spring and summer of 1945.
58. Connaughton, Pimlott, Anderson, *The Battle for Manila.*
59. Manchester, 322.
60. TJ was Captain T.J. Davis, MacArthur's aide.
61. Ferrell, 54.

BIBLIOGRAPHY

Books

Abend, Hallet. *Ramparts of the Pacific* (New York, 1942).

Agoncillo, Teodoro A. *The Fateful Years: Japan's Adventure in the Philippines, 1941–1945,* Vol I (Quezon City, 1965).

Agoncillo, Teodoro A. *The Vargas-Laurel Collaboration Case* (Manila, 1984).

Aluit, Alfonso J. *Corregidor* (Manila, 1997).

Anderson, Duncan. "Douglas MacArthur and The Fall of the Philippines, 1941–1942" in Brian Bond (eds). *Fallen Stars* (London, 1991).

Arnold, H.H. *Global Mission* (London, 1951).

Ashworth, Chris. *RAF Coastal Command, 1936–1968* (London, 1992).

Baldwin, Hanson W. *Great Mistakes of the War* (New York, 1950).

Bartsch, William H. *Doomed at the Start: American Pursuit Pilots in the Philippines, 1941–1942* (Texas A & M University, 1992).

Beard, Charles A. *President Roosevelt and the Coming of War, 1941* (Yale, 1948).

Beck, John J. *MacArthur and Wainwright* (Albuquerque, 1974).

Bischof, Günther and Dupont, Robert L. (eds). *The Pacific War Revisited* (Baton Rouge, 1997).

Blair, Clay. *Silent Victory: The U.S. Submarine War Against Japan* (Philadelphia, 1975).

Bland, Larry I. and Stevens, Sharon Ritenour (eds). *The Papers of George Catlett Marshall,* Vol 3. "The Right Man for the Job: December 7, 1941–May 31, 1943" (Baltimore and London, 1991).

Borg, D. and Shumpei, O. (eds). *Pearl Harbor as History: Japanese-American Relations, 1931–1941* (New York, 1973).

Brereton, Lewis H. *The Brereton Diaries* (New York, 1946).

Bywater, Hector C. *Sea Power in the Pacific* (Boston and New York, 1934).

Cant, Gilbert. *America's Navy in World War II* (New York, 1943).

Chandler, Alfred D. (ed). *The Papers of Dwight David Eisenhower* (Baltimore, 1970).

Chennault, Claire L. *Way of a Fighter: The Memoirs of Claire Lee Chennault* (New York, 1949).

Churchill, Winston S. *The Second World War: The Hinge of Fate* (Boston, 1950).

Churchill, Winston S. *The Second World War: The Grand Alliance* (Boston, 1951).

Churchill, Winston S. *The Second World War: Their Finest Hour* (Boston, 1949).

Chwialkowski, Paul. *In Caesar's Shadow* (Greenwood Press, 1993).

Chynoweth, Bradford Grethen. *Bellamy Park* (New York, 1975).

Clansen, Henry C. and Lee, Bruce. *Pearl Harbor: Final Judgement* (New York, 1992).

Connaughton, Richard, Pimlott, John, Anderson, Duncan. *The Battle for Manila* (London, 1995).

Considine, Robert. *It's All News to Me* (New York, 1956).

Considine, Robert. *MacArthur the Magnificent* (New York, 1942).

Costello, John. *Days of Infamy* (New York, 1994).

Craven, W. F. and Cate, J.L. *The Army Air Forces in World War II*, Vol I, "Plans and Early Operations January 1939–August 1942" (University of Chicago Press, 1948).

Davis, Richard. *Spaatz and the Air War in Europe* (Washington DC, 1993).

Dod, Karl C. *The United States Army in World War II: The Corps of Engineers: The War Against Japan* (Washington DC, 1966).

Dower, John. *War Without Mercy: Race and Power in the Pacific War* (New York, 1986).

Drea, Edward J. *MacArthur's Ultra: Codebreaking and the War Against Japan, 1942–1945* (University Press of Kansas, 1992).

Dupuy, R. Ernest and Trevor N. *The Encyclopaedia of Military History* (London, 1970).

Edmonds, Walter D. *They Fought With What They Had: The Story of the Army Air Forces in the Southwest Pacific, 1941–1942* (Boston, 1951).

Egeberg, Roger Olaf. *The General: MacArthur and the Man he Called 'Doc'* (Washington DC, 1993).

Eisenhower, Dwight D. *At Ease: Stories I Tell to Friends* (New York, 1967).

Eisenhower, Dwight D. *Crusade in Europe* (New York, 1948).

Elphick, Peter. *Far Eastern File: The Intelligence War in the Far East, 1930–1945* (London, 1997).

Eyre, James K. *The Roosevelt-MacArthur Conflict* (Chambersburg, 1950).

Falk, Stanley L. "Douglas MacArthur and the War Against Japan" in Leary, William M. (ed). *We Shall Return* (University of Kentucky, 1988).

Falk, Stanley J. *The March of Death* (London, 1964).

Farley, James A. *Jim Farley's Story* (New York, 1948).

Ferrell, Robert (ed). *The Eisenhower Diaries* (New York, 1981).

Fine, Sidney. *Frank Murphy: The Washington Years* (Ann Arbor, 1984).

Finer, S.E. *The Man on Horseback: The Role of the Military in Politics* (London, 1962).

Francillon, René J. *Japanese Aircraft of the Pacific War* (London, 1970).

Friend, Theodore. *Between Two Empires: The Ordeal of the Philippines, 1929–1946* (Yale, 1965).

Frye, William. *Marshall: Citizen Soldier* (Indianapolis, 1947).

Gunther, John. *Inside Asia* (New York and London, 1942).

Gunther, John. *Roosevelt in Retrospect* (New York, 1950).

Hamilton, Ian. *A Staff Officer's Scrap Book*, Vol II (London, 1907).

Harrison, Francis Burton. *Origins of the Philippine Republic: Extracts from the Diaries and Records of Francis Burton Harrison* (New York, 1974).

Hayashi, Saburo. *Kogun: The Japanese Army in the Pacific War* (Quantico, 1959).

Hersey, John. *Men on Bataan* (New York, 1942).

Hooker, N.H. (ed). *The Moffat Papers: Selections from the Diplomatic Journals of Jay Pierrepoint Moffat, 1919–1943* (Cambridge, Mass., 1956).

Hough, Frank O., et al. "Pearl Harbor to Guadalcanal," *History of U.S. Marine Corps Operations in World War II*, Vol I (Washington, DC, nd).

Huff, Sid. *My Fifteen Years With General MacArthur* (New York, 1964).

Hunt, Frazier. *The Untold Story of Douglas MacArthur* (New York, 1954).

Ickes, Harold L. *The Secret Diary of Harold L. Ickes*, Vol I, "The First Thousand Days 1933–1936," (New York, 1952). Vol 3 (London, 1955).

Jablonski, Edward. *Flying Fortress* (U.S.A., 1965).

James, D. Clayton. *South to Bataan, North to Mukden: The Prison Diary of Brigadier General W.E. Brougher* (Georgia, 1971).

James, D. Clayton. *The Years of MacArthur,* Vol I, 1880–1941 (London, 1970).

Jopling, Lucy Wilson. *Warrior in White* (San Antonio, 1990).

Jose, Ricardo Trota. *The Philippine Army, 1935–1942* (Manila, 1992).

Karnow, Stanley. *In Our Image: America's Empire in the Philippines* (New York, 1989).

Kennedy, Paul. *The War Plans of the Great Powers, 1880–1914* (London, 1979).

Kirosaki, Wayne S. *A Spy in Their Midst: The World War II Struggle of a Japanese-American Hero* (New York, 1995).

Knox, Donald. *Death March: The Survivors of Bataan* (San Diego, 1981).

Larrabee, Eric. *Commander in Chief Franklin D. Roosevelt, His Lieutenants and Their Wars* (New York, 1987).

Leahy, William D. *I Was There* (New York, 1950).

Lee, Clark and Henschel, Richard. *Douglas MacArthur* (New York, 1952).

Lee, Clark. *They Call It Pacific* (New York, 1943).

Leighton, M. *Mobilizing Consent: Public Opinion and American Foreign Policy, 1937–1948* (London, 1976).

Leuchtenburg, William E. *The Perils of Prosperity, 1914–1932* (Chicago, 1958).

Leutze, James. *A Different Kind of Victory: A Biography of Admiral Thomas Hart* (Annapolis, 1981).

Lewis, Emmanuel Raymond. *Seacoast Fortifications of the United States* (Annapolis, 1979).

Liddell Hart, B.H. *History of the Second World War* (London, 1970).

Lim, Vicente. *To Inspire and to Lead: The Letters of General Vicente Lim, 1938–1942* (Manila, 1980).

Linn, Brian McAllister. *Guardian of Empire: The U.S. Army and the Pacific, 1902–1940* (University of North Carolina Press, 1997).

Lippman, W. *U.S. Foreign Policy* (London, 1943).

Loewenheim, Francis L., Langley, Harold D. and Jones, Manfred (eds). *Roosevelt and Churchill: Their Secret Wartime Correspondence* (London, 1975).

Lohbeck, Don. *Patrick J. Hurley* (Chicago, 1956).

Long, Gavin. *MacArthur as Military Commander* (London, 1989).

Lopez, Salvador P. *Elpidio Quirino: The Judgement of History* (Manila, 1990).

Luvaas, Jay (ed). *Dear Miss Em: General Eichelberger's War In The Pacific, 1942–1945* (Westport, 1972).

MacArthur, Douglas. *Reminiscences* (London, 1964).

Mallonée, Richard C. *The Naked Flagpole* (San Rafael, 1980).

Manchester, William. *American Caesar* (New York, 1978).

Marquardt, Frederick S. *Before Bataan and After* (Indianapolis, 1943).

Martin, Ralph G. *Henry and Clare* (New York, 1990).

Miller, Edward S. *War Plan Orange: The U.S. Strategy to Defeat Japan, 1897–1945* (Annapolis, 1991).

Miller, Ernest B. *Bataan Uncensored* (Long Prairie, 1949).

Miller, Francis Trevelyan. *General Douglas MacArthur: Soldier–Statesman* (Philadelphia, 1951).

Morison, Elting E. *Turmoil and Tradition: A Study of the Life and Times of Henry L. Stimson* (Boston, 1960).

Morison, Samuel Eliot. *The Rising Sun in the Pacific* (Boston, 1948).

Morison, Samuel Eliot. *The Two Ocean War* (Boston, 1963).

Morris, Eric. *Corregidor: The Nightmare in the Philippines* (London, 1982).

Morton, Louis. *The War in the Pacific: Strategy and Command: The First Two Years* (Washington, 1962).

Morton, Louis. "The Fall of the Philippines" in *U.S. Army in World War II: The War in the Pacific* (Washington, 1953).

Mosley, Leonard. *Marshall: Hero of Our Times* (New York, 1982).

Olson, John E. *Anywhere, Anytime: The History of the Fifty–Seventh Infantry (PS)* (1991).

Onorato, Michael. *Leonard Wood as Governor* (Manila, 1969).

Overy, Richard and Wheatcroft, Andrew. *The Road to War* (London, 1989).

Perret, Geoffrey. *Old Soldiers Never Die: The Life of Douglas MacArthur* (New York, 1996).

Petillo, Carrol Morris. *Douglas MacArthur: The Philippine Years* (Indiana University Press, 1981).

Pogue, Forrest C. *George C. Marshall: Ordeal and Hope, 1939–1942* (London, 1965).

Quezon, Manuel. *The Good Fight* (New York, 1944).

Ramsey, Edwin Price and Rivele, Stephen. *Lieutenant Ramsey's War: From Horse Soldier to Guerilla Commander* (New York, 1990).

Reston, James. *Prelude to Victory* (New York, 1942).

Rogers, Paul P. *The Good Years: MacArthur and Sutherland* (New York, 1990).

Romulo, Beth Day. *The Manila Hotel* (Manila, 1987).

Romulo, Carlos P. *I Saw the Fall of the Philippines* (Garden City, 1942).

Romulo, Carlos P. *I Walked With Heroes* (New York, 1961).

Roskill, S. W. *The Art of Leadership* (London, 1964).

Saburo, Sakai. *Samurai: Flying the Zero in World War II with Japan's Fighter Ace* (New York, 1963).

Saulo, Alfredo B. *Let George Do It: A Biography of Jorge B. Vargas* (University of Philippines Press, 1992).

Sayre, Francis B. *Glad Adventure* (New York, 1957).

Schaller, Michael. *Douglas MacArthur: The Far Eastern General* (New York, 1989).

Shadegg, Stephen. *Clare Boothe Luce: A Biography* (New York, 1970).

Sheean, Vincent. *Between the Thunder and the Sun* (New York, 1943).

Sheed, Wilfred. *Clare Boothe Luce* (New York, 1982).

Shores, Christopher, Cull, Brian, with Yasuho, Izawa. "The Drift to War to the Fall of Singapore" in *Bloody Shambles: The First Comprehensive Account of Air Operations Over South East Asia, December 1941–April 1942,* Vol I (London, 1992).

Smith, Robert Aura. *Our Future in Asia* (New York, 1940).

Smythe, Donald. *Guerilla Warrior* (New York, 1973).

Spector, Ronald H. *Eagle Against The Sun* (New York, 1985).

Stauffer, Alvin P. "The Quartermaster Corps: Operations in the War Against Japan" in *The United States Army in World War II* (Washington DC, 1956).

Steinberg, David Joel. *Philippine Collaboration in World War II* (Manila and Michigan, 1967).

Stimson, Henry L. and Bundy, McGeorge. *On Active Service in Peace and War* (New York, 1947).

Sulzberger, C.L. *A Long Row of Candles: Memoirs and Diaries, 1934–1954* (New York, 1969).

Sweetman, Jack. *The Landing at Vera Cruz* (Annapolis, 1968).

Tenney, Lester I. *My Hitch in Hell: The Bataan Death March* (Washington DC, 1995).

Thetford, Owen. *Aircraft of the Royal Air Force since 1918,* ninth edition (London, 1995).

Thomas, David. *Battle of the Java Sea* (London, 1968).

Thompson, George R. et al. *The United States Army in World War II: The Technical Services: The Signal Corps: The Test, December 1941–July 1943* (Washington DC, 1957).

Toland, John. *But Not in Shame* (New York, 1961).

Tsurumi, Shunsuke. *An Intellectual History of Wartime Japan, 1931–1945* (London, 1986).

Tugwell, Rexford G. *The Democratic Roosevelt* (New York, 1957).

Uno, Kazumaro. *Corregidor: Isle of Delusion* (Shanghai, 1943).

Vandenberg, Arthur H. Jr. (ed). *The Private Papers of Senator Vandenberg* (Boston, 1952).

Wainwright, Jonathan. *General Wainwright's Story* (New York, 1946).

Watson, Mark S. *Chief of Staff Pre–War Plans and Preparations* (Washington DC, 1950).

Weintraub, Stanley. *The Long Day's Journey into War: 7 December 1941* (New York, 1991).

Whan, Vorin E. (ed). *A Soldier Speaks: Public Papers and Speeches of General of the Army Douglas MacArthur* (New York, 1965).

Whitman, John W. *Bataan: Our Last Ditch* (New York, 1990).

Whitney, Courtney. *MacArthur: His Rendezvous with History* (New York, 1955).

Willoughby, C.A. and Chamberlain, J. *MacArthur: 1941–1951* (London, 1956).

Dissertations, Reviews, Pamphlets and Articles

Baldwin, Hanson W. "Review of Reminiscences" in *The New York Times Book Review* (September 27, 1964).

Boothe, Clare. "MacArthur of the Far East," *Life* (December 6, 1941).

Boothe, Clare. *Sing High: The History of 90 Squadron Royal Flying Corps and Royal Air Force, 1917–1965,* No 90 Squadron Association, 1989.

Carlson, Adolf. *Joint U.S. Army-Navy Planning on the Eve of the First World War: Its Origin and Its Legacy.* Letort Paper (Carlisle, 1998).

Carswell, Robert M. "Philippine National Defense," *Coast Artillery Journal* (March–April, 1941).

Champlin, Malcolm M. Unpublished account of experiences in the Philippines, including biography of Rear Admiral John D. Bulkeley, U.S.N. (December 7, 1965). Office of Information, Internal Relations Division, Naval History Division.

Doyle, Michael K. "The U.S. Navy and War Plan Orange, 1939–1940: Making Necessity a Virtue," *Naval War College Review* (May–June 1980).

Dufault, David Vawter. *Francis B. Sayre and the Commonwealth of the Philippines, 1936–1942.* PhD Dissertation, University of Oregon.

Engelhart, Carl E. *Trapped on Corregidor.* Unpublished Manuscript, Military History Institute.

Ferris, John. "A British Unofficial Aviation Mission and Japanese Naval Developments, 1919–1929," *The Journal of Strategic Studies* (September 5, 1982).

Fey, Harold E. "Militarizing the Philippines," *Nation,* CXLII (June 10, 1936).

Gole, Henry G. *War Planning at the U.S. Army War College, 1934–1940.* PhD Dissertation, Military History Institute.

Gordon, John. "The Best Arm We Had," *Field Artillery Journal* (November–December 1984).

Hasdorff, James C. "Jerry Lee: Founding Father of the Philippine Air Force," *Aerospace Historian,* Vol 20 (Winter–December 1973).

Hill, Milton A. *Lessons of Bataan,* Military History Institute.

Holt, Thaddeus. "King of Bataan," *Military History Quarterly,* Vol 7, No 2 (Winter 1994).

Jacobs, Bruce. "The Evolution of Tank Units in the Pre–World War II National Guard and the Defense of Bataan," *Military Collector and Historian,* Vol XXXVIII, No 3 (Fall 1986).

Jacobs, Bruce. *The War Diary of General Clyde Selleck, Commanding General 71st Division, USAFFE.* "The Battle for Northern Luzon, The Initial Phase of the Battle of Bataan." Historical Conservation Society (Manila 1985).

James, D. Clayton. "The Other Pearl Harbor," *Military History Quarterly* (Winter 1995).

Johnson, H.K. "Defense Along The Line," *Military Review* 28 (February 1949).

Jose, Ricardo. *Beach Defense: The First Regular Division at Mauban, December 23–26, 1941.* Bulletin of the American Historical Collection (April–June 1989).

Miller, J. Michael. *Shanghai to Corregidor: Marines in the Fall of the Philippines*. Marine Corps History Center (1997).

Mitchell, John H. "The First Bombing Mission of the Army Air Corps in World War II," *AAHS Journal,* Vol 34, No 1 (Spring 1989).

Petillo, Carol. "Douglas MacArthur and Manuel Quezon," *Pacific Historical Review* (February 1979).

Picornell, Pedro. *The Remedios Hospital, 1942–1945.* Unpublished Paper.

Sackett, E.L. *History of the USS Canopus* Naval History Department, (April 28 1947).

Santelli, James S. *A Brief History of the 4th Marines.* Historical Division, HQ U.S. Marine Corps (Washington DC, 1970).

Sherill, Robert G. "Drew Pearson: An Interview," *Nation,* CCIX (July 7, 1969).

Tarkington, H.W. *There Were Others.* Military History Institute.

Wacker, Bob. "The Battling Bastards of Bataan," *The Retired Officer Magazine* (March 1992).

Weaver, James R.N. Report of Operations of the Provisional Tank Group, United States Forces in the Far East.

Wheeler, Gerald E. "National Policy Planning Between the Wars: Conflicts Between Ends and Means," *Naval War College Review* (February 1969).

Wheeler, Gerald E. *Philippine Commonwealth: Office of the Military Adviser.* Report on National Defense (Manila 1936).

Whitman, John W. "Decision that Starved an Army," *Army Logistician* (March–April 1995).

INDEX

Japanese: in Davao, 101; internment of, 144, 189; living in Philippines, 100–101; in Manila, 144
Japanese agents, 101, 102–3, 115, 144, 156, 158, 185, 189
Japanese Consulate (Manila), 145, 157, 298
Japanese Good Friday, 293
Japanese Imperial Rescript, 229
Japanese soldiers: nature of, 9
Japanese students, 8
Java, 13, 50, 113, 128, 173, 228, 278, 283
Java (Dutch cruiser), 283
Java Sea, Battle of, 283
Jennings, zz, 258
Johnson, Harold K., 220
Johnson, Luther, 258
Joint Army and Navy Assessment Committee, 286
Joint Army-Navy Planning Board, 35, 48, 100, 110, 161
Joint Chiefs of Staff Committee, U.S.: creation of, 134
Joint Congressional Committee, 178
Joint Estimate for War Plan Orange, 100
Jones, Albert M., 183, 210, 212–13, 218, 221–22, 241–42, 271, 288, 294
Jose, zz, 67, 213

Kansas City Star, 286
Kato, Kanji, 10
Kellogg-Briand Pact, 59
Kelly, Colin, 181–82, 277
Kenney, George C., 164
KGEI (San Francisco radio), 256
Kihara, Jitaro, 101, 145, 158, 223, 252, 253, 266–67
Kimmel, Husband E., 160, 170, 178, 186, 305
Kimura, Naoki, 243, 244, 245–46, 270
King, Edward Postell, Jr., 120, 263, 293–94, 295, 296, 304
King, Ernest J., 129, 134
Kipling, Rudyard, 1
Kiyoshi, Kiyoshi Uchiyama, 101

Komori, Arthur, 144
Kondo Detachment, 276, 277
Kondo, Vice Admiral, 128
Konoye (prince of Japan), 114
Korea, 5, 6, 14, 264, 308
Korean War, 304
Kota Bharu, 164
Kurile Islands, 150
KZRH (Manila radio), 279, 301

La Monja, 226
La Union, 184, 205
Laguan de Bay, 218
Lamb, Ray, 199
Lamon Bay, 151–52, 193, 198, 209–10, 223
Landon, Alf, 64, 69
Larrabee, Eric, 36, 174, 232
Lassiter, William, 31
Lateral 3. *See* Malinta Tunnel (Corregidor)
Laurel, Jose P., 192, 193, 213, 266–67
Lawrence, Colonel, 217
League of Nations, 12
Leavenworth, Kansas: Army base at, 79
Lee, Clark, 121, 147, 153, 280
Lee, Jerry, 82–83
Lee (Robert E.) mansion, 36
Legaspi, 148, 179, 183, 184–85, 187, 224
Legaspi (blockade runner), 239–41
Lepanto mining stock, 218
Liaotung Peninsula, 5, 6
Liaoyang, Battle of, 7
Libby, McNeil and Libby Corporation, 219
Life magazine, 121, 122, 123, Vicente, 52, 53, 86, 105, 146, 183, 241
Lindbergh, Charles, 291
Lingayen: and American withdrawal to Bataan, 215; and anticipation of Japanese attack on Philippines, 152; and battle for Bataan, 245, 246; and early defense plans, 49; intelligence about, 145; and Japanese invasion and occupation of Luzon, 143, 180–81, 193, 198, 199, 200–201, 204, 205,